Conservative Christians and Political Participation

Political Participation in America
Raymond A. Smith, Series Editor

African Americans and Political Participation,
Minion K. C. Morrison, Editor

East Asian Americans and Political Participation,
Tsung Chi

Gay and Lesbian Americans and Political Participation,
Raymond A. Smith and Donald P. Haider-Markel

Jewish Americans and Political Participation,
Rafael Medoff

Latino/a Americans and Political Participation,
Sharon A. Navarro and Armando X. Mejia, Editors

Native Americans and Political Participation,
Jerry D. Stubben and Gary A. Sokolow

Women and Political Participation, Barbara Burrel

Conservative Christians and Political Participation

A Reference Handbook

Glenn H. Utter
James L. True

A B C ⬥ C L I O

Santa Barbara, California • Denver, Colorado • Oxford, England

Library of Congress Cataloging-in-Publication Data
Utter, Glenn H.
  Conservative Christians and political participation : a reference handbook / Glenn H. Utter and James L. True.
      p. cm. — (Political participation in America)
  Includes bibliographical references and index.
    ISBN 1-85109-513-6 (alk. paper) — ISBN 1-85109-518-7 (eBook)
  1. Religious right—United States. 2. Christianity and politics—United States.
  I. True, James L.   II. Title.   III. Series.

BR526.U86 2004
323'.042'0882773—dc22

                                                                  2004018343

08 07 06 05 04   10 9 8 7 6 5 4 3 2 1

This book is also available on the World Wide Web as an eBook. Visit abc-clio.com for details.

ABC-CLIO, Inc.
130 Cremona Drive, P.O. Box 1911
Santa Barbara, California 93116-1911
This book is printed on acid-free paper.
Manufactured in the United States of America

Contents

Series Foreword

Participation in the political process is a cornerstone of both the theory and the practice of democracy; indeed, the word "democracy" itself means rule by the people. Since the formation of the New Deal coalition in 1932, the study of U.S. politics has largely been organized around the idea that there exist distinct "blocs" of citizens, such as African Americans, women, Catholics, and Latinos. This trend was reinforced during the 1960s when the expansion of the media and the decline of traditional sources of authority promoted direct citizen mobilization. And more recently, the emphasis on "identity politics" has bolstered the notion of distinct groups organized along lines of shared personal characteristics rather than common economic interests.

Although political participation is a mainstream, even canonical, subject in the study of U.S. politics, there are few midrange reference materials available on this subject. Indeed, the available reference materials do not include works that provide both a systematic empirical base *and* explanatory and contextualizing material. Likewise, because of the fragmentation of the reference material on this subject, it is difficult for readers to draw comparisons across groups, even though this is one of the most meaningful ways of understanding the phenomenon of political participation. The Political Participation in America series is designed to fill this gap in the reference literature on this subject by providing key points of background (e.g., demographics, political history, major contemporary issues) and then systematically addressing different types of political participation, providing both substance and context for readers. In addition, each chapter includes case studies that either illuminate larger issues or highlight some particular subpopulation within the larger group.

Each volume of the ABC-CLIO Political Participation in America series focuses on one of the major subgroups that make up the electorate in the United States. Each volume includes the following components:

- Introduction to the group, comprising a demographic, historical, and political portrait of the group, including political opinions and issues of key importance to members of the group
- Participation in protest politics, including marches, rallies, demonstrations, and direct actions
- Participation in social movements and interest groups, including involvement of members of the group in and through a wide variety of organizations and associations
- Participation in electoral politics, including a profile of involvement with political parties and voting patterns
- Participation in political office-holding, including elected, appointed, and "unofficial" offices from the local to national levels

The end of each book also includes an A–Z glossary featuring brief entries on important individuals and events; a chronology of political events salient to the group; a resource guide of organizations, newsletters, websites, and other important contact information, all briefly annotated; an annotated bibliography of key primary and secondary documents, including books and journal articles; excerpts from major primary documents, with introductions; and a comprehensive index to the volume.

Raymond A. Smith
Series Editor

Introduction

The participation of conservative Christians in U.S. politics has a long heritage. Christians and Christian organizations have engaged in political activity since the colonial era. The first Great Awakening, the religious revival beginning in the 1730s, had more than religious significance: It ultimately led to challenges to the royal church and to the government officials who supported it, and it contributed to the rise of the antislavery movement. Christian groups engaged in various reform movements during that era, including campaigns to preserve the Sabbath as a day of rest and to bring assistance to Native Americans. In the nineteenth century, many Christians became involved in the campaign against the manufacture and sale of alcoholic beverages, an effort that ultimately resulted in passage of the short-lived Eighteenth Amendment to the U.S. Constitution, establishing national prohibition.

In the late nineteenth century, with greater numbers of clergy adhering to more progressive understandings of their faith, a split occurred among Christian denominations. On one side were conservatives, often called fundamentalists, who held to traditional, or fundamental, beliefs of Christianity, including biblical inerrancy, the deity and virgin birth of Jesus, the substitutionary atonement (Jesus's death on the cross reconciled human beings with God), and the bodily resurrection of Jesus. These denominations primarily emphasized personal salvation. On the other side of the split were those, called progressives or liberals, who focused their energies on the improvement of society, believing that God had provided for the constant betterment of human beings through human efforts to reform social institutions and minister to the physical needs of the population. Liberals often doubted fundamentalist beliefs, such as the virgin birth and biblical inerrancy.

In the first chapter of this book, we present a brief history of Christians' involvement in the American political process from the early days of the nation to the present. Using General Social Survey data as well as other data sources, we describe who the conservative Christians are today, providing membership totals both for denominations considered mainline (predominantly progressive or liberal) Protestant and for those generally considered fundamentalist or conservative. We discuss three trends—increasing membership in fundamentalist denominations, a decrease in mainline church adherents, and a growing group that refuses to identify with any religion—that suggest an increasing polarity concerning religion in the United States.

In Chapter 2, we examine the participation of conservative Christian individuals and organizations in political protest, a strategy that, in the past forty years, various movements have used as a method of political involvement. Protest often encompasses a delicate balance between confrontation and cooperation with established authorities. We present case studies of antiabortion demonstrations and of protests against a U.S. Supreme Court decision disallowing organized prayer at the start of public high school athletic events. Each case highlights the costs of protesting, as well as the potential gains to be made, for conservative Christians.

Chapter 3 focuses on the activities of conservative Christian social movements and interest groups. We emphasize the need to counter the activities of an opposition group as a major incentive to organize: Conservative Christians generally become politically active to respond to perceived threats from groups that promote objectives that conservative Christians find objectionable. We also note the difficulties that groups in general face when attempting to organize for political activity. Focusing on conservative Christian organizations, we describe the activities of two prominent groups: the Moral Majority, established by Jerry Falwell, Paul Weyrich, and other conservative Christian leaders in 1979, and the Christian Coalition, created by Pat Robertson in 1989 (the same year the Moral Majority came to an end). Each group experienced successes as well as failures, and their histories provide insights into the advantages as well as the limitations that conservative Christian groups face when attempting to achieve their objectives in an essentially secular society. We present several case studies of the activities of conservative Christian organizations, focusing on issues of concern to these groups, such as the display of the Ten Commandments, gay marriage, obscenity and pornography, partial-birth abortion, and the wording of the Pledge of Allegiance.

In Chapter 4, we discuss a turnaround in voter turnout on the part of conservative Christians. Since the 1980s, the religious right has gone from a near political apathy to participation on par with that of the general public. In addition, conservative Christian voters have swung from a preponderance of support for the Democratic party to a routine support (among white conservative Christians) for the Republican party. Yet that partisanship is not carved in stone, and many in the religious right appear to vote for an individual candidate as much as voting for a political party. Our analysis of General Social Survey data and National Election Studies data reveals the voting patterns of conservative Christians in contrast to members of mainline churches. We also discuss African-American conservative Christians, who tend to express attitudes and partisan preferences that are very different from those of whites, indicating that conservative religious beliefs and conservative political views do not always coincide.

Chapter 5 investigates the participation of conservative Christians in government at the local, state, and national levels. Conservative Christian organizations have campaigned to have like-minded individuals elected to state legislatures, city councils, and local and state boards of education. In the year 2000, the Republican party, the favored party of conservative Christian organizations, controlled the presidency and both houses of Congress. Also as the twenty-first century began, the U.S. Supreme Court was one or two appointments away from establishing a decisive conservative majority that likely would be more favorable toward the conservative Christian position on such issues as abortion, same-sex marriage, and separation of church and state. On the other hand, openly conservative Christian candidates have had little direct electoral success, and some fundamentalists remain disappointed in the lack of substantive legislation favoring their position on abortion, tuition tax credits, and oral prayer in public school. There are a variety of factors that work against the political success of the religious right, and those factors may help explain why most of their recent political efforts have focused on state and local offices and issues.

The story of conservative Christians and political participation is a continuing one. Although scholars have predicted the downfall of the religious right at various times over the past thirty-five years, conservative Christian groups have continued to influence various aspects of the American political landscape. In this book, we emphasize two factors in that continuing participation: First, seeing themselves as separate from, but essentially embedded in, a secular society, conservative Christians view political activity as a way of altering the secular culture in ways more amicable to their conception of a good society. Second, conservative Christians perceive a necessity in entering the political arena to do battle with organizations that advocate objectives contrary to the basic values of conservative Christians—interests such as the American Civil Liberties Union, the National Organization for Women, and the National Abortion Rights Action League. The future political success of conservative Christians will depend on the preferences of citizens in general, the political skills of interest groups and their leaders, and the ability of leaders to create alliances with nonreligious organizations, particularly political parties.

Glenn H. Utter
James L. True
Lamar University

1

Overview

The extensive participation of conservative Christian groups in the American political process since the early 1980s does not at all represent a new phenomenon. Throughout the history of the United States, religious groups have become politically active, attempting to influence the opinions of the general population and to affect government decisions on issues of concern to the leadership and members of these groups. The participation of religious groups corresponds to the activities of various other interest groups in a representative democracy. This participation involves a plurality of interests, sometimes cooperating, sometimes competing with each other, all vying for the satisfaction of their special concerns. Opposition from nonreligious groups to the political participation of conservative Christian groups and religious organizations in general also has a long history. Many persons and groups throughout the nation's history have raised questions about the appropriateness of organized religions' involvement in American politics, asking whether such participation is conducive to the republican principles upon which the nation was originally based.

Because the political participation of religious groups has a long history in the United States, we will first offer a brief account of such participation, identifying the groups involved and the issues that led to their mobilization to political action. Then we will delimit the present population of conservative Christians and conservative Christian organizations in the United States and identify various subgroupings based on religious belief and practice as well as political stances. We will compare and contrast the beliefs and goals of conservative Christian denominations and organizations with those of mainline churches. Because American politics so often involves interaction among differing interests, we will comment on the types of alliances that have developed in more recent years between conservative Christian organizations and other groups that may share common goals with them.

Who Are the Christian Conservatives?

Christian conservatives in the modern United States are individuals and Protestant churches that are religiously fundamental and politically conservative. Creedal fundamentalism is distinguished by belief in the inerrancy of the Bible as the inspired word of God, the personal salvation of the individual through Christ (often called a born-again experience), an evangelical or revivalist desire to save and convert others, and an acceptance of most traditional Christian doctrines such as belief in God as the Trinity and the virgin birth of Christ (See Smith 1987 for a discussion of the methods and difficulties in classifying denominations as fundamentalist). Political conservatism is marked by a general belief in the importance of limiting the size and scope of government, yet there is a specific willingness among conservative Christians to use government to restore what is seen as traditional social values. From the conservative or neoconservative perspective, government should be used to limit or ban abortions and to restrict or ban homosexual activities (including a prohibition on same-sex marriages, possibly by ratification of an amendment to the U.S. Constitution). Similarly, this view holds that government should be used to restore oral prayers in the public schools. Conservative Christians may vary in the intensity with which they subscribe to some or all of these creedal and political beliefs, but as we indicate below, these beliefs can be used to distinguish Christian conservatives from other Christians as well as non-Christians in the United States. History can provide us with some insights into how those beliefs came to be.

Religion and Politics in the Colonial and Revolutionary Periods

During the colonial era in the United States, religion and politics were intimately intertwined. In the seventeenth-century Massachusetts Bay Colony, only those residents who were members of the Congregational Church could claim the right as citizens to participate in the political life of the community (Reichley 2002 56). However, religious pluralism began very early in the colonies. Disagreements that arose over theological principles led to factions developing within the religious community. Roger Williams arrived in the Massachusetts Bay Colony in 1630 and soon came into serious conflict with Governor John Winthrop over religious and political matters. In 1636, Williams led a group of followers away from Massachusetts and settled Providence as a refuge from religious persecution. This land, purchased from the Narragansett Indians, became the new colony of Rhode Island. In 1682, William Penn, a Quaker, wished to establish a society that would serve as an approximation of the heavenly kingdom. Penn founded a colony that ultimately became Pennsylvania. Penn's more tolerant view of religious faith led to the nurturing of a variety of religious organizations in Pennsylvania. Maryland became a haven for Roman Catholics, especially after the British Parliament passed the Act of Toleration in 1649, guaranteeing that any person professing belief in Jesus Christ remain unmolested in the free exercise of religious belief (Reichley 2002, 82).

A religious revival called the Great Awakening, initiated by Calvinist minister Jonathan Edwards in Massachusetts, swept across the eastern seaboard in the 1730s and 1740s. The Great Awakening refocused American religious attention on the next world instead of this one. Edwards's vivid depictions of "Sinners in the Hands of an Angry God" re-emphasized the natural depravity of human beings, the inadequacy of good works performed by the individual, and hence the need for individual spiritual rebirth (Christian 1966, 15). The evangelical fervor of the Great Awakening emphasized individual salvation for the next world rather than social improvement and political involvement in this one. Although those less fervent about religious belief tended to dominate in the cities, evangelicals gained ascendancy in the frontier regions of North America. As the Revolution approached, many ministers played a key role in supporting the cause of independence. The majority of Anglican clergy, however, remained loyal to Great Britain. Some recent scholars argue that religion played a central and largely unappreciated role in the nationalistic vision that shaped the early history of the United States. In his study of religion and politics, for example, Kevin Phillips (1999, xii–xiii) declared that "the importance of religion and war in the shaping of nations should not even be debatable. . . . From the birth of Protestantism in the sixteenth century, no Western nation has matched the English-speaking peoples in asserting their destiny as

God's Kingdom." According to Phillips, the eighteenth century colonists uniformly foresaw that "*their* New Israel would stretch to the Mississippi or even the Pacific."

Several leaders of the contemporary Christian right claim that the key founders of the United States during the Revolution and the subsequent writing of the Constitution intended to establish a Christian nation. That claim has validity at least to the extent that Christianity was definitely the prevailing religion in the colonies and the newly established nation. However, the religious views of various notable personages of the time indicate that there likely was not a consensus on whether the framers of the U.S. Constitution intended to establish a Christian society (Mapp 2003). John G. West (1996) presents brief sketches of the religious views of several prominent Americans at the time of the nation's founding. Some (such as John Witherspoon and John Jay) were evangelicals, holding to traditional Christian beliefs. Others (e.g., Thomas Jefferson and John Adams) are most accurately described as deists, believing that God may have created the universe but that after the creation he stepped back to allow the finely structured mechanism to operate without further interference. For deists, formal religious practices were unneeded and claims of supernatural revelation were fallacious.

By the end of the eighteenth century, deism had become a prominent religious attitude among many intellectuals and upper-class Americans. Frank Manuel (2002) considers all of the first three American presidents to have been deists, and it is clear that Thomas Jefferson and John Adams were deists. In an 1803 letter to Benjamin Rush, for example, Jefferson wrote about his views of the Christian religion: "To the corruption of Christianity I am indeed opposed; but not to the genuine precepts of Jesus himself. I am a Christian, in the only sense in which he wished anyone to be; sincerely attached to his doctrines, in preference to all others; ascribing to himself all *human* excellence; and believing he never claimed any other" (Muelder, Sears, and Schlabach 1960, 76). In a letter to Thomas Jefferson in 1816, John Adams, limiting his profession of religious belief to acting well, commented, "The ten commandments and the sermon on the mount contain my religion" (Manuel 2002, 569).

Another noted American often associated with deism is Benjamin Franklin. When questioned seriously about his religion, Franklin replied in 1790 with an answer that provided what scholars have called an almost literal reproduction of the main principles of English deism: "Here is my creed. I believe in one God, the creator of the universe. That he governs it by his Providence. That he ought to be worshiped. That the most acceptable service we render to him is doing good to his other children. That the soul of man is immortal, and will be treated with justice in another life respecting his conduct in this. These I take to be the fundamental points in all sound religion, and I regard them as you do in whatever sect I meet with them" (Muelder, Sears, and Schlabach 1960, 70–71).

Deists saw the core of the various religions to be essentially the same, but for some, God's providence was the perfect operation of his physical laws, and others saw God as taking a more active agency in human affairs. In this sense, George Washington was not a classic deist, for he held closely to the belief that divine providence meant that God did indeed intervene in human affairs. While serving as a general during the Revolution, Washington encouraged soldiers to attend worship services and discouraged profanity among the troops, and as president, he issued two national thanksgiving proclamations.

Whatever specific religious beliefs the nation's founders might have held, they generally agreed that morality was crucial to the success of republican politics and that organized religion was necessary, or at least helpful, in the development of an appropriate morality for the nation. As for deists, because they believed that the core of all sound religions was the same, they emphasized religious tolerance. Many prominent Americans of the time cautiously accepted the idea that reason and revelation could provide mutual support in developing and maintaining the human virtues required for republican government (West 1996, 76).

By the time the Revolution began, all but four of the colonies had some provision for an established church. Ministers who supported American independence tended to interpret the conflict as a struggle similar to the one between Israel and Egypt, with the colonies having been chosen by God as the "New Israel" (Gamble 2003, 10–11). Although the First Amendment to the U.S. Constitution prohibited the establishment of a state religion, the U.S. Supreme Court initially interpreted the Bill of Rights as applying only to the national government and not to the states. Consequently, more than forty years elapsed after the ratification of the First Amendment in 1791 before all of the states had ceased having an established religion. In the decades following the Revolution, the states one by one set aside such religious establishment provisions in their constitutions, until, in 1833, Massachusetts became the last state to end official support of religion. However, even after the elimination of any officially established religions, the states continued to maintain a series of statutes prohibiting blasphemy and Sabbath-breaking, to call for days of prayer, and to require a profession of religious belief from those who desired to hold public office (West 1996, 127). Even the present-day Texas constitution, originally adopted in 1876, contains a provision within its Bill of Rights that prohibits religious tests for any office holder, "provided he acknowledge the existence of a Supreme Being."

Although essentially a deist, John Adams kept his religious views very private and publicly expressed the precepts of orthodox Christianity. When president, Adams issued declarations for fast days as religious observances. Thomas Jefferson's more widely known doubts about traditional Christian doctrine, and his willingness to criticize such tenets of Christian belief as the Trinity and the validity of the miracles recorded in the Bible, resulted in the more conservative clergy's actively opposing his election as president in 1796 and 1800. Such opposition notwithstanding, Jefferson won the presidential election of 1800. He personally supported the development of Unitarianism as the religious position most appropriate to the United States.

However, other citizens preferred a more traditional religion, and another major religious revival, called the Second Great Awakening, occurred in the early nineteenth century and contributed to the prevalence of orthodox Christian beliefs. A significant outcome was that the Methodists and Baptists, benefiting from the evangelical appeal of the revival, became the largest Protestant denominations in the country. This revival also contributed to the creation of the Disciples of Christ out of Presbyterianism as another major evangelical denomination. Sunday schools became a major source of education in the early nineteenth century, mixing basic education with religious instruction. Between 1828 and 1835, the number of children attending Sunday school increased from approximately 127,000 to 1 million (West 1996, 102).

Christians and Politics in the Nineteenth Century

In addition to the more personally oriented religious revival in the early nineteenth century, evangelical leaders such as Lyman Beecher initiated campaigns for social reform. Beecher expected the United States to lead the world in moral and political liberation. He hoped that the country would be an example for all others, replacing violence with intelligence and virtue (Gamble 2003, 19). For instance, Alexander Hamilton's death in a duel at the hands of Aaron Burr in

1804 precipitated a crusade against dueling, and Christian luminaries took the lead in this movement. Beecher preached a well-publicized sermon against dueling, and Yale president and prominent evangelical Christian Timothy Dwight also spoke out against the practice. Religious organizations passed resolutions condemning dueling, and clergymen preached sermons against the practice. Although instances of dueling continued, public opinion began to shift against the increasingly archaic means of resolving personal conflicts. In 1839, after two congressmen participated in a duel in which one of them was killed, Congress finally enacted legislation making dueling illegal in the District of Columbia.

A major evangelical Christian concern during the 1830s was the preservation of the Christian Sabbath as a day of rest. In 1810, Congress had enacted legislation that required post offices to remain open all seven days of the week. In 1828, evangelicals established the General Union for Promoting the Observance of the Christian Sabbath to oppose this policy. One point of contention was that the federal government, by requiring the mails to run on Sunday, had overruled state and local ordinances against breaking the Sabbath. In addition, those opposed to the Sunday mails argued that the federal government was violating the right of conscience by requiring employees to choose between keeping their jobs with the post office by working on Sundays and thus violating their conscience or observing the Sabbath according to their own religious beliefs, thereby risking the loss of their jobs. Therefore, the group argued, the First Amendment protection of free religious practice required the federal government to cease Sunday mail delivery. Supporting the compelling state interest standard, evangelicals argued that the government should refrain from limiting the free exercise of religion in the absence of an overriding reason to do otherwise. Those supporting the Sunday mails publicly accused their opponents of attempting to impair republican government and of restricting religious liberty by imposing a particular day of the week on all citizens as an official day of rest (West 1996, 157). Although the attempt to stop the Sunday mails failed, by the 1840s, many Sunday mail routes had been terminated anyway due to improved systems of communication and transportation.

A second issue of the time inspiring evangelical political involvement was the conflict over Native American lands in Georgia. For many years, the state of Georgia had been attempting to gain additional land concessions from the Cherokee tribe. President Andrew Jackson, sympathizing with Georgia's desire to gain control of more land, decided to leave the fate of the Cherokees completely up to the state. The immediate intervention of evangelicals occurred when Georgia, concerned about whites fomenting discontent among the Native American tribe over the land issue, passed a law that prohibited white people from living with the Cherokees unless the whites declared their loyalty to the state and obtained a license. Attempts by religious groups to defend the Indians' claims to the land failed, even though the Supreme Court upheld the rights of the missionaries and the Cherokees (West 1996, 202). In 1838, more than 12,000 Cherokees were placed in detention camps in preparation for removal and were ultimately transported to Oklahoma. Many of them suffered and died as a result of the removal, and a tribal civil war occurred after they arrived in Oklahoma. Although the support of religious groups failed to protect the Cherokee tribe from suffering the consequences of removal, without the intervention of evangelicals, the tribe would have had no supporters of any consequence.

The Revolutionary period would not be the last time that American clergy took opposing sides in a major conflict. The efforts of religious groups that opposed the Sunday mails and Cherokee removal were initial experiments in religious group involvement in the political process and were a prelude to the struggle over slavery, which would activate many Christians and Christian organizations prior to the Civil War. According to Kevin Phillips (1999), while the first Great Awakening of American religious fervor contributed to the American Revolution in 1775, the Second Great Awakening, beginning in 1799, played a significant role in the subsequent political mobilizations that undergirded the Civil War. In the northeastern United States of the 1830s, fervor over the perfectibility of humankind gave rise to a dozen "isms," from utopianism to abolitionism. This religious revival has been described as second commandment Christianity, as it was concerned with loving or improving one's neighbor through strict keeping of the Sabbath, temperance, and the abolition of slavery (Phillips 1999, 357–359).

In the South, the story was more complicated and varied by social class. In the churches of the lower-class whites, many of whom were Baptists, the Second Great Awakening centered on personal sin and salvation. Unlike the more community-focused, reformist revivals in the northeast, the revivals of the lower-class whites in the South concentrated on changing the individual rather than reforming society. Southern elites in the Episcopalian church, on the other hand, were less interested in change and more concerned with a biblical defense of slavery and in preserving the social and economic status quo (Phillips 1999, 373–375).

Religion provided the context for the different views of politics in these Southern personal revivals and Northern reformist revivals, but politics was also a major force in fashioning U.S. religious denominations. Disagreements over slavery eventually split the three major Protestant denominations into northern and southern groups. The Southern Methodists broke away from the Methodists in 1844, the Southern Baptists from the Baptists in 1845, and the "Old School" Presbyterians divided from the northern "New School" ones in stages from 1837 to 1861 (Phillips 1999, 282–284).

In 1818, the Presbyterian General Assembly declared that slavery was "a gross violation of the most precious and sacred right of human nature" and contrary to the laws of God (Reichley 2002, 180). On the other hand, in 1822, the South Carolina Baptists Association, supporting the institution of slavery, presented the traditional argument that the existence of slavery represented punishment for original sin (Reichley 2002, 181). In 1844, when the Methodist General Conference declared that Bishop James Andrews, because he was a slaveholder, should cease to perform his church functions, fourteen Methodist regional conferences in the South left the General Conference to establish the Methodist Episcopal Church, South. In the 1850s, Henry Ward Beecher (son of Lyman Beecher and brother of Harriet Beecher Stowe, author of the anti-slavery novel *Uncle Tom's Cabin*) was the Congregationalist pastor of Plymouth Church in Brooklyn, New York. Beecher solicited donations from his parishioners to purchase Sharps rifles, which were sent to antislavery groups in Kansas to aid in their defense against proslavery forces. In his sermons, Beecher linked the Union cause to the struggle for liberty everywhere, optimistically foreseeing a grand future for all nations unified in a common mission (Gamble 2003, 19). During the Civil War, religious leaders on both sides proclaimed that God favored their cause. Following the Civil War, northern Protestants tended to identify with the Republicans. Various reasons have been suggested for this general preference for the Republican party, including that party's close ties to the Union side in the Civil War, northern Protestants' preference for Republican economic policies, and an image of the Republican party as the party of morality (Reichley 2002, 190). Despite the general loyalty of Protestants to the Republicans, Democrat William Jennings Bryan, in his first bid for the presidency in 1896, tried to appeal to evangelical Christian sentiments in his campaign. In delivering his famous "Cross of Gold" speech at the Democratic national convention, Bryan intended, at least in part, to attract religious support: "You shall not press down upon the brow of labor this crown of thorns, you shall not crucify mankind upon a cross of gold" (Morison 1965, 798). This appeal notwithstanding, Protestant clergy and lay people generally supported Republican William McKinley as the candidate of the party of order and moral principle.

The Rise of a "Two-Party System" in American Protestantism

In the late nineteenth century, there continued to develop a significant division in Protestantism: The more liberal, humanist groups were associated with the social gospel movement, which focused on serving the earthly needs of human beings, and the more conservative denominations were chiefly concerned with personal salvation. This division would widen still further in the twentieth century. The liberal segment of Protestantism had its origins in the deism of early Americans such as Thomas Jefferson and gained additional support from the Unitarian movement in New England. This humanist element in Christianity avidly supported abolition before the Civil War and advocated southern reconstruction following the armed conflict. Protestant ministers such as Josiah Strong and Walter Rauschenbusch advocated the social gospel perspective.

Church historian Martin Marty (1970) has noted that a "two-party system" developed in American Protestantism between the mainline churches and the more fundamentalist evangelical denominations. The idea of a two-party system usually involved a conservative majority in the mainline churches composed primarily of lay people, and a liberal minority, including a central core of the clergy (Reichley 2002, 198). Contributing to the two-party split within American Protestantism was the increasing influence in the late nineteenth century of a German trend of "higher criticism" of the Bible, a criticism that rejected scripture as the infallible word of God and instead regarded the Bible as subject to the same analysis as any other literary work. By 1910, this more liberal religious outlook had influenced most of the major Protestant seminaries, and by the late 1920s, most fundamentalist Christians—those adhering to the central beliefs of historic Christianity, such as the infallible authority of the Bible, the virgin birth of Jesus, and Jesus' central importance in a person's achieving personal salvation—had left the major Christian denominations, and those denominations had become part of mainline Protestantism. The mainline churches were governed primarily by a clergy committed to a more modern, liberal theology that put into question the tenets of the more orthodox theology of traditional Christianity (Guth et al. 1997, 10).

The orthodox evangelical denominations espoused a more individualist theology, believing that the major problems society faced had their origin in the sinful condition in which individual human beings were snared and that if any improvement were to occur, it must originate in the salvation of individual persons. On the other hand, the "modernist" mainline churches, particularly the leadership and clergy of these churches, focused on social explanations for the various evils found in society and on possible strategies for bringing about the betterment of the human condition in this earthly life. According to this more progressive party within Christianity, people needed sufficient nourishment, shelter, protection, and gainful employment to live honest, peaceful, and productive lives, and Christians must bear the responsibility of creating the institutions capable of delivering these basic human needs.

The division between the liberal, or progressive, and the more conservative, or fundamentalist, factions within Christian denominations was highlighted by their respective responses to World War I. Progressives had expected that, entering the twentieth century, Christian influence on the world would lead to a new era of peace within and among nations. As the European conflict loomed, the more progressive clergy suggested that Christians had to share some of the blame for the war because they focused too heavily on an individualistic gospel and on otherworldly salvation, disdaining their obligations to promote equality and brotherhood in this world (Gamble 2003, 93). Possible Christian blameworthiness for the war notwithstanding, many progressive Christian leaders began to see the war as a valuable opportunity to remake the world. The war became, for many, an opportunity to establish democracy and ultimately to end war for all time.

J. Gresham Machen, the conservative Presbyterian theologian, expressed his objections to the progressive interpretation of the war as a conflict between the absolutes of good and evil. He rejected as foolish the notion that the war was being fought for democracy. Even following the disillusionment that set in at the end of the war, many progressives remained hopeful about the future possibilities for achieving justice in the world. In the 1920s, Machen expressed the view that, despite material advancement, the world had in fact continued to decline (Gamble 2003, 234). The disagreement between liberal and conservative Christians revolved in part around contrasting understandings of what could effect genuine improvement in the human condition. Liberals continued to believe that institutional reforms could eliminate evil, a view that conservatives found naïve.

Some charged that Christians had confused patriotism with religion (Gamble 2003, 237) by regarding the United States as a savior nation for the rest of the world. The liberal Federal Council of Churches, precursor to the National Council of Churches, continued to call for reforms to institute economic and racial justice as well as international disarmament, and it lobbied Congress to allow the United States to participate in the International Court of Justice and to cooperate more closely with the League of Nations (Gamble 2003, 241). More liberal Christians continued to believe in progress and the United States as the source of redemption for the world.

Following World War I, temperance reemerged as a major theme for evangelical Christians. Temperance had become a topic of concern for reform-minded evangelicals in the nineteenth century, and Christian groups had initiated campaigns against the use of alcohol. The American Temperance Society was established in 1826, and by 1828, more than 400 temperance organizations had been created around the nation. In 1846, the first state law instituting prohibition of alcohol had been passed in Maine, and thirteen other states quickly followed with their own statutes. However, by 1865, only two states continued a prohibition policy. In 1869, Frances Willare, president of the Women's Christian Temperance Union, initiated the formation of the Prohibition party, which combined an antialcohol campaign with such other social crusades as women's rights and the call for a more egalitarian economic structure (Reichley 2002, 205).

In 1893, the Anti-Saloon League was formed, which, in order to avoid conflict with more conservative Christians, eschewed issues associated with the social reform movement and focused its efforts completely on prohibition. Finally, in 1919, the states ratified the Eighteenth Amendment to the U.S. Constitution, which stated that "the manufacture, sale, or transportation of intoxicating liquors within, the importation thereof into, or the exportation thereof from the Unites States and all territory subject to the jurisdiction thereof for beverage purposes is hereby prohibited." Ironically, this intervention of religious interests into the political process to regulate the morality of the population in fact led to an era in which a large portion of the American people sidestepped the law of the land to procure alcoholic beverages. A group of entrepreneurs—bootleggers and gangsters—eagerly broke the law in order to provide Americans with a product they themselves had decided to prohibit. This experiment in legalized morality came to an end in 1933 with the ratification of the Twenty-First Amendment, repealing Prohibition. This amendment has been the only one ratified through the alternative constitutional procedure involving state conventions rather than state legislatures, because supporters of repeal in Congress feared that religious groups still wielded very strong influence in state legislatures and therefore would likely have defeated the amendment.

In addition to Prohibition, more conservative Christians faced another battle in the first decades of the twentieth century that was more consonant with fundamentalist Christian opposition to modernism. Ever since Charles Darwin published *Origin of Species* (1856), detailing a theory of evolution through natural selection that portrayed human beings as the result of development from lower forms of life, conservative Christians had mounted a counteroffensive against what they considered a serious threat to the moral and religious foundations of society. In 1925, John T. Scopes, a high school teacher, intentionally violated a Tennessee law prohibiting teaching the theory of evolution in the public schools. When Scopes was put on trial, William Jennings Bryan, a three-time Democratic presidential candidate and the secretary of state during President Woodrow Wilson's first term, agreed to serve as one of the prosecutors in Scopes's trial. Politically, Bryan supported liberal causes such as woman suffrage, a national minimum wage, and a graduated income tax. However, on the issue of evolution, he held a typically fundamentalist Christian position.

The World's Christian Fundamentals Association had asked Bryan to prosecute the case; this was a conservative organization established in 1919 to espouse the traditional beliefs of the Christian faith, including belief in the Trinity, the deity of Jesus, substitutionary atonement, the bodily resurrection of Jesus, and the ultimate bodily resurrection of the just and the unjust. However, other noted fundamentalists failed to provide Bryan with support, leaving him to face by himself the highly skilled defense attorney in the case, Clarence Darrow. Bryan agreed to be cross-examined by Darrow, and Bryan's testimony betrayed his ignorance of the theory of evolution. Although the jury found Scopes guilty, Bryan's public humiliation at the hands of Darrow made the victory seem hollow. Bryan died in his sleep within a week of the trial's end.

Students of Christian conservatism (for example, Reichley 2002, 207) observe that evangelicals largely withdrew from the national political realm following the Scopes trial. However, others (for example, Silverman 2003, 174) suggest that for many years after the trial, public school textbooks approached the topic of evolution very cautiously, indicating a more extensive victory for the conservative Christians than simply the conviction of John T. Scopes for violating a Tennessee law. Conservative Christian denominations and groups still remained an influential force specifically at the state and local levels, where they could pressure more effectively school boards and other governments that had a more direct influence on their everyday lives.

Although analysts (for example, Reichley 2002, 207) point to the notable failures in the crusades against teaching evolution and in support of prohibition as significant reasons for lack of conservative Christian participation in national politics, other, more basic factors led to the withdrawal of many orthodox Christians from the political realm. Premillennialism, the belief that conditions in the world would steadily worsen until Christ returned to fight a major battle with the forces of evil before establishing a thousand-year reign on Earth, was a dominant belief among many evangelicals. Therefore, any concern on their part for secular matters paled in comparison to the conviction that worsening world conditions held the promise of the consummation of biblical prophecy (Guth et al. 1997, 44). Evangelical clergy thus held a more "otherworldly" perspective, which turned them and their congregations away from the social and political concerns of everyday life. On the other hand, mainline Christian clergy sought such engagement. The individualist social theology of evangelicals also contributed to political quiescence, for they perceived the ultimate cause of human problems to lie not in the external political structure but in the individual human heart. Evangelicals concentrated their efforts primarily on saving souls, not fighting political battles. However, direct challenges to the moral beliefs of evangelicals ultimately contributed to their political activism at the national level.

The Twentieth-Century Rise of Christian Political Activism

In the first half of the twentieth century, various Christian denominations, including Methodists, Presbyterians, Baptists, and Lutherans, established offices in Washington, D.C., which demonstrated a willingness to delve into certain areas of politics. In 1950, a group of mainline denominations formed the National Council of Churches (NCC), which was a successor to the old Federal Council of Churches originally established in 1908. In 1941, Carl McIntyre, who claimed that the Federal Council of Churches was too liberal and thus misrepresented the true Christian beliefs of Americans, established the American Council of Christian Churches (ACCC). Members of the ACCC could not also be members of the NCC. After World War II, the ACCC focused on a strong antisocialist and anticommunist agenda, and the NCC followed a more liberal program of social and economic reform.

During the late 1950s and early 1960s, mainline churches were united in the crusade to end racial segregation. The struggle for integration represented just the sort of moral engagement with the world to improve the state of society that more liberal clergy in mainline denominations found appealing, and it proved to be a relatively successful enterprise, producing a high level of unity among denominations. By the late 1960s, the Vietnam War had become another major issue, gaining the attention of mainline clergy such as William Sloan Coffin, Presbyterian minister and chaplain at Yale University. These ministers voiced their strong opposition to U.S. military involvement in Southeast Asia. However, the moral clarity and unity of the civil rights movement could not be reproduced in this new campaign. A significant phenomenon occurred: Although Protestant clergy strongly supported protests against the war, a majority of the Protestant laity voiced opposition to such protests. This gap represented an existing, more general, division within mainline churches between the clergy and laity. Meanwhile, mainline seminaries were graduating a new generation of ministers who had distinctly liberal theological and political views.

The gap between the more conservative views of the membership of mainline churches and the more liberal views of their clergy tended to widen throughout the 1970s. According to Reichley (2002, 262), adding to this gap was a change in the organizational structure of mainline churches: Bureaucratic organization became more important to the operation of church bodies, granting to the clergy greater control over the structure and operation of church organizations. Roberto Michels's (1959) "iron law of oligarchy" came into play: Organizations tend ultimately to be governed by a few people in top decision-making positions. Although church organizations were in structure democracies, they in fact encouraged control by the professional clergy. Resolutions that the leadership introduced at church conventions usually passed with minimal opposition from lay representatives. For instance, the 1981 General Assembly of the Disciples of Christ, at the urging of the clergy, issued a "Peace with Justice" statement supporting disarmament, environmental protection, improved educational opportunities, expanded social welfare programs, and opposition to the Reagan administration's defense policies (Guth et al. 1997, 41).

Guth et al. (1997, 151) note that in the 1960s, while major public attention focused on the activities of more liberal clergy, conservative ministers across the nation became involved in local activities such as supporting the regulation of alcoholic beverages, opposing referenda to legalize gambling, and leading campaigns to place limitations on pornography. A series of political events ultimately led to the rebirth of conservative Christian political activism at the national level in the late 1970s and early 1980s. Among these events were two Supreme Court decisions: the 1962 ruling in *Engel v. Vitale* prohibiting government-sponsored prayer in the public schools and the 1973 decision (*Roe v. Wade*) legalizing abortion. In these types of events, conservative Christians perceived a growing public immorality that was actually being supported by government policy.

The restoration of traditional moral values became the battle cry for conservative Christians as a new group of conservative leaders entered the pubic arena. Paul Weyrich became the director of the National Committee for the Survival of a Free Congress, which was essentially a training center for conservative political candidates. Donald Wildmon organized the National Federation for Decency in 1976 (renamed the American Family Association in 1987); Robert Billings founded the National Christian Action Coalition in 1978; and Edward McAteer established the Religious Roundtable in 1979. Christian Voice, an organization established in 1978, grew out of the anti–gay rights movement in California and gained notoriety for producing "moral report cards" containing information about the voting records of members of Congress on issues of importance to the organization. Christian Voice distributed the "report cards" to churches at election time. In 1979, Billings helped persuade fundamentalist preacher Jerry Falwell to become the leader of the Moral Majority, the most prominent conservative Christian organization in the 1980s. Early in his career as a preacher, Falwell had declined to take part in politics, but as he became convinced that the United States was in moral decline, he agreed to become politically active as a leader of conservative Christians.

Although conservative Christian leaders established organizations for the express purpose of becoming more actively involved in politics, the more prominent leaders themselves did not gain widespread acceptance among the U.S. population. Throughout American history, although their theological credentials have given religious leaders greater visibility in the political realm, once they take an active part in politics, these leaders become as exposed to strong criticism as any other person involved in the political realm. The American people have shown great respect for religious leaders, but at times they have rejected such leaders' more direct involvement in politics. When some religious leaders have attempted to gain high public office, the voters have often rejected them at the polls. In 1988, Pat Robertson, a charismatic evangelical preacher and host of the *700 Club* television program, entered the campaign for the Republican presidential nomination. In the Iowa caucuses, in which the outcome depended on the participation of well-motivated activists, Robertson finished a close second behind Senator Robert Dole. However, in the New Hampshire Republican primary a week later, Robertson received a disappointing 9 percent of the vote. Even in the subsequent southern state primaries, Robertson did not win the largest share of the votes of evangelicals, finishing behind Dole and George H. W. Bush (Reichley 2002, 330). Fellow evangelical leaders such as Jerry Falwell, perhaps uncomfortable with Robertson's Pentecostal affiliation, backed Bush for the nomination. Following his disappointing showing in the 1988 Republican presidential primaries, Robertson formed the Christian Coalition, which campaigned to elect candidates at the local, state, and national levels who expressed appropriate moral values. Jerry Falwell also experienced opposition in the general public. In 1989, Falwell, who was receiving highly negative evaluations in public opinion polls, decided to terminate the Moral Majority, which had been renamed Liberty Federation in 1987 in what proved an unsuccessful attempt to attract nonfundamentalist supporters.

In 2000, Gary Bauer, director of the Family Research Council, entered the race for the Republican presidential nomination as the heir apparent to the support that conservative Christians had previously given to Ronald Reagan. However, Bauer gained little support in the early primaries. Fellow evangelicals did not respond to Bauer's appeal for support, pledging their allegiance instead to George W. Bush. Bauer soon dropped out of the race, endorsing Senator John McCain of Arizona for the Republican nomination. In February, McCain reacted to a smear campaign against him during the South Carolina primary battle, criticizing conservative Christian leaders such as Falwell and Robertson and calling them "agents of intolerance."

Both Falwell and Robertson tended to alienate the general public. For instance, soon after the September 11, 2001, terrorist attacks, Falwell, while a guest on Robertson's *700 Club,* suggested that the attacks indicated God's judgment on immoral elements in American society. Robertson publicly agreed with Falwell's analysis. Following the strong negative response to this from the general public as well as from fellow Christian conservatives, Falwell apologized for his statements, and Robertson admitted that they should not have been made. Soon thereafter, Robertson stepped down as president of the Christian Coalition. Although Robertson predicted that the Coalition would regain its former stature, others suggested that the organization likely had lost its influence in American politics for the foreseeable future. Critics argued that Robertson, by failing to fulfill the organization's agenda (including supporting school prayer and campaigning for a ban on abortion) and by failing to support impeachment efforts against President Bill Clinton, contributed to the demise of the Coalition.

Other conservative Christian organizations proliferated during the 1980s and 1990s, often forming around a narrow group of issues.

Describing Christian Conservative Denominations Today

The denominational landscape in the United States is extraordinarily complex, but as the above historical account of the evolution of activism and beliefs indicates, one can identify Christian conservative and mainline Protestant denominations by the religious and political beliefs of their members. In categorizing denominations as fundamentalist or mainline for the purposes of this book, we have generally followed the research methodology developed by the General Social Survey (GSS). The GSS is a recurring nationwide probability sample of U.S. households. Begun in 1972 and continued to the present, the GSS is an authoritative source of information on U.S. public opinion. Its surveys are conducted for the National Data Program for the Social Sciences at the National Opinion Research Center (NORC) of the University of Chicago, and the GSS data are distributed by the Roper Center for Public Opinion Research at the University of Connecticut (Davis and Smith 2003). Tom W. Smith (1987) describes a multifactor approach to categorization that includes not only the survey answers of denominational members but also prior scholarly classifications, membership in ecumenical associations, and the stated theological beliefs of the denominations.

The mainline churches may have ministers and administrators whose views are generally more liberal than those of their congregations, but the surveyed religious views of the mainline congregations can also be distinguished from the more fundamentalist beliefs of the Christian conservative membership. Individual beliefs, of course, may vary from member to member, but the majority of Christian conservative members adhere to the inerrancy of the Bible, which is seen as a complete and verbally correct guide to life. On the other hand, although the majority of mainline church members regard the Bible as divinely inspired, they tend not to take it literally, word for word, as being factually true. Some mainline Christians may have relatively fundamentalist views, but many of them regard the Bible as metaphor and as a story of the search for meaning. Fundamentalists hold that the Bible is literally true, both as science and as history, whereas mainline members tend to accept secular change and science as important or at least as not being antireligious.

Using the GSS survey responses of denomination members guided us to categorize many current Protestant denominations as fundamentalist. We compared these categorizations with denominational data from the National Election Survey to confirm their reliability. We then investigated the membership and number of adherents of each denomination using the *Religious Congregations & Membership* data of the Glenmary Research Center for 1990 and 2000 (Jones et al. 2002). There appear to be many small congregations for which authoritative data are not available. Independent and nondenominational church members may be interviewed in GSS surveys, but these congregations often do not provide data about membership and number of adherents. Nonetheless, this multiple approach allowed us to produce a list of eight mainline denominations with almost 26 million adherents in 2000 and a list of thirty-six fundamentalist denominations with more than 37 million adherents. With that categorization in hand, we were able to investigate the demographic characteristics of denomination members as well as trends in the growth or decline in the number of adherents from 1990 to 2000.

In many ways, Christian conservatives today are much like their counterparts in the mainline Protestant denominations. The size of the cities in which they live, family income, and several other demographic characteristics do not differ greatly between members of mainline and fundamentalist denominations. But these denominations do

TABLE 1.1   Region of Residence of Fundamentalist and Mainline Christians

	Southern U.S.	Other U.S. Regions
Fundamentalists (n=5,240)	58%	42%
Mainline (n=3,775)	38%	62%

Source: General Social Survey. 2002. *NORC-GSS Cumulative Data File 1972–2000.* Storrs, CT: The Roper Center for Public Opinion Research.

differ in some interesting ways. GSS data from in-home surveys by the National Opinion Research Center from 1972 through 2000 can be combined to produce the following demographic comparisons between interviewees who identified themselves as belonging to the mainline denominations and those who identified themselves as belonging to the fundamentalist denominations (Tables 1.1 and 1.2).

GSS survey data indicate that 58 percent of the members of fundamentalist denominations live in the south, versus 38 percent of mainline members. The Glenmary Research Center data for 2000 indicate that 65 percent of the adherents of all reported denominations were located outside of the south, whereas 35 percent were located in the south. For the purposes of both these surveys, the "south" category consisted of denominational reports from Texas, Oklahoma, Arkansas, Louisiana, Mississippi, Alabama, Tennessee, Kentucky, West Virginia, Maryland, Delaware, Virginia, North Carolina, South Carolina, Georgia, and Florida (Jones et al. 2002). As the following summaries of GSS survey data indicate, although Christian conservatives are demographically similar to their mainline counterparts, they are a bit younger and somewhat less educated than those of the selected mainline denominations.

Trends in Denominational Size and Political Preferences

In an effort to achieve comparability across years and across denominations, the Association of Statisticians of American Religious Bodies compiled data on denominational adherents. They define *adherents* as all full members, their children, and the estimated number of

TABLE 1.2   Demographics for Fundamentalist and Mainline Christians

Size of City of Residence	>50,000	2,500 to 49,999	<2,500
Fundamentalists (n=5,240)	65%	17%	18%
Mainline (n=3,775)	71%	15%	15%

Income in 1986	Less than $5,000	$5,000 to $25,000	$25,000 to $50,000	Greater than $50,000
Fundamentalists (n=5,073)	33%	37%	23 %	8%
Mainline (n=3,775)	29%	30%	26%	14%

Education, Highest Level	< High School	High School Diploma	Jr. College Degree	Bachelor's Degree	Graduate Degree
Fundamentalists (n=5,226)	28%	55%	4%	9%	4%
Mainline (n=3,765)	15%	52%	6%	18%	9%

Age	18–29	30–49	50–64	65+
Fundamentalists (n=5,250)	19%	40%	21%	20%
Mainline (n=3,775)	15%	37%	23%	25%

Source: General Social Survey. 2002. NORC-GSS Cumulative Data File 1972–2000. Storrs, CT: The Roper Center for Public Opinion Research.

other participants, such as "the baptized," "those not confirmed," and "those regularly attending services." In Tables 1.3 and 1.4, we present data on the total number of reported adherents for mainline and evangelical denominations, respectively.

As Table 1.3 indicates, all eight of the mainline Protestant denominations reported declines in their numbers of adherents, and these drops occurred at the same time that the overall U.S. population grew by 13.2 percent, from almost 249 million to more than 281 million people.

TABLE 1.3　Total Reported Adherents for Mainline Protestant Denominations, 1990 and 2000

Mainline Denomination	Adherents in 2000	Adherents in 1990	Percent Change
American Baptist Churches in the USA	1,767,462	1,873,731	–5.7
Christian Church (Disciples of Christ)	1,017,784	1,037,757	–1.9
Episcopal Church	2,314,756	2,445,286	–5.3
Evangelical Lutheran Church in America	5,113,418	5,226,798	–2.2
Presbyterian Church (USA)	3,141,566	3,553,335	–11.6
United Church of Christ	1,698,918	1,993,459	–14.8
United Methodist Church	10,350,629	11,091,032	-6.7
Reformed Church in America	335,677	362,932	–7.5
Total	**25,740,210**	**27,584,330**	**–6.7**
U.S. Total Population	**281,421,906**	**248,709,873**	**13.2**

Sources: Bradley, Martin B., Norman M. Green, Jr., Dale E. Jones, Mac Lynn, and Lou McNeil. 1992. *Churches and Church Membership in the United States, 1990.* Atlanta, GA: Glenmary Research Center; Jones, Dale E., Sherri Doty, James E. Horsch, Richard Houseal, Mac Lynn, John P. Marcum, Kenneth M. Sanchagrin, and Richard H. Taylor. 2002. *Religious Congregations and Membership in the United States, 2000: An Enumeration by Region, State, and County Based on Data Reported by 149 Religious Bodies.* Nashville, TN: Glenmary Research Center.

The Roman Catholic Church in the United States (not shown in Table 1.3) was the only mainline Christian denomination that showed growth in the number of adherents, although it posted a decline in the number of churches. Data indicate that the Catholic church had 22,441 churches and 53,385,998 adherents for 1990 versus 21,791 churches and 62,035,042 adherents in 2000—a decline of 3 percent in the number of churches and an increase of 16 percent in the number of adherents. Reichley (2002, 263) notes that the increase in the number of Catholic adherents can be attributed primarily to immigration from traditionally Catholic Latin American countries. But, aside from this Catholic immigration, the mainline Protestant denominations showed ten-year decreases in the number of adherents that ranged from –1.9 percent to –14.8 percent.

On the other hand, the number of adherents in evangelical Protestant denominations grew substantially from 1990 to 2000. Table 1.4 shows data for 36 fundamentalist denominations with reported adherents of 50,000 or more in the United States. During the 1990s, twenty-two of these denominations increased the number of adherents. Seven of them did not report data for 1990 and were new additions to the 2000 survey, and only six of the thirty-six evangelical denominations indicated declines in the number of adherents.

As in previous decades, evangelical denominations increased in size while mainline denominations lost members. Although the mainline denominations listed in Table 1.3 experienced an almost 7 percent decline in adherents overall, the 36 evangelical denominations listed in Table 1.4 experienced more than an eleven percent increase in adherents from 1990 to 2000. Some evangelical denominations, such as the Assemblies of God and the Christian Churches and Churches of Christ, had increases of between 15 and 20 percent. Other, smaller denominations experienced even larger percentage increases, although their absolute numbers are small compared to those of the major denominations.

Of significance to the political fortunes of the conservative Christian agenda has been the continuing rise in the membership of evangelical denominations and the fall in membership of mainline churches, as well as the strong tendency of mainline church laity to support more conservative political positions and to vote for Republican candidates. Kohut et al. (2000, 32) categorize respondents as more highly committed or less highly committed religiously, basing these categories on the level of religious practice and acceptance of traditional beliefs and noting that the percentage of committed evangelical Protestants increased slightly (from 23.9 percent in 1965 to 25.4 percent in 1996).

The proportion of committed members declined among mainline denominations, Roman Catholics, and black Protestants. Findings from the 1994–1996 Pew surveys regarding religious affiliation and political party identification indicate that 46 percent of committed evangelical Protestants identified with the Republican party, compared to 33 percent of less committed evangelicals, 42 percent of more committed mainline Protestants, and 32 percent of less com-

TABLE 1.4   Total Reported Adherents for Fundamentalist Denominations, 1990 and 2000

Fundamentalist Denomination	Adherents in 2000	Adherents in 1990	Percent Change
Denominations with 50,000 to 100,000 Adherents			
Conservative Congregational Christian Conference	50,940	35,600	43.1
North American Baptist Conference	59,545	54,010	10.25
Cumberland Presbyterian Church	77,686	91,040	−14.67
International Churches of Christ	79,161	NR	NR
Evangelical Presbyterians	80,207	45,464	76.42
Church of God of Prophecy	91,106	91,861	−0.82
Free Methodist Church of North America	96,237	82,766	16.28
Subtotal	**534,882**	**460,741**	**33.5%**
Denominations with 100,000 to 240,000 Adherents			
Pentecostal Church of God	101,921	91,072	11.91
New Testament Association of Independent Baptist Churches and Other Fundamentalist Baptists	132,684	NR	NR
Evangelical Covenant Church	153,116	NR	NR
Vineyard USA	155,170	NR	NR
Mennonite Church USA	156,345	154,259	1.35
Conservative Baptist Association of America	224,306	NR	NR
Church of God (Anderson, Indiana)	238,609	232,876	2.46
Baptist General Conference	238,920	167,874	42.32
Subtotal	**1,401,071**	**646,081**	**116.9**

(continues)

TABLE 1.4 *(continued)*

Fundamentalist Denomination	Adherents in 2000	Adherents in 1990	Percent Change
Denominations with 240,000 to 330,000 Adherents			
International Pentecostal Holiness Church	241,828	157,728	53.32
General Association of Regular Baptists	245,636	NR	NR
Christian Reformed Church in North America	248,938	226,163	10.07
National Association of Free Will Baptists	254,170	293,448	−13.38
American Baptist Association	280,973	NR	NR
Evangelical Free Church	285,699	181,692	57.24
Baptist Missionary Association of America	295,239	289,969	1.82
Presbyterian Church in America	315,293	221,392	42.41
Subtotal	**2,167,776**	**1,370,392**	**58.2**
Denominations with 330,000 to 1,000,000 Adherents			
Christian and Missionary Alliances	331,106	271,865	21.79
International Church of the Foursquare Gospel	347,367	255,092	36.17
Wesleyan	381,459	259,740	46.86
Wisconsin Evangelical Lutheran Synod	405,078	419,928	−3.54
Church of the Nazarene	907,331	888,123	2.16
Seventh-Day Adventist	923,046	903,062	2.21
Independent, Charismatic Churches	935,168	794,254	17.74
Church of God (Cleveland, Tennessee)	974,198	695,074	40.16
Subtotal	**5,204,753**	**4,487,138**	**16.0**

(continues)

TABLE 1.4   *(continued)*

Fundamentalist Denomination	Adherents in 2000	Adherents in 1990	Percent Change
Denominations with more than 1,000,000 Adherents			
Christian Churches and Churches of Christ	1,439,253	1,213,188	18.63
Churches of Christ	1,645,584	1,681,013	–2.11
Lutheran Church— Missouri Synod	2,521,062	2,603,725	–3.17
Assembly of God	2,561,998	2,161,610	18.52
Southern Baptist	19,881,467	18,940,682	4.97
Subtotal	**28,049,364**	**26,600,218**	**5.5**
Total Adherents Reported in 2000 and 1990	**37,357,846**	**33,504,576**	**11.5**

Sources: Bradley, Martin B., Norman M. Green, Jr., Dale E. Jones, Mac Lynn, and Lou McNeil. 1992. *Churches and Church Membership in the United States, 1990.* Atlanta, GA: Glenmary Research Center; Jones, Dale E., Sherri Doty, James E. Horsch, Richard Houseal, Mac Lynn, John P. Marcum, Kenneth M. Sanchagrin, and Richard H. Taylor. 2002. *Religious Congregations and Membership in the United States, 2000: An Enumeration by Region, State, and County Based on Data Reported by 149 Religious Bodies.* Nashville, TN: Glenmary Research Center.

mitted mainline Protestants. Only 19 percent of nonreligious people reported a strong Republican party identification. However, in addition to the increased numbers of conservative Christians, there has been an increase in the number of Americans who do not identify with any religious group (Kohut et al. 2000, 75).

Survey data comparing religious affiliations in 1965 and 1996 indicate that the largest percentage gain was in the secular category, which includes those stating no religious preference as well as respondents stating that they are atheists or agnostics. This category increased from 9.7 percent of respondents in a 1965 Gallup poll to 16.3 percent of those sampled in the 1996 Pew Religion Survey (Kohut et al. 2000, 18). Therefore, two disparate trends can be highlighted: increasing numbers of adherents in more evangelical churches, but also an increasing number of Americans who deny any affiliation with an organized religion. Employing data from the 1996 National Election Study, Kohut et al. (2000, 55) conclude that seculars are more liberal than other religious groups on social, sexual, and cultural issues as well as on defense, although they are slightly more conservative than the general sample on the scope of government activity. The major losers in these two trends are the mainline churches, which have been caught between these opposing pulls. Unlike both mainline and evangelical Protestants, who tend to support the Republican party, those with no religious affiliation are more likely to back the Democratic party. Therefore, the fortunes of the two major political parties may depend to some extent on trends in religious affiliation and nonaffiliation, as well as on the propensity of each group to participate in elections.

The racial composition of fundamentalist denominations is important to understanding the political partisanship of their members. Black conservative Christians may be as religiously conservative as their white neighbors; but while many white conservative Christians have begun to identify themselves as Republicans and independents, most black conservative Christians continue to consider themselves Democrats. Black conservative Christians are an important part of fundamentalist churches. When members of all of the fundamentalist denominations examined in this book were surveyed for the General Social Survey, 79 percent were white and 19 percent were black (2 percent were categorized as "other"). Mainline denomination members, on the other hand, were found to be 90 percent white and 9 percent black.

From 1964 onward, two-thirds or more of black voters have identified themselves as Democrats. In their study of generational change and party identification, Stanley and Niemi (2001, 341) declared that the impact of political events associated with the civil rights movement and national partisan competition for the black vote were so intrusive as to complicate any effort at analyzing changes in black party identification. Similarly, our analyses of voting and partisanship among conservative Christians were also complicated by racial factors. We make a more detailed examination of the effects of race and partisanship within three fundamentalist churches in chapter 4. But the gist is that race matters more than religion in determining the partisanship of most black conservative Christians and that this group can embrace a liberal social issue without surrendering their conservative religious stance.

Conservative Christians and Political Issues

The presidency of Jimmy Carter was one of the factors that led conservative Christian leaders like Jerry Falwell to enter the political arena. Carter, a Southern Baptist, attracted support from evangelicals for his run for the presidency in 1976. However, once he became president, Carter disappointed many evangelicals with the liberal positions he took on issues of concern to them, such as abortion. The leadership of the Christian right largely deserted Carter in the 1980 election, instead backing Ronald Reagan. When Reagan assumed the presidency, he did not disappoint his conservative Christian backers, supporting constitutional amendments to allow prayer in the public schools and to ban abortion.

Although mainline churches supported the notion of the social gospel throughout the twentieth century, more conservative Christian organizations, as they became more active in the 1970s, emphasized what has been called a civic gospel, which involved the reemergence of the old themes of individual salvation and responsibility but with an added emphasis on the Bible as the source of the nation's moral principles. Billy James Hargis was an earlier and more strident example of this propensity to associate biblical principles with a national purpose. In the 1950s, Hargis added patriotism and anticommunism to the fundamentalist Christian theme. Conservative principles were offered as an alternative to the more liberal programs of the mainline churches and the seculars. Advocates of the civic gospel saw a connection between Christian orthodoxy and a free enterprise system. As for social welfare programs, some evangelicals supported cooperation between government and private faith-based organizations, believing that both the physical as well as the spiritual needs of the less advantaged should be addressed. They rejected the perceived standard liberal tendency to focus solely on the physical needs of the poor. Being an orthodox Christian was seen as requiring a particular political commitment. For instance, Guth et al. (1997, 64) report findings from the 1990–1991 Wheaton Religious Activist Study that two-thirds of the most orthodox Christian clergy agree that it would be "hard to be both a true Christian and a political liberal."

Although President Clinton maintained relatively high ratings in the polls for the job he was doing during his second term in office, many Americans were troubled with the perceived lack of moral leadership due to his admitted affair with White House intern Monica Lewinsky and the charges that the president had lied under oath about the affair. For many conservative Christians, such revelations confirmed their belief that the Republican party was the party of stability and moral rectitude and that it should be returned to power. However, Kohut et al. (2000, 93), reporting findings from the 1998 National Election Study, point out that only among committed evangelical Protestants did a majority (56 percent) favor President Clinton's impeachment. Thirty-four percent of both less committed evangelicals and committed mainline Protestants favored efforts to impeach President Clinton. Smaller percentages of other groups supported impeachment efforts. For instance, 19 percent of less committed mainline Protestants, 7 percent of committed black Protestants, and just 3 percent of less committed black Protestants favored impeachment. Among seculars, 21 percent supported removing Clinton from office.

Since September 11, 2001, certain conservative Christian leaders have increasingly perceived the United States and Israel as allies in the struggle against terrorism. In October 2002, Falwell, appearing on CBS television's *60 Minutes,* stated that Muhammad, the founder of Islam, was a terrorist. This statement was the most recent in a series of critical comments made by conservative Christian leaders about the founder of Islam. Pat Robertson had previously referred to Muhammad as "a robber and a brigand," and Billy Graham's son Franklin Graham had labeled Islam an evil and wicked religion. Graham criticized American Muslims for their failure to speak out publicly against the September 11, 2001, terrorists attacks, stating that this silence was evidence that these Muslims agreed that the terrorists were fighting "a just and holy war." The press criticized such statements by conservative Christian leaders, claiming that they were indicative of a hate-filled campaign of intolerance that could have serious consequences for the rights of many Americans. Nonetheless, many Christian groups and publications continued to emphasize the differences between Islam and Christianity and to proclaim the superiority of the Christian faith.

The sometimes avidly anti-Islamic rhetoric of some conservative Christian leaders can be partly explained by a phenomenon called Christian Zionism (Kohut 2000, 50), which predates the September 11 attacks. Many conservative Christians express strong support for the state of Israel. Since the 1980s, Israeli leaders, especially those of the conservative Likud party, have in turn cultivated close relationships with conservative Christian leaders. In 1996, Israeli prime minister Benjamin Netanyahu established the Israel Christian Advocacy Council to nurture support for Israel (Silverstein and Scherer 2002, 58). In July 2002, the Zionist Organization of America recognized Pat

Robertson for his efforts to assist Israel. In his defense of Israel, a San Antonio, Texas, preacher named John Hagee has offered a theological justification for Christian support of the Israeli nation. Hagee has argued that Jews have a unique covenant with God and therefore can receive salvation along with Christians, a claim to which other evangelicals have strongly objected (Utter and Storey 2001, 90). Hagee is reported to have raised more than $1 million to help Jews from the former Soviet Union to resettle in Israel. For such efforts, Hagee received expressions of appreciation from Jewish organizations.

This unlikely alliance between conservative Christians and Israel includes leaders such as Edward McAteer of the Religious Roundtable. Based on their interpretation of Daniel, Revelation, and other prophetic books of the Bible, many conservative Christians view Israel as an important ingredient in what they believe will be the events leading to the end times and the return of Christ. Because President George W. Bush is considered by many to be especially receptive to conservative Christian groups, conservative Christian leaders have pushed hard for the U.S. government to continue its support for Israel. Marshall Wittmann, a former lobbyist with the Christian Coalition, is reported to have identified evangelicals as a major force in communicating the Israeli message to the White House (Silverstein and Scherer, 2002, 59). Critics of evangelical support for Israel claim that evangelicals are more concerned about providing support for that nation than obtaining a peaceful resolution to the Mideast conflict.

When George W. Bush ran for the presidency, he used the theme of compassionate conservatism: Government should show appropriate concern for the economic as well as the moral well-being of the less advantaged. Bush emphasized the so-called faith-based initiative, which involved cooperation between government and religious organizations in providing social welfare services and rehabilitation programs such as treatment for drug addiction. After taking office, President Bush appointed John J. DiIulio Jr., a professor at the University of Pennsylvania, to head the White House Office of Faith-Based and Community Initiatives. However, DiIulio quickly became disillusioned over conflicts that emerged in Congress and among conservative Christians over policy questions regarding the granting of federal funds to religious charities. He resigned in August 2001. In November 2002, in an *Esquire* magazine interview, DiIulio strongly criticized the Bush White House for the overly political nature of its domestic policymaking, calling it "the reign of the Mayberry Machiavellis." In the meantime, because of the strong opposition facing related proposed legislation in Congress, the Bush administration decided to implement a program of faith-based initiatives through executive orders.

Guth et al. (1997, 143–144), in their study of the political activism of Protestant clergy, note that evangelical clergy have a significant advantage over their mainline colleagues: Evangelical church members are more likely to attend services than are mainline church adherents. Mainline laity are less accepting of pastoral leadership than evangelicals, and thus evangelical pastors can rely more confidently on their claim to have biblical sanction for their social and political pronouncements. Guth et al. also observe that the political activism of more liberal clergy slowed considerably when congregations objected to such political involvement (1997, 156). They note that conservative clergy, who have greater support from their congregations, tend to participate politically from the vantage point of traditional religious structures, whereas liberal clergy, who face opposition to pastoral political activism from within their congregations, tend to participate as individuals and not as representatives of their denominations (1997, 167). Evangelical clergy are also in greater agreement with their congregations on political matters than are mainline clergy. However, evangelicals face a limitation on their ability to cooperate across denominational lines. As Ted Jelen (1991) observes, each of these more orthodox groups tends to believe they possess the true faith, to the exclusion of others. For instance, independent Baptist clergy have been hesitant to form alliances with Pentecostals, considering them to be theologically heretical for emphasizing such allegedly questionable concerns as "gifts of the spirit."

Guth et al. (1997) observe that the issues of greatest concern to evangelicals include support for the pro-life position on the abortion question, the teaching of creationism (or at least intelligent design) and the official sanctioning of prayer in the public schools, and opposition to illegal drugs and the gay rights movement. In contrast, mainline churches have emphasized the need to cut defense spending, protect the environment, maintain affirmative action as a means of rectifying discrimination, and establish a national health care system. Although mainline Protestant churches have continued to focus on a "social justice agenda," the evangelical churches have maintained a "moral reform" agenda, striving for major alterations in individual behavior by discouraging such practices as gambling and alcohol consumption and encouraging "family values." Opposition to abortion persists as the primary focus of many conservative Protestants and Roman Catholics.

Sometimes the actions of nonreligious groups and individuals are perceived to confirm conservative Christians' belief that there is a crusade against Christians in the United States, especially when symbols of patriotism are combined with religious themes, as with the Pledge of Allegiance to the American flag. In 2002, a suit was brought by a California man who claimed that the phrase "under God" in the Pledge of Allegiance caused emotional harm to his eight-year-old daughter; the Ninth U.S. Circuit Court of Appeals decided in favor of the father. Many individuals and groups responded quickly to the decision, attacking the court's ruling and defending the reference to God in the Pledge. U.S. senators registered their support by reciting the Pledge en masse in Senate chambers and before the C-Span television cameras. In November 2002, Congress approved legislation—unanimously in the Senate and with just five dissenting votes in the House—reaffirming the reference to God in the Pledge and the phrase "in God we trust" as the national motto that appears on currency. President Bush quickly signed the bill into law. The legislation explicitly criticized the appeals court for its decision. Many on both sides of the appeals court ruling awaited a decision on the issue by the U.S. Supreme Court. An important question was whether the Supreme Court would consider its 1943 ruling in *West Virginia State Board of Education v. Barnette* (in which the justices decided that school officials could not force children to recite the pledge) represented a sufficient protection of individual rights or whether the Court would determine that the reference to God in the Pledge, like prayer in the public schools, must be eliminated in order to ensure the separation of church and state. The Court's ruling, announced in June 2004, did not resolve the ultimate question of the constitutionality of the Pledge. Five justices ruled that Michael Newdow, who brought the suit, lacked standing to bring the case before the courts because he did not have legal custody of his daughter. In concurring opinions, Chief Justice William Rehnquist and Justices Sandra Day O'Connor and Clarence Thomas expressed the view that the Pledge did not violate the First Amendment.

As various religious groups, including evangelical Protestants, have become increasingly involved in politics, the American population appears to have become more accepting of that involvement. A 1968 Gallup poll reported that 53 percent of respondents believed that churches should avoid political involvement and that only 40 percent thought that churches should make known their positions on social and political questions. More than 30 years later, Americans appear to have become more tolerant of the participation of religious groups in American politics. The 1996 Pew Center survey reported a reversal of the earlier findings: 54 percent of respondents agreed that churches should express their views on political matters, and 43 percent believed that churches should not (Kohut et al. 2000, 102). With regard specifically to conservative political involvement, Kohut et al. (2000, 120) report that 7 percent of all respondents claimed to be members of the religious right and 25 percent indicated that they supported the religious right.

Very likely, religious involvement in American politics will continue apace. With such issues as abortion, gay rights, prayer in the public schools, school choice, and pornography remaining on the public agenda, conservative Christians will find sufficient motivation to make their voices heard in the political arena. Groups opposed to the conservative Christian agenda can also be expected to continue their political activity in an attempt to limit the influence of that agenda on American government and society.

Conservative Christians and the Liberal Dilemma

Conservative Christians, like all other interests that participate in the American political process, must take the nature of the political culture into account when determining strategy. Robert Booth Fowler (1999) has argued persuasively that the general public in the United States maintains an overall consensus on classic liberal values, even though intellectuals since the 1960s, both liberal and conservative, have expressed increased disapproval with the claim that an overarching liberal framework continues to prevail. Most Americans today consider liberalism to be characterized by a large central government and the amelioration of the excesses of a market economy, with some features of a welfare state. However, that is not what liberalism has meant in the United States in a classic sense. By classic liberal values, Fowler means primarily a concern for the individual person and "his or her rights, wishes, and self-expression in public life" (1999, 100). Classic liberal values also include a commitment to political equality, equality of economic opportunity, and support for the country's political institutions and the limited market economy. Religious groups do not and cannot exist in a social vacuum if they wish to participate effectively in the political realm, despite the pleas of many conservative Christians to the contrary that faithful Christians must separate themselves from the overall secular society.

Fowler identifies three trends in liberal influence on religious groups in the United States that affect their characteristics and interaction with the rest of society. First, individual authority has increased, and participation in organized religion has become a decidedly voluntary activity. This trend has affected the mainline churches most heavily, as is shown in the membership declines in these denominations in recent years. The second trend involves the increasing pluralism both between and within organized churches, to the extent that, Fowler concludes, many "consider themselves virtually a church of one" (1999, 143). The third trend is the increase in the market characteristics of American religion. As religion has become a more individualized activity, denominations have introduced methods for attracting people who can make individual choices, based on personal preference. Fowler notes that more conservative organizations such as Focus on the Family have succeeded in attracting supporters because they appeal specifically to the area of the family, a significant element in the classic liberal valuation of the private sphere (1999, 146).

If Fowler is correct in his assertion that basic classic liberal values celebrating the ascendancy of the individual predominate in American culture, then it is not surprising that conservative Christian groups often emphasize just these values in their political activities and appeals to the general public. Viewed in this light, oral prayer in the public schools becomes a question of freedom of speech and free exercise of religion. Opposition to abortion becomes an issue of right to life. However, underlying the conservative Christian agenda is a desire to nurture a community of common values based on the Christian tradition, which many consider to have contributed vitally to the foundation of the nation (see, for instance, Novak 2001). The success of conservative Christians in achieving their goals through political participation depends to a large extent on their ability to balance an appeal to the values of classic liberal individualism with the commitment to maintain or create a larger Christian community.

References

Bradley, Martin B., Norman M. Green, Jr., Dale E. Jones, Mac Lynn, and Lou McNeil. 1992. *Churches and Church Membership in the United States, 1990.* Atlanta, GA: Glenmary Research Center.

Christian, Asa Kyrus. 1966. *Tuning in on American History.* New York: Exposition.

Davis, James Allan, and Tom W. Smith. 2003. *General Social Surveys, 1972–2002.* Machine-readable data file. Principal Investigator, James A Davis; Director and

Co-principal Investigator, Tom W. Smith; Co-principal Investigator, Peter V. Marsden, NORC ed. Chicago: National Opinion Research Center, producer, 2002; Storrs, CT: The Roper Center for Public Opinion Research, University of Connecticut, distributor.

Dionne, E. J., Jr., and John J. DiIulio, Jr. 2000. *What's God Got to Do with the American Experiment?* Washington, DC: Brookings Institution Press.

Engel v. Vitale, 370 U.S. 421, 82 S.Ct.1261, 8 L.Ed.2d 601, 20 O.O2d 328 (1962).

Fowler, Robert Booth. 1999. *Enduring Liberalism: American Political Thought since the 1960s.* Lawrence: University of Kansas.

Gamble, Richard M. 2003. *The War for Righteousness: Progressive Christianity, the Great War, and the Rise of the Messianic Nation.* Wilmington, DE: Intercollegiate Studies Institute.

Guth, James L., John C. Green, Corwin E. Smidt, Lyman A. Kellstedt, and Margaret M. Poloma. 1997. *The Bully Pulpit: The Politics of Protestant Clergy.* Lawrence: University Press of Kansas.

Hutchins, S. M. 2003. "Practical Atheism." *Touchstone* 16 (June):5–6.

Jelen, Ted G. 1991. *The Political Mobilization of Religious Beliefs.* Westport, CT: Praeger.

Jones, Dale E., Sherri Doty, James E. Horsch, Richard Houseal, Mac Lynn, John P. Marcum, Kenneth M. Sanchagrin, and Richard H. Taylor. 2002. *Religious Congregations and Membership in the United States, 2000: An Enumeration by Region, State, and County Based on Data Reported by 149 Religious Bodies.* Nashville, TN: Glenmary Research Center.

Kohut, Andrew, John C. Green, Scott Keeter, and Robert C. Toth. 2000. *The Diminishing Divide: Religion's Changing Role in American Politics.* Washington, DC: Brookings Institution Press.

Manuel, Frank. 2002. "Deism." *The New Encyclopaedia Britannica.* Vol. 26.

Mapp, Alf J. 2003. *Faiths of Our Fathers: What America's Founders Really Believed.* Lanham, MD: Rowman and Littlefield.

Marty, Martin. 1970. *Righteous Empire: The Protestant Experience in America.* New York: Dial.

Michels, Roberto. 1959. *Political Parties: A Sociological Study of the Oligarchical Tendencies of Modern Democracy.* New York: Dover.

Morison, Samuel Eliot. 1965. *The Oxford History of the American People.* New York: Oxford University Press.

Muelder, Walter G., Christine K. Sears, and Anne V. Schlabach. 1960. *The Development of American Philosophy,* 2nd ed. New York: Houghton Mifflin.

Novak, Michael. 2001. "A Nation That Believes: America Without Religion Is Not America." *National Review* 53 (December 31):31–34.

Phillips, Kevin. 1999. *Cousins' Wars: Religion, Politics, Civil Warfare, and the Triumph of Anglo-America.* New York: Basic Books.

Reichley, A. James. 2002. *Faith in Politics.* Washington, DC: Brookings Institution Press.

Roe v. Wade, 410 U.S. 113, 93 S.Ct. 705, 35 L.Ed.2d 147 (1973).

Silverman, Herb. 2003. "Inerrancy Turned Political." In Kimberly Blaker, ed., *The Fundamentals of Extremism: The Christian Right in America.* New Boston, MI: New Boston Books.

Silverstein, Ken, and Michael Scherer. 2002. "Born-again Zionists." *Mother Jones* 27 (September–October):57–60.

Smith, Tom W. 1987. "Classifying Protestant Denominations," GSS Methodological Report #43.

Stanley, Harold W., and Richard G. Niemi. 2001. "Party Coalitions in Transition: Partisanship and Group Support, 1952–1996." In Richard G. Niemi and Herbert F. Weisberg, eds. *Controversies in Voting Behavior.* Fourth ed. Washington, DC: CQ Press.

Utter, Glenn H., and John W. Storey. 2001. *The Religious Right.* Second edition. Santa Barbara, CA: ABC-CLIO.

West, John G., Jr. 1996. *The Politics of Revelation and Reason: Religion and Civic Life in the New Nation.* Lawrence: University Press of Kansas.

2

Protest Politics

n the past three decades, conservative Christians have shown an increasing willingness to take part in public protests on issues with which they are particularly concerned. In becoming involved in this more activist type of political activity, conservative Christians have followed the lead of both secular and more liberal religious individuals and organizations, which earlier in history demonstrated their political views on such issues as racial equality and U.S. involvement in Vietnam. Two issues of concern to conservative Christians that we will use as examples in this chapter are abortion and prayer in the public schools. Each issue has invoked strong feelings and led to public protests against government policies and judicial decisions. This chapter will examine the religious beliefs that have led to particular types of protests; the social, political, and institutional conditions that either facilitated or discouraged protest activity; and the motivations of individual participants, especially those who assumed leadership positions.

Political Protest

Andrain and Apter (1995), in their study of political protest and social change, introduce various focuses for their investigation. Protest, they hold, can be nonviolent or violent, public or covert, organized or spontaneous, confrontational or in alliance with other groups and governmental agencies. Government response to protest activities can also affect the nature of protest activities. For instance, if authorities employ coercive tactics, some people may become discouraged and withdraw from participating, but others may be emboldened to engage in more radical behavior. In addition, a protest group's access to various resources, such as money, information, and communication skills, can increase the effectiveness of the protest behavior. Andrain and Apter suggest that individuals are more likely to participate in demonstrations if authorities employ low levels of coercion or are inefficient in the use of coercion, if protesters succeed in achieving high group solidarity, and if the protest movement maintains independence from government control. Alternatively, individuals will be less likely to participate in protest activities if authorities are consistent and effective in using techniques of repression, if protest group members remain disunited, and if government institutions succeed in effectively monitoring the behavior of dissident groups.

These factors are especially important in the case of antiabortion protests, for such activities have often involved walking an indistinct boundary between legal protest and illegal actions that can bring arrest, fines, and possibly a prison sentence. Whether individual protesters are willing to risk such consequences depends upon their perception of the seriousness of the problem with which they are concerned. An antiabortion protester who believes that life begins at conception and that a fetus, no matter how early in the pregnancy, is an unborn child to whom God has granted the gift of life will have a strong aversion to a woman's intention to end her pregnancy and to the physician who will perform the medical procedure. Within this context, antiabortion protests have been called attempts to "rescue" unborn children.

In addition to the perception of the circumstance they face, the strength of their convictions influences protesters' willingness to participate. The greater their religious resolve and the greater the depth of their religious beliefs, the more willing protesters will be to risk the consequences of a protest that crosses the line of legality. If protesters believe that God has sanctioned their cause, they will be more willing to risk the possible adverse consequences of protesting.

Perception of the relationship between religious structures and secular governmental institutions can also play an important role in determining the willingness to challenge current policy. Christians, since the first century C.E., experienced conflicting perspectives regarding their relationship to political authority. Although the early

Christian community existed separately from any secular authority, Paul's epistles to the Christian churches call emphatically for obedience to those in power and for Christians to pay their taxes (Romans 13:1–7). Nonetheless, Paul always assumed that loyalty and devotion to God came first and that loyalty to government was secondary. St. Augustine (354–430 C.E.), a giant among early Christians, supported Paul's view, perceiving Christians as citizens of two cities: their actual earthly city of residence and the spiritual city of God.

Due to what Christians saw as the fallen nature of human beings, the state could provide the means for the maintenance of order and at least a temporary peace, which were necessary conditions for living a good life here on earth. However, Christians believed that they must temper their loyalty to the state with the understanding that they owed ultimate obedience to God. Therefore, although justice involved giving human authorities their due (obedience, taxes, etc.), God must also be given his due. Although Christian philosophers and theologians did not allow for easy disobedience to the state and generally rejected the permissibility of organized rebellion, if the commands of an earthly authority conflicted with God's law, the Christian had a duty to obey God and disobey the earthly authority. This tension that Christian doctrine created for the citizen continues to the present day and can create dilemmas for those Christians contemplating involvement in political movements.

Andrain and Apter note four characteristics of religious protest movements (whether of the left or right) that distinguish them from other political protest movements. First, religious values "represent a form of 'cultural power' or 'symbolic capital' that articulate ultimate purposes, transcendental meanings, and ethical ideals" (1995, 60). The faithful perceive significance in secular events that otherwise would lack clear meaning. Second, religious values can provide an independent basis for justifying or criticizing the current holders of political power. Although public officials may increase support for their actions through appeal to religious values, to the extent that religious organizations are independent of government institutions, they can also represent a basis for evaluating, and perhaps disapproving of, official policies and actions. Third, religious organizations often attempt to convert general ethical values into particular government policies. Religious groups do not draw a sharp boundary between issues of personal morality and questions of public policy. Fourth, religious values influence attitudes toward social and political change and affect perceived opportunities for achieving societal transformations. Reformers of the left or the right perceive the contrast between their religious ideals and actual conditions, which can spur activity to work for change.

Andrain and Apter note an important distinction among liberal, conservative, and fundamentalist religious institutions. Whereas liberal religious institutions and clergy emphasize the need for societal changes to improve the physical condition of human beings, conservatives focus more heavily on personal salvation rather than the need for social change. Andrain and Apter perceive fundamentalists (also referred to as reactionaries) as rejecting the existing order and wanting to return society to an ideal past, restoring traditional religious values that they perceive to have been (at least temporarily) lost (1995, 63). Conservative Christian responses to the issues of abortion and prayer in the public schools conform to this notion of fundamentalism. In each case, activist conservative Christians want to undo contemporary changes in public policy that they consider a reflection of deteriorating moral standards and a violation of God's will.

Antiabortion Protest

During the first half of the twentieth century, many people, including religious groups, advocated a strict policy in the states regarding the ability to undergo an abortion. However, after 1960, attitudes began to change, and by 1970, twelve states had liberalized their abortion laws. In March 1970, Hawaii passed legislation that essentially eliminated abortion restrictions. New York, Alaska, and Washington soon followed with legislation repealing prohibitions on abortion. Because most states maintained strict limitations on abortion, states with more liberalized policies became attractive sites for women seeking to terminate pregnancies. The trend toward a state-by-state reform of abortion policies troubled the Roman Catholic Church, and in 1972, the National Conference of Catholic Bishops established the National Right to Life Committee to lobby against liberalizing state abortion laws.

The first antiabortion demonstration occurred in February 1970 at the office of Planned Parenthood in Dallas, Texas. However, such early demonstrations received little notice and had minimal effect on abortion policy. The nature of the abortion controversy changed dramatically in 1973 with the U.S. Supreme Court decision in *Roe v. Wade*, which marked the true starting point for the antiabortion movement. In the *Roe* decision, the Supreme Court took the issue of abortion out of the arena of political negotiation and compromise by declaring that in the first trimester of pregnancy, states could not prohibit a woman's right to end her pregnancy. Although pro-choice interests concluded that the Court decision resolved the question once and for all, an era of intense and often bitter protest lay ahead.

The number of reported abortions in the United States increased dramatically, rising from 744,600 in 1973 to 1 million in 1975. At its highest point, the number of abortions reached 1.5 million per year, a figure that those opposing abortion found scandalous. Initially, Roman Catholics took the lead in the antiabortion movement with the National Right to Life Committee. Under Catholic leadership, protest demonstrations were essentially peaceful activities with little direct confrontation with authorities or abortion providers. Protestant groups initially did not participate in antiabortion demonstrations, partly because of the traditional animosity they felt toward the Roman Catholic Church.

Unlike Andrain and Apter's model of political protest, the abortion issue involves not simply the confrontation of the protest group with governmental authorities, but also with an opposing political movement. Organizations such as the National Organization for Women, the National Abortion Federation, and the National Abortion and Reproductive Rights Action League support the right of women to have the option of an abortion and thus consider the 1974 Supreme Court decision a major victory for the right of women to determine their own reproductive destiny. In addition, abortion does not involve a government fiat that forces anyone to undergo an abortion; rather, women individually may decide for themselves whether to terminate a pregnancy. Abortion rights groups thus consider abortion a personal decision to be made by a woman in consultation with a physician. Therefore, the original goals of antiabortion protests were varied and were not aimed directly at government authority. They included the narrower objective of making the protesters' concerns known to a broader public by demonstrating at abortion clinics.

Closely associated with the actual protest activities was the intention of encouraging the mass media to report demonstrations to the wider public in order to influence public opinion in the protesters' favor. It cannot be estimated with any confidence to what degree antiabortion protesters influenced public opinion over the years. However, survey results during the 1990s indicated that a majority of respondents consistently expressed support for the statement "The choice on abortion should be left up to the woman and her doctor." In July 1990, 57 percent of a Hart/Teeter Research sample chose that option. That percentage remained fairly stable over time, with 60 percent and 58 percent of respondents selecting that alternative in December 1995 and September 1996, respectively (Ladd and Bowman 1997, 21).

However, abortion activists had other goals beyond attempting to influence public opinion. According to more fundamentalist religious beliefs, abortion involves the literal killing of a baby and hence is murder. Therefore, activists saw their protests as having two equally important goals: to prevent women from having abortions and to prevent doctors from performing the procedure. Protesters engaged in what they called "sidewalk counseling," confronting women as they entered abortion clinics and attempting to dissuade them from undergoing an abortion. Sometimes, demonstrators would attempt to create such a chaotic situation around a clinic that either the clinic personnel would close the facility temporarily or the police would ask that it be closed. In such situations, antiabortion protesters declared victory because no abortions would be performed that day.

Conservative Christian organizations and women's rights groups perceived the issue from starkly different perspectives. Clinic personnel and abortion rights supporters were angered by what they saw as a notable lack of understanding and empathy for women who had made a difficult decision to enter a clinic, and they interpreted the antiabortion tactics of demonstrators as crass attempts to intimidate women and deny them one of their basics rights. Not surprisingly, women's groups responded to the antiabortion protests at clinics with strategies to protect women from the protestors. For instance, such groups provided escorts for women entering clinics and confronted the protesters with counterprotests. In addition, abortion rights groups initiated lawsuits and used such tactics as calling for the prosecution of antiabortion protesters under the 1970 Racketeer Influenced and Corrupt Organizations Act (RICO) and the 1946 Hobbs Act, which provides for the prosecution of those engaged in robbery or extortion involving interstate or foreign commerce.

In the late 1970s and early 1980s, Protestant fundamentalists began to enter the antiabortion movement. Their willingness to use more confrontational tactics shifted the strategy of the movement. Initially, the motivation of antiabortion demonstrators involved in part the notion of suffering. By offering themselves for arrest, protesters were atoning for their failure to speak out against the Supreme Court opinion of 1973. They presented themselves as helpless, just as the fetus was seen as helpless and unable to defend itself.

In the 1980s, a new leadership developed in the movement with a willingness to use more aggressive tactics. The dominant antiabortion organization became Operation Rescue, led by Randall Terry, who began demonstrating at abortion clinics in his hometown of Binghamton, New York. Terry used Proverbs 24:11 as the biblical justification for the protests against legalized abortion and those who conducted the procedure: "Rescue those who are being taken away to death; hold back those who are stumbling to the slaughter." Those involved in the antiabortion movement now wanted not only to make known their opposition to abortion, but also to actually prevent abortions from taking place. They used various tactics to block entrances to freestanding abortion clinics, where the great majority of abortions were being performed. Protesters attempted to persuade women entering abortion clinics not to have an abortion.

Protesters harassed even the women who were entering clinics for procedures other than abortion. Protesters attempted to block clinic entrances and parking lots and at times shouted loudly so that they could be heard by the staff and patients inside clinics. Antiabortion groups measured success by the number of arrests protesters were able to force the police to make and by their ability to prevent any abortions from being performed on the day of the protest. Protesters also gauged success by the amount of media coverage they were able to achieve: the greater the coverage, the more people that would be made aware of their protest. However, the courting of public opinion can be an unsure tactic, with opinion shifting quickly from one side to the other, especially in the local area where the protest is being conducted. People might initially express sympathy for the demonstrators, but they subsequently might become impatient with the disruptions and consider the protesters to be extremists or simply troublemakers.

Antiabortion protests during the 1980s and later extended farther than the picketing of abortion clinics. When they could discover the addresses, protest groups would also picket the residences of abortion clinic physicians. Some abortion foes printed and distributed "wanted" posters for physicians who reputedly performed abortions. For instance, in 1992, abortion opponents circulated such a poster in central Florida with the names of twenty-five doctors listed. The poster stated: "The following physicians are wanted for crimes against humanity. Specifically they kill unborn children for a fee. . . . A $1,000 reward is offered for information leading to the arrest of these so-called physicians or revocation of their [licenses]" (Baird-Windle and Bader 2001, 181). Demonstrators invaded abortion clinics, causing damage to the facilities, and more extreme abortion foes began a bombing campaign against clinics.

In 1994, abortion rights groups successfully lobbied Congress to pass the Freedom of Access to Clinic Entrances (FACE) Act, legislation that prohibited demonstrators from blocking entrances to abortion clinics. Among the provisions of this law, the Department of Justice can bring criminal charges against anyone obstructing the entrance to a clinic. In addition, civil charges could be brought by a state attorney general, clinic staff, doctors, or patients (Baird-Windle and Bader 2001, 210). In February 2003, the Supreme Court, in an eight-to-one decision, ruled that the RICO could not be used to prosecute antiabortion demonstrators because they did not acquire property as specified under the legislation and therefore their actions failed to constitute racketeering violations. Nonetheless, the lawsuits that had been brought had effectively contributed to dampening antiabortion protests. Whether the Supreme Court decision will lead to renewed and intensified protests at abortion clinics is unclear. If protests should increase, abortion rights groups can be expected to counter the tactics of antiabortion forces with renewed fervor.

Antiabortion Protest in Atlanta: A Case Study

By summer 1988, Randall Terry's antiabortion organization, Operation Rescue, had achieved national publicity and attracted thousands of individuals to abortion clinic protests. That summer, Operation Rescue organized demonstrations in Atlanta, Georgia, the city in which the Democratic party would hold its presidential nominating convention. Operation Rescue had conducted protest campaigns in other cities, and Terry was seeking to increase still further his organization's influence. Terry received assistance from evangelical leaders Pat Robertson and Jerry Falwell. Robertson made appeals for Operation Rescue on his Christian Broadcasting Network program, *700 Club,* and he interviewed Terry on the program. That exposure gave Terry a certain level of legitimacy among evangelical churches and persuaded many ministers to encourage their congregations to participate in the Atlanta protests.

For the Atlanta demonstrations, Terry developed a new strategy: abortion clinic protesters would not carry any identification and, if arrested, would identify themselves as Jane, John, or Baby Doe. This strategy increased the administrative load for local authorities as they attempted to do the legal processing of those who were arrested. In addition, Terry neglected to meet with police prior to the demonstrations to negotiate ground rules for the demonstrations. Such negotiations could often be crucial to maintaining the delicate balance between cooperation and confrontation with government authorities. Therefore, Operation Rescue demonstrators, which initially included about 200 individuals, faced an unsympathetic police force intent upon limiting the effects of the demonstrations (Risen and Thomas 1998, 272). To counter the protesters' efforts, police succeeded in establishing a line of police officers around clinics, thus preventing the demonstrators from approaching the clinics themselves. The demonstrators then sat on the sidewalk to be arrested there. In addition to police efforts, the abortion rights leadership attempted to counteract the demonstrations by organizing clinic-defense programs, through which volunteers would act as escorts for women who wished to enter clinics, and by bringing legal charges against antiabortion leaders.

Although both Jerry Falwell and Pat Robertson had provided support for the demonstrations, Terry considered support from the prestigious Reverend Charles Stanley to be crucial to gaining the backing of the local churches. Stanley was senior pastor at First Baptist Church in Atlanta, the largest Baptist church in Georgia, and his sermons were televised nationwide. He was at one point the president of the Southern Baptist Convention. Terry asked Stanley for support for his cause; Stanley visited a protest but waited until the end of August before giving Terry an answer.

Stanley published a booklet that he read in his church as a sermon, refusing to endorse the protests and actually denouncing them (Risen and Thomas 1998, 280). By providing his own Bible quotations, he countered Terry's efforts to use the Bible to legitimize the antiabortion protests. He referred to Romans 13:1 ("Let every person be subject to the governing authorities; for there is no authority except from God, and those authorities that exist have been instituted by God") and Titus 3:1 ("Remind them to be subject to rulers and authorities, to be obedient, to be ready for every good work") to criticize the protests. Stanley's comments reflected the centuries-old conflict that Christians had experienced between God's sovereign ordinances and the biblical admonition to obey the civil authorities. The pastor commented that U.S. law did not require that abortions be performed; it only permitted women to choose whether or not to undergo the procedure. Women, he contended, were "free moral agents responsible before Almighty God for their actions." (quoted in Risen and Thomas 1998, 280). Operation Rescue, Stanley said, would be justified in preventing women from entering abortion clinics only if the U.S. government required women to undergo abortions.

Following Stanley's denunciation of Operation Rescue, other Protestant ministers also refused to endorse the organization's antiabortion protests. Nonetheless, Terry decided to continue into the fall his attempts to blockade Atlanta abortion clinics. In an effort to counter the renewed demonstrations, police, with the sanction of court orders against blockades, established metal barricades to prevent demonstrators from approaching clinic entrances. In addition, the city employed the police department's special operations team, which was granted authority to use "pain compliance," a method that involved such techniques as twisting wrists, bending arms back, and applying pressure to the neck to elicit cooperation from demonstrators who were being arrested (Risen and Thomas 1998, 284). Protesters attempted to crawl under the police barricades in order to reach clinic entrances. However, this tactic proved less than successful because police responded more severely to it with their pain compliance and because the image of demonstrators crawling along the street presented an unfavorable image in the media.

A major objective of any public protest effort is to receive media coverage, and despite the negative image presented by the crawling strategy, Operation Rescue achieved major media exposure. More than 750 arrests had been made by the end of August (Risen and Thomas 1998, 276). The national news media extensively covered the October protests. Two network news programs—ABC's *20/20* and CBS's *48 Hours*—featured presentations on the protests, and the Cable News Network offered frequent updates. The national news coverage encouraged protests at abortion clinics around the country and garnered a greater response to the antiabortionists' fundraising appeals. This increased income allowed Terry to expand his staff, begin publishing a newsletter, and develop a mailing list for subsequent fundraising efforts. The publicity that the Atlanta protests received also encouraged fundamentalist churches around the country to sponsor "rescuers" and "crisis pregnancy centers" (Risen and Thomas 1998, 286). The setback that Operation Rescue experienced with the failure to receive the endorsement of Charles Stanley notwithstanding, Terry was sufficiently encouraged to expand activities still further. He declared October 29, 1988, to be a "National Day of Rescue" and planned another protest in Los Angeles for Holy Week of 1989.

Another significant and ominous consequence of the Atlanta demonstrations and the strict police response to the protesters was the radicalization of several of the activists. The failure of President

Ronald Reagan's administration to push very hard for antiabortion measures, including a constitutional amendment; the unwillingness of a majority of the U.S. Supreme Court to overrule *Roe v. Wade;* and the legal efforts of pro-choice groups to restrict antiabortion protests led antiabortion activists and groups to become increasingly frustrated with their lack of progress in ridding the nation of what they considered to be an intolerable evil. Some, frustrated by the lack of progress, turned to more violent strategies. The nature of the antiabortion movement changed once again, with increasingly violent attacks on abortion clinics and personnel that would include bombings and murder. Those jailed in Atlanta included Shelley Shannon, who later was convicted of shooting an abortion doctor in Wichita, Kansas; John Arena, who was convicted of conducting butyric acid (a foul-smelling substance) attacks against abortion clinics; and James Kopp, who was indicted and convicted for the 1998 shooting and killing of abortion doctor Barnett Slepian in Amherst, New York.

The less committed activists were losing their fervor for the cause and were becoming less willing to undergo arrest and jail sentences, and Terry's arbitrary leadership of Operation Rescue, which involved making decisions without consulting others in the organization, began to alienate Operation Rescue activists. In 1989, Terry was sentenced to 6 months in the Fulton County, Georgia, jail for violating a restraining order and for refusing to pay a $1,000 fine. He also faced an additional 6-month sentence for his refusal to comply with the court order. The Operation Rescue leader chose to serve a jail sentence just when the organization needed his leadership, despite increased misgivings about his domineering decision-making style, in planning a campaign to be held in Washington, D.C., in December 1989.

Terry, who reportedly had a strong aversion to spending time in prison, suffered emotionally from his short term of imprisonment. In January 1990, someone paid Terry's fine anonymously, and he was released from prison. Terry's colleagues in the Operation Rescue leadership had encouraged Terry to submit to the sentence as so many other activists in the antiabortion movement had done. But while he was in prison, others in the group's leadership had been making decisions to which Terry objected. A confrontation among the leaders occurred in March 1990, and Terry discharged those who were demanding changes in the organization's operations. By the end of 1990, with divisions in the leadership and a series of lawsuits pending, Operation Rescue was essentially finished as an effective protest organization.

The Aftermath of Operation Rescue

With the demise of Operation Rescue as the primary organizational structure for nonviolent antiabortion protests, the door swung open for those who advocated more violent strategies to achieve their goal of ending abortion in the United States. Such violent activities further weakened the more moderate protest groups as protest activities became increasingly associated with extremists. A major debate raged within the movement over the use of violent tactics, with some denouncing violence, others defending those who committed violence, and yet others unwilling or unable to take a strong position on the troubling issue. When arrested for illegal activities, defendants attempted to use the "necessity defense," claiming that they were breaking the law in order to prevent what they considered to be a greater evil. Although early on, some local judges were willing to accept the necessity defense, the courts ultimately rejected this legal strategy.

Physicians themselves became targets as the most radical elements in the antiabortion movement resorted to violence. From 1993 until 1998, a total of seven people were killed and four were injured in attacks related to abortion clinics. Six of the victims were shot to death, and one died in a clinic bombing. In 1994, Paul Hill, an antiabortion protester and advocate of "justifiable homicide," shot and killed physician John Bayard Britton and his escort, James Barrett, outside a Pensacola, Florida, abortion clinic. Convicted of the murders, Hill was sentenced to death. Other than making automatic appeals, Hill did not resist the sentence, and he later dismissed his lawyers. He was executed by lethal injection in September 2003.

Despite the tarnished image to the antiabortion movement that resulted from this increased violence, including murder, conservative Christian groups and individuals continued their opposition to abortion and introduced new strategies to combat what they considered a fundamental evil. One new strategy was to organize boycotts against the construction of new abortion clinics. For instance, a construction contractor in Austin, Texas, sent letters to other contractors asking them to boycott the construction of a new Planned Parenthood facility (Brulliard 2003, 29). Ultimately, abortion opponents made so many phone calls and sent so many letters and e-mails to local construction companies that the general contractor withdrew from the job, thus halting construction. In other cases, antiabortion groups have searched for building permit violations in order to close abortion clinics and halt construction on new ones. In the Austin case,

TABLE 2.1   Attitudes toward Supreme Court Rulings on Prayer in Public Schools

Question: The United States Supreme Court has ruled that no state or local government may require the reading of the Lord's Prayer or Bible verses in public schools. What are your views on this—do you approve or disapprove of the court ruling?

Religious Affiliation	Percent Approve	Percent Disapprove
Fundamentalists	27.4	72.6
Mainline Christians	40.7	59.3
All Others Interviewed	41.5	58.5

Source: General Social Survey. 2002. NORC-GSS Cumulative Data File 1972–2000. Storrs, CT: The Roper Center for Public Opinion Research.

Planned Parenthood decided to act as its own contractor, and the organization itself hired workers to continue construction of the clinic.

School Prayer

In September 2000, several individuals and hastily established groups announced their intent to protest a recent U.S. Supreme Court decision in *Santa Fe Independent School District v. Doe.* The decision disallowed officially sanctioned prayer at the start of sporting events—specifically, football games—sponsored by public school districts. The court case arose when two families (one Mormon and the other Roman Catholic), assisted by the American Civil Liberties Union (ACLU), initiated a lawsuit to stop the practice in the Santa Fe, Texas, school district of allowing student-led prayer before the start of each high school football game. The Supreme Court decision and the response of the American public should be examined in the context of more than thirty-five years of court-made policy regarding the relationship between church and state. Table 2.1 presents one set of survey data regarding attitudes toward the Supreme Court's rulings on prayer and Bible reading in U.S. public schools.

As the table shows, the majority of all those surveyed from 1972 to 2000 about their attitudes toward prayer in the public schools expressed disapproval of the Supreme Court rulings that state and local governments may not require reciting of the Lord's Prayer or the reading of Bible verses in the public schools. Those respondents who were members of fundamentalist churches were more likely to disapprove (nearly 73 percent) than members of mainline churches (59 percent) and others interviewed (58 percent). These expressed attitudes toward Supreme Court rulings on school prayer give some hope to school prayer supporters that protest demonstrations will be received sympathetically by the general public.

The school prayer issue, like the abortion issue, has deep roots within conservative Christian communities and is a crucial subject in the so-called culture war, a disparity seen as a battle between the more religiously oriented individuals and groups in American society and those less concerned with religious belief. This similarity between the abortion and school prayer issues notwithstanding, public school prayer has usually generated a more moderate level of protest among conservative Christians than the abortion question. Although in the case of abortion, conservative Christians concerned themselves with stopping a practice that the Supreme Court had decided to allow, in the case of school prayer, conservative Christians wished to continue a practice the Supreme Court had prohibited. In endeavoring to alter abortion policy and practice, abortion opponents not only employed the more regular avenues of political influence, including lobbying legislatures and campaigning for antiabortion candidates, but (as we have previously discussed) they also engaged in public protest demonstrations at abortion clinics in order to gain public attention through the media as well as to reduce the number of abortions performed. In contrast, those supporting school prayer in many instances have wished to continue the tradition of prayer in the public schools despite the Supreme Court rulings to the contrary.

Before 1962, at least twelve states either permitted or required prayer and Bible reading in the public schools. Ever since the U.S. Supreme Court ruled officially sanctioned prayer in the public schools to be unconstitutional in the early 1960s, various conservative Christian groups have been advocating the return of so-called voluntary prayer in the public schools. In *Engel v. Vitale* (1962), the Court prohibited the use of the following nonsectarian prayer in the state of New York: "Almighty God, we acknowledge our dependence upon Thee, and we beg Thy blessings upon us, our parents, our teachers and our Country." The New York State Board of Regents had written the prayer and recommended its use by school districts. One local board of education required students to recite the prayer each school day, thus leading to the lawsuit challenging the prayer policy. Justice Hugo Black, speaking for the majority, stated that it was inappropriate for government "to compose official prayers for any group of the American people to recite as a part of a religious program carried on by government." The Court ruled that even though the prayer was nondenominational and students were not required to participate in reciting the prayer and could be excused from the room during the prayer, the prayer was still unacceptable.

A year later, in *Abington School District v. Schempp* (1963), the Court, in an eight-to-one decision, invalidated a Pennsylvania law that required the school day to begin with a Bible reading and a recitation of the Lord's Prayer. The Court ruled that the state of Pennsylvania, by requiring Bible reading, violated the First Amendment dictate that government remain neutral, "neither aiding nor opposing religion." Although the majority on the Court refused to grant to the "voluntary" nature of the prayer and Bible reading any significance in the decision, Justice Stewart, dissenting from the majority in *Engel*, referred to "sharing in the spiritual heritage of our Nation" and stated, "I cannot see how an 'official religion' is established by letting those who want to say a prayer say it" (quoted in Ackerman 2001, 8). Even one dissenting voice on the Supreme Court can give to those who are dissatisfied with the decision renewed hope that their stand may ultimately be vindicated and can motivate them toward taking action in support of their cause, including engaging in protest.

In a related case, *Murray v. Curlett,* also decided in 1963, the Supreme Court disallowed Bible reading and a prayer recitation mandated by the Board of School Commissioners of Baltimore, Maryland. Madalyn Murray O'Hair, the mother of William J. Murray (the plaintiff in the case), subsequently came to be recognized as a leading advocate of atheism in the United States. In three succeeding decisions, the Supreme Court reaffirmed that government sponsorship of such activities as prayer and Bible reading constitutes an establishment of religion in violation of the First Amendment.

Those favoring school prayer claim that there have been various undesirable consequences of removing prayer from the public schools. For instance, David Barton (2002) presents data showing sharp rises in trends that conservative Christians find troubling, such as the percentage of teenage girls who have had premarital intercourse, birth rates for unwed girls age fifteen to nineteen, sexually transmitted diseases (specifically gonorrhea), rape arrests of those age thirteen to eighteen, and murder arrests of those age thirteen to eighteen. Barton also reports large increases in divorce rates, the number of unmarried couples living together, the number of single-parent households, and the percentage of married men and women who have engaged in extramarital sex. Although social scientists generally doubt a clear cause-and-effect relationship between single variables such as Supreme Court rulings on school prayer and these various social phenomena (several other causal factors are suggested), Barton and other conservative Christians insist on finding severe consequences arising from removing religious observances from the public schools. As Ed McAteer, president of the Religious Roundtable, claimed in 1982, "If we are to stem the tide of lawlessness, drug addiction, and sexual perversion, which adversely affect academic performance, we must start with putting God back into our school systems" (quoted in Provenzo 1990, 75).

One reason that school prayer advocates have attempted to identify such bad consequences of removing prayer from the public schools, other than truly believing in the good effects of religious observance, is this: Unlike abortion, in which the undesirable results of policy are clear to the conservative Christian (the unborn are being killed), with school prayer, no direct adverse results beyond the immediate ending of religious observances can be pointed to in order to encourage opposition to the court-initiated policy. Without more tangible effects, it is possible that few people besides those with deep religious convictions about the need to pray would be drawn to protest. Hence, making claims about the broader injurious effects of the policy provides a rationale for political activity to protest against what is considered a crucial aspect of an antireligious agenda. Potential activists are shown how they have, in fact, been harmed, not only by the "violation" of Christians' rights to the free exercise of religion due to an increasingly interventionist federal government, but also by the ill effects suffered by schoolchildren who are being denied appropriate moral and religious training.

Conservative Christian leaders such as Tim LaHaye and David Noebel (2000) also point to an enemy beyond the government. These leaders identify secular humanism as an anti-Christian religion that considers humankind the best and only hope for the future, rejecting any belief in God. Christians are thereby presented with an enemy that allegedly is trying to destroy the Christian faith and Christian values. In this context, political activism can be understood as a defense of the rights of Christians.

The issue of secular humanism came before the courts when a group of evangelical Christians sued state and local education officials in Alabama in the case *Smith v. Board of School Commissioners* (1987). The plaintiffs claimed that the Mobile public schools supported the religion of secular humanism and that the textbooks selected for use neglected to provide any treatment of religious values. They argued that although the school board prohibited the teaching of Christian values, textbooks presented a worldview composed of the tenets of secular humanism. Although the trial judge ruled in favor of the plaintiffs, the federal appeals court in Cincinnati overturned the verdict, stating that Judge Brevard Hand had transformed the First Amendment requirement of government neutrality regarding religion into "an affirmative obligation to speak about religion" (quoted in Provenzo 1990, 81). In 1988, the U.S. Supreme Court declined to hear the case, so the appeals court decision remained in effect. Nonetheless, the case illustrates the claim made by many conservative Christians that contemporary culture in the United States is hostile to their beliefs and deeply held social values.

One strategy for achieving the goal of overriding the Supreme Court rulings has been to engage in some form of school prayer as inconspicuously and with as little public controversy as possible. For instance, Marianne Meier (2002) refers to a study that Kenneth Dolbeare and Phillip Hammond conducted soon after the 1962–1963 Supreme Court decisions, in which the researchers concluded, "almost every imaginable school religious practice seemingly existed in every community studied, and with no public concern" (2002, 70). Officials in thousands of public school districts in small towns across the nation simply ignored the continuing use of prayer in their local schools, or they misinterpreted the Court rulings in order to allow some forms of religious observance. As long as no students or parents complained publicly, and as long as the local press did not raise a public outcry, these officials were content to allow the status quo to prevail. For school officials to attempt to enforce judicial decisions regarding school prayer could possibly have invited retaliation from the local communities. Meier speculates that, in most circumstances, students and parents who opposed the continuing use of prayer declined to make the issue public, perceiving the community to be solidly in favor of school prayer. In addition, the potential costs of legal representation may have deterred attempts to use the courts to challenge religious observances in the public schools. In the *Santa Fe* case, because the plaintiffs gained the support of the American Civil Liberties Union, they were relieved of much of the financial burden of litigation.

Following the Supreme Court decisions on school prayer in the early 1960s (*Engel v. Vitale* in 1962 and *Abington v. Schempp* in 1963), prominent individuals, taking stands in favor of school prayer, strongly criticized the court decision. Reverend Billy Graham, a prominent evangelist, declared that the decisions were one more step toward the secularization of the United States and that, contrary to the Supreme Court rulings, the constitutional framers intended that citizens should have freedom of religion, not freedom from religion. Former President Herbert Hoover stated that the Supreme Court had brought to an end a sacred element in the American heritage. U.S. senators and members of the U.S. House of Representatives, especially those from the South, added their voices to the outcry against the Supreme Court decisions on school prayer.

The introduction of new constitutional amendments to Congress advocating school prayer became a regular occurrence. In 1966, Senator Everett Dirksen initiated a constitutional amendment stating: "Nothing in this Constitution shall abridge the right of persons lawfully assembled, in any public building which is supported in whole or in part through the expenditure of public funds, to participate in nondenominational prayer" (quoted in Meier 2002, 53). This amendment and others led to a great deal of lobbying on both sides; ultimately, all proposals failed to gain the necessary two-thirds vote in both houses of Congress to be sent to the states for final ratification.

When Ronald Reagan campaigned for the presidency in 1980, he promised to work for the return of prayer to the public schools. True to his word, President Reagan supported an amendment—called the "Reagan Amendment"—that emphasized the voluntary nature of prayer: "Nothing in this constitution shall be construed to prohibit individual or group prayer in the public schools or other public institutions. No person shall be required by the United States or any State to participate in prayer" (quoted in Meier 2002, 59). Prominent conservative Christian figures Jerry Falwell and Pat Robertson supported the Reagan administration on the school prayer amendment issue. As with previous attempts, however, this amendment also failed to gain the necessary two-thirds vote in both houses of Congress. In the meantime, the Supreme Court periodically heard cases dealing with school prayer and Bible reading, generally restricting officially sanctioned religious practice in the public schools. When the Supreme Court agreed to hear *Santa Fe Independent School District v. Doe* on appeal from the Fifth U.S. Circuit Court of Appeals, this was the first time since 1992 that the Court had agreed to hear a school prayer case. In that year, in *Lee v. Weisman,* the Supreme Court had prohibited clergy-led prayers at graduation ceremonies.

Santa Fe, Texas, and School Prayer:
A Case Study

The Santa Fe, Texas, case was somewhat unique, in that the instances of prayer at football games attended by several thousand spectators were far more public than the reciting of prayers within one school or one classroom.

In 1995, two families brought this suit against the school district. At the time the lawsuit was filed, the school district was following an official policy of choosing a minister each school year to present invocations at football games and other school events. The two families, however, were expressing concern about religious activities in the schools beyond these invocations at football games. The Gideons, an organization dedicated to distributing Bibles to individuals and institutions, were granted permission to give Bibles to students, and other organizations were also allowed to hand out religious materials on school property. In addition, at lunchtime, students were instructed to bow their heads and pray. The families also objected to a general climate within the school district that they saw as hostile to those not adhering to the Baptist majority in the community.

Fearing retribution from the community, the families asked to remain anonymous during the legal proceedings. In February 1999, the Fifth U.S. Circuit Court of Appeals, in a two-to-one decision, agreed with the families, stating that official prayers before football games violated the constitutional protection of religious freedom, even though the school district's policy had been altered (students could vote on whether or not to have prayer or an invocation, and if they chose to have the observance, the students would then choose the person to lead prayers prior to the start of games). The school district appealed the decision to the U.S. Supreme Court.

Although the appeals court decision remained binding within the fifth circuit, there were scattered examples of "spontaneous prayer" prior to football games that year, amounting to limited protest demonstrations. For instance, in Stephenville, Texas, fifteen students used a portable public address system to lead sympathizers in prayer. In Santa Fe, the student selected to present a message before football games was told by the school district not to offer a prayer. However, in September 1999, that student's family filed suit in federal district court, claiming that their daughter's free speech rights were being violated. The judge agreed with the family and issued an injunction preventing the school district from punishing the student for presenting a prayer in her pregame address, stating that the school could not censor the student's speech. The student was given access to the public address system, and she prayed for a safe football season. The student's prayer gained nationwide attention as a protest against the appeals court decision and as an appeal to the Supreme Court to rule in favor of continuing the tradition of prayer before high school football games.

In March 2000, the Supreme Court heard oral arguments in the *Santa Fe* case. In the Texas Republican primary that month, 94 percent of voters supported a ballot resolution favoring student-initiated prayer at public school sporting events. George W. Bush, then governor of Texas and a candidate for the Republican nomination for president, filed a brief with the Supreme Court supporting student-led prayer. The Supreme Court, in a six-to-three vote, ruled against the school district, rejecting the argument that student free speech was a primary concern in such cases, and they dismissed the school district's rationale for a majoritarian process by which students themselves could decide whether to have an invocation and who would deliver it.

Justice John Paul Stevens, speaking for the majority, emphasized the importance of minority rights by stating that such a system ensured that "minority candidates will never prevail and that their views will effectively be silenced." Stevens emphasized the school sponsorship involved in the process, which presented the message to "nonadherents" in the audience that "they are outsiders, not full members of the political community, and an accompanying message to adherents that they are insiders, favored members of the political community." Rejecting the freedom of speech argument for student-led prayer, Stevens stated: "The delivery of such a message—over the school's public address system by a speaker representing the student body, under the supervision of school faculty and pursuant to a school policy that explicitly and implicitly encourages public prayer—is not properly characterized as private speech."

The decision drew quick responses from those supporting school prayer. For instance, chief counsel Jay Sekulow of the American Center for Law and Justice, an organization established by Pat Robertson to support the rights of Christians to conduct religious observances, perceived a legal dilemma in the court decision. Reiterating the basic argument that prayer supporters had made, Sekulow claimed that school censorship of a student's oral message in order to prevent religious speech violated students' constitutional rights of free speech and religious freedom. He emphasized the Supreme Court's frequent assertion that students maintain their constitutional rights of free speech while on school grounds and noted that students still had the right to engage in such religious activities as meeting in Bible clubs, engaging in religious discussion, distributing religious literature in the same way that secular literature may be distributed, and praying at mealtimes.

Opponents of the court decision in various communities planned protests involving "spontaneous" prayer before football games during the fall 2000 season. At a Friday night football game on September 1, Jody McLoud, principal of the Roane County High School in Kingston, Tennessee, read a statement over the public address system protesting the Supreme Court decision. McLoud commented: "I can use literature, videos and presentations in the classroom that depict people with strong, traditional, Christian convictions as simple minded and ignorant and call it enlightenment. However, if anyone uses this facility to honor God and ask Him to bless this event with safety and good sportsmanship, federal case law is violated. . . . Apparently, we are to be tolerant of everything and anyone except God and His Commandments." Although not a prayer itself, McLoud's comments amounted to an impassioned plea for the audience to participate in prayer.

A group headquartered in Temple, Texas, calling itself No Pray No Play, encouraged football fans to engage in prayer at Friday night games across Texas. September 1 was the opening game for the Santa Fe High School, at which the pro-prayer group expected a turnout including 10,000 prayer supporters in addition to 5,000 fans. The actual protest fell far short of expectations. In a crowd estimated at 4,550, approximately 200 people attempted to take part in prayer before the start of the game. However, without the aid of the public address system, the spectators were unable to hear the prayer participants. A prayer supporter complained that, following the national anthem, when an invocation was traditionally presented, the official announcer immediately began introducing the visiting team, thus cutting short any opportunity for the fans' attention to be directed toward the prayer protesters.

Protests were also reported at other high school football games. In Merkel, Texas, a group of fans bowed their heads in prayer before kickoff. At the Robert E. Lee High School football game in Tyler, Texas, the school band played a Christian selection during a moment of silence following the national anthem. At the Etowah County High School football game in Attalla, Alabama, a student-led prayer was presented over the public address system. In Hattiesburg, Mississippi, 4,500 fans stood for an invocation prior to kickoff, and in Asheville, North Carolina, several thousand people met in the football stadium for a rally to support the saying of the Lord's Prayer at football games.

These protests appeared to be insufficiently planned and generally fell short of expectations. Supporters of the Supreme Court decision observed that a football game presents a poor opportunity to engage in a genuine prayer experience. Some quoted from the New Testament, in which Jesus encourages his followers to pray in private rather than in public: "And whenever you pray, do not be like the hypocrites; for they love to stand and pray in the synagogues and at the street corners, so that they may be seen by others. Truly I tell you, they have received their reward. But whenever you pray, go into your room and shut the door and pray to your Father who is in secret; and your Father who sees in secret will reward you" (Matthew 6:5–6).

The Aftermath of Santa Fe

In local communities where religious convictions are strong and where local leaders believe they are truly right about the importance of religious education, a Supreme Court decision will not change many minds, and the proclivity to try to maintain in some way religious traditions will be hard to resist. However, with the Supreme Court decision, the status quo began to shift toward omitting prayer from the traditional ceremony preceding high school sporting events. Without the official sanction of local officials, organized prayer is difficult to coordinate and protests tend to be ineffective. Nonetheless, public demonstrations can serve the broader purpose of persuading the faithful as well as the general public that an undesirable trend toward secularization is gaining momentum in the United States. Protests can potentially provide ammunition for future political battles, even though there appears to be little chance that conservative Christian forces will be able to win many outright victories on the issue of school prayer.

Conservatives might be better served in this matter by working through the more regularized channels of political activity, including participation in election campaigns, lobbying legislatures, finding innovative ways of introducing religious observances in public schools, and using litigation when necessary. In 2003, the U.S. Departments of Education and Justice issued a set of rules, titled *Guidance on Con-*

stitutionally Protected Prayer in Public Elementary and Secondary Schools, which public junior and senior high schools must follow in order to be eligible for federal funding. The guidelines state: "Where student speakers are selected on the basis of genuinely neutral, evenhanded criteria and retain primary control over the content of their expression, that expression is not attributable to the school and therefore may not be restricted because of its religious content." The guidelines specify that government should protect religious as well as secular speech on an equal basis and should remain neutral between the two types of speech. Prayer is allowed if it occurs outside the formal classroom and if school officials do not initiate it. The guidelines specify that students may pray at mealtime, pray with other students during recess, organize prayer groups and gatherings before school on the same basis as students can organize other activities, and express their religious beliefs in homework and artwork. Teachers are not allowed to encourage students to pray or discourage students from praying, and teachers may not participate in prayer with students. Schools may not provide for prayer at graduation ceremonies or have speaker selection procedures that favor religious speech.

Nonetheless, cases still arise in which school officials encourage prayer. For instance, in May 2003, an elementary school principal in Sylvia, Kansas, created controversy when she was reported to have asked teachers to stand beside students' desks and "pray for that student, their family and their needs" on the National Day of Prayer (*Houston Chronicle* May 15, 2003, 11A). Public officials sometimes contribute to the confusion about the issue of school prayer by announcing days of prayer. In March 2003, Governor Rick Perry of Texas proclaimed a day of prayer in Texas for the American military forces around the world, including those in the Persian Gulf. President George W. Bush declared September 11, 2003, to be a national day of prayer and remembrance for the victims of the terrorist attacks two years before.

Like abortion, school prayer is another issue on which more conservative fundamentalist denominations distinguish themselves from the leadership in mainline churches, who tend to support the separation of church and state. Given public opinion on the issue of school prayer, it is not surprising that a shift in membership toward more fundamentalist churches has occurred, thus increasing the potential political influence of conservative Christians, who have proven willing to take part in protests and to search for ways to bypass court rulings on school prayer, a tactic that might be called pseudo-protest.

Conclusion

Although the politics of protest can gain the attention of public officials as well as of the general public, there are also liabilities associated with this strategy. As we observed in the case of antiabortion protests, those leading the movement may find it difficult to maintain a high level of commitment among participants, especially when protest activities may be costly not only in terms of time, emotional stress placed on family life, and the sacrifice of personal financial resources, but also in terms of possible arrest and imprisonment. If such costs fail to lead to perceptible results, the consequences can be discouragement and withdrawal from active involvement or, for some activists, an even greater commitment and radicalization. Thus the leaders may lose control of the rank and file members of the movement. Although protest demonstrations have been crucial to the antiabortion movement, in contrast, demonstrations associated with the school prayer issue have tended to play a secondary role to the quieter maneuvering of public officials and lobbyists behind the scenes and the conflict played out in the legal system.

References

Abington School District v. Schempp, 374 U.S. 203, 83 S. Ct. 1560, 10 L.Ed.2d 844 (1963).

Ackerman, David M. 2001. *Prayer and Religion in the Public Schools*. New York: Novinka.

Alcorn, Randy C. 1990. *Is Rescuing Right? Breaking the Law to Save the Unborn*. Downers Grove, IL: InterVarsity.

Alley, Robert S. 1996. *Without a Prayer: Religious Expression in Public Schools*. Amherst, NY: Prometheus.

Andrain, Charles F., and David E. Apter. 1995. *Political Protest and Social Change: Analyzing Politics*. Washington Square: New York University Press.

Baird-Windle, Patricia, and Eleanor J. Bader. 2001. *Targets of Hatred: Anti-Abortion Terrorism*. New York: Palgrave.

Barton, David. 2002. *America: To Pray? Or Not to Pray*. Fifth ed. Aledo, TX: Wallbuilder.

Blanchard, Dallas A. 1994. *The Anti-Abortion Movement and the Rise of the Religious Right: From Polite to Fiery Protest*. New York: Twayne.

Brulliard, Karin. 2003. "If You Don't Build Them, They Won't Come." *Washington Post National Weekly Edition* (December 8–14): 29.

Engel v. Vitale, 370 U.S. 421, 82 S.Ct. 1261, 8 L.Ed.2d 601, 20 O.O.2d 328 (1962).

Houston Chronicle. 2003. "School Prayer Request Draws Fire" (May 15): 11A.

Jurinski, James John. 1998. *Religion in the Schools: A Reference Handbook*. Santa Barbara, CA: ABC-CLIO.

Ladd, Everett Carl, and Karlyn H. Bowman. 1997. *Public Opinion about Abortion: Twenty-Five Years after Roe v. Wade.* Washington, DC: American Enterprise Institute.

LaHaye, Tim, and David Noebel. 2000. *Mind Siege: The Battle for Truth in the New Millennium.* Nashville, TN: Word.

Lee v. Weisman, 505 U.S. 577, 112 S.Ct. 2649, 120 L.Ed.2d 467 (1992).

Manatt, Richard P. 1995. *When Right Is Wrong: Fundamentalists and the Public Schools.* Lancaster, PA: Technomic.

Meier, Marianne M. 2002. *Understanding the School Prayer Issue and the Related Character Education and Charter Schools Movements.* Pittsburgh, PA: Dorrance.

Murray v. Curlett, 374 U.S. 203, 83 S.Ct. 1560, 10 L.Ed.2d 844 (1963).

Provenzo, Eugene F., Jr. 1990. *Religious Fundamentalism and American Education: The Battle for the Public Schools.* Albany: State University of New York Press.

Risen, James, and Judy L. Thomas. 1998. *Wrath of Angels: The American Abortion War.* New York: Basic.

Roe v. Wade, 410 U.S. 113, 93 S.Ct. 705, 35 L.Ed.2d 147 (1973).

Santa Fe Independent School District v. Doe, docket no. 99–62 (decided June 19, 2000).

Smith v. Board of School Commissioners of Mobile County, 827 F.2d 684 (11th Cir. 1987).

Solinger, Rickie, ed. 1998. *Abortion Wars: A Half Century of Struggle, 1950–2000.* Berkeley: University of California Press.

3

Social Movements and Interest Groups

Interest Group Participation

An examination of the general study of interest group formation and operation can contribute insights into the conservative Christian social movement as well as into particular interest groups associated with the religious right. Why do groups of people organize for political action? Lowery and Brasher (2004) identify three distinct approaches to understanding interest mobilization. First, according to pluralist theory, Americans already tend to join organizations but are especially inclined to do so during periods when disturbances occur in established relationships among different groups in society. Various trends in American society can be seen to have motivated many conservative Christians to become active politically—such as increasing divorce and crime rates, challenges to the assumed dominance of Christian values including prayer in the public schools, and the official recognition of a right to abortion. Many of these examples can be considered countermobilizations intended to oppose the actions of groups promoting goals antithetical to the beliefs and values of conservative Christians.

Lowery and Brasher's second approach to interest mobilization, attributed originally to Mancur Olson (1965), is one that they term the transactions school. According to this approach, because the objectives that interest organizations pursue are often collective, individuals tend to perceive little incentive to join and participate actively in the group because they can still receive the benefits achieved by the organization. In effect, they become "free riders" (2004, 33). Collective goods are those that cannot be excluded from nonparticipants and that are indivisible among consumers. Clean air is an example, as are many of the goals of conservative Christian organizations, such as a lower crime rate and a more "moral" society in general. Any organization attempting to achieve collective outcomes faces this difficulty: trying to motivate people to contribute resources—money and time—to the group's efforts even though they will receive the benefits whether or not they participate. The temptation is great to remain a free rider, failing to contribute to the organization while still reaping the benefits achieved. Organizations may use differing strategies to counteract the debilitating influence of the free rider problem, such as "forced riding" (2004, 35) (as with labor unions requiring membership as a condition of employment) and offering selective benefits that can be limited to the members only (for example, special rates on vacations or increased medical benefits).

Lowery and Brasher's third approach to interest mobilization is the "neopluralist school" (2004, 22), which views the difficulties of organization to be less onerous than does the transactions approach. This perspective rests on the claim that selective benefits can extend beyond material rewards. As Peter B. Clark and James Q. Wilson (1961) argue, members can receive an "expressive benefit," which is the psychological gratification experienced from actively supporting an issue of deep concern to oneself. Members of and contributors to conservative Christian organizations certainly do receive such benefits, given that they often feel deeply about issues of concern to them. Members may also receive "solidary benefits" (2004, 38), which result from association with like-minded individuals: These include a sense of group membership and a sense of common accomplishment. Nonmembers simply do not have access to these benefits.

Lowery and Brasher note that existing organizations may expedite mobilization of an interest by providing a location where new members may be recruited. Within an existing organization, potential new members for the interest group can be contacted more easily. Churches are in an especially advantageous position for mobilizing members to group involvement, given the often deep commitment of church members. Another factor affecting mobilization is the presence of interest group entrepreneurs, individuals who have the skills to motivate others and to work hard to establish and maintain an organization. People like Pat Robertson, Jerry Falwell, and Donald Wildmon have served as highly effective interest group entrepreneurs for conservative Christian organizations.

Lowery and Brasher note that many organizations do not survive, so after successful mobilization, group maintenance over time is not a foregone conclusion. Relevant to maintaining an interest organization, Lowery and Brasher introduce "niche theory" (2004, 50), according to which organizations develop distinct sources of membership, financial resources, and issue agendas. An organization tends to stake out an area for activity that distinguishes it from other organizations. Recruitment and retention of members is a significant function of groups. Entrepreneurs can play a crucial role in maintaining an organization's niche and in attracting new members and continued funding. Among conservative Christian groups, the National Legal Foundation is one of several organizations, including the American Center for Law and Justice, the Christian Law Association, and the Liberty Counsel, that represent the legal interests of conservative Christian individuals and groups. The organization argues for its legitimate place among other groups that bring cases to the courts, claiming that each group has a role to play when there are so many potential cases to be considered.

Over the past three decades, the number of conservative Christian groups that have become active in some way in the political process has expanded significantly. Such issues as prayer in the public schools, the legalization of abortion, the proliferation of pornography, and concern about such family-related issues as increasing divorce rates have energized conservative Christians to organize for more effective political activity. Many of these groups have learned the techniques of interest group activity: attracting members and monetary support, communicating their demands to government officials, and assisting in the election of office holders sympathetic to their cause. According to pluralist theory, interests tend to check and balance each other. Opposed to Christian groups that wish to maintain, reestablish, or create a society that recognizes Christianity and Christian beliefs as authoritative and influential in all aspects of human life are various interests that pursue objectives contrary to the fundamental beliefs of conservative Christians—including those associated with more mainline Christian groups—or that advocate the establishment of a more secular society in which religious authority plays a minimal role, such as the Council for Secular Humanism.

This chapter will explore and discuss the activities of various conservative Christian groups. First, we will describe the formation of two prominent organizations: the Moral Majority in 1979 and the Christian Coalition in 1989. The successes, as well as the failures, of these organizations carry lessons for other conservative Christian groups as well as for interest groups in general. We will then investigate the recent participation of conservative Christian organizations in varied issue areas. Christian groups are notable for their firmly held principles, which can conflict with the fundamental nature of politics; political activity often involves the willingness to compromise and accept less than complete victory.

A noted political scientist, Robert Dahl (1967, 53–54), borrowing from sociologist Max Weber, has spoken of the "ethics of responsibility," a realm of political action situated between the extremes of rigid morality and unprincipled politics. Conservative Christians who have organized for political activity have at times found it extremely difficult to discover a comfortable resting place in the middle ground between these two extremes, often considering any compromise as automatically unprincipled. Many have become disillusioned with political participation and have withdrawn from the political realm. Nevertheless, although some groups, such as the Moral Majority, Christian Voice, and the Freedom Council, have fallen by the wayside, many Christian groups and individuals have remained politically active and have achieved impressive successes at the national, state, and local levels.

The Moral Majority

In 1979, conservative political activists Paul Weyrich, Richard Viguerie, Howard Phillips, and Edward A. McAteer, among others, joined with the popular Lynchburg, Virginia, Baptist preacher Jerry Falwell to create the Moral Majority, Inc. They and other conservative Christians wished to provide a voice for those discontented with the path they perceived the United States taking, particularly on the issues of abortion and pornography. Falwell had previously opposed political involvement and had criticized other ministers who had participated in the civil rights movement. However, his perception of some major trends in American politics caused him to change his mind: "I never thought the government would go so far afield, I never thought the politicians would become so untrustworthy, I never thought the courts would go so nuts on the left. We have defaulted by failing to show up for the fight" (Falwell 1980, 202).

Falwell and his conservative Christian colleagues objected to the Supreme Court decisions banning organized prayer in the public schools and prohibiting state restrictions on abortion, to the seeming pervasiveness of obscenity and pornography, and to the increasing call for acceptance of homosexuality and equal rights for gays and lesbians. Falwell's fellow conservative Christians wanted him to lead the new organization, which would focus on getting the Republican party to take firm stands on moral issues, especially abortion (Diamond 1989, 60). Falwell established a board of directors composed of such conservative Christian luminaries as Charles Stanley of the First Baptist Church of Atlanta, Georgia; Tim LaHaye, subsequently a coauthor of the *Left Behind* fiction series; and James Kennedy of Coral Ridge Presbyterian Church in Fort Lauderdale, Florida. The organization would serve as a way for conservative Christians to make their concerns about American society and politics known to the general public.

Among its activities, the Moral Majority established chapters in all fifty states. These chapters were headed mostly by pastors in Falwell's own denomination, the Baptist Bible Fellowship, many of whom had previous political experience in fighting local battles over such issues as gay rights and pornography (Diamond 1998, 67). Falwell had a radio program, *Old Time Gospel Hour,* which broadcast sermons given at his Thomas Road Baptist Church in Lynchburg, Virginia; he used this program and a large mailing list to solicit financial support from listeners for the new group. During its first year, the Moral Majority raised more than $2 million (Diamond 1998, 67).

The organization's initial goal was to register voters for the 1980 presidential and congressional elections. During the 1980 election campaign, the Moral Majority claimed to have registered 4 million new voters (Diamond 1998, 67), but those outside the organization placed the total closer to 2 million, still an impressive effort to assist candidates supporting the organization's agenda (Guth 1983, 37). Although claiming to be nonpartisan, the Moral Majority consistently supported a conservative Republican issue agenda, largely because Republicans were more willing than Democrats to support the conservative positions of the Moral Majority. In 1981, the organization sent its newsletter, *Moral Majority Report,* to more than 800,000 homes, and more than 300 radio stations carried daily commentary from the organization. The Moral Majority claimed a membership of more than 4 million people, but others estimated an actual membership of approximately 400,000 (Diamond 1998, 67).

In the mid-1980s, the organization experienced a decrease in donations, which Clyde Wilcox (1996) has attributed to two factors. First, Ronald Reagan's reelection in 1984 led many supporters to conclude that further contributions were no longer as badly needed, and second, scandals over the financial practices of televangelists such as Jim Bakker and Jimmy Swaggart made many people more resistant to fundraising appeals. In 1986, Falwell renamed the organization Liberty Federation in an attempt to attract a broader membership. Falwell himself lost popularity in the general population, due in part to controversial public statements. For instance, in a fundraising letter, Falwell reported that a gay rights group had been given permission to place a wreath on the Tomb of the Unknown Soldier in Arlington National Cemetery, and he commented that the memorial should be renamed The Tomb of the Unknown Sodomite (Silverman 2003, 178).

Critics of Falwell and the Moral Majority began referring to the organization as "neither moral nor a majority." Falwell, having become more a liability than an asset to the conservative Christian cause, resigned as the organization's president in November 1987. Then, in 1988, the Moral Majority experienced serious cash flow problems. Falwell brought an end to the organization in 1989. Even after the Moral Majority's demise, Falwell attracted condemnation for his public remarks. For instance, in 1999, Jewish groups criticized Falwell for announcing before a meeting of pastors in Kingsport, Tennessee, that the Antichrist is alive today and is Jewish (Silverman 2003, 182).

Other conservative Christian activists attempted to learn from the experience of the Moral Majority. Some believed that Falwell and the Moral Majority focused too much attention on national politics—striving in particular to elect Ronald Reagan in 1980—and that they failed to place sufficient emphasis on organizing at the local level. As Clyde Wilcox commented, "Although the Moral Majority organization looked impressive on paper, in practice most state organizations were moribund" (1996, 37). Following Reagan's election, Moral Majority activists mistakenly assumed that change would come quickly and easily on the various issues of concern to the organization. Other organizations, most importantly the Christian Coalition, learned from the Moral Majority's successes as well as its failures, striving to develop organizational strength at the local as well as the state and the national level.

The Christian Coalition

Founded in 1989 by Pat Robertson, host of the *700 Club* Christian television program, the Christian Coalition replaced the Moral Majority as a leading national conservative Christian organization concerned with the alleged lack of morality in government. Robertson had made a run for the Republican presidential nomination in 1988, but with little success. However, by using the remains of his campaign machine to establish a new organization, Robertson succeeded in continuing his political agenda of family values. In January 1989, Robertson met Ralph Reed, a bright young conservative activist, at a dinner in Washington, D.C., and asked him to help in forming the new organization. The following September, Robertson and Reed attended an organizational meeting at which Robertson introduced Reed to Christian Coalition supporters as the only staff member (Watson 1997, 52). The organization began a campaign to elect candidates to political office, from the local to the national level, who demonstrated sufficient commitment to conservative Christian values.

By early 1991, Robertson and Reed had agreed that the Christian Coalition should focus on organizing at the grassroots level. Therefore, the organization worked especially hard to establish its presence at the state and local levels, particularly within the Republican party. Reed, just 28 years old, was an astute political strategist who had supported Jack Kemp, not Pat Robertson, in the 1988 presidential primaries. However, Robertson was impressed with Reed's political abilities and appointed him the Christian Coalition's executive director (Diamond 1998, 76).

In the early 1990s, Reed and the Christian Coalition achieved significant successes. Reed appeared on numerous television talk shows, presenting a photogenic image of the conservative Christian movement. The Christian Coalition had the advantage of a preexisting mailing list of donors to Robertson's presidential campaign from which to solicit funds and recruit members. The new organization also received a contribution of more than $60,000 from the Republican Senatorial Committee for start-up costs (Watson 1997, 52).

In spring 1990, the Coalition claimed a membership of 25,000, but by 1995, the membership was said to have increased to 1.5 million (Diamond 1998, 79). The organization began distributing three publications: *Religious Right Watch,* a brief monthly report detailing violations of Christians' legal rights; *Congressional Scorecard,* a semiannual summary of the voting records of members of Congress on issues of importance to the Coalition and its supporters; and *Christian American*, a tabloid newspaper containing reports of the organization's activities, with columns written by Robertson and Reed. In 1993, the Coalition opened a lobbying office in Washington, D.C., to push the organization's agenda before Congress.

Efforts during the 1990 election campaign in North Carolina allowed the Christian Coalition to take some of the credit for reelecting Jesse Helms to the U.S. Senate, and in 1991, the organization urged supporters to communicate to senators their support for U.S. Supreme Court nominee Clarence Thomas. In an attempt to broaden support for the organization—something that the Moral Majority failed to do—Reed de-emphasized hardline stands on such issues as abortion and homosexuality and focused instead on questions of concern to the broader public, such as taxes, the federal budget deficit, and crime rates. The organization also attempted to become more inclusive. For instance, at the organization's 1995 convention, Catholic, Jewish, and African-American speakers took to the rostrum. In following a strategy of inclusiveness, Reed demonstrated his political skill, but he also risked alienating the more hardcore supporters of the Christian Coalition.

Reed left the organization in 1997 to establish Century Strategies, a political consulting firm. Robertson, still a prominent figure associated with the Coalition at times experienced the same problem as Jerry Falwell—attracting criticism for controversial comments. He was reported to have claimed that the feminist agenda advocated the killing of children and the practicing of witchcraft and lesbianism (Wilcox 1996, 62). In October 2003, Robertson, criticizing the U.S. State Department, stated in a broadcast that the agency should be destroyed with a nuclear device. Although Robertson later tried to clarify his statement, saying that he had made the comment in a "laughing fashion" while discussing a book that was critical of the State Department, Richard Boucher, a department spokesman, called the original statement "despicable" (*Houston Chronicle* 2003b).

The Christian Coalition was charged by the Internal Revenue Service (IRS) with inappropriate political activity, and in 1999, the IRS denied the organization's tax exempt status. The Christian Coalition was restructured into two organizations: the Christian Coalition of America (CCA), which focused on educational activities, and the Christian Coalition International (CCI), which acted as a political action committee that supports candidates for public office. The organization continued to influence American politics. In 2000, the Coalition reported having distributed 70 million voter guides during the election campaign (Silverman 2003, 182). The Christian Coalition was also reported to have invested more than $18 million in George W. Bush's successful run for the presidency (Silverman 2003, 182).

Presently, the CCA, claiming a membership of 2 million, states that it is "dedicated to equipping and educating God's people with the resources and information to battle against anti-family legislation." Robertson, 73 years old, stepped down from his leadership role in 2003, stating that he wanted to devote more time to his ministry. The criticism that he received for various controversial statements, particularly his agreeing publicly with Jerry Falwell's statement that the United States was ultimately responsible for the September 11, 2001, terrorist attacks, may have played a role in his decision to retire. Also, in February 2003, Robertson announced that he would undergo surgery for prostate cancer (*Houston Chronicle* 2003a). He became president emeritus of the organization and Roberta Combs assumed the presidency. Robertson continued to host the *700 Club* television program. The organization's declared goals include strengthening the institution of the family, opposing abortion, supporting local and parental control of education, decreasing the tax burden on families, punishing criminals and defending victims' rights, protecting young people from "the pollution of pornography," defending the institution of marriage (and opposing same-sex marriage), and advocating religious freedom.

The CCA sponsors Citizenship Sundays in local church congregations, a campaign to increase the number of conservative Christian voters. The organization has backed various legislative initiatives in the U.S. Congress, including a ban on human cloning; a bill intended to prohibit the avoidance of parental-consent laws by making it a crime for anyone but a parent to take a minor to another state in order to obtain an abortion; and the Child Pornography Prevention Constitutional Amendment, proposed in reaction against a U.S. Supreme Court ruling disallowing a federal law prohibiting virtual child pornography because no actual children were involved. Objecting to U.S. Supreme Court decisions on such issues as prayer in the public schools and abortion, the CCA supports efforts to stop "judicial tyranny." The organization backed the Pledge Protection Act of 2003, introduced into the House of Representatives by Congressman Tod Adkin. The bill would prohibit courts from hearing cases dealing with the Pledge of Allegiance. In light of the terrorist attacks of September 11, 2001, the CCA announced that it would initiate a renewal of itself to remake it into an instrument of Christian spiritual response to the challenges the country faces domestically and internationally (http://www.cc.org).

Interest Group Involvement: Case Studies

Conservative Christian organizations have become involved in recent policy conflicts at the state and national levels. We will present several of these conflicts as case studies, describing the issues at stake, other interests making policy claims, and the responses of conservative Christian organizations. The examples highlight many of the values such organizations are working to achieve, including protection for the right to life, respect for divine law as presented in the Ten Commandments, protection for the sanctity of traditional marriage against the push to recognize same-sex unions, freedom from exposure to obscenity, and public recognition of the view that the United States is a nation specially blessed by God.

The Right to Die and the Sanctity of Life: The Case of Terri Schiavo

The case of Theresa "Terri" Schindler Schiavo, the 40-year-old Florida woman who has been in a vegetative state for more than 13 years, has drawn the attention of several conservative Christian organizations concerned about the possible consequences for policies regarding the right to life, the right to die, and euthanasia—the latter being a right that conservative Christians vehemently oppose. Although the Schiavo case is not unique, it has become a cause célèbre among conservative Christians.

In 1990, Terri Schiavo suffered cardiac arrest. Although not fatal, the attack caused severe brain damage, leaving the young woman in a persistent vegetative state. Terri's husband, Michael, ultimately decided that Terri, who was being fed intravenously, should be allowed to die. However, Terri's parents, Robert and Mary Schindler, opposed Michael's choice and fought their son-in-law in the courts. Terri's parents argued that their daughter showed definite signs of responding to them, appearing to smile, react to voices, and make sounds. Unlike people in comas, vegetative patients have nearly normal sleep and wake patterns and at times move their limbs or lips. Michael Schiavo commissioned experts to observe Terri, and they noted that such movement represented only reflex actions and that there was no realistic chance that Terri could recover any true cognitive abilities. In October 2003, a judged granted a court order to Michael, allowing Terri's feeding tube to be removed (Roig-Franzia 2003, 1A). This much-publicized event elicited prompt and fierce reaction from various conservative Christian groups.

D. James Kennedy, senior pastor of the Coral Ridge Presbyterian Church in Fort Lauderdale, Florida, along with his organization, the Center for Reclaiming America, called for saving Terri's life. Kennedy declared that the woman was being condemned to "a horrific, inhumane, barbarous death. . . . an excruciatingly painful death by dehydration that . . . will take 10–14 days." Kennedy stated that this "court-imposed torture" would end in a "criminal death." He called on Florida governor Jeb Bush and the state legislature to defend Schiavo's "constitutional and God-given right to life." Kennedy claimed that this case was a logical outcome of the U.S. Supreme Court decision in *Roe v. Wade,* which limited the authority of states to restrict abortion. He stated that the "sanctity of life ethic," which he identified as a Christian concept, had been replaced by a "quality of life ethic," which he branded a pagan concept. Kennedy urged citizens to contact Governor Bush and urge him to save Terri Schiavo's life (Kennedy 2003).

When Governor Bush called a special session of the Florida legislature to consider whether to override the court order to remove Schiavo's feeding tube, Concerned Women for American (CWA), a conservative Christian organization based in Washington, D.C., urged its members to call the Florida legislature and Governor Bush to register their support for "Terri's Bill," which, CWA declared, would "put an immediate moratorium on all dehydration and starvation deaths currently pending in Florida" (Concerned Women for America 2003). The Family Research Council (FRC) also registered its concerns about Schiavo's impending death. Former FRC president Ken Connor, testifying before the U.S. Senate Special Committee on Aging, declared that the Schiavo case foreshadowed mistreatment of elderly Americans and that human life, a gift originating with God, should be respected "from conception to the grave" (Connor 2003).

The Florida legislature passed the desired narrowly drawn legislation on October 21, authorizing the governor to intervene only in cases in which no living will exists, the patient is in a persistent vegetative state, and family members dispute the removal of feeding tubes. Governor Bush quickly acted, ordering physicians to resume Schiavo's tube feeding (Roig-Franzia 2003, 1A). Soon thereafter, lawyers for Michael Schiavo asked a Florida court to invalidate the new statute and the governor's action, arguing that the law violated the state constitutional right to privacy and amounted to an unconstitutional interference with judicial power. Howard Simon, an attorney with the American Civil Liberties Union, declared that the law represented an unwarranted abuse of power by the state legislature and governor (*Houston Chronicle* 2003e).

In the meantime, the Traditional Values Coalition (TVC) called for Michael Schiavo to be removed as Terri's legal guardian, stating that his "primary goal is to see her starved to death" (Traditional Values Coalition 2003a). In fact, on October 31, the Pinellas County chief judge named an advisory guardian to recommend possible treatment options. A month later, the court-appointed guardian reported that any improvement in Schiavo's condition was unlikely and that there was evidence that she could not eat or drink on her own. During his visits to Schiavo, he noted that although the woman appeared to respond to those around her, those responses did not indicate that she was aware of her surroundings (Stacy 2003, 22A). As the judicial system began a new round of deliberations, conservative Christian groups continued to express their determination to defend Schiavo's right to life as a test case against various perceived threats to this right, including abortion, assisted suicide, and euthanasia, and they attacked the belief that the quality of life, in preference over the sanctity of life, could play an important role in any life-or-death decision.

Displaying the Ten Commandments: A Case Study

Controversy over the display of the Ten Commandments in public places epitomizes the basic cultural struggle between opposing interests. One side of the dispute regards such displays as a fundamental recognition of the Christian origin of the United States and its continuation as a nation that follows God's commands, and the other side protests what they consider the tyranny of attempting to impose upon everyone the religious beliefs of one group—even if that group represents a majority of the population. Between these two sides, many Americans react in puzzlement or dismay over such symbolic battles. The case of Roy Moore, chief justice of the Alabama Supreme Court, and his insistence on maintaining a public display of the Ten Commandments clearly demonstrates the belief of conservative Christian groups that the American legal system depends on God-given law and that the nation must publicly recognize that dependence.

In 2000, Moore, a Republican, ran successfully for the judicial office of Alabama chief justice, referring to himself as "the Ten Commandments judge." After assuming the position of chief justice, Moore designed a 5,280-pound monument to the Ten Commandments and, in 2001, reportedly helped move it into the state judicial building in Montgomery during the middle of the night. Groups opposed to the public display, including the Southern Poverty Law Center and Americans United for Separation of Church and State, sued Moore, contending that the presence of the monument on state property promoted religion and thus violated the establishment clause of the Second Amendment. In August 2003, a federal judge ruled that the monument must be removed, and the judge ordered Moore to obey. Moore filed an appeal with the U.S. Supreme Court for a stay to prevent the removal, an appeal that was quickly denied. Moore's fellow justices on the state supreme court complied with the order, and workers removed the monument on August 27, after 2 years on public display.

Moore faced charges of judicial ethics violations for his refusal to comply with a federal court order and went on trial in November 2003 before the Alabama Court of the Judiciary. State attorney general Bill Pryor, a Bush nominee to a federal court position, prosecuted the case against Moore, arguing that Moore should be removed for his "utterly unrepentant behavior" (Johnson 2003, 3A). Assistant Attorney General John Gibbs stated that Moore's refusal to comply with the court order threatened the integrity of the judicial system. The Court of the Judiciary decided unanimously to remove Moore from his seat on the Alabama Supreme Court. In December 2003, Moore decided to appeal the Court of the Judiciary decision to the Alabama Supreme Court, the same court where he served for three years as the chief justice.

The mainline press emphasized Moore's obligation as a judge to obey the law and applauded his removal. For instance, the *Washington Post* referred to Moore as a demagogue and a "scofflaw"—a person who continuously violates the law or fails to answer court summonses. Judges, the paper noted, should not serve as "generals in the culture wars" (*Washington Post National Weekly Edition* 2003a, 25). However, various conservative Christian organizations came to Moore's defense. The Christian Law Association identified Moore's actions with a struggle to recognize the place many Christians believe God and the Bible played in the founding of the United States and to continue to acknowledge publicly the nation's dependence on God. The organization claimed that the Ten Commandments, once publicly displayed "without complaint," now symbolize the conflict between those who wish to recognize the nation's "Godly heritage" and those who want that heritage to be "obliterated" (Christian Law Association 2003).

Prior to the removal of the Ten Commandments monument, the Center for Reclaiming America urged its supporters to call Alabama attorney general Bill Pryor and demand that he "uphold his constitutional duties to defend both the Alabama Constitution and the United States Constitution" by supporting Moore's resolve to keep the monument on public display (Kastensmidt 2003). At a rally held outside the U.S. Supreme Court building in Washington, D.C., on October 6, 2003, Jan LaRue, chief counsel for Concerned Women for America, declared that the majority of Americans who believed in God would not allow "judicial tyrants" to take away the people's liberties. La Rue asserted the right to "proclaim God in our public life and in our public buildings" (Wong 2003). CWA endorsed such measures as placing the Ten Commandments in state capitols and other public buildings; supported the county commissioners of Barrow County, Georgia, who refused to remove the Ten Commandments from the county courthouse; and petitioned the U.S. Congress to establish a Ten Commandments monument in the U.S. Capitol building. In February 2004, in response to the Ten Commandments controversy, Senators Zell Miller (D-GA) and Richard Shelby (R-AL) introduced a measure that would prohibit federal courts from disallowing state court decisions favoring an "acknowledgment of God" (*Houston Chronicle* 2004c). Miller claimed that the framers of the Constitution did not intend to separate church and state and stated that conditions in the United States required a reintroduction of God into society.

In October 2003, James Dobson's Focus on the Family, referring to the American Civil Liberties Union's "anti-Christianity campaign," reported on the commissioners of Cherokee County, Georgia, who planned to accept two stone tablets containing the Ten Commandments and place them in a public place in the county courthouse (Schneeberger 2003). Focus on the Family asked its supporters to send e-mail messages to the five county commissioners, a task that could be done by visiting the organization's Web site (http://www.family.org). The Family Research Council (FRC), responding to the U.S. Supreme Court's refusal to review the Alabama Supreme Court's ruling to remove the Ten Commandments monument, declared that the struggle would continue at the state and local levels over the issue of separation of church and state. The FRC indicated that the Supreme Court would ultimately be forced to deal with the issue because of the need to clarify confusing judicial interpretations of the First Amendment. The organization also called on Congress to pass the Religious Liberties Restoration Act, a measure that would limit the authority of federal courts to rule on the issues of prayer in the public schools and public displays of the Ten Commandments. Organization supporters were urged to e-mail their congressional representatives via the FRC's Web site and ask them to support the bill. The organization also asked supporters to order Ten Commandments book covers, which they billed as "a great way to bring America's Christian heritage into America's classrooms."

The Chalcedon Foundation, an organization that supports the reconstruction of American government and society according to biblical principles, took a defense of Moore to its logical extreme. The Foundation challenged the assumption that Moore had an obligation to obey an order from another judicial official. Stating explicitly the position implicit in the support the Center for Reclaiming America gave to Moore—that he was defending the Alabama and U.S. Constitutions—the organization claimed that the Constitution itself, and not the opinions of any particular judges, is the law of the land. The Foundation asserted that government officials mistakenly believed that their oath of office involved an obligation to obey the judiciary rather than the Constitution and the laws enacted in agreement with it. Jeffrey Tuomala, in an article distributed by the Foundation, argued that, in contrast to many government officials, Moore understood "the nature of his oath of office," that it was "an oath sworn before God and man to support and defend the Constitution" (Tuomala 2003). Tuomala, an associate dean of academic affairs and associate professor of law at Liberty University School of Law in Lynchburg, Virginia, represented a radical view of the legal system: a public official could sometimes be obligated *not* to obey judicial orders, including such rulings as the U.S. Supreme Court's decision on abortion in *Roe v. Wade*.

For those sympathetic with Moore's stand but holding more moderate views about the legal system, the Chalcedon Foundation's challenge to the common understanding of the judicial process could not lead to any satisfactory resolution to the controversy. Rather, their attention turned to the reality of judicial interpretation and therefore to another political struggle: changing the federal judges interpreting the Constitution by supporting President George W. Bush's judicial nominations and opposing Democratic senators' attempts to block Senate ratification of those nominations.

Whatever future actions Moore would decide to take, he could be assured of having the support of conservative Christian organizations. The removal of the Ten Commandments from the Alabama Supreme Court building undoubtedly confirmed the belief of such organizations that secular forces in the United States were engaged in an effort to remove any reference to God from American public life, and that Christians must engage those forces in order to preserve what they believe is the fundamental Christian character of the nation.

In a related case, the American Civil Liberties Union, on behalf of a local resident, challenged the display of the Ten Commandments on a monument in a city park in Plattsmouth, Nebraska. A federal district judge rejected the municipality's argument that the monument represented an expression of constitutionally protected free speech. The American Center for Law and Justice appealed the case on behalf of the local community to the Eighth Circuit Court of Appeals, which, in February 2004, upheld the lower court ruling that the monument must be removed.

Opposition to Homosexual Rights and Gay Marriage

Many conservative Christian organizations have presented a united front on the issue of homosexuality and gay marriage. For many years, such groups have insisted that homosexuality, which they consider biblically condemned, results from an individual choice rather than being a genetically determined characteristic. The Traditional Values Coalition (TVC) categorizes homosexuality with such self-destructive behaviors as alcoholism and drug addiction; they hold that, like those behaviors, homosexuality can be modified or eliminated to the benefit of the affected individual (Traditional Values Coalition 2004). Responding to the Supreme Court decision in *Lawrence v. Texas* (2003), in which the Court struck down a Texas antisodomy law, Louis P. Sheldon of the TVC commented: "[The decision] is a defeat for public morality and America's families" (Traditional Values Coalition 2003b).

Taking a similar position, Focus on the Family holds that homosexuality is "preventable and treatable," a truth the organization claims is being suppressed. In 1998, Focus on the Family began holding a series of conferences around the country titled Love Won Out, in which participants were told they would learn how to deal with reputed misinformation in the public school system, help to change public opinion, and discover how to use the "power of love" to defeat "fear, hate, or ignorance." Various conference speakers, including Joseph Nicolosi, president and principal research investigator for the National Association of Research and Therapy of Homosexuality, were advertised as having special expertise in helping gays to overcome their homosexuality (Focus on the Family 2003a).

FRC president Tony Perkins urged the Massachusetts legislature to adopt a proposed state constitutional amendment titled Marriage Affirmation and Protection Amendment, and he called on Congress to initiate a marriage amendment to the U.S. Constitution. The National Legal Foundation declared itself ready to fight the so-called homosexual agenda. The organization has become involved in the passage of anti-same-sex marriage laws and lobbied for enactment of the Defense of Marriage Act by the U.S. Congress. Whatever the success of these lobbying efforts, the issue of gay marriage promises to play a significant role in future electoral politics.

To the extent that there is a "culture war" occurring in the United States between more conservative and more liberal groups in the population, the issue of homosexuality plays a key role. A great divide separates homosexual interests from cultural conservatives, including the Christian right. Two court decisions in 2003 affirming gay rights were taken by conservative Christian groups as confirmation of their belief that U.S. courts were out of control; these decisions inspired Christian groups to take action to preserve what they considered the biblical mandate regarding acceptable sexual relations.

The first decision, *Lawrence v. Texas*, occurred in June of that year (2003). The U.S. Supreme Court, in a six-to-three decision, invalidated a Texas antisodomy law, thereby legalizing homosexual relations throughout the United States. Justice Antonin Scalia, one of the more conservative members of the Court, so strongly opposed the majority of judges that he wrote a scathing dissent that exceeded the length of the majority opinion. At an October meeting of the Intercollegiate Studies Institute, Scalia criticized legal scholars for inserting liberal political theory into their interpretations of the Constitution. Immediately following the Supreme Court decision, Rick Scarborough, president of Vision America, a conservative Christian group, commended Justice Antonin Scalia for his dissent in the case, calling the justice courageous. Scarborough called on Christians to defend Scalia and to stop an "out-of-control" federal judiciary, which, he claimed, had assaulted the culture with this decision as well as the *Roe v. Wade* ruling on abortion.

The second decision, *Goodridge v. Department of Public Health,* came from the Massachusetts Supreme Judicial Court in November 2003. The court, in a four-to-three ruling, declared the state's ban on gay marriage unconstitutional and gave the state legislature 180 days to provide a mechanism for putting the decision into effect. The Massachusetts case began when, in 2001, seven gay couples attempted to receive marriage licenses from their city and town governments. When denied the licenses, the couples sued the state for discrimination. However, a state court judge dismissed the suit, ruling that state law did not grant marriage rights to gay couples. The couples then appealed to the Supreme Judicial Court of Massachusetts, arguing that the law prohibiting them from marrying violated their constitutional right to equal treatment. The majority of justices in the case agreed with the couples, stating that the standard definition of marriage resulted in hardship for same-sex couples "for no rational reason."

Conservative public officials and organizations responded immediately, criticizing the decision and supporting a constitutional amendment to the Massachusetts state constitution as well as the national Constitution that would define marriage as a union between a man and a woman. President George W. Bush declared that the Massachusetts court ruling attacked the "sacred institution" of marriage, and he promised to defend the "sanctity of marriage." He indicated that he would consider supporting a constitutional amendment that would "honor marriage between a man and a woman" (Loven 2003, 11A). In July 2003, the Vatican issued a statement opposing the legal recognition of same-sex unions. Roman Catholic bishops in the United States, in a semiannual meeting held in Washington, D.C., in November 2003, declared their opposition to extending marriage rights to same-sex couples. In a vote of 234 to 3, with three abstentions, the bishops approved a document titled *Between Man and Woman: Questions and Answers about Marriage and Same-Sex Unions,* declaring that it would be wrong to alter the definition of marriage to provide benefits to "those who cannot rightfully enter into marriage." They planned to publish and distribute the document as a brochure. The bishops decided not to include in the document proposed amendments that would have labeled homosexual sex as sinful.

In 1996, Congress had passed the Defense of Marriage Act, which President Bill Clinton had signed into law. This legislation withheld federal recognition of same-sex marriages. Thirty-eight states, including Massachusetts, had enacted similar provisions. Conservatives feared that all of these laws could fall before judicial scrutiny and that, therefore, the surest way of preserving their conception of marriage was through a constitutional amendment. Representative Marilyn Musgrave (R-CO) introduced an amendment, drafted by the Alliance for Marriage, into the U.S. House of Representatives. The proposed amendment stated: "Marriage in the United States shall consist only of the union of a man and a woman. Neither this Constitution nor the constitution of any state, nor state or federal law, shall be construed to require that marital status or the legal incidents thereof be conferred upon unmarried couples or groups." Musgrave, a longtime member of the conservative Assemblies of God church, had met with Jerry Falwell at Falwell's Thomas Road Baptist Church in Lynchburg, Virginia, to discuss the amendment.

Senator Wayne Allard (R-CO) introduced the same amendment in the U.S. Senate. Several members of Congress expressed their support for such an amendment, and by December 2003, the Federal Marriage Amendment had attracted more than 100 bipartisan cosponsors in the House of Representatives and three Republican sponsors in the U.S. Senate. Senate Republican majority leader Bill Frist announced soon after the Supreme Court decision invalidating the Texas sodomy law that he would support the amendment.

Matt Daniels, founder of the Alliance for Marriage, claimed (Cooperman 2004, 31) the amendment would not restrict states from instituting so-called civil unions, which would allow gay couples to have the same rights as married couples in such areas as health insurance, inheritance, and pension benefits. However, some conservative Christian groups took a more stringent position on the amendment, opposing any recognition of same-sex unions. Those critical of the proposed amendment raised questions about the wording of the second sentence, and particularly the phrase *legal incidents*, which appeared vague and opened the possibility for prohibiting various rights for gays. Critics also observed that conservatives, who usually called for greater state policymaking authority, were now supporting a federal policy on domestic relations that would overrule states' authority to deal with the issue (Mason 2004, 3A).

National polls conducted since summer 2003 had tracked a consistent resistance among those polled to the prospect of same-sex marriages. In an ABC News poll conducted in September (Allen 2003, 14), 55 percent of respondents said that same-sex marriages should be prohibited. In a New York Times/CBS News poll conducted in December (*Houston Chronicle* 2003g), 55 percent of respondents supported passage of a constitutional amendment restricting marriage to a man and a woman. However, 40 percent of respondents opposed such an amendment, indicating a significant division of opinion among Americans.

A subsequent poll indicated that Americans' views on the issue tended to fluctuate. A *Washington Post*-ABC News poll conducted in March 2004 showed an increase in support for gay unions, with 51 percent of respondents favoring allowing same-sex couples to have civil unions with the same legal rights as married couples. A majority of those polled opposed a constitutional amendment to ban same-sex marriages and supported giving states the authority to determine who was eligible to marry. However, 60 percent of respondents stated that they opposed same-sex marriage (*Houston Chronicle* 2004f).

Although many government officials and political activists expressed a willingness to accept same-sex civil unions, if not marriage, conservative Christian organizations mobilized to defend their understanding of marriage as a God-mandated union between a man and a woman. Tony Perkins, president of the Family Research Council, claimed that the Massachusetts court had defied tradition and democracy as well as common sense, indicating that his organization would help to ensure that the issue would be important in the 2004 elections (Mason 2003b, 1A). He warned that if a federal marriage amendment were not ratified, the institution of marriage would be lost to the nation. James Dobson of Focus on the Family, in a fundraising letter to supporters, warned that the institution of marriage could "descend into a state of turmoil" and claimed that the coming battle could be a "turning point in our nation's history." Gary Bauer, head of American Values and 2000 opponent to George W. Bush in the Republican primaries, stated that he would demand that President Bush do all that he could to defend the institution of marriage, which obviously meant support for the constitutional amendment. Bauer urged the president to put in an effort on this issue similar to his campaign for tax cuts (Fineman and Gegax 2003, 35).

President Bush, in his January 2004 State of the Union address, expressed a more cautious approach to the issue of gay marriage by indicating that a constitutional amendment prohibiting gay marriage should be pursued only if the courts continued to support the idea of gay unions. Following the president's address, Donald Wildmon, executive director of the American Family Association and chair of the Arlington Group, a coalition of twenty conservative organizations established to defend the traditional conception of marriage, expressed the seriousness of the gay marriage issue for conservative Christians by suggesting that evangelicals might stay home on election day if the president did not support the marriage amendment. Louis Sheldon, chair of the Traditional Values Coalition, stated that a constitutional amendment could establish a policy for the entire nation and thus would avoid confusing state-by-state policymaking (Holland 2004, 6A).

On February 4, 2004, the Massachusetts Supreme Judicial Court responded to a request from the Massachusetts state senate to rule on whether a proposed bill that would grant to same-sex couples the rights and status of marriage, but which called such relationships civil unions, would be compatible with the court's November 2003 decision. The court majority stated that such a bill would continue a policy of exclusion that the state constitution prohibited. Thus, the court opened the way once more for marriages of same-sex couples, beginning in May. President Bush criticized the decision, but he still stopped short of directly endorsing an amendment to the U.S. Constitution. The twenty-organization Arlington Group, meeting at the Family Research Council's headquarters in Washington, D.C., issued a response to the Massachusetts court ruling, stating that the Massachusetts legislature must approve an affirmation of marriage amendment and urged President Bush to endorse a marriage amendment to the national Constitution (Kastensmidt 2004).

Lobbying for and against a defense of marriage amendment to the Massachusetts state constitution intensified as the Massachusetts legislature approached a February 2004 session to consider such an amendment that would ultimately overturn the court's ruling. However, opponents of gay marriage could do little to prevent the court ruling from taking effect in May 2004 because any proposed amendment required passage in two successive sessions of the state legislature and then ratification by the state's voters, a process that could not be completed until late 2006. The state legislature met to consider the proposed amendment, with both supporters and opponents heavily lobbying legislators. To add to the tension, many of the legislators would be up for reelection the following November. Legislators defeated three proposed amendments, each of which prohibited same-sex marriages but allowed some form of civil union. Gay-rights supporters condemned the proposals, maintaining that gay people would be relegated to second-class citizenship despite victory in the courts.

The legislators reconvened in March to attempt once again to reach agreement on an amendment, and they finally agreed on a compromise that recognized same-sex civil unions but prohibited same-sex marriage. In the meantime, the Massachusetts court decision had energized those in the U.S. Congress who supported a constitutional marriage amendment. Senator John Cornyn (R-TX), chair of the Senate Judiciary Committee, stated (Gamboa 2004, 6A) that the time had arrived for appropriate congressional committees to begin hearings to determine how to deal with what he considered the harmful effects of judicial activism.

While Massachusetts legislators agonized over the wording of a constitutional amendment, political activities in other states indicated how widespread the issue had become. In Virginia, where same-sex marriage had already been banned, the House of Delegates moved closer to approving legislation that would also prohibit same-sex civil unions. On February 12, 2004, declared "National Freedom to Marry Day" by gay groups, city officials in San Francisco began issuing marriage licenses to gay and lesbian couples and conducting marriage ceremonies for them. Although San Francisco mayor Gavin Newsom praised the marriage ceremonies as the achievement of true justice, Randy Thomasson, executive director of the conservative group Campaign for California Families, declared that the marriages were unlawful (Min 2004, 17A). Lawyers for the Alliance Defense Fund, a Christian legal organization concerned with defending traditional values, appealed to the courts to issue an injunction prohibiting such marriages, basing their complaint on a proposition ratified by voters in 2000 that restricted marriage to a union between a man and a woman.

Because the California courts did not act immediately, the issuing of marriage licenses and marriage ceremonies continued. (In late February, former talk show host Rosie O'Donnell married her partner of six years at the San Francisco city hall.) At the urging of California governor Arnold Schwarzenegger, Attorney General Bill Lockyer asked the California Supreme Court to intervene in the situation, but the court declined to do so immediately. By the first week in March, more than 3,600 same-sex marriages had been performed in San Francisco (Hubler 2004, 13A). Lockyer, along with the Alliance Defense Fund, argued that the California constitution prohibited state administrative agencies from unilaterally declaring laws—in this case, the Defense of Marriage proposition approved by voters—to be unconstitutional. On March 11, the California Supreme Court finally issued a stay prohibiting the continued issuance of marriage licenses to same-sex couples.

During this time, same-sex couples in other parts of the country attempted to marry, thus increasing the legal battles over the issue.

The mayor of New Paltz, New York, performed twenty-five same-sex marriages but was charged with performing marriages without the requisite licenses. At the request of Liberty Counsel, a Florida-based organization, New York Supreme Court Justice Vincent Bradley issued a temporary restraining order against New Paltz mayor Jason West, prohibiting him from conducting any more same-sex weddings. When Multnomah County, Oregon, commissioners began sanctioning same-sex marriages, the Defense of Marriage Coalition filed a lawsuit claiming that the commissioners had violated the state's public meetings law by deciding in a private meeting to change policy regarding the issuing of marriage licenses.

Such challenges to the traditional conception of marriage provided significant incentive to conservative Christians to take steps to counter the push toward official recognition of same-sex marriage in states and local communities. At the national level, President Bush, at the urging of several conservative Christian organizations, finally announced his support for a constitutional amendment prohibiting gay marriage and pressed Congress to begin the amendment process (Roth 2004, 1A). Conservative Christian groups such as the Christian Coalition of America praised Bush for calling for a constitutional amendment. In early March, the House of Representatives had tentatively scheduled hearings to consider an amendment.

Black Christians remained a question mark on the issue of gay marriage. Many black Christians tend to be politically liberal but socially conservative. Advocates on both sides of the gay marriage issue appealed to African-American church leaders for their support. Genevieve Wood of the Family Research Council appealed to black evangelical ministers and lay people to oppose gay marriage, while Donna Payne, a board member of the recently formed National Black Justice Coalition, a group representing black gays and lesbians, appealed to liberal black clergy to recognize the equal right of gays to marry (Clemetson 2004, 1E). Although more traditionally oriented black leaders, basing their position on biblical principles, announced their opposition to gay marriage, others, such as Peter Gomes, chaplain at Harvard University, and Al Sharpton, presidential candidate, supported the rights of gays to marry, comparing the differential treatment of gays to the discrimination that blacks historically had to endure.

Many political figures, both Democrat and Republican, expressed support for limiting marriage to heterosexual couples, but some were more willing to consider the possibility of same-sex civil unions. In 2000, Howard Dean, while he was governor of Vermont, had signed the first state law recognizing civil unions between same-sex couples. As a result, Dean gained significant support from gay and lesbian groups in his bid for the 2004 Democratic presidential nomination. In 2001 and 2002, before becoming a candidate for the Democratic nomination, Dean had spoken to branches of the leading gay organization Human Rights Campaign. In 2002, gays and lesbians reportedly organized all but one of the fundraisers that Dean attended (Edsall 2004, 14A). However, conservative Christians wanted someone in the White House who would work toward attaining their social policy objectives, not least among them the preservation of a traditional concept of marriage.

In July 2004, the Republican leadership brought the Defense of Marriage amendment to the floor of the Senate for debate. However, on July 14, senators decided, by a vote of 48 to 50 (with 60 votes needed to continue consideration of the proposed amendment) to cut off further debate. Leaders of the Arlington Group claimed that the vote did not represent a major defeat, but was merely the first step in gaining the necessary two-thirds vote in both houses of Congress to send the amendment to the states for ratification. Charles Colson, a born-again Christian and former White House assistant to President Richard Nixon, commented that the struggle to ratify the amendment could take ten years (*Houston Chronicle* 2004g).

Controversy over Homosexuality in Mainline Christian Churches

Although the issue of homosexuality has played a key role in the agenda of conservative Christian groups, who particularly oppose the push by gay rights groups to establish legally recognized same-sex marriage, these groups tend not to have significant disagreement over the issue among their own members or clergy. The acceptance of biblical authority and the interpretation of scripture as prohibiting sexual intercourse—including homosexual acts—outside marriage does not allow for varying positions on this issue.

The situation differs greatly within the mainline churches, however, where more liberal factions vocally express dissenting opinions, advocating recognition of homosexuals within the congregation and clergy as well as recognition of same-sex unions. The experiences of the Episcopal Church (USA) (ECUSA) and the United Methodist Church (UMC) illustrate the difficulties a denomination faces when subgroups oppose one another over such an emotional issue.

Although the church was once a significant force in the American political establishment, the ECUSA's membership declined by one-third between 1960 and 2003, down to approximately 2.4 million members (Passantino 2003, 6). Membership decline has also occurred in other mainline churches at the same time that evangelical and fundamentalist denominations have expanded their membership rolls. If disagreements between liberals and conservatives in the mainline denominations have contributed to such membership shifts, then the ordination of a gay bishop may augur future membership decline and hence a further shift of social and political influence from mainline churches to evangelical and fundamentalist denominations.

Although more conservative denominations regard the Bible to be the infallible and inerrant word of God, many in mainline churches such as the ECUSA take a less absolutist position on scripture, believing that fallible human beings wrote the books of the Bible and therefore that the scriptures contain errors and reflect the culture of their authors. Although accepting the basic substance of scripture as being God-inspired, many mainline Christians reject the notion that the specific words of scripture are particularly authoritative.

Elizabeth Cady Stanton, a leader in the nineteenth-century woman suffrage movement, collaborated with several other women to write *The Woman's Bible* (republished in 1993), a volume that questioned the authority of scripture, especially with regard to the treatment of women. More recent critics of the Bible raise similar objections with regard to the Bible's treatment of homosexuality. Liberals in the ECUSA and other mainline denominations regard such prohibitions as the product of a particular culture, arguing that the word *homosexuality* does not appear anywhere in the Bible because those writing the scriptures had no conception of homosexuality as a basic characteristic of some people. They also interpret biblical prohibitions on same-sex relationships as references to prostitution, not to committed relationships between same-sex couples. Therefore, liberals conclude that no definite conclusions can be derived from scripture regarding the traditional condemnation of homosexuality.

For their part, conservatives point to specific biblical passages in both the Old and New Testaments that they regard as definite prohibitions on homosexual behavior. For instance, Leviticus 18:22 states: "You shall not lie with a male as with a woman; it is an abomination," and I Corinthians 6:9–10 states: "Do you not know that wrongdoers will not inherit the kingdom of God? Do not be deceived! Fornicators, idolaters, adulterers, male prostitutes, sodomites, thieves, the greedy, drunkards, revilers, robbers—none of these will inherit the kingdom of God."

The controversy over homosexuality reached a crisis stage for the Episcopal church and threatened to splinter the denomination when, in June 2003, New Hampshire clergy and parishioners elected V. Gene Robinson, an openly gay priest, as the new bishop of New Hampshire. Robinson, divorced from his wife, had been in a fourteen-year relationship with another man. In a general convention in August, ECUSA bishops approved Robinson's selection. The convention also opened the possibility for individual dioceses to bless same-sex unions. In October 2003, a group of conservative Episcopalians, troubled by the selection of an openly gay priest as a bishop, gathered in Dallas, Texas, for a meeting of the American Anglican Council, a conservative group within the Episcopal church. The Council approved a document repudiating Robinson's confirmation and asked the worldwide Anglican Communion, of which the Episcopal church was a member, to intervene over the election of Robinson (Kirkpatrick 2003, 3).

Rowan Williams, the archbishop of Canterbury and spiritual leader of the worldwide Anglican Communion, called a meeting of national church leaders to be held in London to discuss the decisions of the ECUSA. In October 2003, thirty-seven Anglican national church leaders (primates) met to deal with the possible split over the question of Robinson's upcoming consecration as a bishop. Williams stated that the meeting allowed the national leaders to work together, but he also noted that the issue regarding human sexuality remained difficult and divisive for the Anglican Communion (Passantino 2003, 8).

American bishop Frank T. Griswold claimed that the issues that united the members of the Anglican Communion would prevail over the divisiveness the human sexuality question had caused (Kirkpatrick 2003, 20). The bishops as a group issued a statement reaffirming a resolution passed at the 1998 Lambeth Conference of Anglican bishops, which had declared that homosexual practices were "incompatible with Scripture" (Passantino 2003, 8). However, the archbishop of Canterbury had no authority to discipline the national churches, which were self-governing, and so no enforceable policy could result from such a meeting. Nonetheless, the future consequences for the Anglican Communion could be significant, particularly as one-half of the world's estimated 77 million Anglicans reside in Africa (Passantino 2003, 6), and these churches include some of the more conservative members of the Communion.

On November 2, 2003, with analysts (for example, Kirkpatrick 2003, 20) speculating that the Episcopal church could not avoid a split, Robinson was consecrated as bishop of New Hampshire in a ceremony held in Durham, New Hampshire. During the ceremony, two conservative clergy members briefly voiced their objections to Robinson's consecration. Bishops of dissident dioceses quickly began to plan possible strategies to oppose the actions of the national organization. There was potential for controversies to arise over local congregations that attempted to leave the church and take with them the property of the congregation. Those intending to remain loyal to the Episcopal church indicated that they would fight any such move, and they suggested that any split in the church could lead to bitter legal conflict (*Houston Chronicle* 2003c).

In January 2004, a group of 3,000 Episcopalians who opposed the election of an openly gay bishop met in Woodbridge, Virginia, to discuss a possible break with the ECUSA. The conservative American Anglican Council sponsored the conference. Robert Duncan, the bishop of Pittsburgh and a vocal opponent of the policies of the national Episcopal organization, spoke of the possible creation of a new group of Episcopal parishes, tentatively called the Network of Anglican Communion Dioceses and Parishes. Following this conference, a meeting was planned at which the heads of approximately twelve dioceses would formally create the new network. As the more conservative bishops proceeded to establish this alternative network of dioceses, Robinson, whose rise to the status of bishop had begun the crisis in the Episcopal church, officially became the bishop of New Hampshire on March 7.

The specific question of sexual practices that divided liberals and conservatives reflected deeper divisions within the ECUSA as well as more general divisions between fundamentalist and evangelical Christian denominations on the one hand and mainline Christian churches on the other. Within the ECUSA as well as in the wider Christian community in the United States, conservatives viewed the conflict as a struggle over whether Christians would adhere to traditional biblical teachings or would instead bow to the secular culture, elements of which conservatives abhorred. More liberal clergy in the ECUSA, such as retired bishop John Shelby Spong (1998), questioned some of the basic tenets of traditional Christianity, such as Jesus's virgin birth, incarnation, deity, and resurrection from the dead. To the extent that the controversy within the ECUSA represented a cultural divide, conservative Christians faced an especially difficult task in maintaining values that many in the wider society—and perhaps many in the conservatives' own midst—regarded as less than absolutely authoritative. However, politically, the difficulties that the

ECUSA faced could foreshadow, at least in the short run, increasing influence for more evangelical denominations as the mainline churches face divisions among their clergy and laity.

Other Protestant denominations joined with conservative dissidents within the ECUSA to protest the actions taken in the Episcopal church as well as actions taken in their own organizations. The Association for Church Renewal, with executives from more than thirty reform groups in eight mainline denominations, called for the reaffirmation of traditional Christian beliefs (Confessing Theologians Commission 2003). The Confessing Theologians Commission, with representatives from the ECUSA, United Methodist Church, Presbyterian Church (USA) (PCUSA), United Church of Christ, Evangelical Lutheran Church in America, American Baptist Church, and United Church of Canada, met in Dallas, Texas, in September 2003 and produced a document titled *Be Steadfast: A Letter to Confessing Christians,* in which the group presented a strategy for conservative Christians to deal with the issues in their denominations. The theologians urged supporters to remain in their mainline denominations, arguing that members could still proclaim the gospel in their churches and the churches could benefit from their renewal efforts. The theologians noted that Christians must resist the tendency of their churches to compromise with the existing culture, in which atheism represented a constant threat. Church leaders, they stated, must be brought away from moral relativism—accepting as appropriate modes of thought and action that the theologians consider contrary to biblical teaching—and the temptation to "champion fashionable causes." The Association for Church Renewal applauded the theologians for producing the document.

The United Methodist Church (UMC) has also faced internal disagreements over the question of homosexual pastors. In March 2004, the UMC held a church trial to determine whether Karen Dammann, pastor of First United Methodist Church in Ellensburg, Washington, and a self-professed lesbian, should be removed from the ministry. The week before the trial, Dammann had married her female partner in Portland, Oregon, which was situated in Multnomah County, where officials had begun to allow same-sex marriages. At the trial, members of Soulforce, an interfaith organization that backs gay rights, demonstrated in support of Dammann while a small group objecting to homosexuality held a counterdemonstration.

For nearly twenty years, leaders of the Pacific Northwest Conference had tried unsuccessfully at UMC general conferences to have the denomination moderate its policies on homosexuality (Mitchell 2004, 9A). Clergy in the Pacific Northwest Conference had voted to keep Dammann, but in fall 2003, the church's Judicial Council overruled the decision. Church law forbade the ordination of "self-avowed, practicing homosexuals," and the UMC's Books of Discipline stated that homosexuality contradicted Christian teaching. However, the social principles that the church had adopted acknowledged gay rights (Mitchell 2004, 9A). The prosecutor argued that because Dammann had admitted to being a practicing lesbian, the jury had all the evidence necessary to declare her guilty. The church counsel representing Dammann at the proceedings emphasized the church principles of inclusiveness and justice. Following testimony and approximately ten hours of deliberations, the jury of thirteen pastors ruled that Dammann could continue as a UMC minister. However, the controversy appeared to be far from over. For instance, pastors in approximately twelve Houston-area United Methodist churches denounced Dammann's acquittal from their pulpits (Vara 2004, 10A).

The issue of homosexuality has highlighted a dilemma faced by mainline denominations. Although many in the mainline clergy wish to extend their churches' ministry to previously excluded groups, conservatives, including many in the clergy, adhere strongly to traditional biblical understandings. Although the issue of homosexual marriage might possibly be defined in a secular context, the official recognition of homosexual relationships within a church itself has brought a determined reaction from conservative Christians for whom the very foundations of their religious beliefs have been challenged. Once again, the mainline denominations find themselves between the fundamentalist and evangelical churches on the one hand—which may appear as appealing alternatives for the more conservative members of the mainline churches—and the still small but growing number of Americans who do not identify with any religious group on the other. In the politics of mainline denominations, parishioners who lose "votes" within the church may decide to vote with their feet, either joining other denominations or creating theologically more accommodating factions within the larger denomination.

Obscenity and Pornography

As cultural conservatives, conservative Christians object strongly to obscene language in the media and to what they find to be lewd or pornographic displays. In 2003, the issue of obscenity on network television came to the forefront when entertainers used questionable language during prime time broadcasts. In January, during a live broadcast of the Golden Globe Awards, Bono of the rock group U2 used the "f-word" when receiving an award. After receiving over 85,000 complaints from members of the Parents Television Council, an organization that monitors television broadcasts for possible obscenity (Ahrens 2003, 31), the Federal Communications Commission (FCC) ruled that because Bono's language did not refer to a "sexual function," it was not obscene or indecent. Members of Congress and representatives of various conservative groups, as well as other FCC personnel, objected strongly to what they considered an inexplicable ruling by David H. Solomon, chief of the FCC enforcement bureau. FCC commissioner Michael J. Copps commented that the agency was doing "an indecent job enforcing indecency" (Ahrens 2003, 31). FCC chairman Michael K. Powell, in a letter to the Parents Television Council, stated that he found the use of the f-word reprehensible when children have access to the broadcast. Twelve senators, including Ernest F. Hollings (D-SC) and Pete V. Domenici (R-NM), introduced a resolution in the U.S. Senate criticizing the FCC ruling, directing the agency to consider canceling the broadcast licenses of television stations that continue to present programs containing indecent content, and asking the agency to fine each incident of indecency. U.S. Representatives Doug Ose (R-CA) and Lamar S. Smith (R-TX) introduced legislation that would more narrowly limit language on television, listing eight explicitly prohibited words and phrases.

Two months after the highly criticized FCC ruling, during the December 10 Fox Network broadcast of the Billboard Music Awards, the issue of indecency was raised again when Nicole Richie of the reality show *The Simple Life* used what was termed a "vulgar substitute" for the word *shoot,* and also used the f-word (Ahrens 2003, 31). Her statements were broadcast uncensored in some parts of the country. Advocates of First Amendment rights tempered the call for more stringent control of television broadcasting, noting that FCC indecency standards were too vague to enforce and were probably unconstitutional. Such vague standards, they contended, amounted to arbitrarily limiting speech that some individuals simply found unacceptable (Ahrens 2003, 31).

Conservative Christian groups strongly objected to what they saw as media indecency during Janet Jackson's February 1, 2004, Super Bowl halftime show performance. During the show, coperformer Justin Timberlake tore off part of Jackson's costume, exposing her right breast. Following the incident, Congress quickly worked on legislation to increase penalties for radio and television broadcasts that violate prohibitions on the transmission of obscene materials.

Many conservative Christian organizations concentrate on the issue of obscenity and pornography as a major national problem. Usually the two words are used synonymously to refer to literature, films, or other public displays that contain language or images of a sexually explicit nature. Focus on the Family, for example, has reacted strongly to cases of broadcasting obscenity. The organization has urged supporters to contact the five FCC commissioners, providing the commissioners' telephone numbers on the organization's Web site (http://www.family.org). Focus on the Family has also provided its members and supporters the opportunity to send e-mail messages to public officials via Focus on the Family's Web site and encouraged individuals to contact their U.S. senators to ask them to strengthen the legal definition of indecency applicable to the broadcast media. The organization has suggested that people could also file a complaint with the FCC when they object to language used on a specific broadcast.

The National Coalition for the Protection of Children and Families (NCPCF), formerly the National Coalition against Pornography (N-CAP), has developed a program called Model Cities of America, which works to help communities to fight pornography. The organization claims that pornography is a health and safety issue, and they advocate the enforcement of laws against pornography and encourage individual responsibility. Among the literature that the organization currently distributes is the *Library Protection Plan,* a guide to persuade public libraries to limit child access to Internet pornography. The NCPCF encourages supporters to contact U.S. Attorney General John Ashcroft to thank the Justice Department for its efforts against obscenity.

The American Family Association (AFA), founded by Donald E. Wildmon in 1977 as the National Federation for Decency, focuses on the mass media, especially television, and its influence on the traditional family. The organization criticizes the entertainment industry for glorifying sexual relations outside marriage and portraying such sexual activity as the norm. The AFA emphasizes the dangers of pornography to the Christian church and is concerned about the easy availability of pornography on the Internet (see the AFA Website, http://www.afa.net).

Another organization that campaigns against obscenity and pornography is the American Decency Association (ADA), a group that declares its Christian perspective for establishing a community that will protect children from "sexual victimization." The ADA encourages supporters to initiate boycotts against enterprises they believe endorse indecency, largely through influencing companies' use of advertising funds. The organization has conducted a monitoring campaign of the Howard Stern radio program, claiming that making sponsors aware through letter-writing campaigns of specific objections to language and subject matter has led to more than 15,000 advertisers nationwide discontinuing their support for the program (http://www.americandecency.org). In March 2004, the Howard Stern program was suspended due in part to the objections raised by organizations like the ADA. The ADA contends that pornography affects a community adversely and that enterprises selling pornographic material should be limited in their geographical location in a community. The Association invites supporters to sign a petition pledging to (1) rid themselves of their televisions, (2) (apparently if they fail to abide by the first pledge) rid their households of cable and satellite services, (3) regulate household television viewing to a minimum, and (4) educate children in Christian principles.

Although legislatures, including the national Congress, have recently shown greater willingness to accede to the wishes of conservative Christians regarding the control of pornography and obscenity, the courts have generally been less open to such control, being persuaded by arguments that civil liberties should not be violated. For instance, in 1996, Congress passed the Communications Decency Act and the Child Pornography Prevention Act, but the Supreme Court struck down both laws. The Court indicated that the Communications Decency Act was too broad and the Child Pornography Prevention Act prohibited virtual child pornography, which did not harm any actual children. The future success of conservative Christian groups in this policy area may well rest on their ability to affect national and state elections. The president nominates federal judicial candidates, but the Senate ratifies them. The larger the conservative Christian-friendly majority (most likely Republican) in the Senate, the greater the chances that a sympathetic president will successfully appoint judges more likely to agree with the social conservative agenda in such areas as pornography. However, liberal principles about freedom of speech are deeply ingrained in the political understandings of Americans (Fowler 1999, 244), and therefore many public officials of whatever political stripe will likely continue to look upon limitations on speech with great caution.

The Partial-Birth Abortion Ban

When President George W. Bush signed legislation to ban partial-birth abortions in November 2003, this represented the first time since the *Roe v. Wade* decision in 1973 that the national government had limited a particular type of abortion. Conservative Christian organizations could take some of the credit for the legislation's ultimate success because of their lobbying efforts as well as their support for conservative candidates at election time. Both houses of Congress had twice before passed this restriction—in 1996 and 1997—but President Clinton vetoed the bills each time. The House passed the bill in 2002, but the Senate, then controlled by Democrats, failed to consider the measure. In 2003, the legislation passed each house of Congress by significant margins: 281–142 in the House and 64–34 in the Senate. Although the vote largely followed party lines, four Republicans opposed the bill and sixty-three Democrats voted for it. At the signing ceremony, President Bush referred to the late-term abortion procedure being banned as "a terrible form of violence" (Mason 2003a, 1A). Present at the ceremony were representatives from leading conservative Christian groups, such as Traditional Values Coalition founder Louis Sheldon. Those critical of the new legislation noted that women were rarely sighted among the invited guests. Anna Quindlen, *Newsweek* columnist, commented that some men at the bill signing supported restricting other rights of American women: "They are clergy who have twisted the word of God to turn it into an instrument of gender bigotry" (Quindlen 2003, 86).

The late-term abortion procedure, technically termed dilation and extraction but called partial-birth abortion by opponents of the procedure, is performed in the second or third trimester of pregnancy. The procedure involves partially delivering the fetus—either the head or, in the case of a breech delivery, the fetal trunk as far as the navel—before the fetus's skull is punctured. The new law prohibits doctors from performing an "overt act" intended to kill a partially delivered fetus. Doctors who violate the law are subject to a sentence of two years in jail and a fine. The law does not hold liable women who undergo the procedure.

Despite the conservatives' legislative success after eight years of effort, groups supporting abortion rights—including the Center for Reproductive Rights (CRR), the American Civil Liberties Union, and the Planned Parenthood Federation of America—immediately filed objections in federal courts around the country. Priscilla Smith, attorney for the CRR, filed a case in federal court in Omaha, Nebraska, likely because a U.S. Supreme Court case in 2000 invalidated a Nebraska law banning the same procedure. In a five-to-four decision, the Supreme Court ruled that the Nebraska law did not define the procedure adequately and that the measure did not contain a health exemption and therefore placed an "undue burden" on women. The CRP had represented the Nebraska doctor in the 2000 Supreme Court case.

In less than an hour after President Bush signed the legislation, U.S. District Court Judge Richard Kopf granted a limited temporary restraining order against the new law, stating that it contained no exception to protect the health of the woman. The following day, federal judges in New York and San Francisco also blocked enforcement of the law. It appeared that, once again, an issue of major concern to conservative Christians would be decided in the federal courts, an arena that many Christians had come to label as too liberal, out of touch with the majority, and out of control in its various rulings.

Despite the 2000 Supreme Court ruling in the Nebraska case, bill supporters had refused to include an exception to protect the health of the woman. Bill sponsors argued that they had added medical findings demonstrating that the procedure was never justified for health reasons. In addition, they claimed that the definition of the procedure had been made sufficiently clear to pass judicial tests (Abrams 2003, 1A). Abortion rights supporters argued that the measure could be used to prohibit other types of abortion and claimed that abortion opponents intended the bill to be a first step down a "slippery slope" toward prohibiting abortion (Holland 2003, 8A). Nancy Northrup, president of the Center for Reproductive Rights, claimed that under the bill, any mid- or late-term abortion could be declared a criminal offense (Abrams 2003, 1A). Interestingly, key Republicans, including Representative Tom DeLay (R-TX) and President Bush, assured the public that abortion was still legal.

Following passage of the legislation and following the legal challenges made to it, political analysts were unsure what role the abortion issue might play in future elections. Those Democrats seeking the presidential nomination tended to agree that a woman's right to an abortion should be maintained, and so the issue played a minimal role in the party's nomination process (Lester 2003, 6A). However, conservative Christian organizations hoped to keep the abortion question as a major litmus test for election candidates, as did abortion rights groups such as EMILY's List, a political action committee dedicated to assisting candidates who support the right of abortion.

Flip Benham, national director of Operation Save America/Operation Rescue (OSA), declared that the devil could have signed the bill and that the measure would prevent no abortions. He argued that physicians would simply change the procedure sufficiently to avoid the banned method. Benham claimed that the ban lacked any enforcement arm, either in the federal government or at the local level. In addition, he noted that by distinguishing fetuses in the later stages of pregnancy from those in earlier stages, the legislation threatened the biblical foundation of the antiabortion movement (Benham 2003). According to the conservative Christian perspective, a fetus, whether two seconds old or eight months, had an equal right to life. Benham was uncomfortable because some people who otherwise supported the right of a woman to choose abortion nonetheless supported the partial-birth abortion ban legislation. Benham rejected any alliance with pro-choice forces because that would mean cooperation with those who supported legalized abortion, a position that Operation Save America strongly rejected. Noting that President Bush did not advocate a total ban on abortion, Benham called the new law a public relations maneuver with no significant policy effect.

Unlike Operation Save America, the more moderate National Right to Life Committee (NRLC) "strongly commended" President Bush for signing the new legislation (National Right to Life Committee 2003). Unlike OSA (which regarded all abortions as equally wrong), the NRLC regarded the late-term abortion procedure in particular to be a significant problem, claiming that it was performed "thousands of times" each year—usually in the fifth and sixth months of pregnancy—on "healthy babies of healthy mothers." Regarding the court orders in New York, Nebraska, and California that blocked enforcement of the new law, the NRLC urged a quick judicial determination of its constitutionality. Noting that a five-to-four majority on the U.S. Supreme Court had struck down a similar state law in Nebraska, NRLC legislative director Douglas Johnson expressed the hope that when the new case reached the Court, at least a one-vote shift would have occurred (NRLC 2003). In July 2003, Pat Robertson had conveyed a similar hope to his television audience, asking them to pray for the retirement of three liberal Supreme Court justices.

In preparing its defense of the partial-birth abortion ban, the U.S. Justice Department attempted to obtain abortion records from Planned Parenthood of America. However, a U.S. District Court judge in San Francisco rejected the department's request, even though Attorney General John Ashcroft assured the court that personal information would be removed from the records. Judge Phyllis Hamilton ruled that the files were not necessary for the trial.

The American Center for Law and Justice (ACLJ), established by Pat Robertson, focused primarily on questions of free speech for Christians and therefore entered the abortion issue largely by defending the free speech rights of antiabortion protesters. The organization stated that it supported the sanctity of life and opposed abortion "in all circumstances" (American Center for Law and Justice 2004). The organization defended the free speech rights of those protesting outside abortion clinics. In two U.S. Supreme Court cases, *Bray v. Alexandria Clinic* (1993) and *Schenck v. Pro-Choice Network of Western New York* (1997), the ACLJ's lead attorney, Jay Sekulow, argued successfully for the free speech rights of abortion protesters. Consistent with its sanctity of life position, the ACLJ also supported the objectives of banning human cloning, euthanasia, and assisted suicide. For instance, the ACLJ filed an amicus curiae brief in the *Washington v. Glucksberg* case, presenting to the justices its reasons for opposing assisted suicide. The U.S. Supreme Court ruled in this case against any right to physician-assisted suicide.

The Alliance Defense Fund (ADF), supporting the partial-birth abortion ban, held that contemporary culture in the United States failed to support the sacredness of human life (Alliance Defense Fund 2004). The organization became involved in various other legislative questions in addition to prohibitions on late-term abortions, including opposition to the legalization of euthanasia and public funding of abortion, and it supported parental consent laws for minors seeking an abortion. The ADF claimed some credit for the eight-to-one U.S. Supreme Court decision in *Scheidler v. National Organization for Women* (2002) invalidating the convictions of antiabortion protesters under the federal Racketeer Influenced and Corrupt Organizations law and other laws intended to deal with extortion by organized crime (Alliance Defense Fund 2003).

According to abortion rights groups, the partial-birth abortion restriction represented a first step in the effort to overturn the U.S. Supreme Court's decision in *Roe v. Wade,* so the quick challenges to the new legislation played a significant role in the continuing struggle over the issue of abortion (Saletan 2003). Complicating the issue, there were not just two sides facing one another but a variety of positions on the issue. Neither the more intense advocates nor the opponents of abortion were satisfied with the new legislation. The plurality of positions on the abortion question indicated that the fate of the legislation in the courts would not signal a quick end to the conflict, which has continued for more than three decades.

Following passage of the partial-birth abortion ban, those supporting further restrictions on abortion, including President Bush, moved toward establishing a policy that some states had already adopted: making it a separate crime to harm a fetus (Abrams 2004, 4A). Related to that effort, in March 2004, prosecutors in Salt Lake City, Utah, decided to prosecute a woman who refused to have a doctor-recommended Caesarean section delivery of twins. The woman ultimately underwent the procedure, but one of the twins died, thus leading to the charge that, by refusing the surgery for so long, she was responsible for the death of the child. Various groups, including the National Organization for Women, Planned Parenthood, and the American Civil Liberties Union, came to the woman's defense, arguing that the case represented an effort to grant personhood to a fetus and thus would open the door for extensive limitations on the right of a woman to have an abortion (*Houston Chronicle* 2004e).

Also in March of that year, Congress passed a bill making it a crime to injure or kill a fetus while committing a federal crime of violence. Groups on both sides of the issue had engaged in extensive lobbying activities prior to the vote on this bill. The legislation defined a fetus as "a member of the species homo sapiens, at any stage of development, who is carried in the womb" (Dewar 2004, 1A). Abortion rights advocates denounced the legislation because the definition of *life* threatened the right to undergo an abortion as established in *Roe v. Wade*. Senator Dianne Feinstein (D-CA) had proposed an alternative measure that did not recognize the fetus as a person and as a separate victim of violence, but it was narrowly defeated. The conservative Christian movement has lobbied state legislatures for similar measures, and twenty-nine states have passed legislation making the killing or injury of a pregnant woman two separate offenses. Abortion rights groups claimed that the partial-birth abortion bill, as well as the Unborn Victims of Violence Act discussed here, would not signal the end of attempts by abortion foes to place further incremental limitations on abortion rights.

The Pledge of Allegiance

Conservative Christian organizations responded quickly when the Ninth Circuit Court of Appeals in San Francisco ruled in June 2002 in a case brought by an avowed atheist, Michael Newdow, on behalf of his 9-year-old daughter (*Elk Grove Unified School District v. Newdow*). The court decided that requiring public school students to recite the Pledge of Allegiance was unconstitutional because the Pledge contained the words *under God* and thus violated the establishment and free exercise clauses of the First Amendment.

The Pledge has an interesting history. In 1892, Francis Bellamy, a preacher and teacher, proposed the use of the Pledge, which he had authored. After leaflets containing the newly created Pledge—which at the time did not contain the words *under God*—were distributed to schools across the country, it became a standard utterance in public schools. However, some religious groups refused to take part in saying the Pledge because they considered it equivalent to idol worship (Stephens and Schebb 1999, 529). In 1943, a suit was brought before the federal courts by a family of Jehovah's Witnesses (*West Virginia State Board of Education v. Barnette*). In this suit, the U.S. Supreme Court reversed a decision it had rendered three years earlier (*Minersville School District v. Gobitis*) and ruled that public schools could not require students to recite the Pledge. In 1954, when many Americans were concerned about the Cold War conflict between the United States and the "godless" Soviet Union, Congress approved the addition of the phrase *under God* to the Pledge, and President Dwight Eisenhower signed the bill into law.

After the 2002 ruling, those groups supporting the Pledge urged the U.S. Supreme Court to hear an appeal of the lower court decision. For instance, the American Center for Law and Justice (ACLJ) filed an amicus curiae brief with the Supreme Court on behalf of thirty-three members of Congress and more than 150,000 citizens, asking the Court to hear the appeal. When, in October 2003, the Supreme Court agreed to hear the case, the ACLJ announced that it would file an additional brief arguing that the phrase *One nation, under God* was a patriotic expression protected by the Constitution because it did not affirm a particular religious faith.

This case differed from arguments regarding prayer in the public schools because those supporting the Pledge denied that the words constituted a prayer and contended that it therefore did not violate any court prohibitions on prayer in the public schools. The ACLJ also raised questions about Michael Newdow's legal standing to bring the case to the courts, as he did not have legal custody of his daughter and had never married the girl's mother (American Center for Law and Justice 2003). This questioning of Newdow's standing appeared to contradict the position of some conservative Christian organizations that wished to grant to the biological father-to-be a legal standing in situations in which a pregnant woman was considering undergoing an abortion.

Following a somewhat different strategy from that of the ACLJ, the National Legal Foundation placed a petition on its Web site (http://www.nlf.net/Petition.htm), addressed to "all federal, state and local officials," that emphasized the place of prayer in the nation's history. For instance, the petition referred to President Abraham Lincoln, who in 1863 declared a day of humiliation, fasting, and prayer, and to President Ronald Reagan's signing of a bill in 1988 declaring a national day of prayer. Public officials were urged in the petition to do everything they could to ensure that the Pledge of Allegiance remained a proclamation of the United States as "one nation under God" and that schoolchildren would continue to be allowed to recite the Pledge. In defending the Pledge, the Christian Law Association observed that Congress itself added "under God" in 1954 to recognize the dependence of the citizens and the government on moral guidance from God.

Organizations such as the American Family Association (AFA) and the Christian Coalition of America urged passage of the Pledge Protection Act of 2003, which would limit the jurisdiction of the federal courts to rule on cases involving the Pledge of Allegiance. The AFA asked supporters to use the organization's Web site (http://www. afa.net) to contact their members of Congress to determine if they were cosponsors of the bill and, if not, to urge them to become cosponsors. The organization also asked supporters to send the message about the Pledge to friends so that they could take the same action.

On May 27, 2003, D. James Kennedy of the Center for Reclaiming America interviewed Sandra Banning, the girl's mother, on his television program, *Truths That Transform*. Banning stated on the show that she was a Christian and objected to the lawsuit, commenting that her daughter still voluntarily recited the Pledge. As the date for the Supreme Court hearing approached, various groups submitted briefs to the Court, many of which were from organizations that opposed the Ninth Circuit's decision. Texas attorney general Greg Abbott, a strong opponent to the original ruling, filed a brief on behalf of the attorneys general of all fifty states. When the Supreme Court finally heard oral arguments in *Elk Grove Unified School District v. Newdow* in March 2004, Newdow appeared before the Court, personally arguing the case. The Supreme Court issued its ruling in the case on June 14, 2004. In an eight-to-zero decision, the justices avoided the constitutional issue surrounding the Pledge, stating that Michael Newdow did not have the legal right to speak on behalf of his daughter because the mother was the girl's sole legal representative (Reinert 2004, 1A). Both Newdow's supporters as well as Pledge defenders expressed disappointment with the decision, indicating that the conflict over the words "under God" in the Pledge would be renewed in the courts.

Faith-Based Funding

While campaigning for the presidency in 2000, George W. Bush pledged that he would effect changes in federal regulations to allow religious organizations to compete on an equal basis with secular groups for grant funding to support social welfare programs (Walsh 2001, 2). He pledged that these religious organizations would not have to compromise on their unique spiritual character, which many have claimed contributed to their ability to treat effectively such problems as addiction and poverty. However, the so-called faith-based initiative—which initially appeared to have widespread support, especially from religious groups of various types—quickly experienced difficulties in receiving legislative approval from Congress due to objections from liberals as well as conservatives. For instance, Jerry Falwell, Pat Robertson, and Richard Land of the Southern Baptist Convention raised concerns about the initiative, which revolved largely around the extent of federal government regulation of participating religious organizations and the prospect that these organizations ultimately might be required to become more secular (Milbank 2003, 13). Falwell feared that future administrations could place greater restrictions on religious groups' use of government funds (Mason 2001, 6A). In addition, Falwell and Robertson expressed concern that the federal government could fund what these conservative Christian leaders considered cults, perhaps indicating a potential complication in the concept of faith-based funding: Certain religious groups might lobby for the introduction of some test of the appropriateness of an organization's religious beliefs (Steinfels 2001, 331).

More liberal groups feared that public funds would be used to proselytize and that religious organizations would be allowed to discriminate in such areas as hiring and eligibility for assistance. The Bush administration held that religious organizations should have the right to hire those individuals most in tune with their goals and missions (Allen and Cooperman 2003, 14). Therefore, in summer 2003, the administration asked Congress to allow religious groups receiving federal funding to base hiring decisions on religious affiliation and sexual orientation. The Salvation Army, in fact, had already requested such an exemption (*Houston Chronicle* 2004d). However, even if religious groups received an exemption from federal nondiscrimination laws, states could still require these organizations to abide by state laws. Federal law itself contained contradictory provisions. Although Title IV of the Civil Rights Act of 1972 stated that religious groups may take religious belief into account when hiring staff members, some laws authorizing social service programs prohibited discrimination based on religion, age, gender, or race.

By spring 2003, all that the Republican majority in Congress could agree upon was charitable tax incentives for those who donated to faith-based organizations, but this was far less than what the Bush administration had requested. The states also appeared hesitant to engage any further in public support for faith-based charities. Although many states had long ago established agreements with religious organizations, the Rockefeller Institute of Government reported in November 2003 that only fifteen states had begun new initiatives to involve faith-based groups in offering social services (*Houston Chronicle* 2003f).

In late 2002, President Bush sidestepped Congress by issuing executive orders to provide religious organizations an equal chance along with secular groups in competing for federal contracts. Although smaller religious organizations lacked grant-writing expertise or did not have the required structure for providing social services in order to be successful in obtaining federal funding, some larger organizations successfully received grants. For instance, some groups received federal grants to strengthen the institution of marriage. The Marriage Coalition of Cleveland Heights, Ohio, received approximately $200,000 to test materials on the value of marriage and child support for poor single parents. Community Services of Allentown, Pennsylvania, received more than $177,000 to provide services, including marriage education, for unmarried couples in cooperation with local churches. The Alabama Child Abuse and Neglect Prevention Board won $200,000 in grant funds to assist single parents to acquire marital skills and to improve their employment prospects (McDonough 2003, 14A). At the state level, in late 2003, Florida governor Jeb Bush dedicated the Lawtey Correctional Institution, the first faith-based prison. Among its spiritually oriented activities, the prison would offer Bible studies, religious counseling, choir practice, and prayer sessions. The prison was expected to reduce the recidivism rate of prisoners (*Houston Chronicle* 2003h).

Although recognizing the objections of some conservative Christians, the Family Research Council and Focus on the Family both supported greater involvement of faith-based organizations in federal government social welfare programs, arguing that the quality of social services—including job training, community policing, and after-school programs—would increase with greater opportunities for religious organizations to compete for federal funding (Brody and Winn 2002; Sherman 2002). These organizations asked their supporters to contact their members of Congress to support funding for religious organizations. However, both groups cautioned that such organizations must be allowed to maintain the integrity of their religious beliefs. They warned that organizations should retain the right to hire employees with beliefs and values compatible with the organization.

Supporters of faith-based funding such as Marvin Olasky, a conservative Christian thinker, have suggested that the potential problems faced by government involvement in funding religious organizations could be handled by establishing a system of vouchers granted to individuals needing assistance, who could then approach the program of their choice (Rogers 2001, 321). David Barton, president of Wall-Builders, an organization that provides educational materials for Christian parents, concluded that a large number of bills to fund individual programs would have to be passed in order to qualify a larger number of faith-based organizations for federal funding. In February 2004, the U.S. House of Representatives moved to satisfy the concerns of conservative Christian groups by voting to allow religious groups to limit hiring to adherents of the organization's faith.

Creationism, Evolution, and Education Policy

Although the biological theory of evolution won a qualified victory over those fundamentalist Christians seeking to rid the public school systems around the nation of its influence, some conservative Christian groups have attempted to introduce what they consider balanced treatments of alternative understandings of the biological origins of humankind through, for instance, the notion of "intelligent design." Rather than attempting to ban the teaching of evolution or rather than introducing creationism into the public school curriculum as an alternative explanation of the origin of human beings, conservative Christian groups have tried to influence the content of biology textbooks, criticizing what are considered inaccuracies and urging the inclusion of discussions of the weaknesses of evolution theory. The experience of the Texas State Board of Education with the approval of textbooks represents the type of influence conservative groups can have on public education.

In fall 2003, when the Texas State Board of Education was considering biology textbooks, the Discovery Institute, headquartered in Seattle, Washington, made its presence known, identifying what the organization considered to be errors in textbooks and recommending that the errors be corrected before the books received approval (Discovery Institute 2003). Bruce Chapman, president of the Institute, identified examples of reported errors that he believed overstated the evidence for the theory of evolution. For instance, the Institute called for the removal from two textbooks of a set of drawings, "Haeckel's embryos," which claimed to demonstrate early developmental similarities in the embryos of eight different species, including humans, frogs, and chickens. The drawings supposedly offered support for evolution theory. However, the drawings were alleged to have been faked (Chapman 2003). Among other objections, the Institute pointed to the "myth of the peppered moth," which involved research claiming to provide an example of a species adapting to its environment. Institute representatives established a presence during hearings about the textbooks, setting up a reception room close to the location where the Board of Education held a hearing in September. Other groups, including a coalition of religious leaders represented by Steve Lucas, pastor of an Austin, Texas, Baptist church, opposed attempts to compromise what they considered the scientific objectivity of textbooks (Elliott 2003, 29A).

In November, the Texas board decided to approve eleven biology textbooks, first defeating a motion by four board members who wished to vote on the textbooks individually. These members supported texts that they claimed more clearly indicated weaknesses in the theory of evolution (Elliott 2003, 29A). Supporters of the teaching of the theory of evolution generally claimed victory in the decision process. The National Center for Science Education commended the board and textbook publishers for withstanding what the organization considered pressures to compromise scientific accuracy (National Center for Science Education 2003). However, Samantha Smoot, executive director of the Texas Freedom Network, an organization dedicated to limiting the political influence of conservative Christian groups, commented that the changes mandated by the board represented an unwarranted questioning of the theory and deplored the pressure book publishers faced. The textbook selection process in Texas was crucially important to publishers because the state was the second-largest consumer of textbooks, and because other states tended to follow the example that state set (Elliott 2003, 29A).

In January 2004, Kathy Cox, Georgia superintendent of schools, proposed eliminating the word *evolution* from the science curriculum and replacing it with the phrase *biological changes over time* (*Houston Chronicle* 2004a). Cox, a Republican elected to the post in 2002, stated that she proposed the change in part to reduce the controversy faced by teachers in conservative areas of the state where parents object to the teaching of evolution. Her proposal faced opposition from varied groups, including educators, legislators, and conservatives supporting the teaching of creationism. Former president Jimmy Carter, a native of Georgia, a Baptist, and a Sunday school teacher, declared that the theory of evolution did not conflict with religious belief and labeled the proposal an embarrassment. Six days after making the proposal public, Cox announced that it was being dropped (*Houston Chronicle* 2004b).

Conservative Christian organizations continue to monitor public school system policy regarding the teaching of evolution. In addition, groups with varied claims to scientific expertise argue for some version of creationism or intelligent design. Reasons to Believe, a California-based organization, provides empirical evidence for intelligent design, if not for a seven-day creation account, as well as evidence for other events described in the Bible. The Creation Research Society, headquartered in St. Joseph, Missouri, holds to a strict interpretation of the creation story of Genesis. Others, such as Hank Hanegraff of the Christian Research Institute, focus on what they claim to be the weaknesses of the theory of evolution (Hanegraff 2003). Although such groups do not become politically involved directly, their endeavors tend to contribute to conservative Christian efforts to modify the curricula of the public schools.

In addition to focusing on the public schools, conservative Christians advocate the expansion of religion-based private schools as well as homeschooling by Christian parents. At private schools and in schooling their children at home, conservative Christians obviously have a far greater opportunity to introduce creationist accounts of the origins of humankind. In the case of private schools, a key issue is the establishment of voucher systems in states that allow parents to receive public funds to pay tuition at the school of their choice.

The U.S. Supreme Court (*Zelman v. Simmons-Harris,* 2002) has given its approval of such voucher systems, ruling that they do not violate the establishment clause of the First Amendment.

U.S. Foreign Policy

Following World War II, conservative Christian organizations began to pay greater attention to U.S. foreign policy, especially after the United States and the Soviet Union entered the Cold War era. Those organizations established during the Cold War era expressed a strong anticommunist message to the American people and have maintained a small niche, attracting sufficient conservative Christian support to survive.

Billy James Hargis established the Christian Crusade (originally called Christian Echoes National Ministry), emphasizing a strong patriotic and anticommunist theme that the organization still continues to promote. In 1953, Hargis, along with staunchly conservative Presbyterian minister Carl McIntyre, organized a Bible dissemination project in which they floated balloons carrying Bible messages into Communist-controlled countries of Eastern Europe.

Another anticommunist crusader, Frederick C. Schwarz, immigrated to the United States from Australia and established the Christian Anti-Communism Crusade (CACC) in 1953. Schwarz conducted lectures for citizen groups and churches throughout the nation, describing a communist strategy for world domination in order to prepare his audiences to combat the communist threat. The fall of the Soviet Union notwithstanding, the organization continues to warn Americans against communism and similar threats, primarily through its monthly newsletter, *The Schwarz Report.* In the 1990s, Schwarz retired and returned to Australia, but the organization continued under the leadership of David Noebel.

Robert Welch established the John Birch Society in 1958 to oppose communist and socialist influences in the United States and elsewhere. Although not an explicitly Christian organization, the Society was named for a Baptist missionary to China who was killed by Chinese Communists, and it emphasized what it considered the vital need to maintain the traditional values of the Judeo-Christian heritage. Welch (1959) claimed that Communists had already infiltrated and subverted the national government and accused various high government officials with collaboration to hand over the government to Communists. Although Welch's more extreme claims found little support, the Society continued to attract highly committed adherents. The organization still publishes *The New American,* a biweekly magazine.

Conservative Christian organizations during the 1980s and 1990s tended to focus primarily on domestic issues such as welfare reform and family values, opposition to abortion, and prayer in the public schools. Some groups also expressed support for maintaining a strong national defense and advocated U.S. assistance for Israel. Conservative Christian leaders such as Hal Lindsey, Paul Crouch, Jerry Falwell, and John Hagee believed that the difficulties Israel faced were part of biblical prophecy (Diamond 1998, 46). Troubling events in the Middle East signaled to them that the final days were at hand. They asked their followers to contribute financially to Israel, God's original chosen nation. The establishment of Israel as an independent nation once again had signified to many conservative Christians that the end of world history was approaching and the second coming of Christ would soon occur (Walvoord 1990). However, unqualified support for Israel and Israeli policy in the Middle East tended to contradict the official policy of the U.S. government, which was attempting to facilitate a negotiated peace between Israel and its neighboring Arab nations as well as with the Palestinians, who demanded the right to establish their own state.

Following the terrorist attacks of September 11, 2001, many conservative Christians began to contrast their religious beliefs with those of Islam (Biema 2003, 38). Some conservative Christian publications, such as the *Christian Research Journal,* asserted the superiority of Christianity over Islam and suggested to readers how to minister most appropriately to Muslims (Saleeb and Geisler 2002). Often, such discussions tended to emphasize the militant nature of Islam, in contrast to the general message from the Bush administration to the American people that the terrorists were an aberration in the otherwise peaceful religion of Islam.

After September 11, some conservative Christian writers and groups suggested that the battle against terrorism was a struggle between Christianity and Islam (e.g., Zacharias 2002; Sproul and Saleeb 2003), a position that the Bush administration forcefully denied (*Houston Chronicle* 2003d). However, one member of the Bush administration appeared to contradict the official policy. In October 2003, news accounts (for example, Graham 2003, 19A) spread that General William G. Boykin, deputy undersecretary of defense for intelligence and an intensely religious man, had made controversial comments about Islam during several speeches he made before evangelical Christian audiences regarding the U.S. war on terror. Among his statements, Boykin said that the enemy in the war on terror was Satan, that God performed a miracle by placing George W. Bush in the White House, and that Muslim Somali warlord Osman Otto was an idol worshiper (Leiby 2003, 8).

Various news commentators and public officials quickly condemned Boykin's reported statements. A *Washington Post* (2003b) editorial commented that Boykin had the right to his own religious convictions but that, as a general in the U.S. Army, he had exceeded appropriate boundaries separating church and state by commenting that though other countries had lost their values, the United States was still a Christian nation. The editorial recommended that the inspector general examine General Boykin's apparent use of government funds in preparing his speeches. Senator John Warner (R-VA) stated that General Boykin should step down from his position while an investigation was conducted into his alleged comments (Kelley 2003, 4A). Although recognizing Boykin's right to speak, Warner nonetheless indicated that in his position of responsibility, the general was expected to exercise "good, sound judgment." E. J. Dionne, Jr., a columnist for the *Washington Post,* commented that Boykin's statements contradicted the Bush administration's official position that the fight against terrorism was not a religious war (Dionne 2003, 26). President Bush distanced himself from the controversy. Boykin himself attempted to calm the objections raised against his statements about Islam, saying that he had not intended to offend Muslims and apologized to anyone who may have taken offense at his remarks (*Houston Chronicle* 2003d). Regarding his characterization of the Muslim warlord, Boykin claimed that he was not referring to the warlord's religion but to his "worship of money and power."

Although various sources criticized Boykin, several conservative Christian individuals and groups rallied to his defense. Christian organizations, including the Christian Coalition of America and Focus on the Family, resolved the long-standing tension between the call to obey government authority and the obligation to follow what was perceived as God's will by favoring Boykin's right to express his religious beliefs and perceptions of the world (Ammons 2003; Focus on the Family 2003b). News accounts reported that Boykin's parents had been Pentecostals, and he was raised in rural North Carolina, where he received a strong religious upbringing (Leiby 2003, 8). Boykin served in highly secret military operations in such places as Grenada, Panama, and Somalia. In his many presentations to church groups across the nation, Boykin detailed the military operations in which he participated and described the importance of his religious beliefs (Leiby 2003, 8). His story contained just what many conservative Christians believed personified the mission of the United States in the world: Boykin combined intense personal Christian beliefs with the expression of the view that the United States was a Christian nation.

In the view of conservative Christians, Boykin was simply exercising freedom of speech, expressing the obvious association of Christianity with his nation's mission to the rest of the world. Therefore, it was not surprising that in late October 2003, the Christian Coalition of America (CCA) called for an end to the "left-wing" criticism of General Boykin. The organization noted that Boykin's characterization of the war against terrorism as a struggle between good and evil was nothing less than what nearly all Americans believed. The CCA asserted that Boykin, a highly decorated soldier, did not violate any rules by speaking at churches. CCA president Roberta Combs reflected the general conservative Christian response to the criticism Boykin had received by stating: "Liberals in this country need to stop their Christian-bashing. . . . Prejudice against evangelical Christians must end" (Christian Coalition of America, 2003). Combs associated the objections to Boykin's statements with Democratic opposition in the U.S. Senate to President Bush's judicial nominees, another concern of Christian groups. James Dobson, during a November 5, 2003, national radio broadcast of his program, *Focus on the Family,* called for Christians to defend General Boykin against attacks from "liberals in the media and in government." Dobson commented that if an officer could be silenced for what Dobson called "merely articulating his Christian views," then the ability of all Christians to speak out would be endangered. Dobson's organization, Focus on the Family, placed an appeal on the organization's Web site (http://www.family.org), asking Christians to contact the president, the secretary of defense, and members of Congress to express their support for General Boykin. Although members of the Bush administration attempted to distance themselves from Boykin's reported comments and the subsequent publicity, the general maintained his official position (*Houston Chronicle* 2003d).

The Boykin case illustrates the extent to which conservative Christians in the United States perceive a close relationship between faith, the nation, and public policy. They view any questioning of that relationship as an obvious attempt to silence the expression of strongly held religious faith and to ignore what they consider the facts of history and the threat to Christianity in the contemporary world.

References

Abrams, Jim. 2003. "House OKs Abortion Limit." *Houston Chronicle* (October 3): 1A, 4A.

———. 2004. "House Bill: Fetus Can Be a Victim of Violence." *Houston Chronicle* (February 27): 4A.

Ahrens, Frank. 2003–2004. "But Was That Dirty Word an Adjective? An FCC Ruling Rekindles an Old Debate about Obscenity on Live TV." *Washington Post National Weekly Edition* (December 22–January 4): 31.

Allen, Mike. 2003. "Gay Marriage, a Front-Burner Issue." *Washington Post National Weekly Edition* (November 3–9): 14.

Allen, Mike, and Alan Cooperman. 2003. "Praying for a Hiring Exemption: Bush Supports Religious Groups' Employment Rules." *Washington Post National Weekly Edition* (June 30-July 13): 14.

Alliance Defense Fund. 2003. "Pro-Life Speech Affirmed!" http://www.allinacedefensefund.org/story/?id=124 (accessed 2004).

———. 2004. "Guarding the Sanctity of Human Life." http://www.alliance defensefund.org/issues/humanlife.php, (accessed 2004).

American Center for Law and Justice. 2003. "ACLJ Asks Supreme Court to Uphold Constitutionality of Pledge of Allegiance." http://www.aclj.org/news.pressreleases/031219_pledge_brief_filed.asp, (accessed 2004).

———. 2004. "Pro-Life Task Force." http://acljlife.org/resources/index.asp, (accessed 2004).

Ammons, Michele. 2003. "Christian Coalition Chastises Left-Wing Criticism of American Military Hero." http://www.cc.org/press.10232003.php (accessed 2004).

Benham, Flip. 2003. "Partial Birth Abortion Ban: Bogus Piece of Legislation." http://www.operationsaveamerica.org/press/press/031105partialbirthabortion ban-bogus-legislation.htm (accessed 2004).

Biema, David Van. 2003. "Missionaries under Cover: Growing Numbers of Evangelicals Are Trying to Spread Christianity in Muslim Lands." *Time* 161 (June 30): 36–44.

Bray v. Alexandria Clinic, 506 U.S. 263 (1993).

Brody, David, and Pete Winn. 2002. "Bush Implements Faith-Based Initiative." http://family.org/cforum/feature/a0023664.cfm (accessed 2004).

Chapman, Bruce. 2003. "How Should Schools Teach Evolution?" http://www.discovery.org/scripts/viewDB/index.php?program=CRSC&command=view&id =1574 (accessed 2004).

Christian Coalition of America. 2003. "Christian Coalition Chastises Left-Wing Criticism of American Military Hero" (October 23). http://cc.org/content.cfm?id=90, (accessed 2004).

Christian Law Association. 2003. "Defending the Decalogue." http://www.christian law.org/decalogue3.html., (accessed 2004).

Clark, Peter B., and James Q. Wilson. 1961. "Incentives Systems: A Theory of Organizations." *Administrative Science Quarterly* 6: 129–166.

Clemetson, Lynette. 2004. "Black Clergy in Middle of Gay Struggle." *Houston Chronicle* (March 6): 1E, 3E.

Concerned Women for America. 2003. "New Hope in Battle for Terri Schiavo's Life." http://www.cwfa.org/articledisplay.asp?id=4753&department=CWA&categoryid=life., (accessed 2004).

Confessing Theologian Commission. 2003. "Be Steadfast: A Letter to Confessing Christians." http://www.confessingumc.org/conf_theolog_besteadfast.htm (accessed 2004).

Connor, Kenneth L. 2003. "Testimony of Kenneth L. Connor before the Senate Special Committee on Aging, October 20, 2003." http://www.frc.org/get.cfm?i=TS03J01 (accessed 2004).

Cooperman, Alan. 2004. "Taking the Marriage Amendment Seriously." *Washington Post National Weekly Edition* (February 23–29): 31.

Dahl, Robert A. 1967. *Pluralist Democracy in the United States: Conflict and Consent.* Chicago: Rand McNally.

Dewar, Helen. 2004. "Congress Clears Bill Making Harm of a Fetus a Crime." *Houston Chronicle* (March 26): 1A, 17A.

Diamond, Sara. 1989. *Spiritual Warfare: The Politics of the Christian Right.* Boston: South End.

———. 1998. *Not by Politics Alone: The Enduring Influence of the Christian Right.* New York: Guilford.

Dionne, E. J., Jr. 2003. "Taking Satan Seriously." *Washington Post National Weekly Edition* (November 30): 26.

Discovery Institute. 2003. "Q & A about Current Texas State Review of Biology Textbooks." http://discovery.org/scripts/viewDB/index.php?command=view&id=1628, (accessed 2004).

Edsall, Thomas B. 2004. "Support from Gays Gave Dean Momentum." *Houston Chronicle* (January 2, 2004): 14A.

Elk Grove Unified School District v. Newdow, no. 02–1624 (decided June 14, 2004).

Elliott, Janet. 2003. "Biology Book Battle Abates." *Houston Chronicle* (November 7): 29A.

Falwell, Jerry. 1980. *Listen America.* New York: Doubleday.

Fineman, Howard, and T. Trent Gegax. 2003. "'My Mommies Can Marry.'" *Newsweek* (December 1): 34–35.

Focus on the Family. 2003a. "Love Won Out." http://lovewonout.com (accessed 2004).

———. 2003b. "Stand Up for Lt. Gen. Boykin. http://www.family.org/cforum/extras/a0028534.cfm, (accessed 2004).

Fowler, Robert Booth. 1999. *Enduring Liberalism: American Political Thought since the 1960s.* Lawrence: University of Kansas Press.

Gamboa, Suzanne. 2004. "Cornyn in Middle of Gay Marriage Row." *Houston Chronicle* (February 7): 6A.

Goodridge v. Department of Public Health, 440 Mass. 309, SJC-08860 (decided November 18, 2003).

Graham, Bradley. 2003. "General's Religious Remarks Blasted." *Houston Chronicle* (October 17): 19A.

Guth, James K. "The New Christian Right." In Robert C. Liebman and Robert Wuthnow, eds. *The New Christian Right: Mobilization and Legitimation.* Hawthorne, NY: Aldine.

Hanegraff, Hank. 2003. *Fatal Flaws: What Evolutionists Don't Want You to Know.* New York: WPublishing Group.

Holland, Judy. 2003. "Republican Majority May Hasten Ban on 'Partial Birth' Abortions." *Houston Chronicle* (August 31): 8A.

———. 2004. "Bush's Comments Put Ban on Gay Marriage on Hold." *Houston Chronicle* (January 25): 6A.

Houston Chronicle. 2003a. "Robertson Announces He Has Prostate Cancer" (February 14): 28A.

———. 2003b. "Robertson Doesn't Really Want To Nuke Anybody" (October 15): 20A.

———. 2003c. "Episcopal Evangelicals Warn of Split from Church" (October 18): 26A.

———. 2003d. "Rice Tries to Calm Fury over General's Religious Remarks" (October 20): 10A.

———. 2003e. "Husband Challenges Florida Law" (October 30): 9A.

———. 2003f. "States Cold to Religious Initiatives" (November 13): 20A.

———. 2003g. "Strong Support Found for Ban on Gay Marriage, Poll Reveals" (December 21): 8A.

———. 2003h. "Faith-Based Prison Dedicated" (December 25): 25A.

———. 2004a. "Georgia Pondering Ban on 'Evolution'" (January 31): 4A.

———. 2004b. "Georgia Schools to Stick with 'Evolution'" (February 6): 4A.

———. 2004c. "Commandments Flap Spurs Senate Measure" (February 13): 26A.

———. 2004d. "Salvation Army Accused of Bias" (February 25): 7A.

———. 2004e. "Mother's Arrest in C-section Case Raises Alarm from Women's Groups" (March 18): 15A.

———. 2004f. "Support for Gay Unions Rising" (March 10): 13A.

———. 2004g. "Battle Rages On" (July 17): 1B, 3B.

Hubbler, Shawn. 2004. "Senator's Son Challenges Policies in Personal Way." *Houston Chronicle* (March 10): 13A.

Johnson, Bob. 2003. "Ouster of Alabama Judge Urged." *Houston Chronicle* (November 13): 3A.

Kastensmidt, Sam. 2003. "Nation Rallies for Moore" (August 18). http://reclaimamerica.org/PAGES/NEWS/newspage.asp?story=1329&SC=roy%20more (accessed 2004).

———. 2004. "Mass. Supreme Court Demands Gay 'Marriage.'" http://reclaimamerica.org/Pages/News/newspage.asp?story=1538 (accessed 2004).

Kelley, Matt. 2003. "Senator Calls on General to Step Aside." *Houston Chronicle* (October 22): 4A.

Kennedy, D. James. 2003. "Dr. Kennedy Speaks Out to Protect Terri Schiavo." http://www.reclaimamerica.org/pages/NEWS/newspage.asp?story=1395 (accessed 2004).

Kirkpatrick, Frank. 2003. "The Anglican Crackup." *Religion in the News* 6 (Fall): 2–4, 20.

Lawrence v. Texas, 02–102 (decided June 26, 2003).

Leiby, Richard. 2003. "Christian Soldier: Lt. Gen. William Boykin, Inspiring Faith in Some and Doubt in Others." *Washington Post National Weekly Edition* (November 17–23): 8–9.

Lester, Will. 2003. "Lieberman's Abortion Stance Meets Scrutiny after Interview." *Houston Chronicle* (December 27): 6A.

Loven, Jennifer. 2003. "Bush Would Back Gay Marriage Ban." *Houston Chronicle* (December 17): 11A.

Lowery, David, and Holly Brasher. 2004. *Organized Interests and American Government.* New York: McGraw-Hill.

Mason, Julie. 2001. "Black Ministers Back Bush Plan: President Finds Unlikely Allies, Foes of Faith-Based Initiatives Program." *Houston Chronicle* (March 20): 6A.

———. 2003a. "Bush OKs Ban on Late-Term Abortion." *Houston Chronicle* (November 6): 1A, 16A.

———. 2003b. "GOP Will Wait, See on Gay Marriage: Upcoming Ruling to Help Determine Campaign Stance." *Houston Chronicle* (November 11): 1A.

———. 2004. "Cornyn: Gay Marriage Threat to Families." *Houston Chronicle* (March 24): 3A.

McDonaugh, Siobhan. 2003. "Federal Grants Given to Religious Groups to Advance Marriages." *Houston Chronicle* (January 3): 14A.

Milbank, Dana. 2003. "They Couldn't Keep the Faith Part." *Washington Post National Weekly Edition* (April 28–May 4): 13.

Min, Tami. 2004. "Gay Wedding March Continues." *Houston Chronicle* (February 15): 17A.

Minersville School District v. Gobitis, 310 U.S. 586, 60 S.Ct. 1010, 84 L.Ed. 1375 (1940).

Mitchell, Melanthia. 2004. "Supporters Arrested at Gay Pastor's Church Trial." *Houston Chronicle* (March 18): 9A.

National Center for Science Education. 2003. "Textbooks Approved in Texas" (November 7). http://www.ncseweb.org/resources/news/2003/TX/682_text books_approved_in_texas_11_7_2003.asp, (accessed 2004).

National Right to Life Committee. 2003. "National Right to Life Committee Comments on Court Orders and President Bush's Statement." http://nrlc.org/abortion/pba/Release110603.html, (accessed 2004).

Olson, Mancur. 1965. *The Logic of Collective Action.* Cambridge, MA: Harvard University Press.

Passantino, Gretchen. 2003. "Episcopalians Capitulate to Culture, Confirming Practicing Homosexual Bishop." *Christian Research Journal* 26 (3):6–8.

Quindlen, Anna. 2003. "Not a Womb in the House." *Newsweek,* November 17: 86.

Reinert, Patty. 2004. "'Under God' Can Stay in Pledge, Court Says." *Houston Chronicle* (June 15): 1A, 6A.

Roe v. Wade, 410 U.S. 113, 93 S.Ct. 705, 35 L.Ed.2d 147 (1973).

Rogers, Melissa. 2001. "The Breaking Points: When Consensus Becomes Conflict." In E.J. Dionne and Ming Hsu Chen, eds. *Sacred Places, Civic Purposes: Should Government Help Faith-Based Charity?* Washington, DC: Brookings. 321–326.

Roig-Franzia, Manuel. "Brain-Damaged Woman to Resume Tube-Feeding." *Houston Chronicle* (October 22, 2003): 1A.

Roth, Bennett. 2004. "Bush Urges Gay Marriage Amendment." *Houston Chronicle* (February 25): 1A.

Saleeb, Abdul, and Norman L. Geisler. "Understanding and Reaching Muslims." *Christian Research Journal* 24:12–21.

Saletan, William. 2003. "Partial-birth Ban Takes Aim Right at Privacy." *Houston Chronicle* (October 3): 35A.

Scheidler v. National Organization for Women, docket no. 01–1118 (decided February 26, 2002).

Schenck v. Pro-Choice Network of Western New York, 519 U.S. 357 (1997).

Schneeberger, Gary. 2003. "Ga. County Defies ACLU on Ten Commandments." http://www.family.org/cforum/feature/a0028622.cfm (accessed 2004).

Sherman, Amy L. 2002. "The Bush Faith-Based Initiative: Compassionate Conservatism in Action." http://www.frc.org/get.cfm?i=WT01K1 (accessed 2004).

Silverman, Herb. 2003. "Inerrancy Turned Political." In Kimberly Blaker, ed. *The Fundamentals of Extremism: The Christian Right in America.* New Boston, MI: New Boston.

Spong, John Shelby. 1998. *Why Christianity Must Change or Die: A Bishop Speaks to Believers in Exile.* New York: HarperCollins.

Sproul, R. C., and Abdul Saleeb. 2003. *The Dark Side of Islam.* Wheaton, IL: Crossway.

Stacy, Mitch. 2003. "Guardian Sees No Hope for Brain-damaged Woman." *Houston Chronicle* (December 3): 22A.

Stanton, Elizabeth Cady. 1993. *The Woman's Bible.* Boston, MA: Northeastern University Press (original work published in 1895).

Steinfels, Peter. 2001. "Holy Waters: Plunging into the Sea of Faith-Based Initiatives." In E. J. Dionne, Jr., and Ming Hsu Chen, eds. *Sacred Places, Civic Purposes: Should Government Help Faith-Based Charity?* Washington, DC: Brookings, 327–335.

Stephens, Otis H., Jr., and John M Scheb II. 1999. *American Constitutional Law.* Second ed. Belmont, CA: West/Wadsworth.

Traditional Values Coalition. 2003a. "Terri Schiavo's Life Still in Danger from Husband!" http://www.traditionalvalues.org/modules.php?name=News&file=article&sid=1257 (accessed 2004).

———. 2003b. "Supreme Court Texas Sodomy Decision Is a Defeat for Public Morality and America's Families." http://traditionalvalues.org/modules.php?name=News&file=article&sid=1009 (accessed 2004).

———. 2004. "Homosexuality 101: A Primer." http://traditionalvalues.org/pdf_files/Homosexuality101.pdf (accessed 2004).

Tuomala. Jeffrey. 2003. "In Defense of Chief Justice Roy S. Moore." http://www.chalcedon.edu/articles/0310/031001jtuomala.shtml (accessed 2004).

Vara, Richard. 2004. "Sunday Sermons to Decry Lesbian Pastor's Acquittal." *Houston Chronicle* (March 26): 10A.

Walsh, Andrew, ed. 2001. *Can Charitable Choice Work?* Hartford, CT: Leonard E. Greenberg Center for the Study of Religion in Public Life, Trinity College.

Walvoord, John F. 1990. *Armageddon, Oil and the Middle East Crisis: What the Bible Says about the Future of the Middle East and the End of Western Civilization.* Grand Rapids, MI: Zondervan.

Washington Post National Weekly Edition. 2003a. "Inspecting the General." (November 10–16): 24

———. 2003b. "No More Justice Moore" (November 24–30): 25.

Washington v. Glucksberg, 521 U.S. 702, 117 S.Ct. 2258, 138 L.Ed.2d. 772 (1997).

Watson, Justin. 1997. *The Christian Coalition: Dreams of Restoration, Demands for Recognition.* New York: St. Martin's.

Welch, Robert. 1959. *The Blue Book of the John Birch Society.* Appleton, WI: Western Islands.

West Virginia State Board of Education v. Barnette, 319 U.S. 624, 63 S.Ct. 1178, 87 L.Ed. 1628 (1943).

Wilcox, Clyde. 1996. *Onward Christian Soldiers? The Religious Right in American Politics.* Boulder, CO: Westview.

Wong, Pamela. 2003. "Hundreds Rally for Ten Commandments in Washington, D.C." http://www.cwfa.org/articledisplay.asp?id=4688&department=CWA& categoryid=freedom (accessed 2004).

Zacharias, Ravi. 2002. *Light in the Shadow of Jihad: The Struggle for Truth.* Sisters, OR: Multnomah.

Zelman v. Simmons-Harris, docket no. 00–1751 (decided June 27, 2002).

4

Electoral Politics

Surveys done in the past to examine the political participation of evangelical Protestants found low levels of participation and a tendency for this group to identify themselves as Democrats. However, analysis of denominational data in the process of writing this book indicates that voter turnout among Christian fundamentalists since the 1990s has been largely on par with the rest of the American electorate and that the Christian right has shifted from a propensity to support Democratic candidates toward greater support for Republican candidates.

Surveys of the politics of the religious right before 1984, in the case of the General Social Survey, or 1989, in the case of the National Election Studies, had some problems in categorizing various denominations, but according to the NES polls, 9–12 percent fewer "Evangelical Christians" in the 1980s reported having voted compared with all others who were interviewed. Our analysis of fundamentalist Christians' voting after 1990 finds that the level of their voting participation now matches that of the average survey respondent. Since 1992, more white fundamentalists have identified themselves as Republicans than as Democrats, although there is a growing number who consider themselves to be independents.

On the other hand, mainline Protestants remain several percentage points more likely to vote than the average or fundamentalist citizens. The difference is small but statistically significant. A positive influence of church membership on voting and the evolving shift in fundamentalist partisanship are evident both in recent scholarly examinations of American politics and in survey data from the National Election Studies (2003a and 2003b) and the General Social Survey (2002).

Religious influence on voting and politics has a long history. As we saw in Chapter 1, religious identification has played a complex and important role in American politics since before the American Revolution. The importance of religion and politics to each other continues to the present day in the United States, but the relationship remains a complex one. American Protestantism is usually divided into mainline and fundamentalist denominations, but there are important differences even within the fundamentalist denominations. For example, fundamentalists who are white take a markedly different partisan stance than those who are black—even when they are part of the same denomination. As we shall see in greater detail in this chapter, black Christian fundamentalists strongly identify with the Democratic party and Democratic candidates, whereas white Christian fundamentalists have been moving toward the Republican party and Republican candidates. Mainline Protestant denominations, on the other hand, have tended to support the Republican party on election day, with some interesting variance in 1996 and 2000.

Obstacles to Analyzing the Religious Right

Few topics for political analysis present a more formidable array of both general and specific obstacles for analysts than is found in studying the religious right. Creedally fundamental and politically conservative Americans have been difficult to classify. What denominations should be considered part of the religious right? How can we observe their political activities? News media may glibly describe fundamentalist Christians as an important factor in many elections, but reliable data to challenge or support that inference are not readily available.

The first general obstacle applies to all U.S. voting studies: Americans use a secret ballot. One of the early Progressive reforms of American election systems was to separate a voter's identity from that voter's choice. U.S. election studies have sought to overcome this obstacle to analysis by seeking voting information through a variety of surveys. National in-home surveys, telephone polls, and voting place exit interviews have produced a large amount of data and an impressive amount of study, starting with the demographic studies at Columbia University (Lazarsfeld, Berelson, and Gaudet 1968) and the national election studies at the University of Michigan (Campbell, Converse, Miller, and Stokes 1960). However, the fact remains that researchers taking these surveys are asking respondents to recall an election and accurately answer questions about their vote and themselves. We cannot directly observe the voting act as if we were in a laboratory. The U.S. Census Bureau, in its Current Population Surveys, does one of the most authoritative accumulations of data and analyses of U.S. voting; however, the U.S. Census position on religious data poses a second general obstacle.

In the United States, official government-initiated questions about a person's religion raise a fundamental issue about the separation of church and state, and the Census Bureau does not ask them. From 1906 to 1936, the Census Bureau surveyed religious organizations in a "Census of Religious Bodies." That census is no longer done, and, since 1976, Public Law 94–521 has provided that a census may not compel a person to disclose information regarding his or her religious beliefs or membership in a religious body. This amendment to Title 13 of the United States Code also provided for increased fines and/or imprisonment for wrongful disclosure of census information. The current government position on the issue is "the Bureau of the Census is not the source for information on religion" (U.S. Census Bureau 2003). The result of these two general obstacles is that researchers must depend upon polls and surveys by government and private organizations for election information and upon nongovernment polls and surveys for information that involves religion or religion and elections.

Studying religious denominations in the U.S. is additionally complicated by their wide variety and by a continually changing landscape of religious bodies that includes the start-up of new denominations and nondenominational congregations, various combinations and changes in existing denominations, and even the demise of some former denominational entities. Keeping track of this changing panoply of denominations is vexingly difficult (Smith, 1987; Wald and Smidt, 1993). For example, in its National Election Studies, the University of Michigan, a long-standing and authoritative source of data on religion and voting, has had to use five different coding schemes for religion in its efforts to stay current on U.S. denominations. In creating a fifth coding scheme in 1989, the NES project analysts noted that the previous coding did not have separate codes for the fastest-growing denominations. Perhaps worse, its categorizations had lumped together groups with very different political characteristics (National Election Studies 2003a).

This categorization problem casts doubt upon some earlier analyses and inferences about politics and religion in the United States. It is difficult to have confidence in a study if its supporting data combined very different subdenominations into the same category, and clearly that has happened in the past. For example, NES surveys from 1960 to 1989 categorized all Presbyterians as a single group without further specification. Yet this denomination includes the fundamentalist Cumberland Presbyterian Church and the fundamentalist Presbyterian Church in America as well as the decidedly mainline Presbyterian Church in the USA. (As discussed in Chapter 1, fundamentalist denominations may be distinguished from others by a preponderance of belief in the inerrancy of the Bible, the importance of a "born again" experience, and a revivalist concern with converting others.) By grouping such very different types of congregations into a single category, earlier analysts may have been unable to sharpen their analyses of the relationship between religion and politics in the United States. Yet if we are interested in understanding the relationship of religion and politics over time, we must go to the existing records and data sources, remembering that a measure of caution may be in order in interpreting them.

Modern analysis of religion and politics in the United States must not only start with an appropriate categorization of denominations; it must also consider the political effect of the racial makeup of the denominations. Since the 1930s, black Americans have become strongly associated with the Democratic party as part of the traditional New Deal coalition. That coalition involved broad support of the Democrats by white southerners, labor union and working-class households, African-Americans, Jews, and, to a lesser extent, Catholics. In some respects, the elections of 1994 and 1996 signaled the demise of that coalition, particularly as conservative white southerners began to consider themselves Republicans (Stanley and Niemi 2001a 387). Nonetheless, African-American support of the Democratic party has continued virtually unchanged, as we examine in greater detail later in this chapter.

Finally, creating a denominational categorization scheme that is complex enough to be accurate has produced a new problem with analyzing the relationships between politics and religion. That problem is insufficient sample size. The National Election Studies and the General Social Survey conduct interviews of nationwide samples of roughly 1,500 to 2,500 people. Although that sample size is perfectly adequate for many questions, it does not capture sufficient interviews in the smaller denominations in any single year to be statistically reliable. For example, the NES for the year 2000 correctly placed the fundamentalist Presbyterian Church in America (PCA) in a separate category from the mainline Presbyterian Church in the USA. But although there were usable data from 323 interviews with mainline Presbyterians, there were only five interviews with PCA fundamentalists. By themselves, five interviews are insufficient for virtually any statistically valid result. In the section below, we address the steps taken in this project to overcome this and the other problems.

A Method for Overcoming the Obstacles to Understanding

For this project, we collected data from multiple sources. We gathered denomination and church population data from the 1990 and 2000 enumerations of religious congregations conducted by the Association of Statisticians of American Religious Bodies and the Glenmary Research Center (Jones et al. 2002). We gathered survey voting and partisanship data by denomination from the biennial and cumulative data files of the National Election Survey (NES) and from the cumulative data files of the General Social Survey (GSS) conducted biennially by the Roper Center for Public Opinion Research (General Social Survey 2002; National Election Studies 2000, 2003a, 2003b).

We employed previous research (Smith 1987) and our own judgment on classifying denominations and organizations as fundamentalist or mainline Protestants to produce a list of fundamentalist church organizations for which some survey and census data were available. We began this listing with the Glenmary censuses of church organizations for 1990 and 2000 (Bradley et al. 1992; Jones et al. 2002). We then used NES and GSS denominational categorizations for a tentative system of classification for fundamentalist or mainline Protestants. We last examined survey data for available information on particular denominations and compiled data files of survey responses for individuals who identified themselves as members of a specific denomination. Beginning with the organizational censuses was useful because by comparing the two Glenmary censuses, we were able to see whether a denomination was growing or shrinking as well as to get some ideas about new start-ups. By seeking information about specific fundamentalist and mainline denominations, we were able to make inferences about reported beliefs and political activities.

The General Social Survey and the National Election Studies have both made serious efforts at classifying denominational responses to their surveys and interviews. Tom W. Smith's methodology for the GSS categorization employed five different techniques for categorizing denominations: (1) prior scholarly classifications, (2) membership in a theologically ecumenical organization as a sign of religious liberalism, (3) survey responses from denominational members, (4) surveys of denominational clergy, and (5) stated theological beliefs. He found that, as mentioned above, fundamentalist Protestants were distinguishable from other Protestants by a preponderance of beliefs in the inerrancy of the Bible, the imminent second coming of Christ, and a personal "born again" salvation experience as well as an evangelical or revivalist desire to save and convert others (Smith 1987).

By using the GSS and NES categorization of denominations, surveyed responses concerning the inerrancy of the Bible and a "born again" experience, and in some cases additional investigation of stated doctrinal positions, we were able to produce the list of eight mainline Christian churches and the list of thirty-six fundamentalist Christian churches found in Chapter 1. Data were obtained on all eight of the mainline churches from past surveys. Data were also compiled on all of the listed fundamentalist churches, but some survey questions had responses from only eighteen of the listed fundamentalist churches, and few questions had responses from more than twenty-eight of them. Three of the fundamentalist Presbyterian organizations were represented in past GSS surveys by data coded "Other Fundamental Presbyterians." One fundamentalist church (the Evangelical Covenant Church) was represented in past surveys by data coded "Independent Charismatic Churches," and most questions had insufficient individual survey data for tracking seven of the smaller and newer fundamentalist churches.

Jehovah's Witnesses represented a special case. The denomination did not report organizational results for the Glenmary censuses. Their individual survey responses indicated that they were creedally conservative, but they did not appear to be politically active. We elected to include survey responses from Jehovah's Witnesses in our files even though these responses are somewhat different from others in the religious right.

The result of all these analytical efforts was a multifaceted data set for eighteen to thirty-six fundamentalist and seven to eight mainline Protestant churches. These can, if necessary, be aggregated into fundamentalist and mainline groupings to obtain sufficient numbers of survey responses for statistical reliability, and for most purposes, this covers elections and surveys from 1976 through 2000. Although earlier categorizations of religions have problems, the aggregations of the NES and GSS along with the voting reports of the U.S. Census Bureau were available to provide a broader context for this present study when needed.

A Look at Christian Conservatism

The nexus of fundamentalist politics and religion may be seen in a variety of social and political issues important to Christian conservatives. For example, fundamentalists generally, but not universally, take conservative views on issues involving abortion, homosexuality, and school prayer (see Chapter 3), as well as support for a strong military defense. Abortion is often seen as a violation of the sanctity of life, homosexuality as biblically prohibited, prayer in the public schools as central to inculcating appropriate values in children, and a strong national defense as necessary to protect the United States, a uniquely blessed nation (the "New Israel" or "City on a Hill"), from foreign threats.

Fundamentalist Protestants are more likely to be pro-life and antiabortion than the mainline Protestants or than all others who answered the religion and abortion questions in the General Social Survey. Of the fundamentalists interviewed (see Table 4.1), 28 percent thought that it should not be possible to get a legal abortion even if there was a strong chance of serious birth defects, and only 9 percent of mainline Protestants opposed abortion in that circumstance. Seventy percent of the fundamentalists felt that not wanting any more children was not sufficient reason for an abortion, while mainline Protestants split almost down the middle on that aspect of abortion policy. Yet 86 percent of the interviewed fundamentalists would support a legal abortion in the case of a pregnancy that seriously endangered the woman's health, and 95 percent of the mainline Protestants would agree (General Social Survey, 2002).

Fundamentalists generally take a more restrictive stand on homosexuality than mainline Protestants do; however, the numbers in opposition vary depending on the circumstances. As Table 4.2 shows,

TABLE 4.1   Survey Responses to Selected Questions about Abortion

Please tell me whether or not you think it should be possible for a pregnant woman to obtain a legal abortion. . .

A. If there is a strong chance of serious birth defects in the baby?

	Yes	No
Fundamentalists	71.9%	28.1%
Mainline	90.7%	9.3%
All Interviewed	81.4%	18.6%

B. If she is married and does not want any more children?

	Yes	No
Fundamentalists	29.5%	70.5%
Mainline	53.2%	46.8%
All Interviewed	44.0%	56.0%

C. If the woman's own health is seriously endangered by the pregnancy?

	Yes	No
Fundamentalists	85.6%	14.4%
Mainline	95.3%	4.7%
All Interviewed	90.0%	9.9%

Source: General Social Survey. 2002. *NORC-GSS Cumulative Data File 1972–2000.* Storrs, CT: The Roper Center for Public Opinion Research.

two-thirds of interviewed fundamentalists would allow a homosexual to speak in their community, and one-half think that a homosexual should be allowed to teach in a college or university, versus 80 percent and 69 percent of the mainline Protestants, respectively. Almost one-half of the interviewed fundamentalists would favor removing a book advocating homosexuality from their public library, whereas only 30 percent of the mainline Protestants would support such a removal. In short, fundamentalist opposition to homosexuality is, to a degree, situational and may be tempered by their support for free speech.

Opinion polls concerning U.S. defense spending indicate that more fundamentalists than others think the government is spending too little on defense, but the proportions do not stray very far from the typical and mainline responses. Figure 4.1 suggests that, over

TABLE 4.2   Survey Responses to Selected Questions about Homosexuality

And what about a man who admits that he is a homosexual?
A. Suppose this admitted homosexual wanted to make a speech in your community. Should he be allowed to speak, or not?

	Yes	*No*
Fundamentalists	64.0%	36.0%
Mainline	79.9%	20.1%
All Interviewed	73.3%	26.7%

B. Should such a person be allowed to teach in a college or university?

	Yes	*No*
Fundamentalists	52.4%	47.6%
Mainline	68.8%	31.2%
All Interviewed	63.6%	36.4%

C. If some people in your community suggested that a book he wrote in favor of homosexuality should be taken out of your public library, would you favor removing this book?

	Yes	*No*
Fundamentalists	48.9%	51.1%
Mainline	30.4%	69.6%
All Interviewed	36.4%	63.6%

Source: General Social Survey. 2002. *NORC-GSS Cumulative Data File 1972–2000.* Storrs, CT: The Roper Center for Public Opinion Research.

time, a reasonable amount of fundamentalist and mainline opinion changes to fit changing circumstances. Page and Shapiro (1992) argue that aggregate public opinion generally responds rationally to changing objective circumstances. In this case, fundamentalist support for more defense spending generally parallels the responses from others. That support peaked in 1980 after the 1979 failed military rescue mission for U.S. hostages held in Iran, after the 1979 Soviet military invasion of Afghanistan, and after increases in U.S. military spending were supported by both Democratic president Jimmy Carter and Republican candidate Ronald Reagan in the 1980 presi-

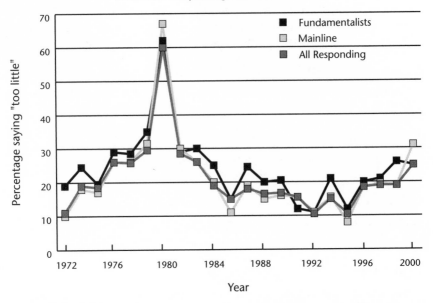

FIGURE 4.1   Public Opinion on Government Spending for U.S. National Defense
Source: General Social Survey. 2002. *NORC-GSS Cumulative Data File 1972–2000.* Storrs, CT: The Roper Center for Public Opinion Research.

dential election. Some fundamentalist Protestants, such as the Mennonites and Jehovah's Witnesses, have a pacifist tradition that can place them at odds with other fundamentalists on this issue. Generally, however, fundamentalists, like other conservatives, remain supportive of a strong U.S. military, and they are usually (but not always) more supportive of it than mainline Protestants.

As we saw in Chapter 1, deeply held beliefs about the importance of religion in society have raised questions about using government policy to make a better society, about supporting an official or established religion, and about whether and when to separate government from religion. We began to look at the political tension inherent in the separation of church and state in Chapter 2 with the issue of a government-supported religious monument in Alabama. In this chapter we trace the political tensions that continue to arise from these questions by examining the issue of school prayer throughout

TABLE 4.3   Views on School Prayer, 1990–1998

Question: Which of the following views comes closest to your opinion on the issue of school prayer?

	1. Should Not Be Allowed	2. Scheduled Silent Prayer	3. General Verbal Prayer	4. Chosen Christian Prayer	5. Other/ Do Not Know
Fundamentalists	5.9%	51.8%	26.1%	13.2%	3.0%
Mainline	8.8%	53.6%	28.5%	7.0%	2.0%
All Others Interviewed	15.8%	50.2%	22.6%	8.7%	2.7%

Sources: National Election Studies. 2003. *National Election Studies (NES) Study and Data Resources 1948–2000,* http://www.umich.edu/~nes/ (accessed November, 2003); National Election Studies. 2003. *National Election Studies (NES) Guide to Public Opinion and Electoral Behavior,* http://www.umich.edu/~nes/nesguide/nesguide.htm (accessed June 2003).

the United States. Modern fundamentalist support for prayer in the public schools is widespread, as is their opposition to Supreme Court rulings to the contrary. As we saw in Chapter 2, 73 percent of the fundamentalists who were interviewed disapproved of court rulings that no state or local government may require the reading of Bible verses or the Lord's Prayer in the public schools. The National Election Studies also asked respondents when they thought school prayer should be allowed. Results are shown in Table 4.3.

Table 4.3 presents the responses from 1990 through 1998 to the question "Which of the following views comes closest to your opinion on the issue of school prayer?" The possible responses to the survey question were as follows:

1. By law, prayer should not be allowed in public schools.
2. The law should allow public schools to schedule time when children can pray silently if they want to.
3. The law should allow public schools to schedule time when children as a group can say a general prayer not tied to a particular religious faith.
4. By law, public schools should schedule a time when all children would say a chosen Christian prayer.
5. Other or do not know (NES Codebook, VCF 9043).

The most popular response for all groups was number 2, a scheduled time for voluntary silent prayer. More than one-half of each group chose number 2, and about one-fourth of all others chose number 3, a scheduled time for a group verbal prayer of a general nature. Nonetheless, there are differences among the responses of fundamentalists, mainline church members, and all others interviewed. Six percent of fundamentalists said that public school prayer should not be allowed, versus 16 percent of other interviewees and 9 percent of mainline Protestants. And almost twice as many fundamentalists (13 percent) as mainline Christians (7 percent) said that that, by law, public schools should schedule time when all children would say a chosen Christian prayer. Possible fundamentalist political reactions to Supreme Court decisions concerning abortion and school prayer are discussed below in the section on voter turnout.

U.S. Voter Turnout: Dwindling and Changing

The proportion of the U.S. population that votes in presidential elections has diminished almost every year since 1964 (Jamieson, Shin, and Day 2002). The U.S. Census Bureau reports that voting rates in the 2000 election were only fractionally higher than the all-time low set in 1996. The Census Bureau used a nationally representative sample to relate a variety of demographic characteristics with the votes that were cast. Based on that sample, the Bureau estimated that 110.8 million Americans voted in the November 2000 presidential election. That figure would be 55 percent of the U.S. population age 18 and older, compared to 69 percent of the adult population in 1964, 59 percent in 1980, and 54 percent in 1996. But not all of the U.S. population over 18 is eligible to vote. After the 1996 election, it became apparent that large numbers of immigrant noncitizens living in the United States meant that previous calculations of turnout were understated (Bruce 1997).

When the Census Bureau recalculated the voting participation rates for U.S. citizens only, the presidential election turnouts for 1996 and 2000 were 70.9 percent and 69.5 percent, respectively (Jamieson, Shin, and Day, 2002). The National Election Studies estimated voter turnout at 73 percent for both 1996 and 2000 (National Election Studies 2003b). Whether the calculations are based on the total U.S. voting age population or just the citizen voting age population, the proportion of those who report voting in elections continues to dwindle.

Indeed, actual participation is slightly less than what is reported in surveys. In presidential elections, official counts are tabulated by each state's board of elections and reported to Congress by the Clerk of the House. When the official counts are compared with the national estimates from survey reports, we find that, typically, 5–12 percent more survey respondents report that they voted than the total votes in the official count. In 2000, the U.S. Census Bureau estimated that 110.8 million Americans voted, but the official count was 105.6 million—about 5 percent less than reported (Jamieson, Shin, and Day 2002, 11–14).

Voting and Religion

Before 1989, problems in correctly categorizing the multiple denominations of religion in the United States made the analytical picture cloudier than more recent efforts. However, the differences between the groups that were previously classified as evangelical Protestants and as mainline Protestants are large enough to infer a greater early reluctance on the part of the evangelicals to participate in elections.

Table 4.4 shows the percentage of survey respondents who stated they had voted in the past election by year from 1964 through 1988. The NES created the categories of "Evangelical Protestant" and "Mainline Protestant" by aggregating responses to a series of questions about the respondents' religion (e.g., "Is your religious preference Protestant, Catholic, Jewish, or something else?" and "What church or denomination is that?"). Although the categorization was later found to be problematic, in all of these elections, the percentage of evangelical Protestants who answered that they had voted was smaller than the percentage of mainline Protestant voters and smaller than the average responses from all interviewed. During this period, a larger proportion of mainline Protestants voted than the average of all interviewed, and a smaller than average proportion of evangelical Protestants voted in these presidential election years. Indeed, in every year, fewer evangelicals voted than the average of all interviewed, and at the same time, more mainlines reported voting.

All three categories of respondents followed the typical seesaw pattern of higher turnout during presidential elections (1964, 1968, etc.) than during the off-year elections (1966, 1970, etc.). As discussed above, the pre-1989 NES categorization of religions has several problems that work against its accuracy. Nonetheless, the differences

TABLE 4.4   Percentage of Respondents Reporting that They Voted in the Fall Election

	Evangelical Protestants	Mainline Protestants	All Interviewed
1964	66	83	78
1966	51	66	62
1968	66	82	76
1970	50	64	59
1972	62	77	73
1974	47	66	53
1976	67	78	72
1978	45	60	55
1980	65	76	71
1982	55	70	60
1984	65	77	74
1986	47	59	53
1988	60	77	70

Sources: National Election Studies. 2003. *National Election Studies (NES) Study and Data Resources 1948–2000,* http://www.umich.edu/~nes/ (accessed November 2003); National Election Studies. 2003. *National Election Studies (NES) Guide to Public Opinion and Electoral Behavior,* http://www.umich.edu/~nes/nesguide/nesguide.htm (accessed June 2003).

among the three reported categories are large, and they indicate lesser involvement in national elections on the part of the evangelical Protestants. Reported evangelical participation in the 1970s averaged 54 percent, 8 percent lower than the average of all interviewed. Evangelical participation in the 1980s averaged 58 percent, 7 percent lower than the average of all interviewed.

The NES numbers of evangelical Protestants who did or did not vote in these early years shows little impact from events that might be thought politically mobilizing for the Christian right. For example, the Supreme Court's 1962 decision on school prayer seems to have made no change in the numbers voting or not voting in 1964. The 1962 decision in *Engel v. Vitale* found that officially required prayers in public schools violated the Constitutional prohibition of the establishment of a national religion; however, generally lax compliance with the Court's ruling (see Anderson 2003, 234) may have muted protest votes against it. On the other hand, the Supreme Court's 1973 ruling on abortion in *Roe v. Wade* may well have been a factor in the 5 percent increase in voter turnout for evangelicals between 1972 and 1976. However, evangelical voting participation decreased again in 1980 and 1988. We must turn to the more recent and more accurate classification of denominations for a clearer picture of the influence of religion on voting in the United States.

Combining the NES results for elections from 1990 through 2000 for each of the denominations selected for this study allows us to provide a statistically stable comparison of the voting participation of members in selected fundamentalist denominations with that of mainline church members and others who participated in the surveys. This 12-year period covers six congressional election years and three presidential election years. Voting turnout remained lower for off-year elections than for presidential elections, but combining NES survey results for these six elections produces a large enough sample to examine some results by individual denomination. We find that individual voting participation for selected fundamentalist denominations in these years was 62.4 percent. As we shall see below, the reported fundamentalist participation is now on par with that of the population as a whole over the 12-year period, and there are interesting differences from one denomination to another, as may be seen in Table 4.5.

Some of the fundamentalist denominations had markedly less voting participation than the others. In four denominations, more members reported not voting than reported voting over this period. Also, a majority of responses from the Church of God of Prophecy, Vineyard Fellowship, and Seventh-Day Adventists reported not voting, although the number of responses from these denominational members is much too small for drawing any inferences at the level of the specific denomination. Sixty of the total Jehovah's Witnesses that were interviewed during the period responded that they had not voted, yielding a voting participation rate of only 12 percent.

Similarly, forty-seven members of the American Baptist Association indicated that they had not voted, for a voting participation rate of 52 percent. In this latter case, however, there appears to be some confusion between responses from members of the fundamentalist American Baptist Association and those from the more mainline American Baptist Churches in the USA. (Race may also be a factor in the case of the American Baptist Association, and we address racial makeup later in this chapter.) Aside from a current similarity in names, confusion may also have arisen from the more northern-centered American Baptist Churches in the USA having changed its name twice in the past forty years. Such name confusion may be the reason 26 percent of the Baptists who were interviewed were unsure

TABLE 4.5 Voter Turnout of the Christian Right in Six Elections,1990–2000. Responses to "Did you vote in the election this November?"

Fundamental Denomination	No	Yes
Cumberland Presbyterian Church	1	5
Evangelical Presbyterian	1	2
Church of God of Prophecy	2	1
Pentecostal Church of God	1	4
Vineyard Fellowship	1	0
Mennonite Church	3	3
Conservative Baptist Association of America	0	5
Church of God (Anderson, Indiana)	5	18
International Pentecostal Holiness Church	1	2
General Association of Regular Baptists	2	4
Christian Reformed Church in North America	6	18
National Association of Free Will Baptists	1	7
American Baptist Association	47	52
Evangelical Free Church	2	7
Baptist Missionary Association of America	19	24
Presbyterian Church in America	0	5
Christian and Missionary Alliance	3	6
International Church of the Four Square Gospel	1	13
Wesleyan	5	6
Wisconsin Evangelical Lutheran Synod	3	10
Church of the Nazarene	23	31
Seventh Day Adventist	17	12
Church of God (Cleveland, Tennessee)	16	19
Jehovah's Witnesses	60	8
Churches of Christ	54	94
Lutheran Church Missouri Synod	34	166
Assembly of God	57	91
Southern Baptist	354	582
Total Fundamentalist Responses	**719**	**1,195**
Percentage	**37.6%**	**62.4%**

Source: Project List of Denominations and National Election Studies, Cumulative Data File, Crosstabulation of Questions VCF 0152 (Religion of Respondent), VCF 0702 (Did Respondent Vote in Election), and Year of Study.

of their exact denomination, whereas only 13 to 14 percent of Lutherans and Methodists did not know their exact denomination. (See Smith 1987 for a discussion of this possible confusion.) If the American Baptist Association and the Jehovah's Witnesses were to be excluded from the fundamentalist statistics, fundamentalist voting

TABLE 4.6   Voter Turnout of Mainline Denominations and Others, 1990–2000

Survey Question: "Did you vote in the election this November?"		
Mainline Denomination	No	Yes
American Baptist Churches in the USA	41	69
Christian Church (Disciples of Christ)	16	66
Episcopal Church	62	200
Evangelical Lutheran Church in America	77	221
Presbyterian Church USA	78	237
Reformed Church in America	5	9
United Methodist Church	213	545
United Church of Christ	26	102
Total Mainline Responses	518	1,449
Percentage	35.7%	64.3%
All Other Valid Responses	**2544**	**4136**
Percentage	**38.1%**	**61.9%**

Sources: National Election Studies. 2003. *National Election Studies (NES) Study and Data Resources 1948–2000*, http://www.umich.edu/~nes/ (accessed November 2003); National Election Studies. 2003. *National Election Studies (NES) Guide to Public Opinion and Electoral Behavior*, http://www.umich.edu/~nes/nesguide/nesguide.htm (accessed June 2003).

participation over the 12 years would be 65 percent rather than the 62 percent shown in Table 4.5.

Similarly, we compared national election participation for members of the eight selected mainline denominations with that of the fundamentalists in Table 4.5 and with that of all other respondents for those years. Voter turnout for the mainline denominations and for all others appears in Table 4.6. The mainline participation rate of 64.3 percent continues to be slightly higher than the participation of all others, who reported voting in 61.9 percent of the responses from 1990 through 2000. Mainline participation is higher than the 62.4 percent of the fundamentalists, but the apparent earlier reluctance of evangelical Protestants to vote has disappeared. Our denominational analysis shows that fundamentalist Christians are now participating in national elections at essentially the same rate as other Americans, and some of the fundamentalist denominations are participating at the same high level as the mainline churches.

The influence of religion on voting participation does not appear to be large, but it is also not likely to be the result of random chance.

Chi-square tests, a common statistical technique, on the totals in Table 4.6 indicate that there is less than one chance in one thousand that there really is no difference between the underlying results for all others and those for mainline Christians. Mainline Christians are 2–3 percent more likely than others who were surveyed to report having voted. For the fundamentalist figures in Table 4.5 above, however, if the American Baptist Association and Jehovah's Witnesses figures are included in the figures, we cannot be sure that the 0.5 percent greater participation of fundamentalists over all others represents a real difference. Chi-square tests do not rule out the possibility that the fundamentalist and all-other populations were voting at essentially the same level during this period.

Our clearer picture of selected fundamentalists' voting participation shows that it is not less than average and may even be above average by a slight proportion. It is possible that there was some mobilization effect of fundamentalist Protestants from 1989 Supreme Court decisions, as their participation in the 1990s was on par with the rest of the American electorate. However, mobilization influences from the Court would likely have been mixed. With three Reagan appointees on the Court, it made rulings that affected government policy on school prayer and abortion. In 1989, the Court let stand an appeals court ruling that banned religious invocations at public high school football games (Anderson 1997, 260–261). (The Supreme Court again supported that position in 2000 when it upheld another appeals court ruling in a Texas case banning religious invocations at public high school football games (Anderson 2003, 234). For a discussion of some conservative Christians' responses to these cases, see Chapter 2.) On the other hand, in 1989, the Court partially backed away from its *Roe v. Wade* abortion ruling when it upheld the state of Missouri's right to prohibit the performance of abortions in their public hospitals and clinics as well as prohibiting the use of state funds for counseling women about abortion (Anderson 2003, 55–56). Whatever the reason, our clearer picture of selected fundamentalist denominations in the 1990s shows that they reported participating in elections at the same or slightly higher rates than the average.

If overall voting participation in the United States continues to dwindle, relatively small differences in participation may become more important in deciding which candidates from what party are elected. The religious right has gone from voting at proportions that are less than other groups to voting at proportions that are on par with or that exceed the participation of most other Americans. Voting in an election makes it more likely that one will vote in the next election, for, in a sense, voting is habit-forming (Gerber, Green, and Shachar 2003). Voting behavior tends to persist, so increased levels of political participation from the religious right may remain important to partisan politics for some time to come. The next section will examine what political parties and candidates have been supported by fundamentalist Protestants in the United States.

Understanding Partisanship and Religion in the United States

Americans express partisanship both by how they vote and by how they view their relationship with a political party. The two expressions of partisanship often agree, but sometimes they do not. Often a citizen will vote for candidates from the Democratic or Republican party and will similarly describe himself or herself as a Democrat or Republican. But it is possible for a person to consider himself or herself a member or supporter of the political party into which he or she was socialized, and yet to vote consistently for the other party's candidates. For example, there was a tendency in the past for southerners to consider themselves to be Democrats, yet to vote for Republican presidential candidates (Stanley and Niemi 2001a). It is also possible to consider oneself an independent and still participate actively in elections. As self-conceptions of party identification and actual voting can differ, scholars of political behavior study both aspects of partisanship, and this chapter examines both voting in presidential elections and self-identification of partisanship.

Presidential Support from the Religious Right

We turn again to our aggregation of selected fundamentalist and mainline denominations to examine who received their votes for president of the United States from 1976 through 2000. Table 4.7 presents aggregations of the reported vote of those who identified themselves as members of various denominations. In the earliest years, these aggregations are limited to eleven fundamentalist and seven mainline denominations, because accurate data were not available for the other listed denominations. After 1989, aggregate figures for eighteen to twenty-one fundamentalist denominations and eight mainline denominations are presented.

TABLE 4.7   Presidential Voting, 1976–2000

Year	Candidate	Fundamentalist	Mainline	All Interviewed	Actual Vote
1976	Carter	57.4	39.7	48.3	50.1
	Ford	38.9	56.4	47.0	48.0
	Other	3.7	3.9	4.8	1.9
1980	Carter	52.6	36.1	39.4	41.0
	Reagan	40.4	56.6	50.8	50.7
	Other	7.0	7.3	9.8	8.3
1984	Mondale	42.2	36.3	41.1	40.6
	Reagan	56.9	61.5	57.3	58.8
	Other	0.9	2.2	1.6	0.6
1988	Dukakis	45.9	42.5	46.6	45.6
	Bush	52.8	56.6	52.3	53.4
	Other	1.3	0.9	1.1	1.0
1992	Clinton	43.7	38.5	47.6	43.0
	Bush	43.7	39.1	33.9	37.4
	Perot	12.0	21.8	18.1	19.0
	Other	0.7	0.6	0.4	0.6
1996	Clinton	48.1	49.0	52.9	49.2
	Dole	41.0	44.6	38.3	40.7
	Perot	9.9	5.6	7.2	8.4
	Other	0.9	0.8	1.6	1.7
2000	Gore	43.8	51.7	50.6	48.4
	Bush	53.9	45.7	45.5	47.9
	Nader	2.3	1.7	2.8	2.7
	Other	0	0.9	0.9	1.0

Sources: National Election Studies. 2003. *National Election Studies (NES) Study and Data Resources 1948–2000,* http://www.umich.edu/~nes/ (accessed November, 2003); National Election Studies. 2003. *National Election Studies (NES) Guide to Public Opinion and Electoral Behavior,* http://www.umich.edu/~nes/nesguide/nesguide.htm (accessed June, 2003); Ragsdale, Lyn. 1998. *Vital Statistics on the Presidency,* rev. ed. Washington, DC: Congressional Quarterly, p. 118; Stanley, Harold W., and Richard G. Niemi. 2001. *Vital Statistics on American Politics.* Washington, DC: CQ, p. 28–29; *The World Almanac and Book of Facts.* 2004. New York: World Almanac Books.

In one sense, the election of 1984 represented a transition year in fundamentalist voting. Before 1984, fundamentalists generally favored Democratic presidential support. After 1984, they favored Republican candidates, with the single exceptions of a tie in 1992 and 1996 when Ross Perot was on the ballot. Fundamentalists may be voting for the person rather than the party. In 1976 and 1980, the majority of fundamentalist Protestant voters supported the born-again Democratic candidate, Jimmy Carter, in his victory over Republican Gerald Ford and in his later loss to Republican Ronald Reagan. In the 1980 campaign, all three of the major candidates (Carter, Reagan, and John Anderson) stated that they had been born-again (Jelen, Smidt, and Wilcox, 1993, 199), but a clear majority of the fundamentalist vote went to Jimmy Carter. In 1984, however, a larger proportion of the fundamentalist vote went to Republican Ronald Reagan. In sum, fundamentalists had a choice between a born-again Democrat and a born-again Republican in 1980, and 53 percent of them voted for Carter. But when born-again Reagan ran against Democrat Walter Mondale, 57 percent of the fundamentalists voted for Reagan.

In 1988, Pat Robertson, an evangelical preacher and the host of *The 700 Club* television program, entered the presidential race and placed second in the Iowa Republican caucus. The three leading candidates for the Republican nomination in 1988 were George H. W. Bush, Bob Dole, and Pat Robertson, and Iowa rated Dole first, Robertson second, and Bush third. However, that was the high point of the Robertson campaign. George Bush swept the south on Super Tuesday. Pat Robertson ended up third in this political effort (Barone and Ujifusa 1989, xxxiii; Ragsdale 1996, 58–59). Robertson did not attract many votes from the fundamentalist denominations studied in this project. Fifty-three percent of the fundamentalist vote in the general election went to Republican Bush. Fifty-seven percent of the mainline Protestant vote went to Bush, continuing the traditional mainline support for Republican presidential candidates. That mainline tradition would change when Ross Perot became a presidential candidate in the election of 1992.

Ross Perot entered the 1992 presidential race as a third-party candidate and garnered 12 percent of the fundamentalist vote, 22 percent of the mainline Protestant vote, and 19 percent of the official total vote. In 1988, the fundamentalist vote had favored Republican Bush over Democrat Dukakis by 7 percent. In 1992, with 12 percent of the fundamentalist vote going to Perot, the remaining fundamentalist vote was split evenly between Republican President Bush and the Democratic candidate, Bill Clinton. In 1988, the mainline Protestant vote had favored Republican Bush by 14 percent. In 1992, with 22 percent of the mainline vote going to Perot, the remaining mainline voters also split nearly evenly between Bush and Clinton. Others who were interviewed tilted more heavily to Clinton, and Clinton's actual presidential victory featured a plurality of 43 percent of the official popular vote over Bush's 37 percent and Perot's 19 percent.

But every presidential race has its own idiosyncrasies, and it would be overstating the case to assert that Perot drew votes only from the Republican candidate. The attractiveness of the candidates and the importance of the issues can also influence the decision to vote. Exit polls of some Perot voters indicated that if Perot had not been on the ballot in 1992, 38 percent of them would have voted for Bush and 38 percent for Clinton (Holmes 1992, B4). If Perot had not been a candidate, how many of those Perot voters would have stayed home and which party would have benefited are questions we cannot answer authoritatively. We can say that Perot supporters made the largest showing for a third-party candidate since Teddy Roosevelt ran as the Progressive Party candidate against Howard Taft and Woodrow Wilson in 1912. Polls characterized Perot supporters as mainly white, under age 45, self-described independents who expressed a deep distrust of government. Nonetheless, 88 percent of fundamentalist Protestants, who share many of those demographic characteristics, split their vote evenly between the two major parties, producing the lowest level of 1992 Perot support, as shown in Table 4.7.

Ten percent of the vote from fundamentalist Protestants returned to Perot when he ran again in 1996, 48 percent went for incumbent Democratic President Clinton, and 41 percent for Bob Dole, the Republican challenger. Indeed, fundamentalist presidential voting mirrored that of the actual total vote in 1996. Mainline Protestants supported Perot less and Dole more, but the largest share of their votes went to President Clinton. Using network exit poll data, Stanley and Niemi (2001b, 122) reported that 53 percent of white Protestant voters voted for Republican Dole, and 38 percent voted for Democratic President Clinton. The Monica Lewinski and Whitewater scandals that would later lead to impeachment efforts were not issues in the 1996 election. When the actual votes were compiled, Clinton won reelection handily with 49.2 percent of the popular vote and 379 of 539 votes in the electoral college.

The major presidential candidates in 2000 were Democrat Al Gore and Republican George W. Bush. The total popular vote in the 2000 election was split almost evenly between Gore and Bush, but this election also featured a third-party candidate, Ralph Nader of the Green party. Some Democrats complained that Nader was siphoning Democratic votes from Gore, but Nader himself rejected that suggestion, and indeed Gore won several states where Nader also drew strong support (Freedberg 2000).

There were major voting differences between fundamentalist and mainline Protestants in the election of 2000. After Governor Bush said in a debate that his favorite political philosopher was Jesus, he gained public support from many of the leaders of the religious right, including Jerry Falwell and Pat Robertson (Goodstein 2000). One South Carolina Baptist called Bush's statement that Christ had changed his life "a defining moment" in the campaign (Niebuhr 2000).

On election day, fundamentalists favored Bush over Gore by 10 percentage points, and mainline Protestants favored Gore by 6 percent. Bush even won Gore's home state of Tennessee, but the election came down to court determinations and a few contested votes in Florida. At the initial count in Florida, Bush led Gore by less than one-half of 1 percent, and according to state law, a recount was automatically conducted. When the recount resulted in an even narrower Bush victory, the Florida Democratic party sued the Florida secretary of state to extend the election deadline to allow for full manual recounts in selected counties. The Florida Supreme Court agreed, but the U.S. Supreme Court overruled them. A year later, a consortium of eight news media finished a 10-month recount of disputed ballots and concluded that if the Florida court's recount had not been stopped by the Supreme Court, Bush still would have won by a margin of 493 votes (Fessenden and Broder 2001). As it stood, however, Florida's secretary of state had earlier certified a Bush victory margin of 537 votes, and Florida's electoral votes went to Bush. Bush became president with 47.9 percent of the national popular and 271 electoral college votes, versus Gore's 48.4 percent of the national popular vote and 266 electoral college votes.

Fundamentalist Protestant participation in U.S. presidential elections since 1976 suggests that they tend to vote for the person rather than the party. They favored born-again Jimmy Carter, a Democrat, over Republican Gerald Ford by 19 percent in 1976, and they favored Carter over Republican Ronald Reagan by 12 percent in 1980. Yet the conservative Reagan was able to attract 15 percent more of the fundamentalist vote in 1984 than Democratic contender Walter Mondale. That margin dropped to 7 percent more fundamentalist votes in 1988 for George H. W. Bush than for Democratic contender Michael Dukakis. In 1992, with Perot in the race, fundamentalists split their votes equally between Republican President Bush and Democrat Bill Clinton. In 1996, they gave Democratic President Clinton 7 percent more votes than Republican opponent Bob Dole. But the knife-edge electoral decision of 2000 showed the potential importance of a modest amount of votes, and the 10 percent edge that the fundamentalists accorded to the candidate who cited Jesus as his favorite political philosopher underscores the willingness of the religious right to support a candidate seen as a conservative Christian.

With voter turnout among the fundamentalist Protestants now on par with the rest of the electorate, the ability of a candidate to attract this particular support could become a deciding factor in American elections in the future.

Shifting Support for the Political Parties

When it comes to describing oneself as a Republican, Democrat, or independent, fundamentalist Protestants have traditionally seen themselves as more Democrat than Republican, and mainline Protestant respondents have traditionally seen themselves as more Republican than Democrat. But as we shall see, that characterization is incomplete and may not accurately reflect current political trends.

For many years, the interviewers for the National Election Studies have asked their respondents a series of questions to identify their support for a political party. They typically asked, "Generally speaking, do you usually think of yourself as a Republican, a Democrat, an independent, or what?" If the answer was Republican (or Democrat), they next asked, "Would you call yourself a strong Republican (Democrat) or a not very strong Republican (Democrat)?" If the answer was independent or no preference, they then asked, "Do you think of yourself as closer to the Republican or Democratic party?" The result was a seven-category scale of Strong Democrat, Weak Democrat, Independent Leaning Democratic, Independent Independent, Independent Leaning Republican, Weak Republican, and Strong Republican. If we combine this partisan scale with the NES categorizations of evangelical Protestants and mainline Protestants, the responses for 1990 through 1996 produce the results found in Table 4.8.

The categorizations in Table 4.8 indicate that evangelicals described themselves mostly as Democrats and independents and that mainlines described themselves as Republicans and independents. Evangelical Protestants were 40 percent Democrat, 33 percent inde-

TABLE 4.8 Number and Percentage of Respondents Identifying with a Political Party, 1990–1996

	DEMOCRAT		INDEPENDENT			REPUBLICAN		APOLITICAL
	Strong Dem	Weak Dem	Dem Leaning	Independent	Rep Leaning	Weak Rep	Strong Rep	
Evangelical Protestant	487	382	266	203	248	298	273	35
		869		717			571	35
		39.6%		32.7%			26.0%	1.6%
Mainline Protestant	232	248	189	162	215	336	286	7
		480		566			622	7
		28.7%		33.8%			37.1%	0.4%
All Valid Responses	1,441	1,480	1,059	816	930	1,159	962	86
		2,921		2,805			2,121	86
		36.8%		35.4%			26.7%	1.1%

Sources: National Election Studies. 2003. *National Election Studies (NES) Study and Data Resources 1948–2000,* http://www.umich.edu/~nes/ (accessed November 2003); National Election Studies. 2003. *National Election Studies (NES) Guide to Public Opinion and Electoral Behavior,* http://www.umich.edu/~nes/nesguide/nesguide.htm (accessed June 2003).

pendent, and 26 percent Republican. Mainline Protestants, on the other hand, were only 29 percent Democrat, 34 percent independent, and 37 percent Republican. The total of all those who responded to the referenced questions self-identified their political party as Democrat in 37 percent of the responses, as independent in 35 percent of the responses, and as Republican in 27 percent of the responses from 1990 through 1996. Most of the mainline Protestants favored the Republican party, and most of the evangelical Protestants favored the Democratic party. But as we shall discuss below, the more detailed categorizations in this project indicate that the religious right is more complicated than this NES categorization may suggest.

One major complicating factor is the racial composition of some of the denominations and the predilections for African-Americans to identify with the Democratic party. Figures 4.2–4.4 below provide a look at the racial nature of partisanship in three fundamentalist denominations: one with about one-half of its reported membership being black, one with about one-third of its membership being black, and one with very few reported black members. Figure 4.2 displays the responses to the partisanship questions for the fundamentalist American Baptist Association from 1990 through 2000. As discussed earlier, some of these denominational responses may be confused as to the specific denomination, but the relationship between race and party self-identification appears fairly clear. About one-half of the survey respondents who identified themselves as members of this particular denomination were African-Americans, and the largest part of that group (75 percent) identified with the Democratic party.

Figure 4.3 shows partisanship responses for individuals who were members of the Southern Baptist Convention from 1990 through 2000. Twenty-five percent of the Southern Baptist respondents were African-American, and 74 percent of that group identified themselves as Democrats. The partisanship responses for members of the Assemblies of God from 1990 through 2000 appear in Figure 4.4. Less than 7 percent of the interviewees from the Assemblies of God were black, and the partisanship of the black members was almost evenly divided among Democrat, independent, and Republican.

Clearly, race is an important factor. Black members of denominations in which blacks make up an appreciable fraction of the membership tend to identify themselves as Democrats, and scholars have found little evidence to indicate that African-Americans' preference for the Democratic party is changing. On the other hand, there is some evidence that white southerners are becoming less strongly

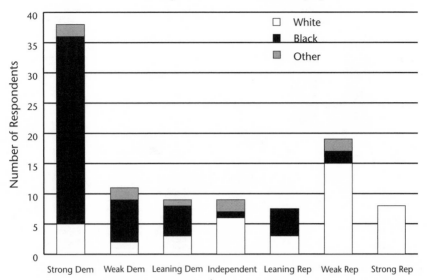

FIGURE 4.2   Partisanship by Race for the American Baptist Association,
1990–2000
Sources: National Election Studies. 2003. *National Election Studies (NES)
Study and Data Resources 1948–2000,* http://www.umich.edu/~nes/ (accessed
November 2003); National Election Studies. 2003. *National Election Studies
(NES) Guide to Public Opinion and Electoral Behavior,* http://www.umich.edu/
~nes/nesguide/nesguide.htm (accessed June 2003).

Democratic and somewhat more likely to see themselves as Republican (Stanley and Niemi 2001a; Niemi and Weisberg 2001). If we are
to examine surveys and polls for evidence of a change in partisanship, then we must distinguish between fundamentalist Protestants
who are African-American and those who are not.

Of the thirty-eight fundamentalist denominations on the list in
Chapter 1, only the American Baptist Association and the Southern
Baptist Convention have more than fifty African-American partisanship responses for the period under study. By going to the biennial
NES surveys and cross-tabulating the Baptist group of respondents
with the partisanship scale, we can produce statistics for these denominations without the responses of their reported black members.
Combining those results with responses from the other fundamentalist denominations on our list produces a clearer picture of the partisanship changes that are under way.

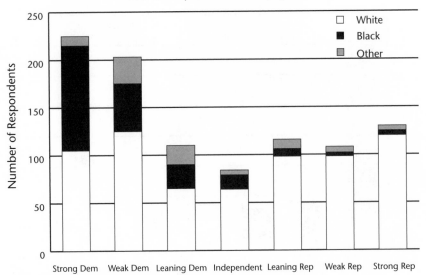

FIGURE 4.3   Partisanship by Race for the Southern Baptist Convention, 1990–2000
Sources: National Election Studies. 2003. *National Election Studies (NES) Study and Data Resources 1948–2000,* http://www.umich.edu/~nes/ (accessed November 2003); National Election Studies. 2003. *National Election Studies (NES) Guide to Public Opinion and Electoral Behavior,* http://www.umich.edu/~nes/nesguide/nesguide.htm (accessed June 2003).

Figure 4.5 presents the partisanship data for white fundamentalists by year for the six elections from 1990 through 2000 after excluding black fundamentalists from the figure. Beginning in 1992, slightly more white fundamentalist Protestants have been identifying themselves as Republicans than as Democrats. There was a peak in 1994, the year Newt Gingrich organized a Contract with America and mounted what proved to be a successful campaign to create a Republican majority in the U.S. House of Representatives. In that year, 40 percent of the selected fundamentalists identified themselves as Republican, versus 30 percent as independent and 28 percent as Democrat. But that Republican preponderance did not last.

The Republican edge over Democratic self-identification, at 12 percent in 1994, fell to 3 percent in 1996, 8 percent in 1998, and 0.5 percent in 2000. In 2000, when fundamentalists were supporting Re-

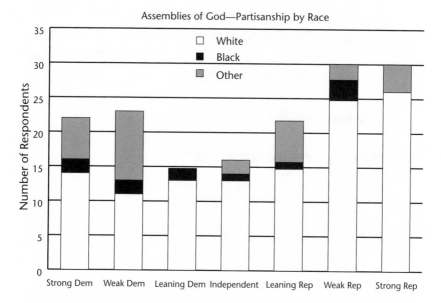

FIGURE 4.4   Partisanship by Race for the Assemblies of God, 1990–2000
Sources: National Election Studies. 2003. *National Election Studies (NES) Study and Data Resources 1948–2000,* http://www.umich.edu/~nes/ (accessed November 2003); National Election Studies. 2003. *National Election Studies (NES) Guide to Public Opinion and Electoral Behavior,* http://www.umich.edu/~nes/nesguide/nesguide.htm (accessed June 2003).

publican Bush over Democrat Gore by 10 percent in the presidential election, fundamentalist Protestants were almost equally split between the two parties when it came to self-identification with those parties. The 1994 plurality of white fundamentalist Protestants who identified themselves as Republican had virtually evaporated by 2000, but a healthy plurality of fundamentalists supported Bush, the conservative Christian, nonetheless.

The former characterization of fundamentalists as strong members of the Democratic party has not been an accurate description of white fundamentalist partisanship since 1992. The Republican party attracted a plurality of support in 1994 and thereafter. A nationwide survey in 2003 found that the Republican party was more widely seen as friendly to religion than the Democrats, although there was a difference between the views of white and black respondents. By more than two to one, white respondents viewed the Republican

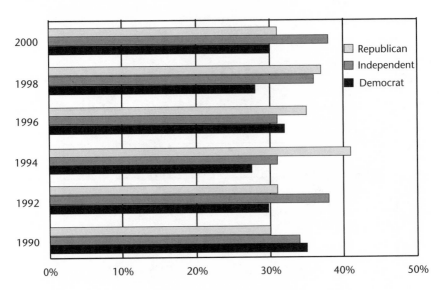

FIGURE 4.5 Partisanship of White Fundamentalists by Year
Sources: National Election Studies. 2003. *National Election Studies (NES)*
Study and Data Resources 1948–2000, http://www.umich.edu/~nes/ (accessed
November 2003); National Election Studies. 2003. *National Election Studies*
(NES) Guide to Public Opinion and Electoral Behavior, http://www.umich.edu/
~nes/nesguide/nesguide.htm (accessed June 2003).

party as friendly toward religion rather than neutral (58 percent to 26 percent). For the Democratic party, white respondents were more divided in their assessment (41 percent friendly, 37 percent neutral, and 13 percent unfriendly toward religion). African-Americans, on the other hand, were nearly twice as likely to say that the Democratic party was friendly toward religion (53 percent) rather than neutral to (27 percent) (Pew Research Center, 2003).

But a remarkable number of fundamentalists are now identifying themselves as independents. Since 1990, about one-third of the fundamentalists in our data set have identified themselves as independent. Even during the Republican peak of 1994, 31 percent first said they were independent, and by the year 2000, that proportion had risen to 38 percent. Partisan independence now constitutes the largest category, although some of those who say first that they are independent will admit to leaning toward one or another of the parties at any one time.

Understanding the Politics of the Religious Right

The lesson for election analysts is clear. Fundamentalists are more likely to vote now than they were before 1990, and from 1976 through the 2000 election, they were supportive of presidential candidates seen as conservative Christians. Fundamentalists are now voting at about the same levels as other Americans, and the margin of support they provide for candidates who are seen as conservative or born-again Christians can be an important factor in who gets elected. Yet, even after the congressional elections of 1994 and the presidential election of 2000, the Republican party has not captured the loyalty of many fundamentalist Protestants. African-American fundamentalists remain loyal to the Democratic party and white fundamentalists have begun to favor the Republican party over the Democrats, but many fundamentalists see themselves as independents, and courting their support will require a new effort for every new election.

References

Anderson, James E. 1997. *Public Policymaking*, 3rd ed. Boston, MA: Houghton Mifflin.

———. 2003. *Public Policymaking*, 5th ed. Boston, MA: Houghton Mifflin.

Barone, Michael, and Grant Ujifusa. 1989. *The Almanac of American Politics 1990*. Washington DC: National Journal.

———. 1993. *The Almanac of American Politics 1994*. Washington, DC: National Journal.

Bradley, Martin B., Norman M. Green, Jr., Dale E. Jones, Mac Lynn, and Lori McNeil. 1992. *Churches and Church Membership in the United States 1990*. Atlanta, GA: Glenmary Research Center.

Bruce, Peter. 1997. "How the Experts Got Voter Turnout Wrong Last Year." *The Public Perspective* (October/November): 39–43.

Campbell, Angus, Philip E. Converse, Warren E. Miller, and Donald E. Stokes. 1960. *The American Voter*. New York: Wiley.

Engel v. Vitale, 370 U.S. 421 (1962).

Fessenden, Ford, and John M. Broder. 2001. "Study of Disputed Florida Ballots Finds Justices Did Not Cast Deciding Vote." *New York Times* (November 12): A1, A16.

Freedberg, Louis. 2000. "Nader Denies Spoiling Gore's Shot at Victory." *San Francisco Chronicle* (November 8): A3.

General Social Survey. 2002. *NORC-GSS Cumulative Data File 1972–2000*. Storrs, CT: Roper Center for Public Opinion Research.

Gerber, Alan S., Donald P. Green, and Ron Shachar. 2003. "Voting May Be Habit-Forming: Evidence from a Randomized Field Experiment." *American Journal of Political Science* 47 (July):540–550.

Glenmary census of church organizations for 1990. See Bradley et al. 1992.

Glenmary census of church organizations for 2000. See Jones et al. 2002.

Goodstein, Laurie, 2000. "Conservative Church Leaders Find a Pillar in Bush." *New York Times* (January 23): 16.

"Governor's Races: Georgia." 2002. *New York Times* (November 6): B6.

Holmes, Steven R. 1992. "An Eccentric But No Joke." *New York Times* (November 5): A1, B4.

Jamieson, Amie, Hyon B. Shin, and Jennifer Day. 2002. "Voting and Registration in the Election of November 2000." *Current Population Reports, P20–542*. Washington, DC: U.S. Census Bureau, U.S. Department of Commerce.

Jelen, Ted G., Corwin E. Smidt, and Clyde Wilcox. 1993. "The Political Effects of the Born-Again Phenomenon." In David Leege and Lyman Kellstedt, eds. *Rediscovering the Religious Factor in American Politics.* Armonk, NY: M. E. Sharpe.

Jones, Dale E., Sherri Doty, Clifford Grammich, James E. Horsch, Richard Houseal, Mac Lynn, John P. Marcum, Kenneth M. Sanchagrin, and Richard H. Taylor. 2002. *Religious Congregations & Membership in the United States 2000.* Nashville, TN: Glenmary Research Center.

Lazarsfeld, Paul Felix, Bernard Berelson, and Hazel Gaudet. 1968. *The People's Choice,* 3rd ed. New York: Columbia University Press (original edition published in 1944).

Leege, David C., and Lyman A. Kellstedt, eds. 1993. *Rediscovering the Religious Factor in American Politics.* Armonk, NY: M. E. Sharpe.

National Election Studies. 2000. *NES 1948–2000 Cumulative Data File Variable Documentation.* http//www.umich.edu/~nes (accessed June 2001).

———. 2003a. *Codebook.* http://www.umich.edu/~nes (accessed June 2003).

———. 2003b. *National Election Studies (NES) Guide to Public Opinion and Electoral Behavior.* http://www.umich.edu/~nes/nesguide/nesguide.htm (accessed June 2003).

Niebuhr, Gustav. 2000. "Evangelicals Found a Believer in Bush." *New York Times* (February 21): A13.

Niemi, Richard G., and Herbert F. Weisberg, eds. 2001. *Controversies in Voting Behavior,* 4th ed. Washington, DC: CQ.

Page, Benjamin I., and Robert Y. Shapiro. 1992. *The Rational Public: Fifty Years of Trends in Americans' Policy Preferences.* Chicago: University of Chicago Press.

Pew Research Center and the Pew Forum on Religion and Public Life. 2003. *Religion and Politics: Contention and Consensus.* http://pewforum.org/docs (accessed February 2004).

Phillips, Kevin. 1999. *The Cousins' Wars: Religion, Politics, and the Triumph of Anglo-America.* New York: Basic.

Ragsdale, Lyn. 1996. *Vital Statistics on the Presidency.* Washington, DC: Congressional Quarterly.

———. 1998. *Vital Statistics on the Presidency,* rev. ed. Washington, DC: Congressional Quarterly.

Roe v. Wade, 410 U.S. 113, S.Ct. 705,35 L.Ed.2d 147 (1973).

Sherman, Mike. 2003. "Moore Appeal Defeated." *Montgomery Advertiser* (July 2), State and Government section.

Smith, Tom W. 1987. "Classifying Protestant Denominations: GSS Methodological Report No. 43," rev. ed. Storrs, CT: Roper Center for Public Opinion Research, University of Connecticut (original report published 1986 and revised in 1987).

"South: States Go Solidly to the G.O.P. with a Big Exception." 2000. *New York Times* (November 8): B8.

Stanley, Harold W., and Richard G. Niemi. 2001a. "Party Coalitions in Transition: Partisanship and Group Support, 1952–1996." In Richard Niemi and Herbert Weisberg, eds. *Controversies in Voting Behavior,* 4th ed. Washington, DC: CQ.

Stanley, Harold W., and Richard G. Niemi. 2001b. *Vital Statistics on American Politics.* Washington, DC: CQ.

U. S. Census Bureau. 2003. Home page, http://www.census.gov/prod/www/religion.htm (accessed July 2003).

Wald, Kenneth D. 2003. *Religion and Politics in the United States.* Lanham, MD: Rowman and Littlefield.

Wald, Kenneth D., and Corwin E. Smidt. 1993. "Measurement Strategies in the Study of Religion and Politics." In David Leege and Lyman Kellstedt, eds. *Rediscovering the Religious Factor in American Politics.* Armonk, NY: M. E. Sharpe.

The World Almanac and Book of Facts. 2004. New York: World Almanac Books.

5

Political Office Holding

The conservative Christians who compose the religious right have become an important part of the Republican party. Although their direct electoral success has largely been limited to local and state offices, they have had a strong and interesting influence on both state and national candidates and office holders, and they have clearly had an important role in including moral issues in contemporary political debates. To appreciate the nature and importance of their influence on national party leaders, we must first understand the conflicting pressures upon the religious right regarding political participation. In this chapter, we will examine the grassroots beginnings of conservative Christian activism, its foray into national politics, and its refocusing on state and local politics. We look for reasons for entry into the national arena and the reasons for this group's lack of national electoral success. We discuss the levels of their success in two state Republican parties (South Carolina and Texas), and we close with the relationship of President George W. Bush with the religious right.

Reasons for Expansion

There are social, institutional, and ideological reasons for the start of the religious right's expansion into political activism in the 1970s. Kenneth Wald, a respected scholar of religion and politics, found three types of pressures driving the new political activism of the religious right. He categorized those forces as social influences, institutional influences, and values. We have previously defined theologically conservative Christians in terms of their basic beliefs, including the inerrancy of the Bible as the word of God, the centrality of a personal born-again experience, and the importance of evangelistic outreach to others. Those creedal characteristics have persisted from before the 1940s, but the social and demographic characteristics of this group have changed over the years.

With regard to the social pressures presented by Wald, the conservative Christians of the 1970s and later were more educated, were more urban, and had a higher socioeconomic position than their predecessors in the 1940s and 1950s. Rural and small-town America remains a stronghold for fundamentalist beliefs, but a large number of adherents to these beliefs have moved to the cities and have also gotten higher-paying jobs and joined the middle class. In the 1970s and thereafter, middle-class conservative Christians had more resources in terms of time and money, as well as improved skills in communication and organization, than their antecedents had. And the greater wealth of the new generations gave them a new interest in the politics of low taxation and limited government. As opposed to the Democratic party identification and the relative political inaction of earlier southern conservative Christians, the interests of this "New Christian Right" led them to greater involvement in politics and to a greater identification with the Republican party.

Wald also identified institutional pressures toward political activity. The expansion of "electronic" churches, the rise of so-called super churches (like Jerry Falwell's Thomas Road Baptist Church in Lynchburg, Virginia, and John Hagee's Cornerstone Church in San Antonio, Texas), and the expansion of member services among the more typical local churches have provided institutional support for increased political activism from Christian conservatives. "Electronic" churches refer to the audiences that identify with television and radio evangelism such as the *700 Club* and the PTL network. It is difficult to provide an exact count, but in the 1990s, there were more than 250 religious television stations, more than 1,600 full-time religious radio stations, and more than 20 religious cable networks

(Wald 2003). Super churches, with over 15,000 members, have their own radio, television, and videotape programs. In terms of political mobilization, these stations and programs provided important communication and outreach capabilities.

The size of the electronic churches also brought conservative Christian leaders into potential conflict with the Federal Communications Commission, which at one point was rumored to be considering limiting the access of religious groups to the public airways (Wald 2003). Similarly, expanded social services such as church-provided education, day care, and counseling brought church members into contact with government regulation in areas such as teacher certification, curriculum control, desegregation mandates, and challenges to the churches' tax exempt status. Conflicts arose in local communities over such issues as zoning regulations and the use of public arenas for religious meetings. One result was a series of clashes that pitted the government's interest in regulating social services against the churches' claims to immunity under the First Amendment and the right of free exercise of religion (Wald 2003). These clashes of interest between governments and religious organizations also provided topics for discussion on the churches' expanded communications networks and occasions for mobilization for political activism.

The third source of pressure for fundamentalists to mobilize was their strong position against what was seen as the decay of public morality and the erosion of traditional values. Until the 1970s, the theology of southern evangelicals was seen as the source of their focus on personal salvation through a belief in Jesus and a born-again experience and their lack of concern for the doings of the temporal world. Modern mainline churches may have sought to reform the world as part of their social theology, but earlier conservative Christians adhered to a premillennial eschatology and did not focus on social reform. Nineteenth-century conservative Christians in the north were involved in political issues concerning the abolition of slavery and the prohibition of alcoholic beverages. In the south, however, those earlier Christian conservatives either focused on personal sin and salvation or found biblical defenses for slavery and the status quo ante (Phillips 1999). The focus on personal, rather than social, salvation persisted in the South until after World War II, and it still remains a major theme for many conservative Christians.

In the 1970s and 1980s, however, many conservative Christians began to exercise their organizational and communication skills in political conflicts over such moral issues as liquor licensing, sex education, and what was seen as government support for pornography in the form of Supreme Court decisions on free speech. In short, Christian conservative leaders were outraged at what they saw as a growing national immorality. They became interested in the sin and salvation of society, and they called on their increasingly affluent constituency, expanded organizations, and enhanced communications to counter these threats to traditional values (Wald 2003).

From Otherworldliness to Political Activism

The transformation of Jerry Falwell from otherworldliness to political engagement illustrates the shift in the religious right from an emphasis on personal to social salvation. In the 1960s when liberal clergy were joining antiwar protests and lobbying for civil rights, Falwell argued that churches should focus on transforming individuals through the saving power of Jesus instead of on reforming institutions. But in the 1970s, Falwell's view of the United States came to include rising divorce rates, gay "rights," the spread of pornography, public schools without public prayers, and the Supreme Court's support of abortion in *Roe v. Wade*. Falwell proclaimed that his earlier statements were "false prophecy" and began to work with conservative political activists to form a new national organization, the Moral Majority (Baranowski 1989, 135–136). Falwell declared, "I never thought the government would go so far afield, I never thought the politicians would become so unworthy, I never thought the courts would go so nuts on the left" (quoted in Blaker 2003, 178).

With the advantage of hindsight, we can now see that the "New Christian Right" experienced three waves of political mobilization. With newfound resources and skills, Christian conservatives first experienced some local successes in grassroots political activism; next expanded to national politics, with mixed results; and most recently have turned to local and state activities, including restructuring county and state Republican parties.

Starting at the Grassroots

Kenneth Wald traced this history, beginning in the 1970s with a series of uncoordinated local reactions against policies that included a gay rights referendum in Florida, public school textbooks in West Virginia, and the near-adoption of the Equal Rights Amendment to the U.S. Constitution.

In a mining valley of West Virginia, the wife of a fundamentalist minister led protests against the English textbooks in the local public schools; she charged that they were disrespectful of authority and religion.

In Dade County, Florida, a new organization called Save Our Children arose against a county ordinance prohibiting discrimination on the basis of sexual orientation. The ordinance was voted down in a popular referendum.

The proposed Equal Rights Amendment to the Constitution stirred Phyllis Schlafly to form Stop-ERA. The amendment ultimately died three states short of ratification.

In each case, evangelical Protestants banded together in defense of traditional values and against what they saw as a growing immorality. These grassroots political activists did not always get everything they wanted, but they demonstrated that conservative Christians could have political influence when they worked together (Wald 2003).

Expanding to National Politics

In the 1980s, various leaders sought to build on grassroots political successes and on the broader effort focused on defeating the Equal Rights Amendment. Four political activists with little previous evangelical involvement, and Jerry Falwell, who had little previous political activism, stood out in the effort to build a bridge between political conservatism and religious conservatism at the national level. Howard Phillips of the Conservative Caucus, John "Terry" Dolan of the National Conservative Political Action Committee, Paul Weyrich of the National Committee for the Survival of a Free Congress, and Richard Viguerie, who was a major fundraiser, hoped to enlist Christian conservative activism against liberal gun control policies, nonrestrictive abortion laws, compulsory unionization, and defense cutbacks (Wald 2003).

The major conservative Christian figure working early to bridge conservative religion and conservative politics was Jerry Falwell, founder of the Moral Majority. A conservative Christian organization based in the Bible Baptist Fellowship, the Moral Majority sought to be a national organization with members and chapters in every state.

Moral Majority chapters encouraged church members to register to vote and to support conservative candidates (Wald 2003). The Moral Majority mobilized opposition to pari-mutuel betting in Virginia, and it had early successes in that heavily Protestant state, where white evangelicals made up about 25 percent of the state's population (Rozell and Wilcox 2003).

The Moral Majority shared a common moralistic agenda with other large organizations such as the Religious Roundtable and the National Christian Action Coalition, and it shared a common interest with other organizations in mobilizing conservative Christians to political action. Nonetheless, when these organizations moved into the national political arena, they had only limited success. They fostered a strong presence in the growing state Republican parties in the south, but at the end of the 1980s, the religious right had made little headway in getting its members elected to Congress. Table 5.1 provides information on the religious affiliation of U.S. Representatives when the 101st Congress was seated in January 1989. Like other data from this time, this historical congressional data is hampered by an inadequate categorization of religious denominations. Nonetheless, in the ten years of efforts from 1979 to 1989, there had been no change in the number of Baptists in the House, despite an 8.1 percent decrease in the number of members affiliated with mainline religions. Some observers and participants concluded that conservative Christians had accomplished little in the way of concrete electoral results in the Congress by the end of the 1980s.

In the U.S. Senate, the picture was little different. In the ten years from the 96th Congress to the 101st Congress, the Senate had lost two Democratic Baptists and gained three Republican Baptists for a 9.1 percent gain, which was a better showing than the mainline Protestants, who lost another 12.5 percent during that period. Table 5.2 provides information on the religious affiliation of the 100 senators who made up the Senate in 1989, as well as percentage changes from 1979 to 1990.

The Republican Party did provide symbolic results for the religious right despite the conservative Christians' modest electoral successes at the national level. Republicans opened the 1984 convention with a prayer by Texas evangelist James Robison and closed it with Jerry Falwell's benediction, which referred to the nominees as "God's instruments in rebuilding America" (Wald 2003, 211).

Despite symbolic gains and continued efforts in the 1980s, the religious right not only had little to show in terms of national election gains, but, more to the point, it also had not made any national leg-

TABLE 5.1   Religious Affiliations of U.S. House of Representatives and
Percentage Changes from 96th Congress (1979–1980) to 101st Congress
(1989–1990)

Year Seated	House: 101st Congress, 1989–1990			Percentage Change, 1979–1989		
Party	Democrat	Republican	Total	Democrat	Republican	Total
Fundamentalist Protestants						
Baptist	33	10	43	0.0	0.0	0.0
Mainline Protestants						
Episcopalian	22	21	43	–24.1	–4.5	–15.7
Methodist	38	25	63	18.8	–3.8	8.6
Presbyterian	16	26	42	–36.0	–3.7	–19.2
Mainline Subtotal	76	72	148	–11.6	–4.0	–8.1
Catholic	81	39	120	–12.9	69.6	3.4
Jewish	26	5	31	44.4	0.0	34.8
All Other	44	49	93	–6.4	8.9	1.1
Totals	260	175	435	–6.1	10.8	0.0

Source: Ornstein, Norman J., Thomas E. Mann, and Michael J. Malbin.
2002. *Vital Statistics on Congress 2001–2002.* Washington, DC: AEI.

islative breakthroughs on an antiabortion law, tuition tax credits, or
voluntary school prayer (Baranowski 1989, 138).

The one bright spot for the conservative Christians was their support for Ronald Reagan as president; however, it now appears that the
leaders of the religious right may have initially claimed more credit
for Reagan's election than they were due. In 1980, most of the religious right leadership supported Republican candidate Ronald Reagan, but many of the rank and file voted for born-again Democrat
Jimmy Carter in his losing bid for a second term. In 1984, the leadership and rank and file of the Christian right were closer together,
for the religious right came out solidly behind Republican Reagan in
his bid for a second term. Conservative Christians in 1984 were part
of a majority that gave Reagan 59 percent of the popular vote.

TABLE 5.2   Religious Affiliation of U.S. Senate and Percentage Changes
from 96th Congress (1979–1980) to 101st Congress (1989–1990)

Year Seated	Sentate: 101st Congress, 1989–1990			Percentage Change, 1979–1989		
Party	Democrat	Republican	Total	Democrat	Republican	Total
Fundamentalist Protestants						
Baptist	4	8	12	-33.3	60.0	9.1
Mainline Protestants						
Episcopalian	7	13	20	40.0	8.3	17.6
Methodist	9	4	13	–30.8	–33.3	–31.6
Presbyterian	7	2	9	–30.0	0.0	–25.0
Mainline Subtotal	23	19	42	–17.9	–5.0	–12.5
Catholic	12	7	19	33.3	75.0	46.2
Jewish	5	3	8	0.0	50.0	14.3
All Other	11	8	19	0.0	–20.0	–9.5
Totals	55	45	100	–6.8	9.8	

Source: Ornstein, Norman J., Thomas E. Mann, and Michael J. Malbin. 2002. *Vital Statistics on Congress 2001–2002.* Washington, DC: AEI.

The Religious Right and the Iowa Caucuses

In 1988, Iowa provided an important testing ground for the religious right. In that year, some of the Christian right supported the presidential candidacy of Pat Robertson, but more did not. Donald Racheter, Lyman Kellstedt, and John Green (2003) called Iowa the Crucible of the Christian Right. In their view, religious conservatives began organizing in Iowa in the mid-1970s over the right-to-life issue of abortion. By the 1980s, both the Moral Majority and Christian Voice organizations were active in Iowa, and they were soon joined by the Freedom Council, headed by Pat Robertson. The religious base of the Moral Majority was fundamentalist Baptists, and that of the Freedom Council was charismatics and Pentecostals (Racheter, Kellstedt, and Green 2003, 123–124). Although Iowa has a population of only 2.8 million people, the Glenmary Research Center found, in its 1990 census of churches and church membership, 4,560 active churches in Iowa. They also calculated that these churches had an estimated 1.6 million adherents, a category that includes both members and an estimate of their children. In short, 60 percent of Iowa's total population were adherents of a religious denomination. This census also found 131 Assembly of God churches, 28 International Foursquare Gospel churches, and 12 Church of God of Prophecy churches in Iowa at the end of the 1980s (Bradley, Green, Lynn, Jones, and McNeil 1992). Thus, the potential existed for an important political mobilization of conservative Christians in Iowa in 1988, and Pat Robertson tried to bring this about. Indeed, with satellite transmission capability, his Christian Broadcasting Network provided a technologically advanced and well-financed base (Linenthal 1989, 351–352).

Despite these advantages, Robertson's bid for the Republican party's presidential nomination quickly lost momentum. The Iowa caucuses of 1988 were the high point of the Robertson campaign. Robertson placed second there in his competition with George H. W. Bush and Bob Dole for the Republican nomination for president, but he never did so well again in subsequent primaries and caucuses. The Republicans in Iowa did not prove to be representative of those in the nation as a whole. Despite Robertson's advantage gained from his Christian Broadcasting Network, George H. W. Bush swept the Super Tuesday Republican primaries, indicating that Bush had greater appeal among the 242 million Americans who lived outside of Iowa in 1988. During the presidential campaign, Bush appealed to conservative Christians, emphasizing profamily themes, and on election day, he garnered 53 percent of the fundamentalist vote identified in this project and 53 percent of the national vote overall, versus 46 percent for Democratic candidate Michael Dukakis.

Looking back on efforts and results in national policy and for national office holders, some observers saw the Robertson failure as indicative of broader problems. Steve Bruce (1988) predicted the end of the religious right or New Christian Right as a political force. Bruce acknowledged that efforts to mobilize Christian conservatives would continue, but he concluded that, as a social and political movement, it was dead. Despite some efforts to represent a "shared Judeo-Christian tradition," the religious right had failed to expand its base to include religious conservatives of other faiths such as conservative Catholics, Mormons, and Jews. To Bruce, that failure meant that the religious right could not have a lasting political impact on American society (Bruce 1988, 126–127).

Constraints against National Expansion

Kenneth Wald (2003) carefully analyzed the forces that have limited the reach of the religious right, and he drew a different conclusion. He cited five major constraints on the conservative Christian political movement: cultural barriers, the political diversity of American religion, evangelical sectarianism, the Republican electoral dilemma, and the movement's political style. Each area was a source of constraint on the political activism of the religious right, but Wald saw them as marking limits rather than an end for the active political engagement of the New Christian Right.

First, American political culture typically celebrates individualism and is generally skeptical of government as a moral leader, which tends to put conservative Christian political candidates at a disadvantage. Second, the world of American religion is very diverse, featuring charismatics, evangelicals, fundamentalists, neoevangelicals (like the Billy Graham ministry), mainline Protestants, Catholics, and a host of non-Christian faiths. If the religious right could attract support from outside of its fundamentalist base, it would be an extraordinarily powerful political group. But the religious right does not attract many followers outside of the evangelical Protestant denominations. Consequently, its political power remains limited. Third, even within these conservative Christian denominations, many people resist the appeals of religious right organizations that campaign in their names. Surveys of these denominations found that barely a majority had heard of the Christian right and only about one-third claimed to support it (Rothenberg and Newport 1984; Wilcox 1989; and Smith 2000, cited in Wald 2003).

Fourth, as a new major force within the Republican party, the religious right brings a conservative social agenda and an intensity of belief that can clash with the economic conservatism of party regulars. Reagan administration Republicans were staunch economic conservatives, but some of them took an almost Libertarian view against using government for social control. The religious right, on the other hand, wants to use government to regulate entertainment, set standards for sex education, and generally to bring individuals and families under the moral authority of church and "right-thinking" government. Fifth, the religious right typically takes a purist stance in political campaigning. Their position on an issue is seen as the will of God, and any opposition is seen a rebellion against God's authority. This purist stance may be typical of true believers, but compromising in order to obtain political allies becomes difficult for those who take this position (Wald 2003, 224–235).

Wald, however, concludes that these negative factors did not end the influence of the religious right because it had transformed itself during the 1990s. Its leaders had adopted mainstream language, its organizations went beyond televangelism and direct-mail lobbies to include well-established membership organizations, and it refocused its political attention on state and local politics. This next generation of the religious right built an infrastructure within state Republican parties and created a network of organizations with a relatively broad base in the population.

Typical of these next-generation organizations was the Christian Coalition. Pat Robertson had founded the Christian Broadcasting Network (CBN) in 1961 (the same year he was ordained as a Southern Baptist minister), and his *700 Club* was nationally syndicated in 1972. The format of the *700 Club* resembled that of secular television programs, and its content blended news with prayer and Christian social commentary (Linenthal 1989, 351). After his unsuccessful presidential bid in 1988, Robertson founded the Christian Coalition, asserting that the real battles of concern to Christians were in neighborhoods, school boards, city councils, and state legislatures. He then hired Ralph Reed, a veteran of conservative political campaigns, as the organization's executive secretary (Wald 2003, 205–213). Robertson's social engagement with the nation, then, ranged from the early "spiritual television" of CBN, to the blend of prayer and social commentary of *The 700 Club*, and ultimately to the clearly politically focused Christian Coalition.

Under Reed's leadership, the Christian Coalition could claim 1.6 million members in more than 1,600 local chapters, yet the presidential election of 1992 proved to be disappointing to them. The Christian Coalition announced that it was sending out 40 million voter guides comparing the three presidential candidates on issues such as abortion, prayer in school, and homosexual rights (*New York Times,* October 31, 1992, I1). Nonetheless, Bill Clinton, the former governor of Arkansas and a candidate who was liberal on all the issues the conservatives valued, won the general election. Clinton won in 1992 with 43 percent of the popular vote, and surveys indicate that he garnered 44 percent of the votes cast by the fundamentalist denominations discussed in this book (data from National Election Studies 2003a and 2003b). At the national level, there appeared to have been some differences in what the leadership of the New Christian Right supported and how the rank and file voted.

Refocusing on States and Localities

In the 1990s, the religious right largely redirected its political efforts at the state and local levels, and at those levels, they experienced a modest amount of success with candidates and policies. Colorado provides an interesting case study of the gap between local and national voting of the religious right in 1992.

Conservative Christians in Colorado gained national attention by promoting a ballot initiative called Amendment 2, which called for amending the state constitution to prohibit any gay rights laws, including those already passed in the liberal areas of Aspen, Boulder, and Denver. The center of the Amendment 2 promotion was Colorado Springs, the home of several evangelical Christian organizations, including Focus on the Family led by Dr. James Dobson. The antigay amendment passed with 53.4 percent approval, but the state's voters went on to give Colorado's electoral votes to Democratic candidate Bill Clinton. Amendment 2 was later ruled unconstitutional by the U.S. Supreme Court (Zwier 2003, 187–188), but the simultaneous approval of the antigay amendment and of Clinton, who had the support of gay and lesbian organizations, suggests both the influence of Christian organizations at the local level and their less immediate influence at the national level.

In other state and local elections, candidates endorsed by the religious right fared better than President Bush did in 1992. People for the American Way, a watchdog organization founded by television producer Norman Lear, announced that conservative Christian candidates won about 40 percent of the 500 elections monitored by that organization. They cited gains in Iowa, Kansas, Florida, Texas, and Oregon. Rex Reed, then executive secretary of the Christian Coalition, agreed with those numbers, and he added that the Christian right had gained big victories on school boards and in state legislatures (*New York Times*, November 21, 1992, I1).

Supporting the Republican Contract with America

Religious right organizations were especially active in the midterm elections of 1994. Newt Gingrich and House Republicans had proposed a "Contract with America" calling for welfare reform, family tax relief, and term limits, and organizations like the Traditional Values Coalition and the Christian Coalition made major efforts to drum up support for new Republican candidates. The Christian Coalition alone handed out about 33 million voter guides and manned a large network of phone banks shortly before the election. The results were impressive. Voter turnout appears to have been high among conservatives, and in many Republican victories, observers credited the 1994 mobilization to two key constituencies: gun owners and Christian conservatives (Wald 2003, 239). In the U.S. Senate, the 1994 election resulted in a body of forty-seven Democrats and fifty-three Republicans, including seven who were Baptists. Seventy-three Republican freshmen were elected to the House of Representatives, and Republicans had 230 members of the House, versus 204 for the Democrats. The Republican party took control of both the House and Senate for the first time since 1954. The Republican Congressional landslide of 1994 may have had many reasons, but the efforts of the religious right were clearly among them.

The Christian Coalition announced its own Contract with the American Family on the steps of the U.S. Capitol in mid-1995. This "contract" included the secular issues of lowering taxes, dismantling welfare programs, and increasing penalties for convicted criminals, but its major focus was on family issues such as restricting abortion, pornography, and obscene art and promoting school prayer and laws shielding Christian schools and homeschoolers from state regulation (Wald 2003, 216).

The original Republican Contract with America quickly passed the House. But it became bogged down in the Senate and produced few substantive laws; however, its focus on welfare clearly played a role in the 1996 passage of the Personal Responsibility and Work Opportunity Reconciliation Act. Part of Public Law 104–193, this Act made major changes in the sixty-year-old system of federal welfare entitlements, including eliminating Aid to Families with Dependent Children and replacing it with the work-related Temporary Assistance to Needy Families (Rahm 2004, 82). This 1996 welfare reform legislation also included a little-noticed provision sponsored by Republican senator John Ashcroft of Missouri. The provision allowed faith-based organizations to receive federal tax money for providing various services to the needy without divesting their programs of religious content (Utter and Storey 2001, 55).

The Republican Congress elected in 1994 produced some legislation that the religious right could view as policy successes in 1996. Senator Ashcroft's inclusion of faith-based organizations in the restructuring of the national welfare system could be seen as a victory. And the profamily and antigay stance of conservative Christians coincided with the priorities of the congressional conservatives who passed the Defense of Marriage Act of 1996 (P.L. 104–199). The marriage legislation amended federal judicial code to specify that no state shall be required to recognize any marriage between persons of the same sex under the laws of another jurisdiction. On the other hand, this act has yet to be challenged in the courts, and many of the issues highlighted in the Contract with the American Family resulted in little or no immediate policy change.

Presidential Disappointments

The 1994 Republican congressional successes with the Contract with America encouraged the religious right and counteracted their growing disappointment with the first term of Bill Clinton, but the 1996 presidential campaign held little but disappointments for politically active conservative Christians. In September of 1996, the Christian Coalition convened a national conference in Washington, D.C., and invited candidates to speak with them. Ross Perot appeared but refused to give his views on abortion, school prayer, and same-sex marriage (*New York Times,* September 14, 1996, I9). The Republican vice presidential candidate, Jack Kemp, was a featured speaker and presented a strong antiabortion message. Bob Dole made a surprise appearance and was cheered by the rank and file, but Pat Robertson said that it would take a "miracle from Almighty God" for Dole to win the presidency. Robertson said that Dole could win only if he would take moral issues (like those Perot would not address) and make them the core of his campaign (*New York Times,* September 15, 1996, I38). Dole, however, refused to do so. Indeed, Dole focused on Clinton's untrustworthiness instead of on the volatile (and potentially divisive) social issues that Republican strategists had earlier thought could bring down Clinton. By October, those issues had essentially disappeared from the Dole campaign (*New York Times,* October 9, 1996, D17).

The reelection of President Bill Clinton in 1996 and the Senate's failure in 1999 to convict him on the impeachment articles voted by the House of Representatives were sources of disappointment to leaders of the religious right. The fundamentalist voters identified in this book gave Clinton a plurality of 48 percent, Dole 41 percent, and Perot 10 percent in the 1996 presidential election. And 76 percent of these denominational respondents said they went to the polls in 1996. That plurality, however, included the votes of fundamentalist

African-Americans, who voted overwhelmingly for Clinton. When we focus exclusively on white Christian fundamentalists, a different picture emerges. Corwin Smidt and James Penning (2003) used exit polls in Michigan to estimate that white Christian conservatives voted overwhelmingly for Dole (67 percent) and not Clinton (only 28 percent) in 1996 when all other Michigan voters gave Clinton a majority and the state's electoral votes (Smidt and Penning 2003, 112). The tendency of white Christian conservatives to support Republican candidates is well documented, but Dole virtually avoided the social conservative issues that energize the religious right. At any rate, President Clinton was reelected in 1996 and spent much of his second term successfully defending himself against impeachment charges.

Paul Weyrich (1999), a spokesman for the Christian right, expressed his disappointment with the presidential election of 1996. Weyrich was a shrewd political analyst who had worked to energize Protestant fundamentalists and Catholic conservatives for conservative political causes. He was the author of the phrase, *the moral majority* (Utter and Storey 2001, 123). For Weyrich, the public's continuing support for Clinton even after the president's sexual misbehavior became widely known meant that the battle for a moral America had been lost. If the public accepted decadent behavior by an American president, then Weyrich concluded that Christians should abandon politics, retreat from the world, and construct their own counterculture (Weyrich 1999, cited in Wald 2003).

Joining the War against Public Immorality

Some conservative Christians did retreat from political activism, but others did not. Many moved their efforts from national organizations and strategies to state and local ones. Others changed their emphasis from elections to influencing social policy and American culture. Paul Weyrich was one of these who changed emphasis. He continued as president of the conservative Free Congress foundation until 2002, when he became chairman and chief executive officer and remained an active contributor. As indicated by the foundation's description of itself, rather than retreating completely from the national level, it emphasized its social mission to oppose moral decay:

> Free Congress Foundation is politically conservative, but it is more than that: it is also culturally conservative. Most think tanks talk about

tax rates or the environment or welfare policy and occasionally we do also. But our main focus is on the Culture War. Will America return to the culture that made it great, our traditional, Judeo-Christian, Western culture? Or will we continue the long slide into the cultural and moral decay of political correctness? If we do, America, once the greatest nation on earth, will become no less than a third world country. (Free Congress Foundation 2004)

The political activism of many in the religious right did change in the late 1990s. Some were disenchanted with what had not been accomplished in terms of school prayer, abortion restrictions, and other conservative social issues. But almost all shared a larger dissatisfaction with what was seen as public immorality in the form of abortion, homosexuality, drugs, and debauched movies and television. And some members of the religious right chose to focus their political activities at the state and local levels.

In the South, the disenchantment of the religious right with the liberal policies of the Democratic party in Washington was an intimate and important part of the southern conservative move to the Republican party. The rebirth of the Republican party in the solidly Democratic south provided many opportunities for conservative Christians to assume leadership roles, and they took advantage of these opportunities. The story of the growth of the Christian right in the Republican party can be grasped by looking at their efforts and successes in South Carolina and in Texas.

Religion and Politics in South Carolina

In South Carolina, the revitalization of the Republican party in the 1970s at first featured a variety of groups. The early state-level Republicans were primarily from mainline Protestant churches, with a few Southern Baptists. But more conservative religious groups soon joined the Republican party and became important by taking advantage of the openness of the skeletal Republican party to well-organized forces. By 1976, independent Baptists under the aegis of Bob Jones University (BJU) had captured the county GOP organization in Greenville, a stronghold of the growing party. What was called the Bob Jones Contingent was soon largely integrated into the state GOP, with party regulars cultivating the new activists and mediating intraparty disputes. These independent Baptists in the BJU group largely eroded the base upon which Jerry Falwell's Moral Majority depended, and it did not become a strong political force in the state (Vinson and Guth 2003, 21–24).

In 1987, however, Pat Robertson's Christian Coalition infiltrated precinct meetings and almost captured the South Carolina state convention. Robertson's key constituency was made up of charismatic and Pentecostal Protestants, who did not make up a large portion of the South Carolina population but who were well organized. However, in 1988 (when Robertson placed second in the Iowa caucus for the Republican nomination for president), a large fraction of conservative Christians in the state (including most Southern Baptists) voted for George Bush. Christian Coalition leaders skirmished with Republican party regulars over the next few years, but the group was weakened in 1997 when Ralph Reed left the Coalition to form his own political consulting firm. Vinson and Guth (2003) concluded that the Christian Coalition had virtually disintegrated in South Carolina by 2002. The numbers of people associated with selected fundamentalist and mainline denominations in South Carolina in 2000 appear in Table 5.3.

In sum, although the conservative Christian movement in South Carolina was larger than just the Christian Coalition, it still did not dominate the state GOP. Nonetheless, conservative Christians remained a major force within the state Republican party and an essential part of any winning election coalition. Although Christian conservatives have not made much headway in obtaining desired policy changes, they have installed some of their people in party leadership positions. And since their entry into South Carolina politics, few, if any, candidates can avoid at least talking about family and moral issues in their campaigns (Vinson and Guth 2003, 24–38).

Religion and Politics in Texas

In their analysis of politics and religion in Texas, James Lamare, Jerry Polinard, and Robert Wrinkle found that religion has often been at the foundation of Texas politics, even before the rise of the New Christian Right. The state constitution's protection of religious freedom comes with a proreligious touch. Article I, Section 4 of the Texas Constitution prohibits using any religious test to qualify for public office as long as the candidate acknowledges "the existence of a supreme being." A U.S. Supreme Court decision nullified this provision decades ago, but it still is there, and it still provides a glimpse at

TABLE 5.3 Membership of Selected Fundamentalist and Mainline Denominations in South Carolina, 2000

Denomination	Number of Churches	Number of Adherents	Percent of State Total Population
American Baptist Association	9	832	—
Assemblies of God	112	18,219	—
Church of God (Anderson)	45	2,856	0.1
Church of God (Cleveland)	297	56,612	1.4
Church of God of Prophecy	130	5,763	0.1
Church of the Nazarene	64	12,824	0.3
Churches of Christ	118	13,091	0.3
International Four-Square Gospel	11	11,036	—
Lutheran—Missouri Synod	16	3,440	0.1
Pentecostal Holiness Church	249	33,820	0.8
Presbyterian Church in America	98	23,313	0.6
Southern Baptist Convention	1,878	928,341	23.1
Episcopal Church	138	52,486	1.3
Evangelical Lutheran Church in America	167	61,380	1.5
Presbyterian Church (USA)	325	103,883	2.6
United Methodist Church	1,047	302,528	7.5
All Reported South Carolina Denominations	5,522	1,908,638	47.6

Source: Jones, Dale E., Sherri Doty, Clifford Grammich, James E. Horsch, Richard Houseal, Mac Lynn, John P. Marcum, Kenneth M. Sanchagrin, and Richard H. Taylor. 2002. *Religious Congregations and Membership in the United States 2000: An Enumeration by Region, State, and County Based on Data Reported by 149 Religious Bodies.* Nashville, TN: Glenmary Research Center.

the infusion of religion into politics in the state (Lamare, Polinard, and Wrinkle 2003, 61).

Religion is an important part of personal and political life in Texas. Surveys have found that some 86 percent of Texans say they pray at home at least once per week, and 70 percent of Texans say that they attend religious services at least once per month, a statistic that is twice the national average and 12 percent greater than it was fifteen years ago. Texans are 60 percent Protestant (with more than one-third of those being Baptists) and 25 percent Roman Catholic (Lamare, Polinard, and Wrinkle 2003, 60–61).

TABLE 5.4   Membership of Selected Fundamentalist and Mainline Denominations in Texas, 2000

Denomination	Number of Churches	Number of Adherents	Percent of State Total Population
American Baptist Association	380	61,272	0.3
Assemblies of God	1,291	228,098	1.1
Baptist Missionary Association	473	123,198	0.6
Church of God (Anderson)	87	4,669	—
Church of God (Cleveland)	230	38,259	0.2
Church of God of Prophecy	84	2,906	—
Church of the Nazarene	323	50,528	0.2
Churches of Christ	2,188	377,264	1.8
International Four-square Gospel	94	12,501	0.1
Lutheran—Missouri Synod	346	140,106	0.7
Pentecostal Church of God	136	11,592	0.1
Pentecostal Holiness Church	119	10,265	—
Southern Baptist Convention	4,973	3,519,459	16.9
Episcopal Church	427	177,910	0.9
Evangelical Lutheran Church in America	412	155,019	0.7
Presbyterian Church (USA)	549	180,315	0.9
United Methodist Church	2,110	1,022,342	4.9
All Reported Texas Denominations	18,466	11,573,549	55.5

Source: Jones, Dale E., Sherri Doty, Clifford Grammich, James E. Horsch, Richard Houseal, Mac Lynn, John P. Marcum, Kenneth M. Sanchagrin, and Richard H. Taylor. 2002. *Religious Congregations and Membership in the United States 2000: An Enumeration by Region, State, and County Based on Data Reported by 149 Religious Bodies.* Nashville, TN: Glenmary Research Center.

Table 5.4 provides a look at the diversity and spread of organized religion in Texas. It reflects the year 2000's enumeration of religious congregations and members by the Glenmary Research Center, which compiles this information from reports from 149 religious bodies. The table does not include many independent congregations or other denominations that chose not to report their statistics in 2000. Yet it provides a view of organized religion in Texas that tends to support the Texas poll information from Lamare, Polinard, and Wrinkle. The 2000 enumeration found more than 18,000 churches in

107 reporting denominations. With a population of more than 20 million, Texas can count more than 55 percent of that population as adherents of a reporting denomination. The dominance of the Southern Baptist Convention is clear, for it can count almost 17 percent of the state's population as adherents. There are a variety of fundamentalist and Pentecostal churches, and except for the United Methodist Church, mainline churches in Texas are eclipsed (at least in membership) by both the Churches of Christ and the Southern Baptists. Organized religion is an important part of Texas society, and it is not surprising that the Christian right found Texas ripe for recruitment and mobilization.

Conservative Christians in Texas have found many religiously oriented political organizations to join. By the late 1970s, the Moral Majority and Religious Roundtable were formed in Texas. There is little evidence that they played a direct role in the state's political parties or elections then; however, that would soon change. By the late 1980s, conservative religious Texans were reacting to what was seen as moral decay (and government-sponsored moral decay, at least insofar as their perspective on abortion and pornography issues were concerned). This beginning of the culture war in Texas fomented a host of new conservative Christian organizations. Lamare, Polinard, and Wrinkle (2003, 63) found five organizations to be foremost among these. They were Texas Eagle Forum (an affiliate of Phyllis Schlafly's Eagle Forum); Concerned Women for America of Texas; two major antiabortion organizations (American Family Association of Texas and Texans United for Life); and the Texas Christian Coalition, the largest and politically most powerful of the five.

As we saw in South Carolina, the Christian right also found a political home in the growing Republican party of Texas by joining and organizing at the precinct level. The party's ranks had begun to swell as Republicans from other states migrated to Texas and as conservative Texans who once filled the Democratic party defected from what they saw as a party drifting to the left. But it was the Christian right that became the core of the state Republican party as it began to win statewide elections in the 1980s and 1990s. The Texas Christian Coalition took advantage of the party rules by voting in the primary elections and then attending the precinct conventions that elected precinct chairs and county delegates. The county conventions then selected delegates to the state party convention. With the support of Christian activists in 1994, Tom Pauken unseated the more moderate Fred Meyer as state party chair, even though Pauken was not the choice of Republican gubernatorial candidate George W. Bush. In

1997, Susan Weddington, a Sunday school teacher, former Democrat, and active participant in the Christian right, succeeded Pauken as state party chair (Lamare, Polinard, and Wrinkle 2003, 67–69). Thus, the burgeoning Republican Party in Texas consisted of economic or business conservatives, who were influential nationally, and Christian conservatives, whose focus was often more local and who had largely taken charge of the party platform.

The 2002 State Republican party platform reflected the religious conservatism of the Christian right. It contained some economically conservative statements, but it also made declarations regarding issues of special concern to conservative Christians:

> (1) Abortion: "We believe that human life is sacred because each person is created in the image of God, that life begins at the moment of conception and ends at the point of natural death, and that all innocent human life must be protected."
>
> (2) Same-sex marriage and family values: "We believe that traditional marriage is a legal and moral commitment between a man and a woman. We recognize that the family is the foundational unit of a healthy society and consists of those related by blood, [heterosexual] marriage, or adoption. The family is responsible for its own welfare, education, moral training, conduct, and property."
>
> (3) Public, private, and religious schooling: "We believe that a well-educated population is fundamental to the continued success of our Republic; and that parents have the right, as well as the duty, to direct their children's education and to have the choice among public, private, and religious schools."
>
> (4) Homosexuality: "The Party believes that the practice of sodomy tears at the fabric of society, contributes to the breakdown of the family unit, and leads to the spread of dangerous, communicable diseases. Homosexual behavior is contrary to the fundamental, unchanging truths that have been ordained by God, recognized by our country's founders, and shared by the majority of Texans. . . . [and] The Party opposes the decriminalization of sodomy." (Texas State Republican party 2004a)

The strong socially conservative stance of the Christian right in the Texas Republican party has created a new fissure in party politics in the state. When the Democratic party dominated Texas, there was a cleavage between the economic or business conservative wing of the party and its liberal and populist wing. The conservatives dominated the political scene. Before the 1970s, Democratic business conservatives controlled party rules, distributed patronage and desirable policies, and commanded the lion's share of the money involved in campaigns and elections (Barbour et al. 2003, 858). Although the liberals could get an occasional populist governor elected, their base and resources were different from those of the conservative wing of the Texas Democratic party. But with the election of Republican governor Bill Clements in 1978, and with the conservative shift toward the Republican party during the "Reagan Revolution" of the 1980s, many Texas business conservatives changed over to the Republican party. However, their domination of the Republican party was successfully challenged by the social conservatives of the religious right.

Religious conservatives gained prominence and a large measure of control in the Texas Republican party by organizing successful grassroots efforts that began at the precinct level. In the end, they dominated the state convention and constituted at least half of the delegates to the national GOP convention in 2000 (Lamare, Polinard, and Wrinkle 2003, 69); however, they have not been able to nominate and elect their own candidates because Republican campaign contributors prefer economic conservatives over social conservatives (Barbour et al., 2003, 861).

The religious right in Texas has had only mixed success in local elections, and even its highly energized campaign to elect new members to the state board of education (SBOE) failed to reach expectations. The fifteen-member SBOE contains one member from each of fifteen geographical districts and is responsible for overall policy for the state's primary, secondary, and vocational schools, including statewide textbook approvals. Religious beliefs are an important part of an individual's decision to run for a school board—not just in Texas, but throughout the country (Deckman 2001). And the Christian right can sometimes view textbooks as the battleground between religion and secular humanism. Nonetheless, after expending much effort over ten years, the Christian right was able to win only six seats on the board, which was two short of a majority. Although the SBOE deliberations have since then become acrimonious, the board is still not under the clear control of the religious right (Lamare, Polinard, and Wrinkle 2003, 70), and such control appears likely to remain elusive for some time to come.

In the 2004 primary elections in Texas, a socially conservative Republican beat a more moderate Republican from the conservative Woodlands area north of Houston. Some parts of Texas have become so solidly Republican that winning the primary is tantamount to winning the election, and that is the case in Montgomery County and city of The Woodlands. At the time this book went to press, the winning socially conservative Republican was unopposed in the general election. Her election would keep ten Republicans on the fifteen-member board, but only five of those Republicans said that they were socially conservative. The five did not agree on all issues. Incumbent Terri Leo, a conservative from Spring, Texas, said, "We vote very differently at times on things like charter schools" (Zuniga 2004). It appeared likely that this important board would continue to be fractious and that control of it could not be taken for granted, even with ten Republican members.

George W. Bush and the Religious Right

Republicans with national ambitions have made overtures to the religious right in Texas without necessarily publicly siding with the more radical positions of the social conservatives. In the late 1990s, as Texas governor George W. Bush prepared to seek the GOP nomination for president, he hired Ralph Reed as an adviser. Reed had just left his position with the Christian Coalition to found his own political consulting firm. In another example, the defining moment for the Christian right in the 2000 campaign came when Governor Bush said in a debate that his favorite political philosopher was Jesus. After that, he gained public support from Jerry Falwell, Pat Robertson, and other leaders of the religious right (Goodstein 2000). He did this without having to take divisive stands on many of the "hot-button" issues of the socially conservative Christian right.

Gary Bauer, another national favorite of the religious right, did not handle his supporters as adroitly as Bush did. The head of the Family Research Council and an associate of Focus on the Family's James Dobson, Bauer sought to repeat Pat Robertson's campaign success in Iowa by mobilizing nondenominational evangelicals. However, others also sought the support of the Christian right in 2000, including Pat Buchanan, publisher Steve Forbes, ambassador Alan Keyes, and former vice president Dan Quayle. Bush paid his respects to the Christian right during the campaign, and he won the caucuses with 41 percent of the vote (Racheter, Kellstedt, and Green 2003, 139). But Bauer's troubles with his conservative Christian constituency did not end there.

After losing the Iowa caucuses and the New Hampshire primary, Gary Bauer dropped out of the presidential race (Meckler 2000) and gave his endorsement to John McCain as McCain headed into the

South Carolina primaries. McCain initially welcomed Bauer's support, but when some of the religious right launched some very negative ads against him, McCain struck back with a controversial speech that criticized the divisiveness of Pat Robertson and Jerry Falwell comparing them to the Reverend Al Sharpton and Louis Farrakhan. Later on the campaign bus, McCain said that he was trying to battle "the forces of evil" in the Republican party. Bauer quickly urged McCain to retract his comments, but McCain did not back away from his remarks (Heath 2000). As a consequence, Bauer, a leader among Christian conservatives, was now not only out of the race, but he was also left with his endorsement of a candidate who had attacked two of the icons of the religious right. In September, Bauer lost his position with the Family Research Center, which named a Florida lawyer to replace him.

Texas governor Bush went on to win the nomination and the 2000 presidential election. He addressed gatherings of the religious right and courted their support, but he did so without publicly promising to rectify what many Christian conservatives saw as wrongheaded government policies on moral issues. Bush's public positions on these issues did not contradict those of the religious right, but he did not promise rapid initiatives on abortion, homosexuality, religious schooling, and pornography.

At the 2002 party convention in Texas, the religious right faction of the state Republican party made a spirited effort to mandate candidates' support of the platform as a requirement for party funding for campaigns. Their method was to be the imposition of Rule 43. The proposed rule was designed to stop Republican candidates from ignoring the party platform by denying state party funds to any candidate who failed to declare whether he or she approved, disapproved, or was undecided about each plank in the platform. Rita Davis, a vocal Christian Republican from San Antonio, said, "We've been working on it ever since we took over the party." However, Davis and other Christian conservatives did not get their way. When it came to a vote on adopting the rule, there were choruses of yeas and nays. Rules chairman Tina Benkiser declared that the nays had it, and she gaveled the session quickly to a close (Bernstein 2002). Ms. Benkiser was later selected as chairman of the state Republican Party (Texas State Republican Party 2004b).

The final statement on candidate loyalty to the Texas Republican party platform contains a less draconian formulation:

> Any person filing as a Republican candidate for a public or Party office
> shall be provided a current copy of the Party platform at the time of

filing. The candidate shall be asked to read and initial each page of the platform and sign a statement affirming he/she has read the entire platform. . . . We direct the Executive Campaign Committee to strongly consider candidates' support of the Party platform when granting financial or other support (Texas State Republican party 2004a)

Rather than alienating moderate voters by adhering strictly to the policy desires of the Christian right, President Bush and other elected Republicans have been able to retain the conservatives' support seemingly without disaffecting supporters outside of the religious right. Economic conservatives can be happy with reduced taxes and increased defense, but Republican Christian conservatives can also point with pride to legislation that outlaws partial-birth abortions and curtails fetal stem cell research as well as to Senate hearings and presidential support for a proposed constitutional amendment to prohibit same-sex marriage (Hulse 2004). Within Texas, Republican governor Rick Perry, Bush's successor, sought to bridge the gap between the economic and religious wings of the party. He appointed Susan Weddington, the former state Republican party chair, as president of OneStar Foundation. One part of the foundation's role is to open the Texas Office of Faith-Based and Community Initiatives to serve as a single point of contact with similar federal and state offices (Perry 2003). President Bush and Governor Perry seem to have found a faith-based perspective on government-supported volunteerism that can please Christian conservatives without disaffecting other Republicans.

In return, members of the religious right in Texas have voiced their support for President Bush's policies. When asked about the coming war in Iraq, Harold O'Chester, pastor of Great Hills Baptist Church (of the Southern Baptist Convention), said, "Our bent is very patriotic, and we're going to back our president. I think he's a good man, a godly man." James Linderman, Texas district president of the fundamentalist Lutheran Church—Missouri Synod, said that he did not second-guess the president. He added, "President Bush doesn't tell the pastors in the Texas district how to preach, and I don't tell him how or when to go to war" (Flynn 2003).

In 2004, the Congress with which George Bush had to deal presented a fairly friendly face to the religious right. Ninety-nine of its members were likely to be members of fundamentalist denominations. There was a bit of uncertainty in that number, because some Baptists were not fundamentalists and some Presbyterians were. The religious affiliations of the 108th Congress appear in Table 5.5.

TABLE 5.5   Religious Affiliations of Members of the 108th Congress

	House			Senate			Congress
	Dem	Rep	Total	Dem	Rep	Total	Total
Fundamentalist Denominations							
Baptist	32	33	65	1	5	6	71
Christian Reformed Church		2	2				2
Christian Scientist		5	5				5
Mormon	3	9	12	1	4	5	17
Pentecostal		4	4				4
Seventh-Day Adventist	1	1	2				2
Mainline Denominations							
Christian Church	3		3				3
Disciples of Christ	1		1				1
Episcopalian	10	24	34	3	7	10	44
Lutheran	9	10	19	3	1	4	23
Methodist	16	33	49	7	5	12	61
Presbyterian	11	26	37	3	10	13	50
Other Denominations							
African Methodist Episcopal	4		4				4
Eastern Orthodox		5	5	1	1	2	7
Protestant Unspecified	12	22	34	2	2	4	38
Roman Catholic	71	53	124	14	11	25	149
Unitarian	1	1	2	1		1	3
United Church of Christ/Cong.		2	2	3	2	6	8
Unspecified Other	7		7		1	1	8

Source: Hawkings, David, and Brian Nutting, eds. 2003. CQ's *Politics in America 2004:* The 108th Congress. Washington, DC: CQ.

George W. Bush took office in January 2001, and on February 1 of that year, the Senate voted to confirm John Ashcroft as U.S. attorney general. When he was in Congress, Ashcroft had amended the Welfare Reform Act to allow government funding to go to faith-based organizations when they were providing social welfare. In addition,

Congress has passed several pieces of legislation favored by the religious right, including a ban on partial-birth abortions.

Conclusion

The electoral successes of the religious right have proved to be spotty, yet they have changed the context of American politics. Few candidates (and very few Republican candidates) today would begin their campaigns without some reference to moral issues. Once noted for concentrating on the next world and personal sin, religious conservatives are now involved in political struggles to hold back the forces of moral decay. Social conservatives and the religious right have become central features in most state Republican parties and a key factor in many winning coalitions for party candidates. Candidates from the religious right win elections only occasionally, but their issues and their language helps to frame the political debates of the United States in the twenty-first century.

References

Baranowski, Shelley. 1989. "Jerry Falwell." In Charles H. Lippy, ed. *Twentieth-Century Shapers of American Popular Religion*. New York: Greenwood.

Barbour, Christine, Gerald C. Wright, Christine Thurlow Brenner, Bruce Drury, Lori Cox Han, Christy Woodward Kaupert, J. Aaron Knight, and James Riddlesperger. 2003. *Keeping the Republic: Texas Edition*. Boston: Houghton Mifflin.

Bernstein, Jake. 2002. "Elephant Wars: The Christian Right Flexes Its Muscle at the Republican Convention." *The Texas Observer* (July 5), available at http://www.texasobserver.org.

Blaker, Kimberly, ed. 2003. *The Fundamentals of Extremism: The Christian Right in America*. New Boston, MI: New Boston.

Bradley, Martin B., Norman M. Green, Jr., Dale E. Jones, Mac Lynn, and Lori McNeil. 1992. *Churches and Church Membership in the United States 1990*. Atlanta, GA: Glenmary Research Center.

Bruce, Steve. 1988. *The Rise and Fall of the New Christian Right: Conservative Protestant Politics in America 1978–1988*. New York: Oxford University Press.

Deckman, Melissa. 2001. "Religion Makes the Difference: Why Christian Right Candidates Run for School Board." *Review of Religious Research* 42(4):349–371.

Flynn, Eileen E. 2003. "Religion Underlies Much of the Debate about Possible War." *Austin American-Statesman* (March 10, 2003): A1.

Free Congress Foundation. 2004. Home page, http://www.freecongress.org (accessed March 2004).

Goodstein, Laurie. 2000. "Conservative Church Leaders Find a Pillar in Bush." *New York Times* (January 23, 2000): 16.

Green, John C., Mark J. Rozell, and Clyde Wilcox, eds. 2003. *The Christian Right in American Politics: Marching to the Millennium*. Washington, DC: Georgetown University Press.

Hawkings, David, and Brian Nutting, eds. 2003. *CQ's Politics in America 2004: The 108th Congress*. Washington, DC: CQ.

Heath, Jena. 2000. "Bauer Urges McCain to Retract Comments," *The Austin American-Statesman* (March 2): A1.

Hulse, Carl. 2004. "Senate Hears Testimony on a Gay Marriage Amendment." *New York Times* (March 4), available at http://www.nytimes.com/2004/03/04/politics.

Jones, Dale E., Sherri Doty, Clifford Grammich, James E. Horsch, Richard Houseal, Mac Lynn, John P. Marcum, Kenneth M. Sanchagrin, and Richard H. Taylor. 2002. *Religious Congregations and Membership in the United States 2000*. Nashville, TN: Glenmary Research Center.

Lamare, James W., Jerry L. Polinard, and Robert D. Wrinkle. 2003. "Texas: Religion and Politics in God's Country." In John C. Green, Mark J. Rozell, and Clyde Wilcox, eds., *The Christian Right in American Politics*. Washington, DC: Georgetown University Press.

Linenthal, Edward Tabor. 1989. "Pat Robertson." In Charles H. Lippy, ed. *Twentieth-Century Shapers of American Popular Religion*. New York: Greenwood.

Meckler, Laura. 2000. "Bauer Drops Out of GOP Lineup for President," *The Seattle Times* (February 4): A7.

National Election Studies. 2003a. *Codebook*. http://www.umich.edu/~nes (accessed June 2003).

———. 2003b. *National Election Studies (NES) Guide to Public Opinion and Electoral Behavior*. http://www.umich.edu/~nes/nesguide/nesguide.htm (accessed June 2003).

Ornstein, Norman J., Thomas E. Mann, and Michael J. Malbin. 1996. *Vital Statistics on Congress 1995–1996*. Washington, DC: Congressional Quarterly.

———. 2002. *Vital Statistics on Congress 2001–2002*. Washington, DC: AEI.

Perry, Rick. 2003. Press release (October 17). http://www.governor.state.tx.us/divisions/press/pressreleases/PressRelease. 2003–10–17.5303.view (accessed July 2004).

Phillips, Kevin. 1999. *The Cousins' Wars: Religion, Politics, and the Triumph of Anglo-America*. New York: Basic.

Racheter, Donald P., Lyman A. Kellstedt, and John C. Green. 2003. "Iowa: Crucible of the Christian Right." In John C. Green, Mark J. Rozell, and Clyde Wilcox, eds. *The Christian Right in American Politics*. Washington, DC: Georgetown University Press.

Rahm, Diane. 2004. *United States Public Policy: A Budgetary Approach*. Belmont, CA: Thomson Wadsworth.

Rothenberg, Stuart, and Frank Newport. 1984. *The Evangelical Voter*. Washington, DC: Free Congress Research and Education Foundation.

Rozell, Mark J., and Clyde Wilcox. 2003. "Virginia: Birthplace of the Christian Right." In John C. Green, Mark J. Rozell, and Clyde Wilcox, eds. *The Christian*

Right in American Politics: Marching to the Millennium. Washington, DC: Georgetown University Press.

Smidt, Corwin E., and James M. Penning. 2003. "The Christian Right's Mixed Success in Michigan." In John C. Green, Mark J. Rozell, and Clyde Wilcox, eds. *The Christian Right in American Politics: Marching to the Millennium.* Washington, DC: Georgetown University Press.

Smith, Corwin. 2000. *Christian America? What Evangelicals Really Want.* Berkeley: University of California Press.

Texas State Republican Party. 2004a. *2002 State Republican Party Platform.* http://www.texas gop.org (accessed March 2004).

———. 2004b. "Tina J. Benkiser." http://www.texasrepublicanparty.org/leadership/chairman.php (accessed July 2004).

Utter, Glenn H., and John W. Storey. 2001. *The Religious Right: A Reference Handbook,* 2nd ed. Santa Barbara, CA: ABC-CLIO.

Vinson, C. Danielle, and James L. Guth. 2003. "Advance and Retreat in the Palmetto State: Assessing the Christian Right in South Carolina." In John C. Green, Mark J. Rozell, and Clyde Wilcox, eds. *The Christian Right in American Politics: Marching to the Millennium.* Washington, DC: Georgetown University Press.

Wald, Kenneth D. 2003. *Religion and Politics in the United States.* Lanham, MD: Rowman and Littlefield.

Weyrich, Paul. 1999. "A Moral Minority?" Free Congress Foundation Web site, http://www.freecongress.org (accessed February 1999).

Wilcox, Clyde. 1989. "Evangelicals and the Moral Majority." *Journal for the Scientific Study of Religion* 28:400–414.

Zuniga, Jo Ann. 2004. "Board of Education's Social Conservatives Gain Ground." *Houston Chronicle* (March 15): A11.

Zwier, Robert. 2003. "The Christian Right and the Cultural Divide in Colorado." In John C. Green, Mark J. Rozell, and Clyde Wilcox, eds. *The Christian Right in American Politics: Marching to the Millennium.* Washington, DC: Georgetown University Press.

6
Conclusion

Our examination of conservative Christian political participation has yielded several conclusions regarding the characteristics of those associated with the conservative Christian movement, what issues have tended to activate conservative
Christians, the types of political activity they have engaged in, the results of that activity, and the prospects for continued political engagement and the possibility of success in a society that has become
increasingly pluralistic and secularized.

A History of Involvement

The political history of the United States demonstrates that the religious commitments of Americans have long resulted in consistent, if
not always successful, political involvement. From the pre–Civil War
activism of abolitionists to the campaign against alcoholic beverages
and on to the crusade against the teaching of the theory of evolution
in the public schools in the 1920s, many Christians have organized
for political involvement. Numerous examples of political participation involve more liberal, or progressive, factions within the structure
of Christian denominations. Focusing on the requirement to minister to the needs of fellow human beings and the possibility of altering social structures for the betterment of conditions for human beings, progressive denominations and church leaders more naturally

became involved in social and political activism than their more conservative brethren.

More conservative groups at first tended to shy away from political involvement, particularly in the American South. This reluctance was partially because conservative religious adherents tended to have lower income and education levels, two characteristics that are generally associated with lower political participation. In addition to socioeconomic factors, religious beliefs and past political defeats also may have contributed to their lack of previous political participation. Christian conservatives have tended to concentrate on the expected degeneration of conditions in this world in anticipation of the arrival of God's future kingdom, and so political involvement appeared far less important than tending to spiritual matters and the saving of souls. Past political defeats may also have contributed to the hesitancy of the leadership in fundamentalist denominations to engage in political activity or to encourage their congregations to participate.

The Scopes "Monkey Trial" of 1925, in which the state of Tennessee prosecuted John T. Scopes for violating a recently passed state law prohibiting the teaching of evolution in the public schools, received national attention when journalists heaped ridicule on the "backward" fundamentalist Christians. At the time, leaders of the World's Christian Fundamentals Association shied away from direct involvement in the case, perhaps a wise decision given the rough treatment William Jennings Bryan, a member of the prosecution, received at the hands of defense attorney Clarence Darrow.

New Reasons for Conservative Christian Activism

By the 1970s and 1980s, these reasons for lack of political involvement no longer had as significant an influence on the behavior of conservative Christians. A new generation of members of the more fundamentalist denominations experienced a marked improvement in income and education, which would suggest that their political participation would also increase. The expanded institutions of the religious right aided a new activism. The growth of super churches with very large memberships and their own television and radio programs as well as the growth of television evangelism provided new encouragement for engaging in politics to oppose what was seen as growing public immorality.

In addition, there appears to have been a change in the previous complex interaction in the past between the eschatological beliefs of more conservative Christians and their hesitancy to become involved in the mundane world of politics. As conservatives came to view the issues facing the nation as directly threatening their traditional cultural understandings—such as with the prohibition on prayer in the public schools, the legalization of abortion, and a national government that appeared to support pornography in the name of free speech—some conservative Christian leaders began to develop an alternative perspective to the premillennial view of the end times. A few leaders emphasized reconstructionism, the view that Christians must restructure society according to God's law as presented in the Bible. Conservative Christians tended to view the United States, despite all of its faults, as a Christian nation from its very founding, and therefore they wanted to maintain the Christian character of the nation, return the society to Christian principles, or further develop the nation toward a millennium that human obedience to God's law could bring about.

Obstacles to Political Success

Yet the religious right has faced and still faces difficult political problems. The movement consists of different and disparate groups. They are what social scientists call a grouping, rather than a group. A grouping is a largely artificial construct of people who share some characteristics in common. For example, in this book, we have aggregated all denominations that are creedally fundamental and politically conservative, but these denominations do not often interact with each other. To be a group or an interest group in the United States, these denominations would have to communicate and interact with one another to press their claims on government.

It is in the area of cooperation and interaction that the many factions of the religious right have difficulty. In one sense, televangelists can bring together their listeners into a group, but that communication is primarily only one-way, from the evangelist to the listeners. The upsurge of politically oriented, religiously based organizations like the Moral Majority sought to bridge this gap of communication and interaction among the adherents of various fundamentalist churches. Yet these organizations were disappointed when they tried to influence national elections. Local and state organizations of the religious right have had more success in influencing state Republican parties and local and state elections. To be a force in the pluralistic politics of the United States, an interest group must present a united front, yet the religious right is often divided within itself about the proper response to specific issues and about the priority to be placed on their efforts.

There is another political difficulty that the religious right faces: There is something of a gap between its leadership and its members. For example, in the 1980 presidential election, Jerry Falwell of the Moral Majority and Colonel Doner of Christian Voice both claimed credit for Ronald Reagan's success, yet our research has discovered that more of the rank and file religious right voted for born-again Jimmy Carter in 1980 than for Reagan. There is no doubt that the Moral Majority and Christian Voice encouraged members' turning out to vote, but not all of those members voted the way their leaders wanted. Nonetheless, both the leadership and the rank and file of the religious right remain concerned about the moral decay they see around them in the United States.

The prospect of same-sex marriage represents for conservative Christians a prime example of the concern for the impingement of a more secularized world on their most dearly held moral and religious beliefs. This prospect, therefore, like other issues in the past, acts as a strong spur to political involvement. The proposal for an antigay constitutional amendment illustrates this draw toward the political realm. Cultural conservatives generally hesitate to resort to constitutional amendments because, politically, they tend to prefer state authority to national authority, but the prospect of same-sex marriage is so objectionable to them that many conservatives believe such an extreme strategy is the only option to bring a halt to what is considered the otherwise inevitable ruin of a sacred institution that they believe lies at the very foundation of a moral society. However, that is not a universal position among members of the religious right.

Grand Rapids, Michigan, is usually thought of as the center of what amounts to a small northern Bible Belt, yet interviews there reveal that some evangelical churchgoers are ambivalent about the proposed constitutional amendment. Some interviewees mentioned friends who were gay; others questioned whether an amendment was the right answer. A survey by the University of Akron found that evangelical Christians were divided over whether gays should have the same rights as other Americans. Corwin Smidt, who helped conduct the Akron study, said, "Evangelicals do not march in lock step" (Kirkpatrick 2004). Although usually supporting a privileged status for state over national authority, some conservatives have expressed a willingness to grant to the national government the power to define marriage for the entire country. Whether correct or not in their evaluation of the threat to the social structure, these conservative Christians have demonstrated their intense feelings about the issue and indicated their willingness to engage in an ardent political battle with proponents of gay marriage and civil unions.

Although we distinguished between fundamentalist and mainline denominations in this book, we also emphasized the fairly obvious point that the variations in political preferences within a denomination often are fairly high, if not as pronounced as variations between denominations. As with labor unions, the fundamentalist leadership cannot guarantee unanimous support of the membership for the organization's official position. Political opinions can vary considerably within each organization. Also, the views of specific organizations can vary, thus representing the varied concerns of conservative Christians.

Conservative Christian organizations can also have different sources of denominational support. For instance, fundamentalist denominations tend to hold different views from Pentecostal groups with regard to the status of the gifts of the spirit in the church today. Although Jerry Falwell tended to derive support from fundamentalists, Pat Robertson's core of backers came from the Pentecostal tradition. Such differences can lead to an unwillingness to collaborate on political goals. However, certain goals may be so strongly held that leaders of different religious traditions may find it possible to cooperate. For example, evangelical Protestants have been able at times to form an alliance with Roman Catholics to organize protests against abortion clinics.

In addition to discussing the various groups associated with conservative Christian causes, we have included in the Organizations section several groups that advocate goals in opposition to the mission of conservative Christians. From a pluralist perspective—similar to Sir Isaac Newton's third law of motion, stating that for every action there is an equal and opposite reaction—the advancement of one interest tends to encourage the development of opposing forces. Conservative Christian organizations do not act in a vacuum but react to and compete against other organized interests. These interests, in turn, attempt to blunt the influence of conservative Christian groups. We highlight such organizations as the American Civil Liberties Union, Americans United for Separation of Church and State, and the Interfaith Alliance, as well as groups more critical of the very idea of religiosity, such as the Freedom from Religion Foundation and the Council for Secular Humanism, the latter advocating the a worldview that many conservative Christians find inimical to what they believe to be the purpose of human existence.

Conservative Christian organizations often take stands on issues not directly tied to their religious beliefs, such as support for the free enterprise system and opposition to government involvement in the economy and society (except when government is perceived as an instrument to be used to support the values advocated by the organizations, such as limiting abortion, prohibiting obscenity, and maintaining a strong national defense). Such stands not directly related to religious concerns do not necessarily correlate with a more fundamentalist theology because, as we noted, African-American Christians tend to hold very different positions on such issues, thus suggesting that influences other than religious beliefs have led to such policy preferences. A conservative political environment, when combined with more fundamentalist religious beliefs, results in a characteristic, but not necessarily inevitable, combination of issue preferences.

A Strong Faction in the Republican Party

Conservative Christian organizations, in a more pronounced way than the rank and file members of fundamentalist denominations, support the Republican party and have increasingly denounced the Democratic party for holding positions regarded as contrary to true Christian values, especially on such issues as abortion. The progressive, or liberal, theological drift of the mainline denominations, particularly among their clergy, may well be associated (in the general population of conservative Christians as well as among the more politically active ones), with the labeling of the Democratic party as the more liberal political force in American politics.

The future success of the conservative Christian movement may be closely tied to the fortunes of the Republican party. However, the success of the Republican party may not always result in greater political success for conservative Christians. Many members of the religious right do, on a case-by-case basis, support Republican candidates. For example, many are pleased with George W. Bush's faith as a born-again Christian, and many are pleased with policy such as the ban on partial-birth abortions (Niebuhr 2000; Allliance Defense Fund 2004). The intrinsic nature of American politics is bargaining and compromise. The distaste of many in the religious right for compromise will continue to dilute the influence of their religious principles on party politics.

Another Crossroads for the Religious Right

Scholars have predicted the demise of the religious right at various times over the past thirty years. However, conservative Christian organizations have fairly consistently reorganized themselves, and they have the capacity to do so again. After the dissolution of the Moral Majority, for example, the Christian Coalition quickly emerged as a significant lobbying force representing the concerns of conservative Christians. Various entrepreneurs have established organizations that appeal to the apprehensions of Americans with regard to various cultural issues. As long as other groups generally opposed to the conservative Christian agenda advocate such objectives as the official recognition of gay marriage, the removal of religious signs and symbols from public buildings, and the continued legal status of abortion, conservative Christians can be depended on to continue their attempts to counter what they see as unacceptable policies and social conditions.

A final consideration regarding the future success of the conservative Christian movement involves the general religious preferences of Americans. Although the Republican party in recent years may have gained increasing support from evangelical Protestants as well as Roman Catholics, an interesting trend has been observed in attitude surveys: the unwillingness of some respondents to identify with any religious group (Duncan 2003). Although still representing a relatively small proportion of the total population, these so-called nones may reflect the increasingly secularized nature of the American population. This group might have an increasing influence on the political landscape and thus may, to some extent, blunt the electoral and policy successes of the conservative Christian movement. Such a trend could also indicate an increasing polarization of American society.

Yet the ability of the religious right to reformulate itself when its influence flags may mean that it will face a series of crossroads in the future. It has already successfully negotiated several crossroads so far. As we have previously observed, although the more mainline denominations appear to be losing members, the more fundamentalist churches have increased their numbers of adherents, and the proportion of the population abandoning all religious affiliation has also increased. This trend might most accurately reflect the so-called culture war in which conservative Christians have perceived themselves to be engaged, and it suggests that the political participation of the religious right will not be a transient feature in American politics.

References

Alliance Defense Fund. 2004. "ADF Statement on the Federal Marriage Amendment," http://www.alliancedefensefund.org/ (accessed July 2004).

Duncan, Otis Dudley. 2003. "The Rise of the Nones," *Free Inquiry* (December 2003/January 2004) 24:24–27.

Kirkpatrick, David D. 2004. "Gay-Marriage Fight Finds Ambivalence from Evangelicals." *New York Times*, http://www.nytimes.com (accessed February 2004).

Niebuhr, Gustav. 2000. "Evangelicals Found a Believer in Bush." *New York Times* (February 21, 2000): A13.

Documents and Quotations

We include in this section selected documents, including acts of Congress, Supreme Court decisions, and speeches, on such issues as abortion, prayer in the public schools, homosexuality and same-sex marriage, and charitable choice and the faith-based initiative. The second section includes quotations that present conservative Christian views on the importance of political participation and the appropriate strategies to be used, as well as on such issues as abortion, faith-based funding, gay marriage, and family values.

Defense of Marriage Act of 1996

This legislation was initiated in response to attempts by gays and lesbians to have state legislatures approve legislation that would recognize same-sex marriages. The legislation allows states to ignore same-sex marriages that may be recognized in another state. The constitutionality of the legislation has been questioned, and therefore several members of Congress have called for a constitutional amendment that defines marriage as a union between one man and one woman.

Sec. 2. Powers Reserved to the States

(a) IN GENERAL—Chapter 115 of title 28, United States Code, is amended by adding after section 1738B the following:

Sec. 1738C. Certain acts, records, and proceedings and the effect thereof

"No State, territory, or possession of the United States, or Indian tribe, shall be required to give effect to any public act, record, or judicial proceeding of any other State, territory, possession, or tribe respecting a relationship between persons of the same sex that is treated as a marriage under the laws of such other State, territory, possession or tribe, or a right or claim arising from such relationship."

Partial-Birth Abortion Ban Act of 2003

After several attempts, Congress finally passed this ban on a late-term abortion procedure that involves partial delivery of the fetus. President Clinton had vetoed two previous bills that were sent to his desk. Almost immediately after President George W. Bush signed the ban, several lawsuits challenging the legislation were introduced into the federal courts. Those challenging the act claimed that it failed to provide for possible exceptions and was sufficiently vague that physicians performing other types of legal abortion would be subject to arrest and prosecution.

Section 2 Findings

The Congress finds and declares the following:

(1) A moral, medical, and ethical consensus exists that the practice of performing a partial-birth abortion—an abortion in which a physician delivers an unborn child's body until only the head remains inside the womb, punctures the back of the child's skull with a sharp instrument, and sucks the child's brains out before completing delivery of the dead infant—is a gruesome and inhumane procedure that is never medically necessary and should be prohibited.

(2) Rather than being an abortion procedure that is embraced by the medical community, particularly among physicians who routinely perform other abortion procedures, partial-birth abortion remains a disfavored procedure that is not only unnecessary to preserve the health of the mother, but in fact poses serious risks to the long-term health of women and in some circumstances, their lives. As a result, at least 27 States banned the procedure as did the United States Congress which voted to ban the procedure during the 104th, 105th, and 106th Congresses.

(3) In *Stenberg v. Carhart* (530 U.S. 914, 932 [2000]), the United States Supreme Court opined "that significant medical authority supports the proposition that in some circumstances, [partial birth abor-

tion] would be the safest procedure" for pregnant women who wish to undergo an abortion. Thus, the Court struck down the State of Nebraska's ban on partial-birth abortion procedures, concluding that it placed an "undue burden" on women seeking abortions because it failed to include an exception for partial-birth abortions deemed necessary to preserve the "health" of the mother.

(4) In reaching this conclusion, the Court deferred to the Federal district court's factual findings that the partial-birth abortion procedure was statistically and medically as safe as, and in many circumstances safer than, alternative abortion procedures.

(5) However, the great weight of evidence presented at the Stenberg trial and other trials challenging partial-birth abortion bans, as well as at extensive Congressional hearings, demonstrates that a partial-birth abortion is never necessary to preserve the health of a woman, poses significant health risks to a woman upon whom the procedure is performed, and is outside of the standard of medical care. . . .

(13) There exists substantial record evidence upon which Congress has reached its conclusion that a ban on partial-birth abortion is not required to contain a "health" exception, because the facts indicate that a partial-birth abortion is never necessary to preserve the health of a woman, poses serious risks to a woman's health, and lies outside the standard of medical care. Congress was informed by extensive hearings held during the 104th, 105th, and 107th Congresses and passed a ban on partial-birth abortion in the 104th, 105th, and 106th Congresses. These findings reflect the very informed judgment of the Congress that a partial-birth abortion is never necessary to preserve the health of a woman, poses serious risks to a woman's health, and lies outside the standard of medical care, and should, therefore, be banned . . . .

§ 1531. Partial-birth abortions prohibited

(a) Any physician who, in or affecting interstate or foreign commerce, knowingly performs a partial-birth abortion and thereby kills a human fetus shall be fined under this title or imprisoned not more than 2 years, or both. This subsection does not apply to a partial-birth abortion that is necessary to save the life of a mother whose life is endangered by a physical disorder, physical illness, or physical injury, including a life-endangering physical condition caused by or arising from the pregnancy itself. This subsection takes effect 1 day after the date of enactment of this chapter.

(b) As used in this section—

(1) the term "partial-birth abortion" means an abortion in which

(A) the person performing the abortion deliberately and intentionally vaginally delivers a living fetus until, in the case of a head-first presentation, the entire fetal head is outside the body of the mother, or, in the case of breech presentation, any part of the fetal trunk past the navel is outside the body of the mother for the purpose of performing an overt act that the person knows will kill the partially delivered living fetus; and

(B) performs the overt act, other than completion of delivery, that kills the partially delivered living fetus; and

(2) the term "physician" means a doctor of medicine or osteopathy legally authorized to practice medicine and surgery by the State in which the doctor performs such activity, or any other individual legally authorized by the State to perform abortions: Provided, however, that any individual who is not a physician or not otherwise legally authorized by the State to perform abortions, but who nevertheless directly performs a partial-birth abortion, shall be subject to the provisions of this section.

(c) (1) The father, if married to the mother at the time she receives a partial-birth abortion procedure, and if the mother has not attained the age of 18 years at the time of the abortion, the maternal grandparents of the fetus, may in a civil action obtain appropriate relief, unless the pregnancy resulted from the plaintiff's criminal conduct or the plaintiff consented to the abortion.

(2) Such relief shall include

(A) money damages for all injuries, psychological and physical, occasioned by the violation of this section; and

(B) statutory damages equal to three times the cost of the partial-birth abortion.

(d) (1) A defendant accused of an offense under this section may seek a hearing before the State Medical Board on whether the physician's conduct was necessary to save the life of the mother whose life was endangered by a physical disorder, physical illness, or physical injury, including a life-endangering physical condition caused by or arising from the pregnancy itself.

(2) The findings on that issue are admissible on that issue at the trial of the defendant. Upon a motion of the defendant, the court shall delay the beginning of the trial for not more than 30 days to permit such a hearing to take place.

(e) A woman upon whom a partial-birth abortion is performed may not be prosecuted under this section, for a conspiracy to violate this section, or for an offense under section 2, 3, or 4 of this title based on a violation of this section.

Unborn Victims of Violence Act of 2004

This legislation makes it a separate crime to injure or kill a fetus in an attack on a pregnant woman. Although supporters argued that the legislation had no effect on the right of abortion, opponents expressed concern that the act was one step toward criminalizing abortion.

Sec. 1841. Protection of unborn children

(a) (1) Whoever engages in conduct that violates any of the provisions of law listed in subsection (b) and thereby causes the death of, or bodily injury (as defined in section 1365) to, a child, who is in utero at the time the conduct takes place, is guilty of a separate offense under this section.

(2) (A) Except as otherwise provided in this paragraph, the punishment for that separate offense is the same as the punishment provided under Federal law for that conduct had that injury or death occurred to the unborn child's mother.

(B) An offense under this section does not require proof that—

(i) the person engaging in the conduct had knowledge or should have had knowledge that the victim of the underlying offense was pregnant; or

(ii) the defendant intended to cause the death of, or bodily injury to, the unborn child.

(C) If the person engaging in the conduct thereby intentionally kills or attempts to kill the unborn child, that person shall instead of being punished under subparagraph (A), be punished as provided under sections 1111, 1112, and 1113 of this title for intentionally killing or attempting to kill a human being.

(D) Notwithstanding any other provision of law, the death penalty shall not be imposed for an offense under this section. . . .

(c) Nothing in this section shall be construed to permit the prosecution—

(1) of any person for conduct relating to an abortion for which the consent of the pregnant woman, or a person authorized by law to act on her behalf, has been obtained or for which such consent is implied by law;

(2) of any person for any medical treatment of the pregnant woman or her unborn child; or

(3) of any woman with respect to her unborn child.

(d) As used in this section, the term "unborn child" means a child in utero, and the term "child in utero" or "child, who is in utero" means a member of the species homo sapiens, at any stage of development, who is carried in the womb.

John Geddes Lawrence and Tyron Garner, *Petitioners v. Texas,* docket no. 02-102 (2003)

This Supreme Court decision overruling a Texas sodomy law sent shock waves through conservative groups. Conservative Christians became fearful that the next step in the "gay rights agenda" would be a demand for the legal recognition of gay marriages. When the Massachusetts Supreme Judicial Court declared unconstitutional a state law prohibiting same-sex marriages, many conservative Christians began to call for a constitutional amendment defining marriage as a union between one man and one woman. Following is the dissent to the majority opinion registered by Justice Scalia, which Chief Justice Rehnquist and Justice Thomas joined.

Justice Antonin Scalia, with Chief Justice William Rehnquist and Justice Clarence Thomas, dissenting

I turn now to the ground on which the Court squarely rests its holding: the contention that there is no rational basis for the law here under attack. This proposition is so out of accord with our jurisprudence—indeed, with the jurisprudence of *any* society we know—that it requires little discussion.

The Texas statute undeniably seeks to further the belief of its citizens that certain forms of sexual behavior are "immoral and unacceptable," *Bowers, supra,* at 196—the same interest furthered by criminal laws against fornication, bigamy, adultery, adult incest, bestiality, and obscenity. *Bowers* held that this *was* a legitimate state interest. The Court today reaches the opposite conclusion. The Texas statute, it says, "furthers *no legitimate state interest* which can justify its intrusion into the personal and private life of the individual," *ante,* at 18 (emphasis added). The Court embraces instead *Justice Stevens'* declaration in his *Bowers* dissent, that "the fact that the governing majority in a State had traditionally viewed a particular practice as immoral is not a sufficient reason for upholding a law prohibiting the practice," *ante,* at 17. This effectively decrees the end of all morals legislation. If, as the Court asserts, the promotion of majoritarian sexual morality is not even a *legitimate* state interest, none of the above-mentioned laws can survive rational-basis review. . . .

Justice O'Connor seeks to preserve [state laws limiting marriage to opposite-sex couples] by the conclusory statement that "preserving the traditional institution of marriage" is a legitimate state interest. *Ante,* at 7. But "preserving the traditional institution of marriage" is just a kinder way of describing the State's *moral disapproval* of same-sex couples. Texas's interest in §21.06 could be recast in similarly euphemistic terms: "preserving the traditional sexual mores of our society." In the jurisprudence *Justice O'Connor* has seemingly created, judges can validate laws by characterizing them as "preserving the traditions of society" (good); or invalidate them by characterizing them as "expressing moral disapproval" (bad).

Today's opinion is the product of a Court, which is the product of a law-profession culture, that has largely signed on to the so-called homosexual agenda, by which I mean the agenda promoted by some homosexual activists directed at eliminating the moral opprobrium that has traditionally attached to homosexual conduct. I noted in an earlier opinion the fact that the American Association of Law Schools (to which any reputable law school *must* seek to belong) excludes from membership any school that refuses to ban from its job-interview facilities a law firm (no matter how small) that does not wish to hire as a prospective partner a person who openly engages in homosexual conduct. See *Romer, supra,* at 653.

One of the most revealing statements in today's opinion is the Court's grim warning that the criminalization of homosexual conduct is "an invitation to subject homosexual persons to discrimination both in the public and in the private spheres." *Ante,* at 14. It is clear from this that the Court has taken sides in the culture war, departing from its role of assuring, as neutral observer, that the democratic rules of engagement are observed. Many Americans do not want persons who openly engage in homosexual conduct as partners in their business, as scoutmasters for their children, as teachers in their children's schools, or as boarders in their home. They view this as protecting themselves and their families from a lifestyle that they believe to be immoral and destructive. The Court views it as "discrimination" which it is the function of our judgments to deter. So imbued is the Court with the law profession's anti-anti-homosexual culture, that it is seemingly unaware that the attitudes of that culture are not obviously "mainstream"; that in most States what the Court calls "discrimination" against those who engage in homosexual acts is perfectly legal; that proposals to ban such "discrimination" under Title VII have repeatedly been rejected by Congress . . . that in some cases such "discrimination" is *mandated* by federal statute . . . and that is some cases such "discrimination" is a constitutional right, see *Boy Scouts of America v. Dale*, 530 U.S. 640 (2000).

Let me be clear that I have nothing against homosexuals, or any other group, promoting their agenda through normal democratic means. Social perceptions of sexual and other morality change over time, and every group has the right to persuade its fellow citizens that its view of such matters is the best. That homosexuals have achieved some success in that enterprise is attested to by the fact that Texas is one of the few remaining States that criminalize private, consensual homosexual acts. But persuading one's fellow citizens is one thing, and imposing one's views in absence of democratic majority will is something else. I would no more *require* a State to criminalize homosexual acts—or, for that matter, display *any* moral disapprobation of them—than I would *forbid* it to do so. What Texas has chosen to do is well within the range of traditional democratic action, and its hand should not be stayed through the invention of a brand-new "constitutional right" by a Court that is impatient of democratic change. It is indeed true that "later generations can see that laws once thought necessary and proper in fact serve only to oppress," *ante,* at 18; and when that happens, later generations can repeal those laws. But it is the premise of our system that those judgments are to be made by the people, and not imposed by a governing caste that knows best. . . .

At the end of its opinion—after having laid waste the foundations of our rational-basis jurisprudence—the Court says that the present case "does not involve whether the government must give formal recognition to any relationship that homosexual persons seek to enter." *Ante,* at 17. Do not believe it. More illuminating than this bald, unreasoned disclaimer is the progression of thought displayed by an earlier passage in the Court's opinion, which notes the constitutional protection afforded to "personal decisions relating to *marriage,* procreation, contraception, family relationships, child rearing, and education," and then declares that "[p]ersons in a homosexual relationship may seek autonomy for these purposes, just as heterosexual persons do." *Ante,* at 13 (emphasis added). Today's opinion dismantles the structure of constitutional law that has permitted a distinction to be made between heterosexual and homosexual unions, insofar as formal recognition in marriage is concerned. If moral disapprobation of homosexual conduct is "no legitimate state interest" for purposes of proscribing that conduct, *ante,* at 18; and if, as the Court coos (casting aside all pretense of neutrality), "[w]hen sexuality finds overt expression in intimate conduct with another person, the conduct can be but one element in a personal bond that is more enduring," *ante,* at 6; what justification could there possibly be for denying the benefits of marriage to homosexual couples exercising "[t]he liberty protected by the Constitution," *ibid.?* Surely not the encouragement of procreation, since the sterile and the elderly are allowed to marry. This case "does not involve" the issue of homosexual marriage only if one entertains the belief that principle and logic have nothing to do with the decisions of this Court. Many will hope that, as the Court comfortingly assures us, this is so.

The matters appropriate for this Court's resolution are only three: Texas's prohibition of sodomy neither infringes a "fundamental right" (which the Court does not dispute), nor is unsupported by a rational relation to what the Constitution considers a legitimate state interest, nor denies the equal protection of the laws. I dissent.

Santa Fe Independent School District v. Doe (2000)

The following is the dissenting opinion to the Supreme Court's ruling on organized prayer at high school sporting events. The issue of school prayer has energized many conservative Christians, who believe that the religious freedom of children is being restricted by such rulings. Supporters of the ruling argue that this is another example of the Court overruling the attempt to impose religious observances on unwilling participants.

Chief Justice William Rehnquist, with Justice Antonin Scalia and Justice Clarence Thomas, dissenting

The Court distorts existing precedent to conclude that the school district's student-message program is invalid on its face under the Establishment Clause. But even more disturbing than its holding is the tone of the Court's opinion; it bristles with hostility to all things religious in public life. Neither the holding nor the tone of the opinion is faithful to the meaning of the Establishment Clause, when it is recalled that George Washington himself, at the request of the very Congress which passed the Bill of Rights, proclaimed a day of "public thanksgiving and prayer, to be observed by acknowledging with grateful hearts the many and signal favors of Almighty God." . . .

Even if it were appropriate to apply the *Lemon* test here, the district's student-message policy should not be invalidated on its face. The Court applies *Lemon* and holds that the "policy is invalid on its face because it establishes an improper majoritarian election on religion, and unquestionably has the purpose and creates the perception of encouraging the delivery of prayer at a series of important school events." *Ante,* at 26. The Court's reliance on each of these conclusions misses the mark.

First, the Court misconstrues the nature of the "majoritarian election" permitted by the policy as being an election on "prayer" and "religion." . . . To the contrary, the election permitted by the policy is a two-fold process whereby students vote first on whether to have a student speaker before football games at all, and second, if the students vote to have such a speaker, on who that speaker will be. . . . It is conceivable that the election could become one in which student candidates campaign on platforms that focus on whether or not they will pray if elected. It is also conceivable that the election could lead to a Christian prayer before 90 percent of the football games. If, upon implementation, the policy operated in this fashion, we would have a record before us to review whether the policy, as applied, violated the Establishment Clause or unduly suppressed minority viewpoints. But it is possible that the students might vote not to have a pregame speaker, in which case there would be no threat of a constitutional violation. It is also possible that the election would not focus on prayer, but on public speaking ability or social popularity. And if student campaigning did begin to focus on prayer, the school might decide to implement reasonable campaign restrictions.

But the Court ignores these possibilities by holding that merely granting the student body the power to elect a speaker that may choose to pray, "regardless of the students' ultimate use of it, is not acceptable." *Ante,* at 25. The Court so holds despite that any speech that may occur as a result of the election process here would be *private,* not *government,* speech. The elected student, not the government, would choose what to say. Support for the Court's holding cannot be found in any of our cases. And it essentially invalidates all student elections. A newly elected student body president, or even a newly elected prom king or queen, could use opportunities for public speaking to say prayers. Under the Court's view, the mere grant of power to the students to vote for such offices, in light of the fear that those elected might publicly pray, violated the Establishment Clause. . . .

[I]t is easy to think of solemn messages that are not religious in nature, for example urging that a game be fought fairly. And sporting events often begin with a solemn rendition of our national anthem, with its concluding verse "And this be our motto: 'In God is our trust.'" Under the Court's logic, a public school that sponsors the singing of the national anthem before football games violates the Establishment Clause. Although the Court apparently believes that solemnizing football games is an illegitimate purpose, the voters in the school district seem to disagree. Nothing in the Establishment Clause prevents them from making this choice.

Prepared Remarks of Attorney General John Ashcroft

White House Faith-Based and Community Initiatives Conference, Denver, Colorado, January 13, 2003 (excerpts)

President George W. Bush entered the White House as a major supporter of public funding for faith-based organizations that provide social services. The faith-based initiative has raised serious questions about the separation of church and state. Some argue that such programs could involve government funds being used for religious purposes, while others fear that government regulation of religious institutions might accompany any funding.

Under Charitable Choice, organizations cannot be excluded merely because they have a cross on their wall or a rabbi on the board of directors. Faith-based organizations cannot be denied the opportunity to meet needs simply because they hire workers who share their religious beliefs. And they cannot be forced to change or to compromise their beliefs or their mission in order to qualify for participation in federal programs.

Charitable Choice has played a fundamental role in delivering services to those in need, particularly in easing the path from welfare to work for millions of Americans. While the legislative framework has been in place since the 1990s, it was not until President George W. Bush took the oath of office that faith-based organizations serving our communities began to receive encouragement from the federal government. This encouragement and support expands their unique capacity to serve America and meet human needs.

George W. Bush came to office with the belief that charities, grassroots organizations and faith-based groups fill needs that government, no matter how well intentioned, generously funded, or carefully designed, cannot possibly fill.

For the first time in a long time, our leaders in Washington understand what Americans of all religious backgrounds have long held to be true: Through faith, all things are possible.

• Faith ministers to the less fortunate. Eighty percent of the more than 300,000 religious congregations in America provide services to those in need.

• Faith shapes lives. Over 90 percent of urban congregations provide social services, ranging from preschool to literacy programs to health clinics.

• Faith shepherds communities. Polls estimate that between 60 and 90 percent of America's congregations provide at least one social service, and about 75 percent of local congregations provide volunteers for social service programs.

• Faith nurtures children. One out of every six child-care centers in America is housed in a religious facility. The nation's largest providers of child-care services are the Roman Catholic Church and the Southern Baptist Convention.

• And perhaps most significantly, faith inspires the faithful to love their neighbors as they'd love themselves. Nearly one-quarter of all Americans volunteer their time and effort through faith-based organizations.

Many of America's best ideas—and best results—for helping those in need have come not from the federal government but from grassroots communities, private and faith-based organizations of people who know and care about their neighbors. For years, America's churches and charities have led the way in helping the poor achieve dignity instead of despair, self-sufficiency instead of shame.

A government check may relieve hunger, but it cannot supply hope. It can provide temporary shelter, but it cannot offer the long-term integrity of independence. . . .

With each act of kindness, a heart is changed. With each act of mercy, hope is rekindled. And each act of faith introduces values that can change lives.

Thank you for your work. Thank you for your leadership. Thank you for your faith. May God bless you, your ministries, and may God bless the United States of America.

Southern Baptist Convention Resolution, on Thirty Years of *Roe v. Wade* (June 2003)

For three decades, opposition to abortion has been a major rallying cry for many conservative Christians. This resolution, passed by the Southern Baptist Convention, presents a clear conservative Christian position on the issue, renouncing a prochoice stance of some previous Baptist leaders.

WHEREAS, Scripture reveals that all human life is created in the image of God, and therefore sacred to our Creator (Genesis 1:27; Genesis 9:6); and

WHEREAS, The Bible affirms that the unborn baby is a person bearing the image of God from the moment of conception (Psalm 139:13–16; Luke 1:44); and

WHEREAS, Scripture further commands the people of God to plead for protection for the innocent and justice for the fatherless (Psalm 72:12–14; Psalm 82:3; James 1:27); and

WHEREAS, January 2003 marked thirty years since the 1973 United States Supreme Court *Roe v. Wade* decision, which legalized abortion in all fifty states; and

WHEREAS, Resolutions passed by the Southern Baptist Convention in 1971 and 1974 accepted unbiblical premises of the abortion rights movement, forfeiting the opportunity to advocate the protection of defenseless women and children; and

WHEREAS, During the early years of the post-*Roe* era, some of those then in leadership positions within the denomination endorsed and furthered the "pro-choice" abortion rights agenda outlined in *Roe v. Wade;* and

WHEREAS, Some political leaders have referenced 1970s-era Southern Baptist Convention resolutions and statements by former Southern Baptist Convention leaders to oppose legislative efforts to protect women and children from abortion; and

WHEREAS, Southern Baptist churches have effected a renewal of biblical orthodoxy and confessional integrity in our denomination, beginning with the Southern Baptist Convention presidential election of 1979; and

WHEREAS, The Southern Baptist Convention has maintained a robust commitment to the sanctity of all human life, including that of the unborn, beginning with a landmark pro-life resolution in 1982; and

WHEREAS, Our confessional statement, The Baptist Faith and Message, affirms that children "from the moment of conception, are a blessing and heritage from the Lord"; and further affirms that Southern Baptists are mandated by Scripture to "speak on behalf of the unborn and contend for the sanctity of all human life from conception to natural death"; and

WHEREAS, The legacy of *Roe v. Wade* has grown to include ongoing assaults on human life such as euthanasia, the harvesting of human embryos for the purposes of medical experimentation, and an accelerating move toward human cloning; now, therefore be it

RESOLVED, That the messengers to the Southern Baptist Convention meeting in Phoenix, Arizona, June 17–18, 2003, reiterate our conviction that the 1973 *Roe v. Wade* decision was based on a fundamentally flawed understanding of the United States Constitution, human embryology, and the basic principles of human rights; and be it further

RESOLVED, That we reaffirm our belief that the *Roe v. Wade* decision was an act of injustice against innocent unborn children as well as against vulnerable women in crisis pregnancy situations, both of which have been victimized by a "sexual revolution" that empowers predatory and irresponsible men and by a lucrative abortion industry that has fought against even the most minimal restrictions on abortion; and be it further

RESOLVED, That we offer our prayers, our love, and our advocacy for women and men who have been abused by abortion and the emotional, spiritual, and physical aftermath of this horrific practice; affirming that the gospel of Jesus Christ grants complete forgiveness for any sin, including that of abortion; and be it further

RESOLVED, That we lament and renounce statements and actions by previous Conventions and previous denominational leadership that offered support to the abortion culture; and be it further

RESOLVED, That we humbly confess that the initial blindness of many in our Convention to the enormity of *Roe v. Wade* should serve as a warning to contemporary Southern Baptists of the subtlety of the spirit of the age in obscuring a biblical worldview; and be it further

RESOLVED, That we urge our Southern Baptist churches to remain vigilant in the protection of human life by preaching the whole counsel of God on matters of human sexuality and the sanctity of life, by encouraging and empowering Southern Baptists to adopt unwanted children, by providing spiritual, emotional, and financial support for women in crisis pregnancies, and by calling on our government officials to take action to protect the lives of women and children; and be it further

RESOLVED, That we express our appreciation to both houses of Congress for their passage of the Partial-Birth Abortion Ban Act of 2003, and we applaud President Bush for his commitment to sign this bill into law; and be it further

RESOLVED, That we urge Congress to act swiftly to deliver this bill to President Bush for his signature; and be it finally

RESOLVED, That we pray and work for the repeal of the *Roe v. Wade* decision and for the day when the act of abortion will be not only illegal, but also unthinkable.

Excerpts from Scholarly Literature

The following quotes are found in literature from, and about, conservative Christians. Although not necessarily representative of all conservative Christians, these quotes provide insights into their beliefs and goals, as well as the intensity with which they hold those beliefs.

By forgetting not only our heritage but also the Biblical truth of Proverbs 29:2 [When the righteous are in authority, the people rejoice; but when the wicked rule, the people groan], we began to extract ourselves from public affairs. Many Christian leaders, while encouraging young people to become pastors or missionaries, discouraged them from entering the legal, political, or public arenas. Little by little, the church-at-large not only embraced but even began to teach the heresy that Christians and politics were incompatible and should be divorced.

> *Barton, David. 2002.* America: To Pray? Or Not to Pray?, *5th ed. Aledo, TX: WallBuilders, 117.*

We are in a moment of enthusiasm about the role that religious organizations play in our social welfare system, and a moment of high interest in expanding that role and creating new kinds of partnerships between government and religious organizations. These partnerships are portrayed by some as the potential cornerstone of our future welfare system and the solution to many difficult problems caused by poverty. They are portrayed by others as the harbinger of disaster. I think they are neither. Religious organizations will play an important role in our future social welfare system, but that is not new. Welfare reform has brought with it some new opportunities and dangers in this arena, and I think we should chart a course that avoids both naive triumphalism about the opportunities and exaggerated fears about the dangers.

> *Chaves, Mark. 2001. "Religious Congregations and Welfare Reform: Assessing the Potential." In Andrew Walsh, ed.* Can Charitable Choice Work? Covering Religion's Impact on Urban Affairs and Social Services. *Hartford, CT: Leonard E. Greenberg Center for the Study of Religion in Public Life, 136.*

In the end, any successful reform movement must work within *both* political parties. Where would Martin Luther King have been without

Nelson Rockefeller and other Republicans sympathetic to civil rights? The central figure in the passage of the Civil Rights Act of 1964 was Everett Dirksen, the Republican leader of the U.S. Senate. Liberal feminists advanced the Equal Rights Amendment commensurate with their ability to attract support from prominent Republicans like Betty Ford and Mary Dent Crisp. Once the Equal Rights Amendment was dropped from the Republican party platform in 1980, it was only a matter of time before it went down to defeat. Likewise, the religious conservative movement must resist the temptation to identify its fortunes solely with those of the Republican party. Political parties lose power as quickly as they gain it, while social movements have a larger responsibility to advance an agenda that transcends electoral politics. That leads us to consider the new challenges facing the pro-family community as it struggles to make active faith a real factor in American politics.

> *Reed, Ralph. 1996.* Active Faith: How Christians Are Changing the Soul of American Politics. *New York: Simon and Schuster, 235.*

The most urgent challenge for pro-family conservatives is to develop a broader issues agenda. The pro-family movement has limited its effectiveness by concentrating disproportionately on issues such as abortion and homosexuality. These are vital moral issues, and must remain an important part of the message. To win at the ballot box and in the court of public opinion, however, the pro-family movement must speak to the concerns of average voters in the areas of taxes, crime, government waste, health care, and financial security.

> *Reed, Ralph. 1993. "Casting a Wider Net."* Policy Review *(Summer): 31.*

Homosexual living arrangements under the guise of marriage are not only sterile, incapable, and insufficient, they are destructive to the very fabric of our society. The strategy to inculturate active homosexual practice into our society as a favored institution is synonymous with injecting a cancer into a healthy body. Homosexual marriage directly attacks the family which is the most vital cell in society. The family is the first government, the first church, and the first school. We must not allow this vital cell, the rock upon which society is built, to be inculturated with a perversion that will destroy it, and with it the future of our children and grandchildren.

Fournier, Keith. 1998. "In Defense of Marriage."
Law and Justice *(January), 4–5. Quoted in Sara Diamond.*
Not by Politics *Alone. New York: Guilford, 171.*

As I began to pray about abortion in America, I just had these ideas flooding my head about how to fight abortion. To have people in front of abortion mills. To help women place their babies in Christian homes once they were saved from having abortion, to reeducate the public to the value of human life, from a Bible-based perspective. Because only the Bible gives us value. We were praying, and I had all these thoughts rushing through my head and I really thought God was impressing me to do something to fight abortion. It did not fit my theology, it did not fit my plans for my life. We broke up this prayer meeting with this strong sense that I was supposed to do something.

Terry, Randall. Quoted in Risen, James, and Judy L. Thomas. 1998. Wrath of Angels: The American Abortion War. *New York: Basic, 238.*

How would you answer these questions: Do you approve of pornographic and obscene classroom textbooks being used under the guise of sex education? Do you approve of the present laws legalizing abortion-on-demand that resulted in the murder of more than one million babies last year? Do you approve of the growing trend towards sex and violence replacing family-oriented programs on television?

If you are against these sins, then you are exactly the person I want on my team. I have put together a Clean Up America campaign that is going to shake this nation like it has never been shaken before. I cannot do it alone. Together we must awaken the moral conscience of our nation. The battle has just begun.

Jerry Falwell. Quoted in Strober, Gerald, and Ruth Tomczak. 1979. Jerry Falwell: Aflame for God. *Nashville: Thomas Nelson, 174–175.*

Christian thinking is under assault. Values which Judeo-Christianity has held sacred for thousands of years are falling to sophisticated pagan reasoning. Sadly, many Christians—even Christian leaders—are being taken in.

One of the greatest challenges facing the Church is to resist the temptation to let the secular idea of relativism infect the Christian view of revelation—objective truth. Will Christians have the ability and tenacity to resist the siren-song of carnal thinking? Or will they fall for—and into—both relativism and propaganda?

> *Spencer, James R. 1995.* Bleeding Hearts and Propaganda: The Fall of Reason in the Church. *Lafayette, LA: Huntington House, 27.*

To interpret Jesus and his significance in *purely* political terms would be to reduce Jesus. But we should also be reducing Jesus if we were to exclude the political dimension of his life and fate. Because the Kingdom of God he served embraces the whole of human life, and because he identified in love with human beings whose lives were affected by political structures and policies, his mission impinged on the political along with other dimensions of life. Politics, as we have observed a number of times, is not everything; nor is the political dimension a watertight, autonomous sphere of life; it interacts with all other dimensions of life. Thus we may expect to find that Jesus' life, death and resurrection, while not reducible to politics, have a political dimension.

> *Bauckham, Richard. 1989.* The Bible in Politics: How to Read the Bible Politically. *Louisville, KY: Westminster/John Knox, 142.*

We were led to believe that . . . it was okay to give religious "lip service" in the political arena, but the "real" world of "dirty" politics was much too stringent and abrasive. How could a truly spiritual man or woman ever survive in such dog-eat-dog surroundings? It just wasn't practical, or so we were told. It was, after all, the "Real" world, not some etherial [*sic*] stained-glass existence. . . .

Unlike Jesus' First Century disciples, we are citizens of a democratic nation whose primary power rests constitutionally on the shoulders of the people. The true vortex of power in our country is among those who participate in the political process.

Failure to act positively creates a natural vacuum into which falsehood and negativity rushes. This is exactly what has happened. As a result we have seen our freedoms threatened.

The foremost question, then, is how to reverse that dangerous trend—how to re-establish those founding principles set forth by our Forefathers.

> *McLellan, Vern. 1986.* Christians in the Political Arena. *Charlotte, NC: Associates, 110, 112.*

The Bible says we are to . . . rule. If you don't rule and I don't rule, the atheists and the humanists and the agnostics are going to rule. We should be the head of our school board. We should be the head of our nation. We should be the Senators and the Congressmen. We should be the editors of our newspapers. We should be taking over every area of life.

Weiner, Bob. The Forerunner *television program aired on Concord, California's KFCB, December 7, 1985. Quoted in Sara Diamond 1989.* Spiritual Warfare: The Politics of the Christian Right. *Boston: South End, 45.*

Whether you are talking about abortion or childcare or the influence of pornography or these issues about what's on the TV screen during prime time, what tends to motivate most of our folks is a fear that their children are being peeled away, seduced by the popular culture, or that what they are trying to do at home is being undermined either intentionally or unintentionally by the government and the culture at large.

Bauer, Gary. Interview by Duane Murray Oldfield, March 6, 1989. Quoted in Duane Murray Oldfield. 1996. The Right and the Righteous: The Christian Right Confronts the Republican Party. *Lanham, MD: Rowman and Littlefield, 65.*

[Americans] have fallen easily into the Manichean habit of dividing the world into darkness and light, Evil and Good, past and future, Satan and Christ. They have seen themselves as a progressive, redemptive force, waging war in the ranks of Christ's army, or have imagined themselves even as Christ Himself, liberating those in bondage and healing the afflicted. From the time of the earliest colonial settlements, for good or ill, the metaphors of the cross of Christ and of the mission of His Church have been deeply embedded in the story of the American people and their relations with the rest of the world.

Gamble, Richard M. 2003. The War for Righteousness. *Wilmington, DE: ISI, 5.*

You wait until the Sunday before the election and you distribute them [voter guides] all in one day. The election is held on Tuesday. Now why do we distribute them the Sunday before? It needs to be fresh in the voter's mind. Voters do not have a particularly long retention period.

Number two, it does not give that liberal candidate that we're opposing time to go run back to all the churches screaming that he's not really that way, which is what they try to do if you give them a chance. Thirdly, when that liberal National Council of Churches minister stands in front of the pulpit and denounces the report card in the church service, it's too late because you've distributed it on Sunday, the election was held on Tuesday, and the minister denounces it the next Sunday, you see.

> *Doner, Colonel. Speech at the July 1986 conference of the Coalition on Revival, Washington, D.C. Quoted in Sara Diamond. 1989.* Spiritual Warfare: The Politics of the Christian Right. *Boston: South End, 62.*

There has been no consistent treatment of marriage over time. Perhaps it is wrong to use the government to dictate the details of this precious institution, and perhaps marriage needs to return to the Church. Cultures evolve, and not always for the better. American law follows cultural trends, but American law has wisely (at least up until now) sought to permit a maximum of individual freedom to associate not only for economic ends but for spiritual ones. The Court's articulation of myopic individualism, for the time being, is balanced by its understanding that the most important individual right is to gather in association. Taking advantage of that understanding may be the best thing that we can do for marriage.

> *Presser, Stephen B. 2004. "Marriage and the Law: Time for a Divorce?"* Chronicles *(March), 22.*

[T]he senior editors [of *Touchstone*] agree that the Democratic party has in the last generation undergone changes that make it impossible for a knowledgeable Christian to support it in good conscience, just as it was once impossible for a knowledgeable Christian in Germany to vote in good conscience for the Nazi party, whatever good that party may have done, and however many religious allies it might have had."

> *Hutchens, S. M. 2003. "Practical Atheism."* Touchstone *(June), 5.*

The strongest defenders of traditional marriage defend it because they believe it was instituted by God. They believe that government merely *recognizes* marriage, and cannot redefine something it did not create. The strategy of the gay activists is to remove marriage from this vaunted status and bring it down to earth, where mankind can tinker with it. Their claim is that government—not God—has the sole authority to define sex and marriage. With the wind of some bizarre Supreme Court rulings at their backs (holding that the law may reflect irreligion but not religion), the gay activists have reason for optimism.

Mersereau, Adam G. 2003. "Defining Marriage Down."
Touchstone *(November), 18.*

For now, the Boy Scouts and the churches have a legal privilege to practice what the legal and media cultures consider to be irrational discrimination, whether on the basis of sexual orientation or of religious belief, but I would not give that privilege a long life expectancy. . . . A private organization may defy the dominant moral creed as long as it remains below the media radar screen, but pressure can be brought to bear whenever the dominant forces decide that some obstacle to their control of the culture has become intolerable.

For now, the law may allow the Boy Scouts to exclude atheists and homosexuals, but is it right for them to do so? That question will trouble the Scouts continually until the culture is persuaded again that God really is our creator rather than merely a product of the human imagination, and that he cares about what we do sufficiently to build a moral code into the bedrock of reality.

Johnson, Phillip E. 2003. "Scouts and God."
Touchstone *(March), 17.*

The sodomite [homosexual] must admit that he is what God says he is, a sinner, and realize that God hates his sin and must punish it. Then he must believe that Jesus Christ paid for his sins on the cross of Calvary, be willing to turn from his sins, and receive Jesus Christ as his personal Savior. After having taken Christ as Lord and Savior, the homosexual will have experienced the joy of sins forgiven, a new life in Christ, and will quit his gay lifestyle.

Houke, Arthur, 2004. The Servant *19 (February), 1.*

It is said that Christians should leave human governments to the management of the ungodly, and not be diverted from the work of saving souls, to intermeddle with human governments.

To uphold and assist good government is not being diverted from the work of saving souls. The promotion of public and private order and happiness is one of the indispensable means of doing good and saving souls. It is nonsense to admit that Christians are under an obligation to obey human government, and still have nothing to do with the choice of those who shall govern.

> *Finney, Charles. Quoted in Billy James Hargis. 2000.*
> *"Christians Challenged to Get Involved in Politics."*
> Christian Crusade *48 (April), 4.*

That sodomy is an inalienable right would no doubt come as a big surprise to the Constitution's framers. They are, of course the last constitutional experts the Supreme Court would ever consult. The Supreme Court, judging from the majority opinion's slavish attention to Europe's regard for sodomy, is much more interested in the thoughts of modern Danes than dead Americans. . . .

The majority on the Supreme Court declares that anti-sodomy laws compromise the "dignity" of homosexuals. The framers would reverse the judgment: it is sodomy that compromises their dignity, and it is the rule of law which points to and protects that dignity. The framers belonged to communities that passed such laws so as to safeguard a moral culture in which human dignity is possible.

> *Neumayr, George. 2003. "U.S. Supreme Court: Yes, to Sodomy!"*
> The Schwarz Report *43 (August), 1.*

Will your child "accept the responsibility for preserving the earth for future generations" if she doesn't believe in birth control or abortion? And, why teach students to embrace "personal adaptability to change"? In 1938, patriotic Germans resisted change, while others adapted to Hitler's "new Germany." How do you grade a child in "appreciating racial, ethnic, religious, and political systems"? A youngster should be taught about political differences. But, should every political system, including Marxism, be "appreciated"? Should religions such as Wicca be "appreciated"? People—not ideologies—should be "appreciated."

> *Luksik, Peg, and Pamela Hobbs Hoffecker. 1995.*
> Outcome-Based Education: The State's Assault on
> Our Children's Values. *Lafayette, LA: Huntington House, 14.*

The early church was prepared for persecution because they knew that it was coming. The Lord had told them. The apostles had told them. They had believed that they were in the midst of tribulation. They were. Yet, we still ignore the teachings of Scripture to be ready. Being ready requires preparedness. Our children need to know that these things are coming. They need to understand the reasons why, so that they can stand in the evil day. They need to be taught that God will honor their endurance, and provide grace in their hour of need. They need to understand that this world's goods will mean nothing in that day!

> *Parks, Jerry. 1993.* False Security: Has the New Age Given Us a False Hope? *Lafayette, LA: Huntington House, 156.*

Never forget that our blessed Lord Jesus Christ warned against wolves in sheep's clothing (Matthew 7:15). God's people need to test every organization and religious leader to see if some aspect of liberalism and compromise is believed and promoted.

> *Colas, Ralph G. 2002. "USA/WCC Report."* The ACCC Report, *4.*

All the world has an important stake in Middle East developments. In many respects, peace in the Middle East is even more important to the growing power and prosperity of a new Europe than it is to the United States. Now, most of the world is involved in the conflict in the Middle East, and the prosperity of the world depends on some mechanism to guarantee peace and a continued flow of oil from the region. This is precisely what biblical prophecy predicts. The Middle East is the battleground for the road to Armageddon and the second coming of Christ, the prophesied stage for the final drama of world history. With world attention on the Middle East, Israel already back in her ancient land, and the world in a mood for someone to guarantee peace, the major components of the end time are in place.

If these facts are true, present events are a call to faith and repentance, a turning to God and to Jesus Christ who is the final Judge of every individual and nation. God's dramatic intervention into human history, as spelled out in biblical prophecy, may be very near.

> *Walvoord, John F. 1990.* Armageddon, Oil and the Middle East Crisis: What the Bible Says about the Future of the Middle East and the End of Western Civilization. *Rev. ed. Grand Rapids, MI: Zondervan, 15.*

In the 1970s, reacting against the hesitancy of many premillennialists to enter the public arena, some evangelicals abandoned premillennialism altogether to embrace "Reconstruction" or "Dominion" theology, a kind of fundamentalist postmillennialism committed to achieving a Christianized world in the present age. Drawing on the work of theologian Rousas J. Rushdoony, Reconstructionists insisted that Christians must take seriously God's command to Adam and Eve to exercise "dominion" over the earth and "subdue" it. This meant, they argued, aggressive action to impose Christ's rule on the world now, *before* His return at Armageddon. While postmillennialists of an earlier day had focused on issues of social justice, the Reconstructionists were more preoccupied with imposing their own (they saw it as Christ's) stern morality on the world.

> *Boyer, Paul. 1992.* When Time Shall Be No More: Prophecy Belief in Modern American Culture. *Cambridge, MA: Belknap, 303.*

Whether the awful events of September 11 occasion a deep and long-lasting infusion from this nation's spiritual roots depends on how we take hold of the moment. The first moral obligation is to think clearly: We need to end the long bifurcation of reason and faith in the mental habits of recent generations. In the founding generation, those two wings beat very nearly as one, but in generations both before and after there has been a tendency to exalt either reason at the expense of faith, or the reverse. This is a foolish, unnecessary, and destructive mistake. . . .

Further, we need to recognize that the serious partisans of liberty and truth are few; and that we need each other's contributions, faults and all. It was wrong of Jerry Falwell to point the finger at his secular adversaries as if they were responsible for God's "anger" at the United States, and just as wrong of Michael Lind and Andrew Sullivan (and many others) to point their fingers at Jerry Falwell as if he were a soul mate of bin Laden.

> *Novak, Michael. 2001. "A Nation That Believes: America without Religion Is Not America."* National Review *(December 31), 34.*

Key People

Jim Bakker (1939–)

James Orson Bakker was born in Muskegon, Michigan, the fourth son of a tool and die maker. In his youth, he was interested in photography and public speaking. In high school, he was a disc jockey who emceed school dances. Although he had attended Muskegon Assembly of God Church as a child, Bakker said he did not know God until 1958. One night that year, as he was driving with his girlfriend in his father's car, he ran over a little boy in the church's parking lot. The child survived, but Bakker said that his soul searching after that incident led him to feel a call to preach (Lippy 1989).

He entered North Central Bible College of Minneapolis, Minnesota, in 1959, and there he met Tammy LaValley from International Falls, Minnesota. Ms. LaValley was attending North Central Bible College with hopes of becoming an evangelistic missionary. Jim and Tammy dropped out of college in order to get married in 1961, for the college forbade students to marry. The couple began their marriage as traveling evangelists, preaching in small churches in North Carolina (Lippy 1989).

In 1965, the Bakkers went to Portsmouth, Virginia, to work with Pat Robertson's Christian Broadcasting Network. In 1966, Bakker launched what was probably the first Christian talk show; however, he resigned in 1971 and moved to Santa Ana, California, where he founded Trinity Broadcasting Systems with Paul Crouch. Crouch had been the assistant pastor of Bakker's childhood church in Muskegon, but he and Bakker disagreed about Trinity. Bakker resigned in 1973, and half of the Trinity staff followed him to Charlotte, North Carolina, in January 1974. In November of that year, Bakker became the host of a talk show that he named the *PTL Club* for "Praise the Lord" and "People That Love."

The *PTL Club* soon became more than a television program. Its early studio was a furniture showroom in Charlotte, but in 1976, Bakker moved his headquarters to Park Road, a converted colonial mansion. In 1978, Bakker broke ground on his "Total Learning Center" in Fort Mill, South Carolina, an enterprise that later became Heritage USA, a Christian-based theme park. The Heritage complex included a 504-room hotel, campsites, a $10 million water park, a pyramid-shaped executive office building, condominiums, and a new television studio. By 1986, more than 6 million people were visiting Heritage USA each year, and Bakker began planning an even larger endeavor that would have included a multiacre re-creation of old Jerusalem with dramas, a bazaar, and a lodging area as well as a 30,000-seat "PTL Ministry Center" patterned after London's Crystal Palace (Lippy 1989). But before he could realize these dreams, Bakker's earlier indiscretions began to catch up with him.

Bakker's preaching focused on salvation and prosperity, and he and Tammy lived that message and preached it as well. On the *PTL Club* program, Jim and Tammy would plead for money from their audience and praise Jesus when the money came in. Some of that money went for luxuries. At one time or another, the Bakkers owned a Rolls-Royce, a Mercedes-Benz, and a houseboat. The Bakkers fans appeared to love basking in the couple's reflected glamour. Although more socially conscious Christians may have disapproved, the Bakkers' gospel of salvation and prosperity appealed to many of their listeners. Between 120,000 and 160,000 people contributed $1,000 or more to become "Lifetime Partners" of PTL. Bakker promised that each $1,000 contribution earned the donor three free nights' stay at Heritage USA (Lippy 1989).

Jim Bakker's 1987 downfall began with a story of sexual misconduct and continued on through his conviction and imprisonment for fraud. It appeared that, in 1980, Jim Bakker had a sexual encounter with Jessica Hahn, a former church secretary (Lippy 1989). Accused of adultery and financial misconduct, Bakker turned control of his empire over to Jerry Falwell, who became embroiled in a struggle to retain PTL against the claims of its many creditors. Falwell asked for contributions to see PTL through these trying times, but revelations about the misconduct of Jim Bakker and fellow evangelist Jimmy Swaggart of Baton Rouge, Louisiana, soured the viewers on making more contributions (Utter and Storey 2001). Falwell soon withdrew and left PTL and Heritage USA in the hands of the bankruptcy court. Oral Roberts University made a successful bid to buy the television network of PTL. In 1989, Jim Bakker was convicted of mail fraud, wire fraud, and conspiracy and sentenced to 45 years in prison in addition to a $500,000 fine.

In prison, Jim Bakker wrote an account of his misuse of donated funds and announced that he had had a change of heart, discovering fellowship among those in suffering. In his 1996 book, *I Was Wrong,* he criticized the "health and wealth" gospel that he had previously proclaimed and expressed remorse for his actions. In his 1998 book, *Prosperity and the Coming Apocalypse,* he explained his beliefs about the end of the world. He declared that contemporary Christians had developed a dependency on money, material things, and all the conveniences of modern society and that these things often became substitutes for God. Bakker added that Christians would have to undergo at least some of the great tribulations prophesied in the biblical book of Revelation.

Believing Bakker's expressions of remorse, a federal judge reduced his 45-year sentence to 8 years and eliminated the $500,000 fine. In December 1994, Bakker received an early release after 5 years and 2 months in prison. Bankruptcy court awarded $49 million to Heritage USA's creditors but made no award to the small contributors, the "Lifetime Partners." Another court ordered Bakker to pay $130 million to former contributors; however, a different jury in 1996 decided in favor of Jim Bakker and against the followers who had been seeking refunds of their contributions for "partnerships" in a multimillion-dollar lawsuit.

In 1992, Tammy Faye divorced Jim while he was in prison. She married Roe Messner in 1993 and stayed married to him while he served a twenty-seven–month prison sentence for federal bankruptcy fraud. In 2003, Tammy Faye Messner hosted charity fundraisers for Alliance AIDS Service, including a fashion show with twelve drag queens and a "drag bingo" fundraiser. She also was one of six personalities in WBTV's *Surreal Life,* in which cameras followed Tammy Faye and other media personalities such as actor Erik Estrada, singer Vanilla Ice, and adult film star Ron Jeremy twenty-four hours per day for thirteen days in a Los Angeles mansion. Tammy Faye made plans for a new Christian television program to be called *Tammy Faye's House Party,* but in 2004 she announced on CNN's *Larry King Live* that she had inoperable lung cancer.

In 2003, Jim Bakker returned to televangelism with an hour-long, 5-day-per-week program, *The New Jim Bakker Show,* broadcast from Branson, Missouri, despite an earlier assertion from Bakker that he did not ever plan on being in television again. He and his second wife, Lori, had moved to Branson at the urging of local business-man Jerry Crawford. Crawford credited Bakker's PTL ministry with helping to save his marriage, and he said that he had been born again during a 1986 visit to PTL headquarters. Crawford paid for a café and television equipment, and then offered them to Bakker to use for a television show to be broadcast from the Studio City Cafe. Crawford let Bakker and his wife live rent-free in a home he built near his own. Bakker's new show featured religious music, guest in-terviews, and party hats for café diners who were celebrating birth-days. Bakker has said that he made $16,000 in 2003 and still owed about $7 million in penalties and interest as of 2004. He also said that he worried about so-called prosperity preachers who follow his previous philosophy of "give to receive." "It's very, very dangerous when we focus on material things," he said. "Especially the church—to focus on material things is opposite of what Jesus taught." (Smith 2003).

Gary L. Bauer (1946–)

Gary Bauer worked for many years for conservative Christian causes. James Dobson's Focus on the Family chose Bauer to be its congres-sional lobbyist, and Bauer headed the Family Research Center, an off-shoot of Focus on the Family, until he resigned after his 2000 presi-dential campaign. As of this writing in 2004, he serves as president of American Values and as chairman of Campaign for Working Families, both based in Arlington, Virginia. Bauer created the Campaign for Working Families in 1997 as a political action committee.

Bauer was reared in Newport, Kentucky, and he graduated with a B.A. from Georgetown College in Kentucky in 1968. He received a J.D. from Georgetown University in 1973. After working for a trade association, he joined the 1980 Reagan presidential campaign as a se-nior policy analyst. After being successful in the election, Reagan se-lected Bauer for various positions in his administration, including chairman of the president's Special Working Group on School Disci-pline and undersecretary in the Department of Education. In 1988 and again in 1996, Bauer expressed his displeasure with the Republi-can presidential candidates, lamenting their lack of serious conservative credentials. He decided to remedy the situation by running for president himself in 2000 (Utter and Storey 2001).

During the Iowa caucuses, the first shakeout of presidential candidates, a fierce battle developed between Bauer and Alan Keyes to be recognized as the conservative alternative. At the same time, conservative Steve Forbes was also competing with Texas governor George W. Bush, as well as conservative Utah senator Orrin Hatch. During his campaign, Bauer opposed legalized abortion (including advocating a constitutional amendment against abortion), gay rights, and the right to die. He advocated additional welfare reform and tax cuts for families. In addition to these orthodox conservative Christian positions, Bauer also advocated a patient's bill of rights and campaign finance reform. The Republican caucus results disappointed Bauer. They showed Bush winning (with 41 percent of the vote), followed by Forbes (30 percent), Keyes (14 percent), Bauer (9 percent), and Hatch (1 percent). Moderate Republican John McCain gained the other 5 percent of the vote, even though he did not campaign in Iowa (*Boston Herald,* January 25, 2000, 5).

After finishing last in the New Hampshire primaries as well, Bauer became the sixth Republican contender to drop out of the presidential race. At that time, he said he would not support either Bush or McCain unless they joined him in supporting efforts to outlaw abortion and to halt U.S. trade with the People's Republic of China. However, Bauer surprised some of his supporters in February 2000 when he gave his endorsement to candidate McCain, who had beaten Bush in the New Hampshire primary (*Houston Chronicle,* February 17, 2000, 19). In South Carolina, Christian Coalition founder Pat Robertson gave his endorsement to Governor Bush, and a series of anti-McCain ads were printed or aired (*Austin American-Statesman,* February 18, 2000, A7). Bauer was on stage at a political rally with Senator McCain when McCain lashed out at Pat Robertson and Jerry Falwell, comparing them to Al Sharpton and Louis Farrakhan as "agents of intolerance." Later on his campaign bus, McCain said he was trying to battle "the forces of evil." Bauer urged McCain to retract his remarks, but McCain did not do so (*Austin American-Statesman,* March 2, 2000, A1). Religious conservative leaders expressed shock and disappointment with Bauer's endorsement of McCain, whose pro-life stance was questioned by conservatives who worried that he was soft on abortion. Bauer's own Family Research Council and longtime ally, James Dobson, publicly criticized Bauer's endorsement of McCain, which Dobson called "troubling" and "hard to understand" (Colorado Springs, CO, *Gazette,* April 2, 2000, A8).

As of 2004, Bauer was heading a political action committee, Campaign for Working Families, as well as American Values, his organization to fight the "culture war" in the United States. From these positions, Bauer has made efforts to influence both national policy and American morality. Addressing a Washington conference of conservative Christians and Jewish Zionists in May 2003, Bauer joined in the attacks on President Bush's "Road Map" for peace in the Middle East. Bauer said, "The land of Israel was originally owned by God. . . . Since He was the owner, only He could give it away. And He gave it to the Jewish people." Bauer added that terrorists did not understand "why Israel and the United States are joined at the heart." Instead of the Bush Road Map plan for the Middle East, Bauer proposed that U.S. policy should focus on Israel's retention of "the lands God promised to Abraham, Isaac, and Jacob" (*Washington Times*, May 19, 2003, A1). Bauer also authored an open letter to President Bush supporting the war in Iraq but opposing Bush's road map for Israel (Religious Freedom Coalition 2003). Addressing a gathering at Cornerstone University in Grand Rapids in 2004, Bauer heaped praise on President Bush's decision to back a constitutional amendment banning gay marriage. Bauer said, "We're in the middle of not one, but two wars—one where we're fighting terror, and the second war is just as important: It's a war about the definition of America." He said that President Bush had declared a cultural war with his decision to back the antigay marriage amendment. Bauer thought this issue would rouse the Christian conservatives to action in the 2004 election (*The Grand Rapids Press*, March 4, 2004, A1).

Robert J. Billings (1926–1995)

Robert Billings served in the Reagan administration as secretary of education, where he was a major supporter of Christian schools. Billings graduated from Bob Jones University in Greenville, South Carolina, and worked early on as a high school principal. He left that position, however, because he felt that there was excessive government interference and a dominance of secular humanism in public education generally. He and his wife established Christian schools across the nation. He later served as president of Hyles-Anderson College in Crown Point, Indiana. In 1976, he campaigned unsuccessfully for Congress (Utter and Storey 2001).

Billings was active in conservative Christian organizations. He founded the National Christian Action Coalition in 1978, a successor to Christian School Action. The organization's major goal was to oppose government involvement with Christian schools over issues of teacher certification, curriculum control, desegregation mandates, and tax exempt status. Billings directed an effort against the Internal Revenue Service when that agency sought in 1978 to deny tax exemptions to Christian schools that were allowing racial discrimination. In 1979, he helped persuade Jerry Falwell to form a new organization, Moral Majority, and assisted in rallying support for it. He served as the organization's first executive director.

Billings left the Moral Majority in 1980 to serve as a religious advisor in Ronald Reagan's presidential campaign. He was named the director of regional offices in the Department of Education in that administration. There, he continued to oppose the Internal Revenue Service's efforts to tax religious schools. Nonetheless, the U.S. Supreme Court, in 1983, overruled the administration's decision to grant tax exempt status to Billings's old alma mater, Bob Jones University. In 1988, he supported Senator Bob Dole's unsuccessful bid for the Republican nomination for president. Billings reportedly said that people did not wish to think for themselves but desired leadership and wanted to be told what to think by those who were more closely involved with politics (Utter and Storey 2001).

William G. Boykin (1948–)

Army lieutenant general William G. Boykin made the national news when it became known that he had addressed evangelical Christian audiences and likened the war against Islamic militants to a battle against Satan. Television news showed film clips of the general appearing in dress uniform and making such comments before a religious group in Oregon in June 2003 (*The Washington Times,* October 24, 2003, A1). General Boykin had given other speeches at evangelical Christian churches in which he cast the war on terrorism as a religious battle between Christians and the forces of evil. Boykin said Islamic extremists hated the United States "because we're a Christian nation, because our foundation and our roots are Judeo-Christian. . . . And the enemy is a guy named Satan" (*Los Angeles Times,* October 16, 2003, A1). He later apologized for his remarks, saying "I am not anti-Islam or any other religion"(*Los Angeles Times,* October 18, 2003, A11).

William Boykin was born in Wilson, North Carolina, on April 19, 1948. He was and is a career army officer. As a brigadier general,

Boykin commanded the army's Delta Force in 1992 and the army's Combat Applications Group and Task Force Rangers in Somalia in 1993. Two of his men in that latter unit were awarded posthumous Medals of Honor for their actions on October 3, 1993, to protect the wounded crew of a downed helicopter in Mogadishu (Department of Defense 1996a, 1996b). That action entered popular culture in the movie *Black Hawk Down*. Boykin also served in the Pentagon as deputy director of special activities on the Joint Intelligence Coordination Staff and as Deputy Director for Operations, Readiness, and Mobilization on the army staff. From 1998 to 2000, General Boykin commanded the Special Forces Command. In 2000 he became the commanding general at the U.S. Army John F. Kennedy Special Warfare Center, Fort Bragg, North Carolina.

It was in North Carolina that Boykin attracted press attention by inviting a large group of predominantly Southern Baptist pastors to Fort Bragg to participate in a military-themed motivational program for Christian evangelists (*New York Times*, April 6, 2003, 24). The 2003 invitation apparently sprang from the close friendship between Boykin and the Reverend Bobby H. Welch. Welch was a Southern Baptist minister in Daytona Beach, Florida, where he started an evangelistic campaign called FAITH Force Multipliers. Welch later said that he was a Vietnam veteran who had trained at Fort Bragg and who had sought to apply military principles to evangelism. He later added that he had held a previous FAITH Force Multipliers session at General Boykin's invitation in 2002. A few of the invited ministers had been offended at the close melding of church and state at the event. In April 2003, however, the ministers' visit was scaled down after the press reported the invitation (*New York Times*, April 6, 2003, 24).

In June 2003, the Department of Defense nominated Major General Boykin for promotion to lieutenant general and for assignment as deputy undersecretary of defense for intelligence. Also in June, he spoke at a religious meeting and reportedly likened the war against Islamic militants to a battle against Satan, but the report of the speech did not surface until October 2003. Then the *Los Angeles Times* reported that, in one of his speeches, Boykin had said of Islamic warlord Osman Otto of Mogadishu, "I knew that my God was a real God, and his was an idol." NBC News broadcast segments of such speeches the general had made while in uniform. A *Los Angeles Times* columnist had secretly recorded the comments at churches in Oklahoma, Oregon, and Florida (*Los Angeles Times*, October 16, 2003, A1).

Reaction to the press stories quickly came from supporters, detractors, and those who sought to distance themselves from Boykin. Senator John Warner, Virginia Republican and chair of the Senate Armed Services Committee, joined with Senator Carl Levin, the ranking Democrat on the committee, to ask Secretary of Defense Donald Rumsfeld to conduct an internal investigation to determine whether General Boykin had acted inappropriately. They also asked for the general to temporarily resign his Pentagon post until the investigation was complete. Representative Todd Tiahrt, a Republican from Kansas, and other members of Congress defended Boykin. Tiahrt asked Secretary Rumsfeld not to discipline Boykin because elected officials and military leaders have talked about God and spiritual matters throughout U.S. history (*Grand Rapids Press*, October 21, 2003, A4). Boykin requested an investigation by a military inspector general, and Secretary Rumsfeld agreed (*St. Louis Post-Dispatch*, October 22, 2003, A4), but he did not temporarily relieve Boykin as Warner had asked. President George W. Bush said, "General Boykin's comments don't reflect the administration's comments. . . . He doesn't reflect my point of view or the point of view of this administration" (*New York Times*, October 23, 2003, A7). After that, the press found little to report on. In 2004, Boykin continued to serve as deputy undersecretary of defense for intelligence.

James C. Dobson (1936–)

A former associate professor of pediatrics at the University of Southern California School of Medicine, Dobson was the founder and chairman of Focus on the Family. He earned his Ph.D. from the University of Southern California in 1967, and he has received various honorary degrees as well. The Focus on the Family organization was concerned with social issues affecting the traditional family structure. It produced his syndicated radio and television programs, including his popular 30-minute weekday program, *Focus on the Family*. In the 1990s, his radio and television programs reached approximately 28 million people every week (Utter and Storey 2001). His organization reported in 2004 that he was heard daily on more than 3,000 radio facilities in North America and in translation in 116 countries, including being carried by state-owned radios in the People's Republic of China. These translations could mean that Dobson's commentaries were heard daily by more than 200 million people (Focus on Family 2004).

Although Dobson emphasized traditional Christian values in the advice he gave about the problems people faced in contemporary family life, he did not present the explicitly biblical messages found with other radio evangelists. His book, *Dare to Discipline* (1970), became a popular evangelical treatise on the subject of parenting. In it, he criticized permissive parents and emphasized the need for discipline within a loving parent-child relationship. This first edition of the book sold more than 3 million copies. Dobson later revised and updated it as *The New Dare to Discipline*. Altogether, Dobson's books for the family have sold more than 16 million copies. Focus on the Family's revenues for 2003 exceeded $130 million, including $112 million in contributions and $6 million in sales. The organization had a staff of more than 1,300, including several licensed family counselors to deal with emergency situations. Dobson's organization was headquartered in Colorado Springs, Colorado.

Dobson's concern for families has led to his involvement in national politics. He was called to a White House conference on the family during the Carter administration, and he served on six government panels during the Reagan administration, including the Commission on Pornography that was headed by Attorney General Ed Meese. Concerned that his and his organization's views were not being given enough attention in Washington, in 1988, Dobson merged his organization with the Family Research Council, a policy advocacy group then headed by Gary Bauer. This arrangement not only increased Bauer's prestige, but it also gave Dobson a venue for promulgating his conservative positions on abortion, homosexuality, and teen sex. However, concerned with endangering its tax exempt status, Focus on the Family severed its legal ties with the Family Research Council in 1992. (See the entry for Gary Bauer in this appendix, as well as the appendix of organizations, for more information on Focus on the Family and the Family Research Council.)

Dobson is the son, grandson, and great-grandson of Nazarene preachers, and he brings an emphatically moral perspective to processes of policymaking and politics, especially concerning the traditional family. The Web site for Focus on Family (http://www.family.org), for example, asks if homosexuality can be cured, and its answer is: "Focus on the Family is promoting the truth that homosexuality is preventable and treatable." Similarly, Focus on the Family asks members to write to Congress regarding strengthening protection for the unborn, and it provides instructions for writing to one's local newspaper editor regarding support for a constitutional amendment against same-sex marriage. In this regard, Focus on the

Family shares a purist attitude with many of the leaders of the religious right. But a purist typically sees no value in compromise, and as a result can have serious difficulty in attracting enough allies to constitute a majority position. For Dobson, "It's either God's way, or it is the way of social disintegration" (Utter and Storey 2001). Consequently, he chastises more pragmatic efforts.

In 1996, Dobson faulted Ralph Reed for not attacking Colin Powell more aggressively for his position on abortion. In 1998, Dobson threatened havoc to the national Republican party unless it took more solid stands on issues important to social conservatives (Utter and Storey 2001). In 2000, he was troubled by his old comrade Gary Bauer when Bauer endorsed John McCain following Bauer's own withdrawal from the race. After Jerry Falwell and Pat Robertson characterized the September 11, 2001, attacks on the United States as God's wraith against a sinful nation, Dobson wondered, "how a God of justice can bless and preserve a nation in which murder is its centerpiece, and sexual immorality is its pastime" (Infield 2001). Dobson's purist stance on abortion and homosexuality not only made it difficult to compromise on public statement and policy initiatives, but it also typified the Republican party's difficulty with the religious right. If the party catered directly to the right's very conservative views, it faced the possibility of alienating more moderate Republicans and more moderate independent voters.

Colonel V. Doner (1949–)

Colonel Doner was one of the cofounders of the American Coalition for Traditional Values and of the Christian Voice, one of the oldest of the Christian right groups. Christian Voice grew out of an unsuccessful attempt by California evangelicals to get a state law passed that would limit the public employment of homosexuals. Composed primarily of members of Assembly of God churches, Christian Voice concentrated its activities on influencing elections. Doner and his colleagues claimed that they were responsible for defeating President Jimmy Carter and thirty incumbent Congress members in the 1980 election. Conventional wisdom in 1980 did credit the religious right as being an important part of Reagan's election. On the other hand, surveys by the National Election Studies found that evangelicals' turnout for voting in the 1980s averaged 58 percent, 7 percent lower than the average voting of all who were interviewed for the survey. During the 1980 election, Christian Voice published moral report cards on congressional Democrats and ran controversial campaign ads, including one that identified President Carter with the homosexual rights movement. Doner appeared on national television programs such as *60 Minutes* and *Phil Donahue,* where he was noted for his combative style. He was chairman of the national Reagan/Bush Christian voter registration and mobilization campaign in 1984.

In his 1989 book, *The Samaritan Strategy,* Doner examined the political activities of the religious right and its association with the Republican party, including the extent of Republican support in his 1984 establishment of the American Coalition for Traditional Values and the curtailment of that support when Republican leaders began to fear the coalition's influence. In 1986, Doner left Washington after concluding that the religious right had failed to achieve its main objectives. Later, he came to believe that the religious right had erred in not caring enough about the plight of the needy, such as homeless and abandoned children. In 1988, he published *Responsible Parents' Guide to TV.* He began to seek contacts with more liberal evangelical Christians to increase their service to the needy. Doner became the chairman of the Children's Hunger Relief Fund. In that role, he accused the government of Sudan of a genocide campaign against the people of the upper Nile region.

More recently, Doner has presented his thoughts on religion and politics in the *Chalcedon Report,* a print and e-mail publication of the Chalcedon Society. Doner and Chalcedon published a booklet, *The Late Great GOP and the Coming Realignment,* and its three-part e-version, *Collapse of the GOP and the Coming Realignment.* In these, Doner expressed his deep disappointment with the Republican party in the 1990s for a host of sins. The party, he said, had failed to keep faith with its basic principles, gotten out of touch with average Americans, failed to mobilize the "moral majority," and demonstrated moral bankruptcy in not restoring the nation's Christian heritage. His solution was for conservative evangelicals to abandon their unofficial alliance with the Republican party in order to seek to establish a third force in American politics, based on an alliance with others who shared their social conservatism. Such potential partners, he suggested, could include populists, independents, and "suburban-value" Democrats. Doner also criticized evangelical Christians for not recognizing the authority of the Old Testament and its relevance to contemporary society.

Jerry Falwell (1932–)

Probably the most controversial and prominent spokesman for the religious right has been Jerry Falwell. His transformation from other-worldliness to political engagement is an archetype of the change in the religious right from personal to social salvation.

In the 1960s, Falwell argued that churches should focus on transforming individuals through the saving power of Jesus instead of on a social message to reform institutions. But in the 1970s, Falwell saw a nation that featured disintegrating families, gay rights, the spread of pornography, public schools without public prayers, and government support of abortion rights. Falwell proclaimed that his earlier statements were "false prophecy," and he turned to conservative political activists to form a new national organization, the Moral Majority (Baranowski 1989, 135–136).

Reared among bootleggers in the hill country of central Virginia, Falwell gave no early hint that he would later become the minister of one of the largest Baptist churches in the country. After he became a Christian in 1952, he attended Bible Baptists College in Missouri. When he returned to Lynchburg, Virginia, he established an independent Baptist church in a vacant bottling plant. He soon launched a thirty-minute radio program and a television program. From 35 members in 1956, his Thomas Road congregation had grown to nearly 20,000 by the early 1980s Thomas Road Baptist Church (TRBC) remained a "super church" in terms of membership size and electronic outreach in 2004. Falwell's Sunday service was carried to an estimated audience of 21 million via 681 radio and television stations as *The Old-Time Gospel Hour*. With an audience of this size, Falwell was an impressive fundraiser. He generated enough contributions to fund TRBC, Lynchburg Christian Academy, a home for alcoholics, a children's day school, an inner-city program, and a college (Liberty University in Lynchburg). In fact, by 2003, Liberty University and TRBC had grown so large as to raise fears of overdevelopment from the Lynchburg city council. Falwell was able to assuage the council's concerns, and it rezoned an 83-acre property to allow desired expansions of Falwell's University (Battle 2003).

But it was as a political spokesman for the religious right that Falwell gained his greatest recognition. With the help of conservative political strategists such as Paul Weyrich and Edward McAteer, Falwell cofounded the Moral Majority in 1979. Its purpose was to give a political voice to the growing numbers of Christian fundamentalists who were disturbed by the perceived immorality in American politics and culture. These fundamentalists had traditionally abstained from political struggle but could no longer stay uninvolved in the face of Supreme Court decisions on public school prayer, abortion, and obscenity. Movies and television with immoral pictures and stories, gay rights, and the near passage of the Equal Rights Amendment struck Falwell and his followers as reasons for political activism to reassert traditional values (Baranowski 1989). When Ronald Reagan was elected to the presidency in 1980, the Moral Majority and other leaders of the religious right claimed credit. There was no doubt that they had made vigorous efforts to register and mobilize voters and that they had targeted liberal Democrats for defeat. However, it is not clear just how much effect these efforts had and what these effects were. Many members of the religious right voted for Jimmy Carter, a Southern Baptist who had been born again. But, as discussed in Chapter 4, others did support Reagan. Although it claimed to be nonpartisan, the Moral Majority appeared more at ease with the conservative Republican agenda than with that of the Democrats (Utter and Storey 2001).

The Moral Majority was never very successful at attracting members from outside its core of Christian fundamentalists. In an effort to broaden the base, Falwell renamed it Liberty Foundation in 1986. However, that was the year in which Praise the Lord (PTL) leader Jim Bakker was tried and convicted of misappropriation of funds. The fallout from the Bakker scandal swept over other televangelists, including Jerry Falwell. A Gallup poll indicated that 62 percent of the American public viewed Falwell unfavorably (Utter and Storey 2001). In 1989, he dissolved the Moral Majority, three years after its activities had been shifted to the newly formed Liberty Foundation, and began to devote more attention to his local congregation and his college, Liberty University, in Lynchburg, Virginia. If Liberty University was any example, Falwell preferred authority over liberty—at least insofar as students were concerned. Under university rules, students could not participate in unauthorized demonstrations, were obliged to attend church, and could be expelled for participating in petition drives or demonstrations not approved by the administration (Wald 2003, 314).

Falwell continued to generate controversy with his public statements. In early 1999, he announced that the Antichrist was a Jewish man who probably was alive today, and he declared that Tinky Winky, one of the *Teletubbies* characters on children's television, was gay and therefore a menace to American youth. Falwell maintained a relatively low profile in the 2000 presidential race. He largely worked behind the scenes in support of George W. Bush, but he did work to register at least 10 million voters for the November election, calling the project "People of Faith 2000."

After the September 11 destruction of the World Trade Center and the suicide plane crashes into the Pentagon and in Pennsylvania, Falwell appeared on Pat Robertson's *700 Club* program and said that God was punishing the United States because of its immorality. In his statement, he said that this terrorist assault might seem minuscule "if God continues to lift the curtain and allow the enemies of America to give us probably what we deserve." Host Robertson added, "The abortionists have got to bear some of the burden for this because God will not be mocked." Speaking of "the pagans and the abortionists and the feminists and the gays and the lesbians," Falwell continued, "I point the finger at you and say, 'You made this happen'" (Knight Ridder/Tribune News Service, September 14, 2001). Outraged reaction against these statements was fairly widespread, and Falwell later apologized. He conceded that his remarks were "insensitive, uncalled for at the time, and unnecessary as part of the commentary on this destruction." Robertson, on the other hand, blamed his producers for inviting Falwell and insisted that he did not understand what Falwell was saying and that the group that transcribed his remarks may have taken them out of context (Lowe 2001).

It remained difficult for Falwell to stay away from controversy. In a 2002 television interview, he said, "I think Muhammad was a terrorist." He said that he had concluded from reading Muslim and non-Muslim writers that Islam's prophet was "a violent man, a man of war" (*Cincinnati Post,* October 4, 2002). Falwell later said he was honestly answering a question about whether he considered Muhammad a terrorist on a program that was examining conservative Christian support of the nation of Israel. Yet Falwell joined with Jay Sekulow at the White House in November 2003 to witness President George W. Bush's signing of the Partial-Birth Abortion Ban Act. Whether commenting on the September 11 attack or on other issues, Falwell appeared to always be engaged with the combination of religion and politics, and he seemed to be able to stir controversy with his statements.

William ("Billy") Franklin Graham (1918–)

Billy Graham represented the neoevangelists of the religious right, a group that was guarded about both fundamentalism and the charismatic approach. Within the mainstream of evangelism, neoevangelists have proved to have reservations about the political stance of the religious right. Billy Graham personified this more moderate stance. Early in his career, he exhibited some of the political and social tendencies typical of fundamentalist Protestants. But over the years, Graham racially integrated his crusades, spoke out in favor of civil rights legislation, and advocated limits on the nuclear arms race. Graham warned that any attempt to identify a particular political agenda with Christianity was likely to bring discredit on religion and to interfere with evangelization (Wald 2003, 230).

Billy Graham practiced a biblically based and passionate style of evangelism that set the standard for many others, and in so doing, he helped to make evangelical Christianity acceptable once again to the general American public. He has been accepted at both Democratic and Republican White Houses, and when actor Mel Gibson produced his controversial movie, *The Passion of the Christ,* Gibson visited Graham in 2003 and convinced him of his sincerity. Graham said, "I feel as if I have actually been there. I was moved to tears" (Knight Ridder/Tribune News Service, December 1, 2003).

Billy Graham had a rural upbringing near Charlotte, North Carolina, and an early revival conversion to Christ. Charlotte Jean Ford, Graham's youngest sister, recalled that he was 11 or 12 when they moved into their new two-story, red brick house, and he lived there for 8 years until he left for Bob Jones College in Cleveland, Tennessee, in 1937 (Knight Ridder/Tribune News Service, March 11, 2004). Graham publicly committed his life to Christ at a 1934 revival led by traveling evangelist Mordecai Ham. Unhappy with the restrictions at Bob Jones College, Graham transferred to the Florida Bible Institute near Tampa, Florida, where he was ordained a Southern Baptist minister in 1939 (Lippy 1989).

Graham graduated from Wheaton College near Chicago in 1943 and assumed the duties of pastor at the First Baptist Church in Western Springs, Illinois. In 1943, he married Ruth McCue Bell, whom he had met at Wheaton. She was the daughter of medical missionaries in China. Chicago introduced Graham to radio evangelism also in 1943 when his congregation sponsored *Songs in the Night,* a weekly radio program with Graham preaching. The following year, he became a preacher for the Youth for Christ organization, leading evangelistic campaigns targeted at adolescents and young adults in the United States and Europe. From 1947 to 1952, Graham also served as president of Northwestern Schools in Minneapolis, Minnesota, despite his increasing commitment to a career as an evangelist.

In 1949, Graham's evangelical campaign in Los Angeles, California, had such a rousing response that it was extended from three weeks to two months. The Los Angeles revival made Graham a celebrity. In 1950, Graham first used the word *crusade* to describe his evangelistic campaign in Columbia, South Carolina. The attendance of Governor Strom Thurmond at a service and Thurmond's endorsement of Graham began the long association of Billy Graham with political figures. Also in 1950, he formed the Billy Graham Evangelistic Association to coordinate his expanding activities, including his *Hour of Decision* radio broadcasts. In 1952, he resigned from Northwestern Schools and moved to Montreat, North Carolina. In 1955, he established the conservative journal *Christianity Today* because he believed the existing *Christian Century* was too liberal. President-elect Dwight Eisenhower sought Graham's advice about an inaugural prayer, and in 1965, Graham gave President Lyndon Johnson's inaugural prayer (Lippy 1989).

In the 1950s and 1960s, Graham took a strong anticommunist stance. He maintained his primary focus on the need for personal conversion, but he also was willing to express his opinion on social issues. He uncritically supported U.S. involvement in Vietnam under Presidents Johnson and Nixon, and he took conservative positions on other issues. Graham criticized the Supreme Court's ban on oral prayer in public schools and its perceived leniency toward criminals. He led Sunday worship services at the White House during the presidency of Richard Nixon. After Nixon's resignation, Graham reduced his presence as the "friend to presidents." In the 1980s, Graham raised questions about the dangers of an arms race between the United States and the Soviet Union. Although some conservative Christian leaders have criticized Graham's evangelism as ignoring the importance of political activism, attitude surveys of the general population indicate that Billy Graham remains to the present day one of the more esteemed Americans.

In the 1990s, Graham publicly supported ecumenism, which more fundamental Christians had seen as anathema. Graham said that not only Roman Catholics, but also Muslims, Buddhists, and nonbelievers, could receive God's grace. By the late 1990s, however, Graham's failing health prevented him from continuing his active work schedule. He suffered from Parkinson's disease, prostate problems, and high blood pressure. Graham delegated many of his evangelical duties to his son Franklin. In 2000, his health prevented Graham from attending the National Prayer Breakfast in Washington, D.C., one of the few times he had missed the event since 1993 (Utter and Storey

2001). Early in 2004, at age eighty-five, Graham fell and broke his hip in Jacksonville, Florida. Surgeons immediately performed a partial hip replacement, and Graham was released from the hospital after four weeks of physical therapy (*New York Times,* February 3, 2004). Billy Graham has had a long and impressive career as an internationally known evangelist, but as of 2004, the Billy Graham Evangelistic Association was in the hands of his children.

John Hagee (1940–)

Born in Baytown, Texas, near Houston, Hagee attended Trinity University in San Antonio on a football scholarship. He received his bachelor's degree in 1964. He earned a master's degree from North Texas State University in 1966, and he studied at Southwestern Bible Institute in Waxahachie, Texas. Later, he received an honorary doctorate from Oral Roberts University, and he has been on its board of regents since 1989. Hagee, the son of a Baptist minister, began his evangelism career in 1958. In 1966, he was the founding pastor of what would become Trinity Church, a charismatic congregation in San Antonio. While at Trinity, Hagee divorced his wife to marry a member of the congregation. He left Trinity in 1975 to become the pastor of a very small church in San Antonio called the Church of Castle Hills. Hagee oversaw the church's growth from fewer than 100 members in 1975 to 17,000 members in 2004. Within 2 years, Hagee had built a new sanctuary seating 1,600 people. In 1987, Hagee dedicated another new sanctuary with the capacity to seat 5,000, and the church was renamed Cornerstone.

Cornerstone Church's services included a jazz band and a 125-member choir. His company, Global Evangelism Television, developed a nationwide broadcast ministry with daily and weekly television and radio programs. Pastor Hagee also sold audiotapes and videotapes of his sermons, in which he preached about abortion, environmentalism, feminism, homosexuality, and American foreign policy in the Middle East. Hagee also preached the salvation and prosperity theme that was previously associated with Jim Bakker. According to a San Antonio reporter, Hagee preached, "When you give, it qualifies you to receive God's abundance," and "If you're not prospering, it's because you're not giving" (*San Antonio Express-News,* June 21, 2003, 10H).

Hagee's influence among evangelical Christians outside his church stemmed from his broadcast church services and the sale of audiotapes and videotapes. In 2004, Cornerstone Church services were broadcast on 120 television stations and 110 radio stations. Cornerstone claimed that its broadcasts were heard in 92 million homes. Hagee's speaking style was appealing to many fundamentalist Christians. He was very animated, presented his lessons in a highly confident and uncompromising manner, and offered applications of scripture to listeners' daily lives. He was a best-selling author of books about the millennium and the end of the world (*Beginning of the End* [1996] and *Final Dawn over Jerusalem* [1999]) and about alleged conspiracies in American government and society (*Day of Deception* [1997]).

Despite the popularity of much of his message with others in the religious right, Hagee attracted criticism for claiming that Jews had a separate covenant with God from that of Christians and that Jews, therefore, did not have to be converted to Christianity for salvation (*Washington Times,* July 3, 2002). Hagee opposed anti-Semitism, and Cornerstone's teachings included the belief that the Genesis promise to Israel constituted a sacred covenant with Jews today and with the country of Israel. Cornerstone sponsored a Night to Honor Israel to show the church's support for that nation (*Houston Chronicle,* November 25, 2002). Hagee received accolades from Jewish organizations for, among other things, raising more than $1 million to aid the resettlement of Soviet Jews in Israel. In 2003, Hagee was a cosigner, along with Jerry Falwell, D. James Kennedy, and Ed McAteer, of Gary Bauer's Open Letter to President Bush. The letter argued that the Palestinian leadership must end its propaganda "that teaches Nazi-inspired hatred of Jews and incitements to violence."

Some fundamentalist leaders expressed concern about Hagee's use of the "salvation and prosperity" doctrine. This doctrine held that giving to God's purposes qualified the giver to receive God's great gifts, including personal wealth. The way to wealth, in this view, was through obedience to God's laws and through giving to the church. Despite criticism from some, the salvation and prosperity doctrine remained an important part of Hagee's message.

Hank Hanegraaff (1950–)

A prolific author and the president of the Christian Research Institute (CRI) International, Hank (Hendrik) Hanegraaff was both revered and attacked by others in the religious right. Most fundamentalists would agree with Hanegraaff's strong opposition to abortion and his strong support for creationism (Utter and Storey 2001). However, Hane-graaff has attacked some individuals and evangelical movements for departing from orthodox Christian beliefs. Both his stands and his attacks (and questions about them) formed part of his nationally broadcast daily radio program, *The Bible Answer Man*, and his organization's ministry on the Internet (http://www.equip.org). Hanegraaff also traveled as a guest speaker to church conferences and gatherings. He and his wife Kathy have nine children and live in Southern California.

One of CRI's major purposes is to expose cults that allegedly distort the Christian message. Founded by Walter Martin in 1960, CRI considers the Mormon Church, the Jehovah's Witnesses, and the Masons to be cults. In addition, CRI also criticizes the Trinity Broadcasting Network, its owner, Paul Crouch, and evangelistic personalities such as Benny Hinn and Kenneth Copeland, who appear on the network. They are attacked for departing from the true faith and descending into cultic behavior.

Hanegraaff was raised in the Christian Reformed Church, but he stated that he became a true Christian after investigating the scientific evidence for the creation, the resurrection of Jesus, and the inspiration of the Bible. He was a staff member in D. James Kennedy's Evangelism Explosion and later became associated with Walter Martin, who was then head of the Christian Research Institute. When Martin died in 1989, Hanegraaff took his place in that position, and he became president and chairman of CRI.

Hanegraaff proved to be a prolific writer about contemporary Christian topics, yet his writings remained controversial among evangelicals. His *Christianity in Crisis* (1997) and *Counterfeit Revival* (1999) stirred comment and opposition as well as support, and his *The Covering: God's Plan to Protect You from Evil* (2002) and *The Third Day: The Reality of the Resurrection* (2003) may do the same. In *Christianity in Crisis,* Hanegraaff attacked various televangelists who presented what he considered to be unbiblical messages. He attacked those who espoused the health and wealth gospel, which taught that God rewarded those who demonstrated adequate faith—for example, increasing the believer's personal wealth as a result of increased church giving. In *Counterfeit Revival,* he investigated evangelists who encouraged emotional displays at public meetings as a sign of the presence of the spirit. He focused on Rodney Howard Brown's preaching, in which Brown roused his audience to uncontrollable "holy laughter" and strange behaviors. For Hanegraaff, the health and wealth gospel and "holy laughter" were not only unbiblical, but they also flew in the face of any rational consideration of the facts.

Hanegraaff marshaled his efforts at rationality to attack evolution in *The FACE That Demonstrates the Farce of Evolution* (1998) and to support the factual resurrection of Jesus in *Resurrection* (2000) and *The Third Day: The Reality of the Resurrection* (2003). Computer and Internet literate, Hanegraaff also published *The Millennium Bug Debugged*, in which he criticized the widespread media uproar over the supposed Y2K computer disaster. He also published *The Prayer of Jesus* (2002) and *The Bible Answer Book* (2004). Hanegraaff described *The Covering: God's Plan to Protect You from Evil* (2002) as a sequel to his book *The Prayer of Jesus*. *Covering* called for Christians "to return to the biblical and practical model for spiritual warfare as centered in discipleship and the spiritual disciplines away from the shallow and dangerous contemporary craze of deliverance and exorcism."

Billy James Hargis (1925–)

Born in Texarkana, Texas, Hargis began his studies for the ministry in 1943 at Ozark Bible College in Bentonville, Arkansas, and he was ordained a minister in the Disciples of Christ that year. Hargis left the college in 1945 without a degree. He received a bachelor's degree from Pikes Peak Bible Seminary in 1957, a Bachelor of Theology degree from Burton College in Colorado Springs, Colorado, in 1958, and an honorary doctorate from Bob Jones University in 1961. Hargis served as pastor of the Christian churches in Salisaw, Oklahoma (1944–1946), and Granby, Missouri (1946–1947). In 1966, Hargis left the Disciples of Christ and founded the Church of the Christian Crusade in Tulsa, Oklahoma, as an independent ministry.

Hargis founded the Christian Echoes National Ministry, Inc., in 1948 in Tulsa, Oklahoma, and he remained its president until 1986. In 1953, Hargis joined with Carl McIntire in the Bible Balloon project, a plan to float balloons carrying Bible messages over the Iron Curtain to the countries beyond. In the early 1960s, Hargis became more politically active by urging his followers to work for conservatives in election campaigns (*Sarasota Herald-Tribune,* December 11, 1996).

Throughout the 1950s and 1960s, Billy James Hargis combined Christian fundamentalism with extreme patriotism. Hargis founded a Christian anticommunist ministry called the Christian Crusade. In

1948, he began publishing the *Christian Crusade Newspaper,* and in 1949, he began speaking on *Christian Crusade* network radio broadcasts. Beginning in 1970, Hargis also served as president of American Christian College in Tulsa, Oklahoma, until he stepped down in 1974 following allegations of sexual misconduct.

In the 1960s and early 1970s, Hargis wrote several books in which he identified campus radicals, antiwar protesters, and advocates of black power with communism and with a general decline of moral values in the United States. His works included *Communist America: Must It Be* (1960), *Communism: The Total Lie* (1961), *Facts about Communism and Churches* (1962), *The Real Extremists: The Far Left* (1964), *Distortion by Design* (1965), and *Why I Fight for a Christian America* (1974). In 1970, Hargis founded American Christian College to teach "anti-Communistic patriotic Americanism."

In 1974, a female student, her husband, and three other male students accused Hargis of having sexual relations with them over a period of three years. David A. Noebel, a former associate evangelist with the Christian Crusade and vice president of American Christian College, reported that he and other officials called Hargis back from a Korean tour in October 1974 and confronted him about the allegations. Hargis reportedly admitted his guilt and blamed it all on "genes and chromosomes" (*Time Magazine* 107 (February 16, 1976): 52). The college then arranged for his resignation. Hargis announced that he was giving up his work due to health problems, but Vice President Noebel said that the health reasons for Hargis's resignation were just a cover (Plowman 1976). Hargis spent seven months at his farm in Missouri then returned to Tulsa in September 1975 and resumed his ministries there, with the exception of the college.

Hargis founded the Billy James Hargis Evangelistic Association in 1975 and continued as its president. He continued to serve as pastor of the Church of the Christian Crusade in Tulsa until 1986. Without Hargis's fundraising skills and donor lists, American Christian College closed in 1977. After leaving the college in 1974, Hargis wrote a variety of fundamentalist tomes, including *Thou Shalt Not Kill: My Babies* (1977), *The Depth Principle* (1977), *The Disaster File* (1978), *Riches and Prosperity through Christ* (1978), *The National News Media* (1980), *The Cross and the Sickle: Super Church* (1982), *Abortion on Trial* (1982), *The Federal Reserve Scandal* (1985), *My Great Mistake* (his 1985 autobiography), *Communist America: Must It Be? Vol. 2.* (1986), *Forewarned* (1987), and *Day of Deception* (1991).

After the sex scandal, Hargis found it difficult to get his message on radio and television, yet he continued his various ministries on a somewhat smaller scale. He continued to contribute to his monthly *Christian Crusade Newspaper,* which had, in 2004, a reported circulation of 25,000, and he had largely retired to his Rose of Sharon Farm in Neosho, Missouri.

In the 1960s, Billy James Hargis was known to millions as "America's Crusading Evangelist." Indeed, some observers credit Hargis and his longtime friend Carl McIntyre with giving birth to the anticommunist focus of the Christian right. Each issue of his *Christian Crusade Newspaper* contained the quote, "All I want to do is preach Jesus and save America."

Gary Jarmin (1949–)

Gary Jarmin worked as a legislative lobbyist and, in the 1980s, was one of the religious right's most politically active leaders. By the late 1980s, he was part of an effort to refocus the political efforts of the religious right away from explicitly Christian lobbying efforts and toward a more secular, grassroots orientation, still with a conservative emphasis. Jarmin was the legislative director of Christian Voice and the administrator of the organization's Moral Government Fund, a political action committee that made donations to congressional campaigns. Christian Voice began the controversial practice of rating congressional and state officials on moral issues. Jarmin wrote the *Congressional Report Card* on key family and moral issues and later became president of Christian Voice. Christian Voice grew out of anti–gay rights and antipornography campaigns in California in the 1970s. It was originally named Citizens in 1976, then was briefly called American Christians United. Christian Voice maintained its headquarters in Alexandria, Virginia.

In 1984, Jarmin became field director for the American Coalition for Traditional Values, and in 1987, he became the political director for the American Freedom Coalition. The American Freedom Coalition was headed by Robert Grant and was an organizational product of Grant's, Jarmin's, and others' beliefs that the poor showing of candidates supported by the religious right in 1986 meant that the right should cooperate with other groups to achieve common objectives. The now-defunct American Freedom Coalition reportedly accepted financial assistance from Sun Myung Moon's Unification Church, and several organizational administrators were said to be Unification Church members. This assistance was controversial because of some of the Unification Church's practices and because, in 1982, Sun

Myung Moon was convicted of conspiracy to evade taxes (Utter and Storey 2001).

For Jarmin, a major objective of the American Freedom Coalition (AFC) was to build local organizations to apply conservative pressure on local issues. For Jarmin and Grant, there seemed to be not only an interest in social needs, but also a desire to move away from potentially divisive theological differences and toward greater tolerance and a willingness to build alliances with others interested in the AFC's goals.

Jarmin's most enduring ally proved to be the Republican party. During the Reagan presidency, Jarmin characterized the Republican party as an instrument that could be used to achieve the objectives of the Christian right. Jarmin noted that they had not achieved all the policy goals they had sought during the Reagan years, but that involvement with the GOP and the Reagan administration had provided valuable experience in government and political action (Utter and Storey 2001). In 1996, Jarmin participated in writing the party's national platform, including its strong antiabortion plank. In the closely fought 2000 presidential election, Jarmin introduced a measure of levity when it became apparent that Florida and the courts would have the deciding votes. Learning that the Florida secretary of state, Republican Katherine Harris, had once played Snow White at Disney World in the 1970s, Jarmin quipped, "No doubt this means the seven Supreme Court justices in Florida will forever be known—in GOP circles anyway—as the seven dwarfs of this election" (*Washington Times,* November 24, 2000).

Jarmin also remained politically active in other ways. He has been involved in the Council for National Policy, a coalition of conservative political leaders. He and his wife, Gina Mondres, operate Jar-Mon Consultants, Inc., a Washington lobbying firm that specializes in election campaigns and foreign policy issues dealing with eastern Asia. Jarmin is also the vice president of the Parents' Day Foundation, which annually recognizes model parents on Parents' Day. Unfortunately, the foundation's 1999 selections proved to be former members of the Children of God, a group formed in California by David Berg that became infamous for prostituting its female members and for being linked with child pornography in South America. Jarmin said that, in making the award, the foundation did not ask about religious affiliation and that the 1999 awardees had declined the award. When a *Houston Chronicle* reporter asked about Jarmin's connections with Sun Myung Moon, Jarmin said that the apparent connection was coincidental but that much of the foundation's funding came from Moon-supported organizations (*Houston Chronicle,* August 5, 1999). Jarmin also served as chairman of the U.S.-Cuba Foundation, a political group that represented Republicans who wanted the trade embargo with Cuba ended.

Bob Jones, Sr. (1883–1968)

Born in Alabama, Bob Jones, Sr. came early to religious ardor and activity. He was converted in a Methodist church at age eleven, preached in his first revival at twelve, had a rustic brush-arbor church at thirteen, was a licensed minister at fifteen, and became a circuit rider, covering several churches on a circuit, at sixteen. He was orphaned at age seventeen and enrolled in Southern University in Greensboro, Alabama, but he left after two years to become a full-time evangelist.

Jones was a biblical literalist, and he saw anyone who did not accept the inerrancy of the Bible as approaching heresy. Consequently, he left the Methodist church in search of a more fundamental faith because he believed the church had departed from literalism and embraced modernism. Jones traveled throughout the United States, evangelizing largely in the South but also in Ohio, Pennsylvania, New York, Illinois, and other states. Jones became active in the World's Christian Fundamentals Association, served on the Moody Bible Institute's continuing education faculty, and, in 1926, established his own college, Bob Jones University, where his administrative duties meant a reduction in his evangelistic travels (Lippy 1989).

Bob Jones established his original college at College Point, Florida, but he was a victim of the stock market crash of 1929 and the resulting Great Depression. The loss of contributions and the collapse of the Florida real estate market necessitated relocation, and the school moved to Cleveland, Tennessee, in 1933. Here it succeeded, outgrowing all its available space, and in 1947, the school moved to its present home in Greenville, South Carolina.

Bob Jones University was founded as an explicitly fundamentalist institution, committed to the Bible and Christian ethics. Its creed called for fighting all atheistic, agnostic, pagan, and so-called scientific adulteration of the gospel (http://www.bju.edu/aboutbju/creed/index). The creed was followed by Bob Jones, Sr., as president, by Bob Jones, Jr., who succeeded his father as president, and by Bob

Jones III, who in turn succeeded his father and who was the president in 2004. The university says that it stands without apology for the old-time religion and the absolute authority of the Bible. The school has strict rules regulating the behavior of its students, faculty, and staff (http://www.bju.edu/). Bob Jones has perhaps grown into the largest fundamentalist institution of higher education in the United States, and it assists in fundamentalist homeschooling with materials from its BJU Press and BJ HomeSat.

Starting with Bob Jones, Sr., the strictness of their religious beliefs has separated BJU loyalists from other religious fundamentalists. They prefer to have nothing to do with unbelievers or those who associate with them. In the 1950s and 1960s, students and alumni of Bob Jones University appeared to follow the leadership of the Joneses in denouncing Billy Graham for allowing nonfundamentalists to participate in his crusade. The Joneses also condemned Graham for not directing converts to join fundamentalist congregations (Lippy 1989).

The Bob Joneses (Sr., Jr., and III) were serious in their commitment to separation from unbelievers, those who preached false doctrine, and those who associated with either group. This separatism was evident when they renounced the National Council of Churches and the National Association of Evangelicals. Instead, they joined with Carl McIntire in forming the American Council of Christian Churches as an opposition force.

In the 1980s, the presence of BJU fundamentalists in South Carolina preempted Jerry Falwell's Moral Majority there because Falwell depended heavily upon the very independent Baptists who had been virtually monopolized by BJU in South Carolina. As a consequence, the Moral Majority had virtually no grassroots organizations in that state.

Their conservative religious and political beliefs may make BJU loyalists difficult allies, but they have not prevented BJU loyalists from becoming an important part of the Republican party in South Carolina (Vinson and Guth 2003).

D. James Kennedy (1938–)

Kennedy was born in Augusta, Georgia, was raised in Chicago, and as a teenager moved to Florida with his family. He received a bachelor's degree from the University of Tampa and a Master of Divinity degree from Columbia Theological Seminary. He also received a Master of

Theology degree from the Chicago Graduate School of Theology and a Ph.D. from New York University.

Kennedy's Sunday sermons are televised nationally from his Coral Ridge Presbyterian Church in Fort Lauderdale, Florida. Church programs are broadcast over 500 stations, three cable networks, and three satellite networks (http://www.coralridge.org). Kennedy is a prolific author. Among his many publications are *Truths That Transform: Christian Doctrines for Your Life Today* (1996), *Evangelism Explosion, 4th edition* (1996), *What If Jesus Had Never Been Born?: The Positive Impact of Christianity in History* (1997), *The Gates of Hell Shall Not Prevail* (1997), *Why I Believe* (1999), *Why Was America Attacked?: Answers for a Nation at War* (2001), and *What If America Were a Christian Nation Again?* (2003).

Kennedy is the senior minister in a church that has almost 10,000 members as well as chief executive officer for eight other ministries, including Coral Ridge Ministries television, Coral Ridge Ministries radio, and radio station WAFG-FM (all under the company Coral Ridge Ministries Media, Inc.); the Center for Reclaiming America; the D. James Kennedy Center for Christian Statesmanship; Westminster Academy; Knox Theological Seminary; and Evangelism Explosion International. Kennedy founded Evangelism Explosion International in 1962 as a training program to teach lay people to convert nonbelievers to Christianity. In 1978, Coral Ridge Church became affiliated with the Presbyterian Church of America, a fundamentalist denomination. In 1989, Kennedy began the Knox Theological Seminary, which trains pastors in the reformed tradition and is committed to the inerrancy of the Bible. In addition to his weekly televised sermons on *The Coral Ridge Hour,* Kennedy is involved also in *Truths That Transform,* a daily radio program, and the *Kennedy Commentary,* a daily three-minute radio commentary. In 1971, he founded the Westminster Academy, a K–12 Christian school, in Fort Lauderdale.

Kennedy focused his political activism largely at the national level. He established the Center for Christian Statesmanship in Washington, D.C., in order to minister to people in government and government-related positions there. Since 1994, Kennedy's Reclaiming America for Christ has provided a series of conferences in Fort Lauderdale, and, in addition, the Center for Reclaiming America strives to inform Americans about issues considered crucial to the Christian faith and to motivate them to support the biblical principles on which Kennedy believes the nation was founded. The Center aims to help citizens "reclaim their communities for Christ" (Utter and

Storey 2001). Yet observers in Florida say that neither the Center to Reclaim America nor the Center for Christian Statesmanship has been much involved in Florida politics, preferring instead a primarily national focus (Wald and Scher 2003). In that regard, Kennedy issued a statement applauding President George W. Bush's endorsement of a proposed constitutional amendment "to defend the sanctity of marriage" against efforts to define it as anything other than between a man and a woman (Coral Ridge Ministries 2004).

Tim and Beverly LaHaye (1926–) (1930–)

Tim and Beverly LaHaye may be the man and woman most responsible for identifying secular humanism as the common enemy of the religious right and for popularizing the fundamentalist crusade against it. Since sounding this alert, Tim Lahaye has gone on to co-write the best-selling *Left Behind* fiction series, which chronicles the apocalyptic future of the United States, and Beverly LaHaye became the founder and life-president of Concerned Women of America, a conservative national organization advocating policies concerning women, family, and marriage.

Born in Detroit, Michigan, Tim LaHaye was raised in a devout and conservative Baptist home. His mother was a fellowship director in a local Baptist church, and his uncle was a Baptist preacher. After a brief stint in the U.S. Army Air Force, LaHaye enrolled in Bob Jones University in 1946, where he met Beverly Jean Ratcliffe. They married on July 5, 1947. Beverly dropped out of school to be a homemaker and pastor's wife, and Tim finished his last two years at BJU while serving as pastor of a small Baptist church in Pickens, South Carolina. After he graduated in 1950, the family moved to Minnesota, where Tim was pastor of a Baptist church in Minneapolis. In 1956, they moved to a suburb of San Diego, California, where Tim began a pastorate at Scott Memorial Baptist Church that would last a quarter of a century (Lippy 1989).

The couple's focus on Christian marriage and family led them into broadcasting and education. In 1956, the LaHayes begin appearing on a weekly half-hour television program, *LaHayes on Family Life,* which was later nationally syndicated. The LaHayes expanded their family ministry by publishing articles and books as well as by conducting a national lecture series called "Family Life Seminars." In 1965, the LaHayes established the Christian High School of San

Diego in order to allow children to avoid the humanist influences in the local schools. The school system later grew to include two high schools, an elementary school, and Christian Heritage College, of which Tim LaHaye served as president from 1970 to 1976.

In 1976, Tim LaHaye resigned from Christian Heritage College and joined his wife in a two-year tour carrying the Family Life Seminars to fifty cities, preaching traditional family values while also increasingly preaching about the dangers of secular humanism. Tim LaHaye had written some successful Christian pop psychology books, including *Spirit-Controlled Temperament* in 1966. Successful spinoffs of this first book included *Transformed Temperaments* (1971) and *Understanding the Male Temperament* (1977), as well as Beverly LaHaye's *Spirit-Controlled Woman* (1976) and *Spirit-Controlled Family Living* (1978). The couple's growing dissatisfaction with humanist influences found an outlet in Tim's writing. LaHaye's 1980 book, *The Battle for the Mind,* crystallized his attack on secular humanism. LaHaye defined humanism as a religion that places sole confidence in human beings and acknowledges no need for God. *Battle* was praised by the nation's fundamentalist leaders and, from the time of the book's publication, secular humanism became the new focus for their attacks (Utter and Story 2001). LaHaye followed the book up with two sequels, *The Battle for the Family* (1982) and *The Battle for the Public Schools* (1983).

A theme that developed from the LaHayes' seminars and writing was that of Christian sexuality within marriage. Their co-written book *The Act of Marriage: The Beauty of Sexual Love* (1976), her book *What Lovemaking Means to a Woman* (1984), and his book *What Lovemaking Means to a Man* (1984) advocate greater sexual gratification for Christian married couples. Within a few years of its publication, *The Act of Marriage* had sold more than a million copies, and a new edition was released in 1998 (Utter and Storey 2001). More recently, they have co-written *The Act of Marriage after 40* (2000).

One of the founders of the Moral Majority, Tim LaHaye started Californians for Biblical Morality in 1980 as a branch of Moral Majority. He also created the Council for National Policy, a coalition of leaders of the religious right. In 1983, Tim rallied many of the leaders of the religious right into his own political lobby organization, the American Coalition for Traditional Values (ACTV). The organization's executive committee and board of directors included Jim Bakker, Kenneth Copeland, Jerry Falwell, Jimmy Swaggart, and Thomas Zimmerman, who was also general superintendent of the Assemblies of

God. ACTV conducted a voter registration campaign for the 1984 election.

In 1979, Beverly LaHaye established Concerned Women of America with only nine members. CWA was dedicated to policies dear to the religious right: anti–gay rights, antiabortion, anti-ERA, and pro-prayer in public schools. By 1984, she could claim a membership of more than 500,000 women organized into 1,800 local chapters. In 1985, she moved with her husband to Washington, D.C.——she to establish the new national office of the CWA and he to move the ACTV headquarters to Washington.

Soon after the LaHayes' move to Washington, D.C., reports began to surface concerning financial support from Sun Myung Moon's Unification Church. After Moon was imprisoned for tax evasion in 1982, Tim LaHaye's Coalition for Religious Freedom (a precursor to ACTV) hosted a 1984 "Pageant for Religious Freedom," which hosted pastors from across the country to emphasize the need for active opposition to government intrusion into religious affairs. But, when the pastors learned that the event had been financed by the Unification Church, they protested. LaHaye soon resigned from the coalition, but that did not end his difficulties with the Unification Church. LaHaye later said that because of difficulties in setting up the Washington office of ACTV, he had accepted financial aid from Bo Hi Pak, a top aide to Sun Myung Moon. A link to the Unification Church was worrisome to those fundamentalists who believed that they should separate themselves from anyone who did not share their beliefs, but it was also worrisome to other supporters because of the conviction and imprisonment of Unification leader Sun Myung Moon (Lippy 1989).

In 1996, Tim LaHaye and Jerry Jenkins published *Left Behind,* the first of their novels about a coming apocalypse. The multiple novels of this series routinely are best sellers. The first in the series was made into a movie and is available on audiotape. *Armageddon* (2003), the next to last book in the series, was on the *New York Times* best seller list, and advance sales of *Glorious Appearing* (2004), the last in the series, indicate that it will also be a best seller. *Glorious Appearing* is advertised as based on Tim LaHaye's understanding of the book of Revelation.

Tim LaHaye has also published *Tim LaHaye's Prophecy Study Bible* (2004), and Beverly LaHaye has also co-written her own novels with conservative Christian themes: *Seasons under Heaven* (1999), *Showers in Seasons* (2000), and *Times and Seasons* (2001).

Hal Lindsey (1930–)

Hal Lindsey, like Tim LaHaye, is another member of the religious right who recounts the coming apocalypse and who encourages the belief that Armageddon is upon us. Born in Houston, Texas, Lindsey attended the University of Houston for two years before joining the U.S. Coast Guard. He later worked as a tugboat captain. Formerly an agnostic, Lindsey reported that he was converted to Christianity by reading a Gideon New Testament. From 1958 to 1960, he attended the Dallas Theological Seminary, earning a master's degree in theology, and he spent the next ten years traveling throughout the United States, Mexico, and Canada as a speaker for the Campus Crusade for Christ.

Lindsey's interest in eschatology (the study of the last days of Earth) was revealed in 1970, when he published *The Late, Great Planet Earth*. His book struck a responsive chord in the religious right. It reportedly sold 20 million copies in 52 languages, and it was made into a movie in 1978. Lindsey followed this success with a string of apocalyptic spinoffs. He published *Satan Is Alive and Well on Planet Earth* (1972), *The Terminal Generation* (1976), *Countdown to Armageddon* (1980) and some later books in the genre: *The Final Battle* (1995), *Planet Earth, 2000 A.D.* (1996), *Apocalypse Code* (1997), *Planet Earth: The Final Chapter* (1998), and *Facing Millennial Midnight* (1999). Lindsey's works typically portray current events as the fulfillment of Bible prophecies about the end of time. The restoration of Israel as a state in 1948 and Israel's gaining control of Jerusalem in 1967 convinced Lindsey that the end days were upon us and that we were the "terminal generation."

In *1980s: Countdown to Armageddon*, Lindsey stated that the decade of the 1980s could very well be the last decade of history. In 1996, in *Planet Earth: 2000 A.D.*, he was certain that the Second Advent would occur in the next few years. In 1998, Lindsey changed publishers and removed the date from his title with *Planet Earth: The Final Chapter*. In 2004, Lindsey was providing his explanations of current events as prophecies of the end of days on weekly telecasts from the Trinity Broadcasting Network.

In the 1980s, Lindsey's rather apolitical eschatology began to change when he publicly supported a stronger military to oppose communism abroad and endorsed entrepreneurial values to counter socialist tendencies at home (Lippy 1989). More recently, he has supported Israel's side in its confrontations with the Palestinians. Lindsey has been comfortable with the leaders of the religious right, although he has not engaged in as much electoral activism as Pat Robertson and Jerry Falwell.

In 2004, Lindsey continues to present his interpretations of biblical prophecy and current events in published works and over television. Lindsey is a host for *PTL* (Praise the Lord), he provides a weekly review of events and prophecy on Paul Crouch's Trinity Broadcasting Network, and Lindsey's Web site (http://www.hallindsey.org) provides news and his commentaries.

Edward A. McAteer (1927–)

Ed McAteer is known as one of the godfathers of the political activism of the religious right. He, along with Paul Weyrich, has worked tirelessly to organize conservative Christians into a political force. McAteer was a marketing specialist for the Colgate-Palmolive Company, and he has translated his communication and organization skills into this effort. He retired from Palmolive and became the national field director of the Christian Freedom Foundation, a group dedicated to training evangelicals for positions of leadership in government.

In 1979, McAteer helped establish the Religious Roundtable, and he continues as its president at this writing in 2004. The Roundtable started with a council of fifty-six, the same number of people who signed the Declaration of Independence. Just as Weyrich worked to enlist Jerry Falwell to head the Moral Majority, McAteer worked to bring James Robison, Jerry Falwell, Pat Robertson, D. James Kennedy, and Charles Stanley to serve on the board of directors for the Roundtable. Just as the Moral Majority politically activated the independent Baptist churches, the Religious Roundtable focused on activating the Southern Baptist Convention, the largest fundamentalist denomination in the country.

The Religous Roundtable sponsored the National Affairs Briefing in Dallas, Texas, in August 1980, bringing together attendees from the religious right and the political right. Ronald Reagan was the only candidate to attend the gathering, and although it was billed as nonpartisan, this meeting solidified conservative and fundamentalist support for Republican candidates. The meeting attracted national attention, but the stridency of some of the speakers and the hints of anti-Semitism at the meeting disturbed some Americans (Utter and Storey 2001). McAteer mounted a campaign for the Senate in 1984, and after his defeat, the influence of the Roundtable declined. Although his support of conservative political causes remained strong, McAteer diverged from Weyrich when the latter sought to refocus the objectives of the religious right as a secular "cultural revolution." McAteer could not embrace a political strategy that omitted the Judeo-Christian God, no matter how noble its purposes were (Utter and Storey 2001).

As of 2004, McAteer continued as president of the Roundtable, although his efforts had not been as sweeping as before. He maintained close ties to the fundamentalists who took control of the Southern Baptist Convention in the 1980s. In 2000, McAteer appealed to supporters to join a long-distance telephone company, Lifeline, which would contribute 10 percent of its receipts to the Roundtable.

In 2001, there was a campaign to have McAteer nominated as U.S. ambassador to Israel; however, President Bush selected a career diplomat, who is an orthodox Jew, for the post. In 2003, McAteer joined the Committee for a One-State Solution and was a cosigner of Gary Bauer's open letter to President Bush concerning Israel. Some fundamentalists see a special importance to the state of Israel because of their understanding of the end of the world prophecy in the biblical book of Revelation, and the Bauer letter opposed Bush's Road Map plan for the Middle East. The Religious Freedom Coalition's Web site (http://www.rfcnet.org), which archived the letter, added a proposal that U.S. policy should focus on Israel's retention of "the lands God promised to Abraham, Isaac, and Jacob."

Carl McIntire (1906–2002)

Carl McIntire was a well-known radio evangelist and an independent and unbending fundamentalist Presbyterian pastor. He was an ardent Cold Warrior, and in 1948, he argued that the United States had a moral duty to launch a nuclear strike on the Soviet Union. In 1953, McIntire joined with Billy James Hargis on the Bible Balloon project, a plan to float balloons carrying Bible messages over the Iron Curtain to the countries beyond. Yet over time, McIntire had a difficult time working with others.

The son of a Presbyterian minister, McIntire was born in Ypsilanti, Michigan, in 1906, but the family soon moved to Oklahoma, where his mother's parents had been missionaries to the Choctaw Nation. McIntire later enrolled in Princeton Theological Seminary but was dissatisfied with the growing influence of liberal theologians. In

1929, he followed his mentor J. Gresham Machen, who founded the new Westminster Theological Seminary in Philadelphia. Graduating in 1931, McIntire was ordained into the Presbyterian Church of the United States of America (PCUSA), and he became the pastor of a major fundamentalist congregation, the Collingswood, New Jersey, Presbyterian Church. He would be their pastor until after he was asked to retire in 1998.

After joining with Machen in an effort to promote conservative missionaries over liberal ones, McIntire ran afoul of the PCUSA's ecclesiastical court, which found both men guilty of sowing dissension within the church and which withdrew their ministerial credentials in 1936. The following year, the two established the Presbyterian Church of America, but the new denomination was vexed by McIntire's single-minded insistence on a policy of total abstinence from intoxicating liquor. Machen soon died in 1937, and McIntire and twelve other pastors left the PCA to establish another denomination, the Bible Presbyterian Church.

With financial help from wealthy supporters, McIntire set out to establish a comprehensive evangelical organization. He informed the faithful through columns in the *Christian Beacon,* a journal begun in 1936, and through his thirty-minute radio program, *The Twentieth Century Reformation Hour,* begun in 1955. He provided higher education through his Faith Theological Seminary in Philadelphia and through colleges in Cape Canaveral, Florida, and Pasadena, California. In 1941, he founded the American Council of Christian Churches, an organization that worked to get more conservatives into the military chaplaincy. After World War II, he established the International Council of Christian Churches in order to reveal "the great apostasy which Satan and his agents are glorying in—the World Council of Churches."

McIntire did not shrink from public demonstrations to make his political and religious points. He picketed the meetings of the World Council of Churches, and once he led a march of 14,000 demonstrators in Washington, D.C., demanding victory in the Vietnam War. In 1971, when Nixon was thawing U.S. relations with the People's Republic of China with a sports exchange called "Ping Pong Diplomacy," McIntire set up his own game of table tennis in front of the White House in protest.

At the height of his popularity in the 1960s, his *Twentieth Century Reformation Hour* was carried on more than 600 radio stations largely in the South and Midwest (Lippy 1989). On his program, he railed against Communists, homosexuals, evolution, sex education, the civil rights movement, fluoridated water, and virtually every denomination except his own Bible Presbyterian Church. In 1971, the Federal Communications Commission refused to renew the license of a radio station that carried his program on the grounds that the station was not providing time for replies from those whom McIntire had attacked. Other stations feared for their licenses as well. Soon, McIntire was reduced to a single station in New Jersey. He protested the FCC action as a violation of his right to free speech, and in 1973, he set up a pirate radio station in a former minesweeper. However, the Coast Guard closed the venture after one day. As revenues and listeners dwindled, McIntire's problems were exacerbated.

McIntire's singlemindedness and autocratic methods sparked troubles with many of those he worked with. In 1971, a bitter split at Faith Theological Seminary ended with the school's president, most faculty members, and about half of the students leaving in protest of McIntire's high-handed leadership and his outspoken support of a complete victory in Vietnam. The property in Philadelphia was lost, and the *Christian Beacon* went bankrupt. McIntire continued as pastor of the Collingswood Presbyterian Church, but his voice began to fail, and when his congregation asked him to step down, he refused. The congregation had shrunk in number to fifty, and they felt that McIntire was no longer competent to lead them. After two divisive congregational meetings, McIntire appealed to the Presbytery of New Jersey to retain him, but the Presbytery declared the pulpit vacant. McIntire began to hold Sunday services in his own home, and he threatened court action to gain his reinstatement (Utter and Storey 2001). He died in March 2002 at the age of 95.

Roy S. Moore (1947–)

Roy Moore has become famous among the religious right as the Ten Commandments judge. In 2001, a controversy arose in Alabama over a monument to the Ten Commandments. The issue raised questions about government respect and support for religion, and it was not resolved until Moore, chief justice of the Alabama Supreme Court, was removed from the bench.

Moore was born in Gadsden, Alabama, the first of three boys and two girls born to Roy and Evelyn Moore. In 1992, Republican governor Harold Guy Hunt, who had been a preacher in the Primitive Baptist denomination, appointed Moore, a West Point graduate, to fill the place of a rural circuit judge who had died. Judge Moore posted a hand-carved plaque of the Ten Commandments in his courtroom. In 1994, the American Civil Liberties Union sued over the display. A Montgomery County Circuit Judge ruled in 1996 that Judge Moore's courtroom practice was unconstitutional but that the Ten Commandments could remain on display while the case was appealed. In 1998, however, the Alabama Supreme Court dismissed the case on a technicality.

Running for the office of Alabama Supreme Court chief justice in November 2000 as a Republican and as "The Ten Commandments Judge," Moore was easily elected. On the night of July 31, 2001, the new chief justice had a two-and-a-half-ton stone monument of the Ten Commandments placed in the middle of the state courthouse rotunda (Kleffman 2002). He did so without the advance knowledge of the other eight justices of the Alabama Supreme Court. Three Alabama attorneys filed suit, arguing that the monument violated their First Amendment rights to have diverse religious views without the government officially supporting one set of beliefs. In November 2002, a federal judge ruled that the monument violated the Constitution's ban on government promoting a religious doctrine. The ruling said that the monument could stay in the courthouse but that it would have to be moved from its present public position in 30 days. Chief Justice Moore appealed the decision and refused to move the monument, and hundreds of protesters supported keeping the monument in the rotunda. The 11th U.S. Circuit Court of Appeals ruled against Moore in July 2003. The appeals court affirmed the district judge's order to remove the monument from its public position in the Alabama Judicial Building.

The eight other justices of the Alabama Supreme Court ordered employees to comply with the district judge's order. Chief Justice Moore was suspended in August 2003 for defying a federal court order to remove the monument. In September 2003, Moore addressed an audience of 10,000 men at a Promise Keepers event in Atlanta, and his supporters organized a five-state tour for a Styrofoam replica of Moore's Ten Commandments monument. Newly elected Republican governor Sonny Perdue of Georgia, speaking at a Christian Coalition rally in front of the Georgia state capitol, supported displaying the Ten Commandments in public buildings (*New York Times,* September 30, 2003, A24).

Judge Moore appealed to the U.S. Supreme Court, which refused to hear his appeal. In November 2003, Moore appeared before a special judicial court to face charges of six ethical breaches, including failing to uphold the integrity of the judiciary and bringing the judicial office into disrepute. Alabama's attorney general, Bill Pryor, who had once supported Moore and helped with his legal defense, now urged that Moore be removed from office "based upon his flagrant and totally unrepentant behavior" (Gettleman 2003). The special court agreed, unanimously ordering Moore's removal as chief justice. Afterward, Moore said, "I'd do it all over again" (*New York Times,* November 13, 2003, A18). In 2004, it looked as though Alabama law may allow that to happen. State legislators had sponsored a bill to approve the display of the Ten Commandments in public buildings, and Moore may be eligible to run again for the elected position of chief justice.

Marvin Olasky (1950–)

Olasky wrote thirteen books and many articles, but two of his books (*The Tragedy of American Compassion* and *Compassionate Conservative*) stirred both controversy and the interest of Republican politicians, including President George W. Bush. The *New York Times Magazine* (September 1999) noted that some observers characterized Olasky as the "godfather of compassionate conservatism," others saw him as a "leading thinker and propagandist of the Christian Right" (Utter and Storey 2001), and still others more harshly called his historical judgments "crude and pinched" (*Houston Chronicle,* October 8, 2000, 24). But he had the ear of President Bush, who said, "Marvin offers not just a blueprint for government, but also an inspiring picture of the great resources of decency, caring, and commitment to one another that Americans share" (Utter and Storey 2001, 105).

A member of the journalism faculty at the University of Texas at Austin since 1983, Olasky at times embraced a wide variety of religious and philosophical views. His search for a worldview governed by discernible laws led him from Judaism to atheism to Marxism-Leninism to Christian fundamentalism. He was born in Massachusetts to second-generation Russian Jewish immigrants. Olasky was, in his words, "bar-mitzvahed at thirteen and an atheist at fourteen" (Utter and Storey 2001, 105). He entered Yale University in 1968 and quickly became involved in left-wing political activities against the war in Vietnam and in support of labor. He graduated with a B.A. in 1971, and within the next two years, he married his first wife, became a reporter for the Bend, Oregon, *Bulletin,* joined the communist party, and made a pilgrimage to Russia. By the end of 1973, he had divorced his wife, abandoned communism, and entered the graduate program at the University of Michigan in Ann Arbor.

While studying American culture at the university, he met Susan Northway, a Michigan undergraduate, who became his second wife. While he was getting his M.A. and Ph.D. degrees from the University of Michigan, Olasky's political orientation moved to the right. His doctoral dissertation dealt with politics and American films. He studied classic western movies and was impressed by their strong sense of right and wrong. He prepared a course on early American literature and read numerous Puritan sermons in the process, and he also studied the Christian existentialists. By the end of 1976, he had married his second wife and converted to Christianity.

Olasky lectured at San Diego State University for a year, then the DuPont Company of Wilmington, Delaware, hired him as an executive speechwriter and public affairs coordinator. By the time he joined the faculty at the University of Texas as an assistant professor of journalism in 1983, Olasky had become a Calvinist, a fundamentalist Presbyterian, and an outspoken critic of abortion and the welfare state (http://www.journalism.utexas.edu/faculty/olasky.html).

The timely publication of *The Tragedy of American Compassion* in 1992 meant that he would not remain a rather obscure professor and polemicist. The book came out on the eve of the Republican "Contract with America" and the election of 1994, and it encapsulated the sentiments of many conservatives. Olasky argued for slashing welfare and downsizing government in the name of family values and compassion. He derided the "false compassion" of welfare payments that doled out material aid without providing spiritual guidance or encouraging self-discipline. True compassion, he contended, would nourish the soul as well as the body, and "faith-based" organizations should receive tax support for their superior programs for the needy. Former Secretary of Education William Bennett called *Tragedy* the "most important book on welfare and social policy in a decade" and sent a copy to Republican House Speaker Newt Gingrich. In Gingrich's first address as speaker of the House, he proclaimed, "Our models are Alexis de Tocqueville and Marvin Olasky. We are going to redefine compassion and take it back" (*Wall Street Journal*, March 20, 1995, A16). Suddenly, Olasky was a celebrity of the religious and political right, appearing on talk shows, giving interviews, and lecturing at the Heritage Foundation, a conservative policy-planning organization and think tank.

Olasky also published *The American Leadership Tradition* and *Central Ideas of American Journalism.* He is also editor of *World* magazine, for which he wrote a weekly column. His biography notes more than 800 articles published on journalism, history, poverty fighting, religion, sports, and other matters. He was granted tenure at UT-Austin, and is a full professor in the journalism department.

Olasky's *Compassionate Conservativism* (2000) continued his arguments, describing the seven characteristics of compassionate conservatism as being assertive, basic, challenging, diverse, effective, faith-based, and gradual. In the foreword to the book, President George W. Bush provides a ringing endorsement, saying that government does some things well, but it "cannot put hope in our hearts or a sense of purpose in our lives." The bulk of the book is devoted to vignettes of compassionate conservatism in action. During the summer of 1999, Olasky and his teenage son Daniel visited some of the nation's big cities to see what kinds of antipoverty programs were most effective. They found faith-based programs to be more effective than their government counterparts. Olasky argued that a new approach was needed because the present government approach was not working. *Compassionate Conservativism* raised serious questions about what faith-based organizations could and should do and about how much and what kind of government support was appropriate.

Olasky and President Bush appeared to hold comparable views on welfare and the importance of religion and government in helping the needy (Utter and Storey 2001). Bush is an Episcopalian turned Methodist, and Olasky has traversed many philosophical and religious approaches becoming an elder at Redeemer Presbyterian Church. Olasky seemed to be much more evangelical than Bush, but they shared a belief in compassionate conservativism.

Ralph Reed (1961–)

Ralph Reed was a part of Pat Robertson's Christian Coalition, a political consultant, chairman of the Georgia GOP, and most recently a regional director of the campaign to reelect President George W. Bush. Reed was born in Portsmouth, Virginia, the son of a Navy doctor who frequently moved to new assignments. By the time Reed entered high school in Toccoa, Georgia, the family had lived in seven different towns (Utter and Storey 2001). After Reed entered the University of Georgia, he served a summer internship in the U.S. Senate in 1981. Reed stayed through the fall working for the National College Republicans, and then he returned to the University of Georgia in 1982, completed his degree, and afterward returned to Washington to resume his efforts with the National College Republicans. During the 1984 North Carolina senatorial race between Jim Hunt and Jesse Helms, Reed moved to Raleigh, where he founded Students for America and joined the campaign for Helms, the outspoken conservative incumbent.

Despite his love for electoral politics, Reed enrolled in the graduate program at Emory University in Atlanta on a scholarship to study history. He graduated with a Ph.D. in 1986 and appeared headed for a career in academia; however, three years later, Reed was appointed executive secretary for Pat Robertson's Christian Coalition. In 1982, Reed was a leader among conservative campus Republicans, but shortly thereafter, he gave up smoking and drinking and became a born-again charismatic Christian. "I now realize," he said, "that politics is a noble calling to serve God and my fellow man" (Utter and Storey 2001). Appropriately, his Ph.D. dissertation, which examined the early history of church-related colleges, criticized them for sacrificing their religious heritage in favor of larger endowments.

Despite Reed's support for Jack Kemp over Pat Robertson in the 1988 presidential primaries, Robertson so admired Reed's organizational skills and religious commitment that, when Robertson formed the Christian Coalition, he hired Reed as executive secretary. There, Reed sought to broaden the base of the Coalition by taking a more ecumenical approach. When desirable, he downplayed such issues as abortion, homosexuality, and school prayer in favor of more traditional political issues such as taxes, crime, and education. Even his foes acknowledged that this kind of flexibility made Reed a formidable political opponent (Utter and Storey 2001). Yet his strategy faced the daunting task of attracting more moderate conservatives without alienating its hardcore conservative base.

Following setbacks in the 1996 elections, Reed left the Christian Coalition to found his own political consulting firm, Century Strategies, based in Atlanta. But the path remained difficult. In 1998, Reed claimed a .500 batting record for his clients, but his major clients were uniformly defeated. In Alabama, his client Republican Fob James lost the party's first gubernatorial race in 16 years, losing to Democrat Don Siegelman. In Georgia, the campaign of Reed's client Mitch Skandalakis was blamed for generating a backlash of black voters that knocked off most of the Republican ticket. Reed said that Republicans should recognize that this was a long-term struggle in which there would be gains and losses, but that did not mean retreat (Baxter 1998).

Reed saw more successes in his later efforts on behalf of Republican candidates. In 2000, Reed became a consultant for the George W. Bush campaign. Reed opined that the Christian right would clearly be an important and key element of the Republican coalition (*Atlanta Journal-Constitution*, November 11, 1999, C2). That turned out to be the case, with 54 percent of Christian fundamentalists voting for Bush in November. In 2001, Reed was elected to the chairmanship of the Georgia Republican party. In the 2002 elections in Georgia, President Bush visited the state three times in support of Republican senatorial candidate Saxby Chambliss, and Chambliss defeated veteran Democrat Max Cleland. A former Democratic Georgia state senator, Sonny Perdue, sought Reed's help after his conversion from Democrat to Republican in 1998. Reed advised Perdue in his successful campaign for governor in 2002, ousting Democratic governor Roy Barnes, who reportedly outspent the Perdue campaign by a ratio of seventeen to one. In 2003, Reed resigned from state party chairmanship and signed on as the southeast regional director for the 2004 Bush campaign. He began to train teams to dominate the talk shows, and he began assembling a large new database of supporters and potential supporters. The new jewel of the Republican campaign was an interactive Web site (http://www.georgebush.com) that offered chat rooms, event calendars, and campaign tips. For example, a Bush supporter in Florida could enter his or her zip code and immediately be given both the phone number of every talk radio in the local area and tips on what to say if he or she got on the air.

Pat Robertson (1930–)

Marion Gordon "Pat" Robertson was born in 1930 and reared in Lexington, Virginia, the son of a prominent politician (Senator A. Willis Robertson) and a devoutly religious mother. Robertson was a Phi Beta Kappa graduate of Washington and Lee University, studied at the University of London, and served as a noncombatant with the U.S. Marine Corps in Korea (1951–1952). He enrolled in Yale Law School and was graduated in 1955. He started his business career in the South American manufacturing operation of W. R. Grace and Company.

The young Robertson had not proved to be very religious, as indicated by his fondness for women, whiskey, and poker, but that changed in 1956 with a religious experience that was helped along by a staunch fundamentalist. In his book, *Shout It from the Housetops*, Robertson recounts this experience with evangelist Cornelius Vanderbreggan in an expensive Philadelphia restaurant (Lippy 1989).

Robertson entered the Biblical Seminary of New York City (later renamed the New York Theological Seminary), where he became a charismatic evangelical Christian. In 1959, he returned to Virginia and purchased a television station in Portsmouth. In January 1960, Robertson launched the Christian Broadcasting Network (CBN). Later, he sought donations to cover operating expenses: He asked for 700 listeners to pay $10 per month. This effort evolved first into the 700 Club and then into a television program by the same name. Evangelists Jim and Tammy Faye Bakker joined CBN in 1965, and they were responsible for a large share of the successes of Robertson's fundraising telethons. In 1966, Bakker launched what was probably the first Christian talk show; however, he resigned from CBN in 1971 and moved to Santa Ana, California, where he founded Trinity Broadcasting Systems with Paul Crouch. By 1975, CBN had an estimated 110 million viewers, and in 1979, Robertson opened an international headquarters and founded CBN University at Virginia Beach. By 1987, the CBN empire employed more than 4,000 people and spread over 380 acres (Utter and Storey 2001). CBN continues in affiliations with the American Center for Law and Justice and Operation Blessing International Relief and Development Corporation, which was founded by Robertson in 1978. The university in Virginia Beach, Virginia, continues under the name Regents University.

As a televangelist, Robertson shared with most of the Christian right a series of social concerns. He opposed abortion, homosexuality, pornography, and the Equal Rights Amendment. He supported oral prayers in public schools and tuition tax credits for private schooling (Utter and Storey). In 1988, Robertson attempted to translate his recognition as a television personality and spiritual leader into a bid for the Republican nomination for president. George H. W. Bush, Bob Dole, and Robertson were the three leading candidates for the Republican nomination in 1988, and the Iowa caucuses rated Dole first, Robertson second, and Bush third. However, that was the high point of the Robertson campaign. Bush swept the south on Super Tuesday, leaving Robertson in third place despite his efforts. Robertson subsequently endorsed Bush for the election (*Austin American-Statesman*, February 18, 2000, A7).

In 1989, Robertson founded the Christian Coalition as a replacement for Jerry Falwell's Moral Majority, which Falwell had disbanded. With Ralph Reed as executive secretary, the Coalition quickly became a very politically powerful group of religious conservatives by pursuing aggressive grassroots efforts to topple incumbents who were not profamily from school boards and local and state offices. During the 1994 election, the group handed out 35 million voter guides and 17 million scorecards. The scorecards showed the "moral score" for each Congress member, using information compiled from the voting record on issues important to the religious right. By 1995, the Christian Coalition claimed 1.6 million members in 1,600 local chapters and access to a network of more than 60,000 churches. The high point for the Coalition, however, soon passed. Ralph Reed left in 1997, and the organization lost a 10-year struggle with the Internal Revenue Service (Wald 2003). The IRS ruled that Christian Coalition activities were essentially partisan rather than religious and withdrew the Coalition's tax exempt status. The organization shifted some activities to Bedford, Texas, in 1999 in concert with the Texas Christian Coalition, and it continued in Washington, D.C., as the Christian Coalition in America. Robertson resigned as president and board member of the Coalition.

In 2000, Robertson reaffirmed his ordination vows, resumed the title of Reverend (which he had dropped prior to the 1988 campaign), and announced that his heart was on missions and on "getting people into the kingdom of God." (Utter and Storey 2001). Yet controversy did not stray far from Robertson. In a September 13, 2001, television interview on *The 700 Club,* guest Jerry Falwell said that the September 11 attack would seem small "if God continues to lift the curtain and allow the enemies of America to give us probably what we deserve." Host Robertson added, "The abortionists have got to bear some of the burden for this because God will not be mocked." Falwell agreed "The pagans and the abortionists and the feminists and the gays and the lesbians, I point the finger at you and say 'You made this happen'" (*Knight Ridder/Tribune News Service,* September 14, 2001). The outrage from liberal groups in response to these statements was immediate, and Falwell soon apologized and characterized his remarks as insensitive; however, Robertson did not apologize, saying that he simply did not understand what Falwell was saying (*Roanoke Times,* September 23, 2001, 1). Robertson continues as the spiritual and temporal head of CBN and its affiliates.

Jay Alan Sekulow (1956–)

Jay Sekulow has proved to be an articulate and knowledgeable legal and public advocate for the positions of the religious right. Supporting the right of Christians to proselytize the general public, he made his efforts at persuasion on television programs such as *Good Morning America, Nightline, CNN Crossfire,* and *Larry King Live.* He appears regularly on Pat Robertson's *700 Club.* Indeed, the American Center for Law and Justice (ACLJ), for which Sekulow is chief counsel, began in Virginia Beach, Virginia, as part of Robertson's programs, and ACLJ maintains offices in Washington, D.C., and Virginia Beach and remains affiliated with Robertson's Christian Broadcasting Network.

Sekulow published several books arguing for the right of Christians to speak freely about their faith and to proselytize the public. In *From Intimidation to Victory* (1990), he dealt with issues involving the right of Christians to freedom of speech, to include the rights of parents to speak out against such perceived evils as abortion. He also advised readers about how to employ the strategy of civil disobedience. Sekulow's *Knowing Your Rights* (1993) explained Christian rights, especially free speech and how to exercise it. In *And Nothing but the Truth,* Sekulow and coauthor Keith Fornier related their experiences in waging legal battles on church-state issues. They argued that religious expression was being publicly suppressed and that the central values of society, the nation's Judeo-Christian values, were being displaced. In his booklet *Christian Rights in the Workplace* (1998), he argued that the law did not prohibit religious employees or employers from speaking about their faith in the workplace.

Sekulow graduated from Mercer University with both B.A. and J.D. degrees. He established the ACLJ in Virginia Beach in 1990, and he served as lead counsel and presented oral arguments before the Supreme Court in several cases important to the religious right. In *Board of Airport Commissioners v. Jews for Jesus* (1987), the Court invalidated an airport regulation restricting the distribution of religious literature in airport terminals. In *Board of Education of Westside Community Schools v. Mergens* (1990), the Court ruled that the Equal Access Act was constitutional, thus providing high school students with the right to establish Bible and prayer clubs. In *Lamb's Chapel v. Center Moriches School District* (1993), the Court ruled that the school district had inappropriately banned a showing of the James Dobson film *Turn Your Heart toward Home* in a school facility.

Sekulow is discriminating in his public support. He is supporting the U.S. Department of Justice in U.S. district court cases that defend the law against partial-birth abortions. He publicly supports the teaching of creationism in addition to evolution in public schools. Yet Sekulow joined with Richard Land, president of the Southern Baptist Convention's Ethics and Religious Liberty Committee, in counseling moderation and compliance with the law when Alabama's State Supreme Court justice Roy Moore refused to obey court orders to remove his stone monument to the Ten Commandments from the Alabama Judicial Building.

Despite his skill as an attorney, Sekulow does not always win his cases before the Supreme Court, but he represents his clients zealously. In *Santa Fe Independent School District v. Doe* (2000), the Supreme Court held that districts could not allow student-led prayers at public school football games, despite oral arguments from Sekulow and John Cornyn, then the Texas attorney general. In *Locke v. Davey* (2004), the Court ruled that states that subsidized secular study at the college level could withhold the scholarships from students who were preparing for the ministry, in spite of Sekulow's argument that the state of Washington was unlawfully discriminating in doing so. When asked about his reasons for arguing in high-profile cases, Sekulow said, "For good or ill, the court has tremendous power in this country." He added, "To ignore the courts or to vacate the courts and not be involved would be, in my view, a violation of what Jesus talks about in the Sermon on the Mount about being 'salt' and 'light'" (*Virginia Pilot,* November 1, 2003, A1). Sekulow joined with Jerry Falwell at the White House in November 2003 to witness President George W. Bush's signing of the Partial-Birth Abortion Ban Act.

Cal Thomas (1940–)

Cal Thomas, perhaps the best-known evangelical journalist, is also perhaps the most widely syndicated columnist in the country. A native of Washington, D.C., the 6'7" Thomas played basketball at American University, a private university in that city. Thomas was interested early in broadcast journalism. He became a disc jockey and news reader at age 16, and two years later, he joined NBC News in Washington as a copy boy. He worked as a radio and television reporter for NBC in the 1960s. Thomas was also associated with PBS television, with Fox News, and, when he was in the army, with Armed Forces Radio and Television. His began his newspaper column with the Los Angeles Times Syndicate in 1984, and as of 2004, he could claim that it was carried by more than 550 papers (http://www.calthomas.com).

Thomas is a religious conservative who is influenced by both Richard Halverson, former chaplain of the U.S. Senate, and Francis Schaeffer, a prestigious philosopher-theologian of the religious right. Thomas shares with others in the religious right chagrin and dismay over the gay rights and feminist movements and over increased rates of divorce and abortion in the United States (Utter and Storey 2001). He joined Jerry Falwell's Moral Majority as a vice president in the early 1980s in an effort to stem what was seen as a rising tide of immorality.

Nonetheless, in 1990, Thomas and coauthor Edward Dobson wrote that the religious right had little to show for twenty years of political activism. In *Blinded by Might*, they concluded that "the moral landscape of America" had gotten worse. They wrote: "Two decades after conservative Christians charged into the political arena, bringing new voters and millions of dollars with them in hopes of transforming the culture through political power, it must be acknowledged that we have failed." They contended that although conservative Christians should remain active as voters, they should not expect politics to transform the moral climate of this country. Virtue and morality could not, they said, be imposed on a people by its government. Thus, Thomas and Dobson concluded that the religious right should return to its traditional evangelical emphasis on saving the souls of individual sinners. Its strength lay in the transforming power of the gospel, not in the coercive power of government. The right's best example of constructive change, they said, was the establishment of crisis pregnancy centers by religious conservatives; these centers had contributed more to limiting abortions than any policy efforts.

In his many columns, Thomas covered a wide variety of topics from a conservative Christian perspective, and he also wrote *Gays in the Military: The Moral and Strategic Crisis* in 1993 (when the Clinton administration was sponsoring its "Don't Ask, Don't Tell" policy about gays in the military). Thomas criticized the nasty politics of religious conservatives in the South Carolina Republican primary in 2000, stating that the supposedly higher-principled Christian right could "get down and dirty with the best of the pagans" (Utter and Storey 2001). He criticized Democrats Al Gore and Joe Lieberman in the presidential campaign, reserving his praise for the wisdom of George W. Bush to surround himself with able people.

Thomas also co-wrote *The Wit and Wisdom of Cal Thomas* with Wayne Staykal in 2001. In it, Thomas pithily compared former President Clinton with former President Reagan: "It was said of Ronald Reagan that he had so much respect for the presidency he never removed his suit coat while in the oval office. Clinton respects it so little he has trouble keeping his pants on there."

Paul Weyrich (1942–)

Paul Weyrich was a key figure in the 1960s and 1970s in the move of conservative Christians toward political activism. A Greek Catholic, Weyrich may not have been strictly a member of the religious right, but he clearly saw Protestant fundamentalists as an untapped source of political support for conservative causes (Utter and Storey 2001).

Weyrich was born in Racine, Wisconsin, in 1942 of blue-collar parents. He obtained an associate's degree from the University of Wisconsin in 1962. He worked as a newspaper reporter, political reporter, and newscaster in Wisconsin and as news director for radio station KQXI in Denver, Colorado. He served as press secretary for U.S. Senator Gordon Allott of Colorado from 1967 to 1973 and as special assistant to Senator Carl T. Curtis of Nebraska from 1973 to 1977. In 1973, he was one of the founders and the president of the Heritage Foundation, a think tank whose mission was the formulation and promotion of conservative public policies.

Weyrich was a key figure in the establishment of conservative political organizations. Out of Washington, D.C., he operated the Committee for the Survival of a Free Congress, which was a training school for conservative political candidates. Weyrich saw that certain social issues (e.g., abortion, anticommunism, prayer in public schools) were creating an opportunity to bring Protestant fundamentalists and Catholic conservatives together as a new force in the American political process. He, along with Ed McAteer, Robert Billings, and Howard Phillips, courted Jerry Falwell in 1979 to lead this new force, and Weyrich is credited with coining the name *Moral Majority* (Utter and Storey 2001). In the founders' view, the organization was to bring together religious fundamentalists of any denomination for common political purposes. McAteer's Religious Roundtable organization was seen as an umbrella organization that could coordinate the efforts of various activities of the religious right, such as the Moral Majority and Christian Voice.

Weyrich championed a "cultural conservatism" that would unite religious and nonreligious people in the fight for traditional values on which conservative Protestants, Catholics, Jews, and even atheists could agree. When Ronald Reagan was elected president in 1980, the Moral Majority claimed that its election efforts had been an important part of that victory. Although it claimed to be nonpartisan, the Moral Majority was most comfortable with the conservative Republican agenda (Utter and Storey 2001).

Despite Weyrich's efforts, the Moral Majority never had much success in attracting members from outside its core of Christian fundamentalists. In an effort to broaden the membership base, Falwell renamed it Liberty Foundation in 1986. However, that was the year in which Praise the Lord (PTL) leader Jim Bakker was charged with sexual misconduct and was tried and convicted of fraud. The fallout from the Bakker scandal swept over other televangelists, including Falwell and the Liberty Foundation (Utter and Storey 2001). The Moral Majority was no more.

Disillusioned with the Senate's refusal to impeach President Clinton, Weyrich announced in February 1999 that the "culture war" of the conservatives against immorality had been lost and that politics was a failure. He had come to believe that religious and social conservatives would have more success outside of the political arena (Weyrich 1999). Yet Weyrich stayed engaged in energizing the public on conservative issues. Railing against excessive government intrusion in the aftermath of the September 11 attacks, Weyrich argued in editorials and op-ed pieces that Americans were risking their rights in the rush to be secure. He wrote: "The mechanisms are all in place for the U.S. government to go after its citizens. The government simply has to brand the likes of us who dissent from its policies as potential terrorists. Do I think that George Bush would ever do this? I do not. Do I think that a subsequent liberal government would do so? I most certainly do" (Weyrich 2002).

References

Baranowski, Shelley. 1989. "Jerry Falwell." In Charles H. Lippy, ed. *Twentieth-Century Shapers of American Popular Religion*. New York: Greenwood.

Battle, Emily. 2003. "Lynchburg, Va., Council Approves Rezoning for Falwell's Liberty University." *Lynchburg (VA) News & Advance* (December 17)

Baxter, Tom. 1998. "Election '98 Ralph Reed's 'Tough Day' Holds Lessons for Right." *The Atlanta Journal-Constitution* (November 5): K1.

Board of Airport Commissioners v. Jews for Jesus. 482 U.S. 569, 107 S.Ct. 2568, 96 L.Ed. 2d 500 (1987).

Board of Education of Westside Community Schools v. Mergens. 496 U.S. 226, 110 S.Ct. 2356, 110 L.Ed. 2d 191 (1990).

Department of Defense. 1996a. News Release No. 412–96. http://www. defenselink.mil/releases/1996/b070396_bt412–96.html (accessed January 23, 2004).

———. 1996b. News Release No. 203–96. http://www.defenselink.mil/ releases/1996/b041196_bt203–96.html (accessed on January 23, 2004).

Focus on the Family. 2004. http://www.family.org/docstudy/aboutdrdobson.cfm (accessed March 11, 2004).

Gettleman, Jeffrey. 2003. "Alabama Justice Goes on Trial over Ten Commandments," *New York Times,* November 12. http: //www.nytimes.com/ 2003/11/12/national (accessed November 12, 2003).

Infield, Tom. 2001. "Falwell, Robertson See God's Wrath in Attacks," *Knight Ridder/Tribune News Service* (September 14): K2551.

Kleffman, Todd. 2002. "Monumental Decision." *Montgomery Advertiser,* October 13. http://www.montgomeryadvertiser.com/Specialreports/TENCommandments (accessed October 3, 2003).

Lamb's Chapel v. Center Moriches School District. 508 U.S. 384, S.Ct. Docket Number 91–2024 (1993).

Lippy, Charles H. 1989. *Twentieth-Century Shapers of American Popular Religion.* New York: Greenwood Press.

Lowe, Cody. 2001. "How to Remove Foot from Mouth with Grace," *Roanoke Times.* (September 23): 1.

National Election Studies. 2003a. *Codebook.* http://www.umich.edu/~nes (accessed June 2003).

———. 2003b. *National Election Studies (NES) Guide to Public Opinion and Electoral Behavior.* http://www.umich.edu/~nes/nesguide/nesguide.htm.

Plowman, E. E. 1976. "The Rise and Fall of Billy James." *Christianity Today* 20 (February 27):42–43.

Religious Freedom Coalition. 2003. "Open Letter to President Bush," May 22. http://www.rfcnet.org/news, (accessed on March 26, 2004).

Smith, Bill. 2003. "Downsized Bakker Returns to TV Pulpit in Branson, Mo." Knight Ridder/Tribune News Service (December 3): K3342.

Utter, Glenn H., and John W. Storey. 2001. *The Religious Right.* 2nd ed. Santa Barbara, CA: ABC-CLIO.

Vinson, C. Danielle, and James L. Guth. 2003. "Advance and Retreat in the Palmetto State: Assessing the Christian Right in South Carolina." In John C. Green, Mark J. Rozell, and Clyde Wilcox, eds. *The Christian Right in American Politics.* Washington, DC: Georgetown University Press.

Wald, Kenneth D. 2003. *Religion and Politics in the United States.* 4th ed. Lanham, MD: Rowan & Littlefield.

Wald, Kenneth D., and Richard K. Scher. 2003. "'A Necessary Annoyance'? The Christian Right and the Development of Republican Party Politics in Florida." In John C. Green, Mark J. Rozell, and Clyde Wilcox, eds., *The Christian Right in American Politics.* Washington, DC: Georgetown University Press.

Weyrich, Paul. 1999. "We're Losing the Culture War." *Knight Ridder/Tribune News Service* (February 23): K5947.

———. 2002. "Still Risking Our Rights in the Rush to Be Secure." *Houston Chronicle* (February 14): 35.

Organizations

The organizations listed here have been active in various ways in the political realm, although some have been more successful than others. For each organization listed here, we include contact information, publications, Web site, and a brief description of objectives and activities. We also include the names of group leaders, who often play the crucial role of interest group entrepreneurs, attracting supporters and other resources to the organization. Organizations often do not reveal their total membership, which may be considered a measure of potential political influence. However, these groups frequently request that supporters, or "adherents," take actions such as contacting public officials or taking part in public demonstrations. Even though the total number of members and adherents for a particular organization may not be large, each group has found a particular niche within the population of conservative Christians by appealing to a specific issue or narrow set of issues.

Following the list of conservative Christian organizations, we have included several organizations that oppose the goals of the conservative groups. A major motivating factor for group development is the desire to counteract an opposing movement. Therefore, these differing groups tend to carry on a symbiotic relationship, mutually reinforcing each other by attempting to check each other's influence in the political realm.

Conservative Christian Organizations

Alliance Defense Fund (ADF)
15333 North Prima Road, Suite 165
Scottsdale, AZ 85260
(800) 835–5233; (480) 444–0025
http://www.alliancedefensefund.org

In 1993 several conservative Christian leaders, including James Dobson, D. James Kennedy, Bill Bright, and Larry Burkett, collaborated to create the Alliance Defense Fund, an organization dedicated to restoring what the founders considered a serious loss of religious liberty due to court decisions. The ADF works with approximately 125 other organizations to provide funding for legal cases. The organization also recruits and trains attorneys to represent any of the associated organizations involved in legal cases. The ADF is involved in developing strategies to defend the traditional notion of marriage backed by conservative Christians.

American Anglican Council (AAC)
1110 Vermont Avenue NW, Suite 1100
Washington, DC 20005
(800) 914–2000
http://www.americananglican.org

Groups of Episcopal bishops, laypersons, and scholars, at meetings in December 1995 and June 1996—called Briarwood I and II, respectively—established the American Anglican Council as an organization dedicated to biblical authority and Anglican orthodoxy. Meeting participants were troubled by what they perceived to be the tendency of the Episcopal leadership to move away from the historic biblical Christian faith. The AAC has criticized the leadership of the Episcopal Church USA for failing to deal adequately with what the organization considers a major crisis for the church. The group incorporated in August 1996 as a 501c(3) nonprofit organization in the District of Columbia. When V. Gene Robinson, an openly gay Episcopal priest, was elected bishop of New Hampshire in 2003, the members of the American Anglican Council quickly protested his elevation to such a position of authority. The organization has attempted to defend the rights of parishes where the membership tends to be more conservative. The AAC appears to be unwilling to accept the preservation of unity within the denomination as the primary concern; instead, they favor faithfulness to their understanding of biblical mandates and the tradition of the Anglican church.

American Center for Law and Justice (ACLJ)
1000 Centerville Turnpike
P.O. Box 64429
Virginia Beach, VA 23467
(804) 523–7570; (757) 226–2836 (fax)
http://www.aclj.org

In 1990, Pat Robertson established the American Center for Law and Justice as a law firm dedicated to defending the legal rights of Christian individuals and organizations. The ACLJ has been involved in cases dealing with zoning regulations that allegedly discriminate against churches and religious organizations, denial of equal access for religious organizations to community facilities, and participation in public prayer. The organization has entered the debate over such issues as the Pledge of Allegiance, the free speech rights of antiabortion protesters, pornography and obscenity, and the rights of workers to share their religious beliefs with coworkers during breaks or other free time.

American Council of Christian Churches (ACCC)
P.O. Box 5455
Bethlehem, PA 18015
(610) 865–3009
http://www.amcouncilcc.org

Carl McIntire established the American Council of Christian Churches in 1941 as an alternative to the Federal Council of Christian Churches, which was the precursor to the National Council of Churches (NCC). A year later, the National Association of Evangelicals (NAE) was established, which became the more successful alternative to the more liberal NCC. Member denominations of the ACCC include the Bible Presbyterian Church, the Fellowship of Fundamental Bible Churches, and the Evangelical Methodist Church. At the organization's sixty-second convention in October 2003, delegates approved resolutions that called on Christians to adhere to biblical teachings about homosexuality; urged the community of nations to recognize Israel's right to exist in peace and affirmed Israel's right to defend itself; opposed judicial activism, particularly with regard to the removal of the Ten Commandments monument from the Alabama Supreme Court building; criticized the NAE for its "harmfully inclusive policy"; and commended President George W. Bush "for his integrity, valor, boldness, leadership, and consistency." Its publication, *The ACCC Report,* reports on the monitoring of conventions of other religious organizations such as the NAE, the World Council of Churches, and the National Religious Broadcasters.

American Decency Association (ADA)
P.O. Box 202
Fremont, MI 49412
(231) 924–4050
http://www.americandecency.org

Bill Johnson, former state director of the American Family Association of Michigan, established the American Decency Association to combat pornography, obscenity, and indecency at the local level. The organization attempts to mobilize citizens concerned about pornography in their local communities. The ADA encourages boycotts of businesses it considers to be involved in the sale of sexually explicit materials.

American Family Association (AFA)
P.O. Box 2440
Tupelo, MS 38803
(601) 844–5036; (601) 842–6791 (fax)
http://www.afa.net

Founded in 1977, the American Family Association supports traditional family values, particularly against the influence of the entertainment industry, which the AFA claims glorifies immoral behavior such as premarital sex. Homosexuality and pornography are the organization's primary targets. The AFA regularly contacts supporters on specific issues and recommends actions to be taken, such as encouraging companies not to advertise their products on objectionable television programs.

American Life League (ALL)
P.O. Box 1350
Stafford, VA 22555
(888) 546–2580
http://www.all.org

The American Life League provides a voice for those conservative Christians who strongly oppose abortion for any reason. The organization believes that life begins at conception (fertilization of the human egg) and therefore opposes abortion unconditionally, even in cases of rape or incest. It will not support any legislation meant to regulate abortion rather than ban the procedure completely. In addition to opposing abortion without exception, the ALL objects to various forms of birth control as well as any form of euthanasia, or "mercy killing." The League supports adoption of the "Paramount Human Life Amendment" to the U.S. Constitution, which states, "The paramount right to life is vested in each human being from the moment of fertilization without regard to age, health or condition of dependency." The League publishes its magazine, *Celebrate Life*, six times per year.

American Values
2800 Shirlington Road, Suite 610
Arlington, VA 22206
(703) 671–9700; (703) 671–1680 (fax)
http://www.ouramericanvalues.org

Gary Bauer, former head of the Family Research Council and candidate for the Republican presidential nomination in 2000, established American Values to continue his work to support conservative Christian values. The organization has defended a traditional conception of marriage as a relationship between one man and one woman, considering the push toward recognizing same-sex marriage as a threat to this traditional understanding. Criticizing judicial branch decisions that it considers threats to family values, American Values has supported President George W. Bush's nominees to the federal courts.

Campaign for Working Families (CWF)
2800 Shirlington Road, Suite 605
Arlington, VA 22206
(703) 671–8800
http://www.cwfpac.com

Gary Bauer established the Campaign for Working Families in 1996 as a political action committee, an organization registered with the Federal Election Commission for the purpose of raising funds to contribute to candidates for public office. Before endorsing candidates and providing financial support, the CWF asks each candidate to complete a detailed questionnaire on issues of concern to the organization. The CWF also conducts face-to-face interviews with candidates and monitors their campaigns. The organization supported the partial-birth abortion ban, which Congress passed in 2003, and has lobbied successfully to have "defense of marriage" legislation passed in the states of Alaska, California, Nebraska, Nevada, and Hawaii.

Center for Reclaiming America (CRA)
P.O. Box 632
Fort Lauderdale, FL 33302
(877) 725–8872
http://www.reclaimamerica.org

D. James Kennedy, pastor of Coral Ridge Presbyterian Church in Florida, established the Center for Reclaiming America to provide instruction to Christians interested in influencing the culture of the

United States. The organization has been active in pursuing the conservative Christian position on several issues, including the public display of the Ten Commandments, the Pledge of Allegiance, and homosexuality. The Center holds conferences to train individuals at the grassroots to become effective in political engagement at the local level.

Chalcedon Foundation (CF)

P.O. Box 158
Vallecito, CA 95251
(209) 7736–4365; (209) 736–0536 (fax)
http://www.chalcedon.edu

Established in 1965 by Rousas John Rushdoony, the Chalcedon Foundation advocates the application of biblical faith and law to all aspects of life, including government, the schools, the arts and sciences, law, and economics. The organization claims that solutions to the problems of the modern world are to be found only in the Bible. Therefore, the CF attempts to counter the influence of secular humanism. The organization opposes centralized government, preferring instead a decentralized society and system of government. The issues on which the CF has taken a public stand include the Ten Commandments controversy in Alabama and the preservation of a traditional conception of marriage.

Christian Anti-Communism Crusade (CACC)

P.O. Box 129
Manitou Springs, CO 80829
(213) 437–0941

Fred Schwarz, an Australian physician who emigrated to the United States, founded the Christian Anti-Communism Crusade in 1953 to publicize what Schwarz considered the subversive dangers of communism in the United States and around the world. Schwarz led the organization until his retirement and return to Australia in 1998, when David Noebel assumed leadership of the organization. Since its founding, the CACC has conducted seminars to inform people about the strategies of communist movements in order to prepare them for resisting the communist threat. The organization offers Christianity as the alternative to communism and other left-leaning ideologies. The Crusade distributes literature and publishes a monthly newsletter, *The Schwarz Report,* which includes articles that warn against the influence of liberal individuals and groups and the continuing threat of communism.

Christian Coalition of America (CCA)
P.O. Box 37030
Washington, DC 20013–7030
(202) 478–6900; (202) 479–4260 (fax)
http://www.cc.org

The Christian Coalition of America, founded by Pat Robertson in 1989, has as its basic mission the representation of Christians in government. The organization identifies voter education as its primary duty and reports having distributed 70 million voter guides prior to the 2000 elections. CCA lobbies the national legislative and executive branches on various issues, holds training workshops for Christians around the nation, and organizes community activists to influence local government. The organization supports proposed legislation, including a Houses of Worship bill, that would remove the Internal Revenue Service ban on political speech for churches; a federal marriage amendment to define marriage as a union of one man and one woman; a constitutional amendment to ban child pornography; and bills to limit federal court authority over the public display of the Ten Commandments and the recitation of the Pledge of Allegiance.

Christian Crusade
P.O. Box 977
Tulsa, OK 74102
(918) 665–2345

Billy James Hargis founded the Christian Crusade in 1948 as a combination fundamentalist Christian, patriotic, and anticommunist organization. Originally called the Christian Echoes National Ministry, the organization takes conservative stands on many contemporary issues, including questioning the environmental movement, defending the display of the Ten Commandments in the rotunda of the Alabama judicial building, and supporting minority Christian communities in countries with Islamic majorities. The organization has established a small niche among conservative Christians, distributing a monthly newspaper, *Christian Crusade,* which includes articles that focus on the perceived threats of liberalism, big government, and influences from other religions.

Christian Law Association (CLA)
P.O. Box 4010
Seminole, FL 33775
(727) 399–8300
http://www.christianlaw.org

Established in 1978, the Christian Law Association, with a staff of twelve full-time attorneys and four legal assistants, represents churches and individual Christians in legal cases resulting from government regulation or prohibitions on religious activities. The organization represents only those churches that profess Jesus Christ as the only way to salvation and accept the Bible as "the only Divinely-inspired, infallible, and complete Word of God." Among its activities, the CLA defends the rights of students to express Christian beliefs and the right of teachers to share their beliefs with students. The organization offers legal seminars to help Christian ministries avoid lawsuits. The CLA reports responding to more than 75,000 inquiries and requests for assistance each year.

Christian Research Institute (CRI)
P.O. Box 7000
Rancho Santa Margarita, CA 92688–7000
(949) 858–6100
http://www.equip.org

Walter Martin established the Christian Research Institute in 1960 to advocate "orthodox" Christianity and to expose groups the organization considers to be heretical cults. The organization has criticized the ministries of such televangelists as Benny Hinn, Kenneth and Gloria Copeland, and Trinity Broadcasting Network founder Paul Crouch. When Martin died in 1989, Hank Hanegraff assumed leadership of the CRI and became the host of the organization's radio program, *Bible Answer Man*. Hanegraff has published several books on subjects such as the claimed weaknesses of the theory of evolution and the truth of Christ's resurrection. The organization publishes *Christian Research Journal,* a monthly magazine devoted to exposing cults and cultic behavior.

Concerned Women for America (CWA)
1015 Fifteenth Street NW, Suite 1100
Washington, DC 20005
(202) 488–7000; (202) 488–0806 (fax)
http://www.cwfa.org

Beverly LaHaye established CWA in the late 1970s with just nine members. The organization presently claims a membership of more than one-half million women. CWA focuses on six basic issue areas: defense of the traditional family, opposition to abortion, support for educational reform, opposition to pornography and obscenity, protection of religious liberty, and preservation of U.S. sovereignty. Specific issues on which CWA has spoken include the public display of the Ten Commandments in the Alabama judicial building and elsewhere and the case of Terri Schiavo, the Florida woman in a vegetative state whose husband was attempting to have her life support removed. The organization supported the Unborn Victims of Violence Act and urged the prohibition of mifepristone, the abortion drug. LaHaye announced in March 2004 that CWA president Sandy Rios had been dismissed. LaHaye referred to "irreconcilable differences," but some reports of the dismissal indicated that disagreement over the proposed Defense of Marriage Amendment had led to Rios's leaving CWA.

Creation Research Society (CRS)
P.O. Box 8263
St. Joseph, MO 64508–8263
(816) 279–2312
http://www.creationresearch.org

Ten scientists, after failing to have research favorable to the creationist perspective published in scientific journals, established the Creation Research Society in 1963 in order to found a journal in which like-minded scientists could have their work on "special creation" published. The Society believes that the Bible is the written word of God; that God made all living things, including human beings, during the week of creation as described in the biblical book of Genesis; that the flood described in Genesis was a historic event; and that salvation through Jesus Christ was made necessary by the fall into sin of Adam and Eve, whom they believe to have been the first man and woman. The CRS publishes the *CRS Quarterly,* which focuses on the reinterpretation of scientific data to agree with the creationist perspective. Although the Society does not engage in political activity, the organization's opposition to evolution provides a basis for those politically active conservative Christians who attempt to have alternatives to creationism introduced into the public school curriculum.

Discovery Institute
1511 Third Avenue, Suite 808
Seattle, WA 98101

(206) 292–0401, extension 126
http://www.discovery.org

The Discovery Institute conducts investigations in various substantive areas relevant to society and government, including technology, science and culture, legal reform, national defense, transportation, the environment, and the economy. The organization bases its activities in part on "a belief in God-given reason and the permanency of human nature." The Institute's Center for Science and Culture has focused on science education in the public schools and advocates the inclusion of critical approaches to the study of evolution. The Institute has intervened in state textbook and curriculum decisions, calling for the removal of perceived errors in science textbooks and supporting curricula that treat the theory of evolution critically. The organization holds that although the theory of evolution should be taught, alternatives, including intelligent design (the position that a higher intelligence played a role in the process), can be legitimately included in scientific investigation.

Eagle Forum
P.O. Box 618
Alton, IL 62002
(618) 462–5415
http://www.eagleforum.org

Phyllis Schlafly established the Eagle Forum in 1972. It is a profamily organization that had the original objective of defeating the Equal Rights Amendment to the U.S. Constitution. Currently, the Forum has a long agenda of issues on which it lobbies, including national defense, immigration, education, the display of the Ten Commandments, and the wording of the Pledge of Allegiance. The organization opposes the American Civil Liberties Union and Americans United for Separation of Church and State in their efforts to remove public displays of the Ten Commandments. The Forum questions the wisdom of the national education law, No Child Left Behind, which Eagle Forum regards as an unacceptable compromise to please Democrats with greater government spending and Republicans with promises of higher education standards and accountability.

Faith and Action (FA)
109 Second Street NE
Washington, DC 20002–7303
(703) 257–5593

http://faithandaction.org

Faith and Action attempts to minister to public officials in the legislative, executive, and judicial branches of the federal government. The organization distributes its religious message through news conferences, symposia, panel discussions, literature distribution, and personal contacts with public officials. FA conducts the Ten Commandments Project, which includes presenting stone artwork tablets of the Ten Commandments to public officials and awarding a Ten Commandments Leadership Award. Among the recipients of the award are President George W. Bush, Senator Trent Lott, and Speaker of the House J. Dennis Hastert.

Family Research Council (FRC)
801 G Street NW
Washington, DC 20001
(202) 393–2100; (202) 393–2134 (fax)
http://www.frc.org

Founded in 1981 as the Family Research Group, the FRC supports marriage and the family as the institution crucial to the preservation of civilization, and it advocates adherence to the Judeo-Christian worldview as the basis of a free and just society. The organization engages in public debate on policy proposals geared to protect human life. The FRC has taken positions on a host of issues, including abortion, pornography, sex education, school prayer, faith-based funding, the public display of the Ten Commandments, and gambling. In response to the push for recognition of same-sex unions, the FRC announced a nationwide campaign to support the traditional institution of marriage. In February 2004, the organization began a Marriage Protection Pledge campaign, asking elected officials at the state and federal levels to announce publicly their support for traditional marriage. Voters would then be able to make their decision on the basis of whether a candidate agrees with the FRC's stand on the issue.

Focus on the Family (FF)
8605 Explorer Drive
Colorado Springs, CO 80920
(719) 531–3400; (719) 548–4525 (fax)
http://family.org

Focus on the Family began in 1977 as a Christian organization dedicated to assisting families facing the problems of the contemporary world. FF's primary goal is to maintain the traditional family unit, informed by Christian values. The organization becomes involved in political questions as they influence the Christian conception of the family. FF has supported passage of some form of the faith-based initiative proposed by President Bush and encourages supporters to contact their representatives in the U.S. Congress on the issue. FF regards homosexuality as a preventable and treatable condition and conducts Love Won Out conferences on the topic. The organization has supported the public display of the Ten Commandments as well as General William G. Boykin's public pronouncements about religion.

FRC Action

801 G Street NW
Washington, DC 20001
(800) 225–4008
http://www.frcaction.org

FRC Action, the lobbying group within the Family Research Council, works to reverse the Supreme Court decision in *Roe v. Wade,* to win approval of conservative judicial appointments, to prevent the approval of measures at the state and national levels permitting gay marriage or civil unions, and generally to adopt policies that strengthen the family as a God-created institution. The organization opposed the adoption of a civil union policy for same-sex couples in Vermont.

Free Congress Foundation (FCF)

717 Second Street NE
Washington, DC 20002
(202) 546–3000
http://www.freecongress.org

The Free Congress Foundation focuses primarily on conservative cultural values. The FCF maintains that a necessary relationship exists between traditional Judeo-Christian values and the advancement of Western societies, including economic prosperity, recognition of civil liberties, and equal opportunities to citizens. The organization warns that if traditional beliefs are abandoned, the advantages that resulted from them will be lost. Like other conservative Christian organizations since the September 11, 2001, terrorist attacks, the FCF has warned against what it considers the potentially violent nature of Islam, pointing to passages in the Qur'an that call for violence against unbelievers. The Foundation takes stands on many public policy issues, including passage of a constitutional amendment defining marriage as a union between a man and a woman, support for President Bush's judicial nominees, limiting federal government spending and reducing the size of government, and various profamily measures.

Institute for Creation Research (ICR)
P.O. Box 2667
El Cajon, CA 92021
(619) 448–0900
http://www.icr.org

Calling itself a "Christ-focused creation ministry," the Institute for Creation Research advocates a creationist view of the origins of the world as opposed to the evolution perspective and supports teaching creationism along with evolution in the public schools. The Institute maintains a Museum of Creation and Earth History that provides a Christian and creationist view of the history of the world. Among the ICR's radio broadcasts are the weekly *Science, Scripture, and Salvation* and the daily *Back to Genesis*. The organization publishes two periodicals, *Acts and Facts* and *Days of Praise*.

Institute on Religion and Democracy (IRD)
1110 Vermont Avenue NW, Suite 1180
Washington, DC 20005
(202) 969–8430; (202) 969–8429 (fax)
http://www.ird-renew.org

The Institute on Religion and Democracy has as its primary objective the creation and strengthening of democracy and religious liberty in the United States and around the world. The IRD asserts that the Christian idea of human freedom is best expressed through democracy. The organization calls on churches to engage in ministry that conforms to orthodox biblical principles and that represents the views of their membership. The Institute has supported those in the Episcopal Church USA who objected to the election of an openly gay bishop.

Liberty Counsel (LC)
P.O. Box 540774
Orlando, FL 32854
(407) 875–2100
http://www.lc.org

Calling itself a civil liberties and legal defense organization, the Liberty Counsel invites Christian individuals or groups involved in controversies involving "religious freedom, the sanctity of life or traditional family values" to contact the organization for information and possible pro bono legal assistance. The organization has been involved in cases dealing with restrictions on students distributing religious literature on public school and college campuses; antiabortion picketers; and religious groups wishing to meet in community centers. In February 2004, on behalf of a member of the New Paltz, New York, board of trustees, the Counsel filed two lawsuits against the mayor of the municipality, who had conducted marriage ceremonies for same-sex couples who did not have valid marriage licenses. One of the lawsuits involved a petition to remove the mayor from office. The LC publishes *The Liberator,* a monthly newsletter. Mathew Staver hosts *Freedom's Call,* a daily radio program, and *Law and Justice,* a television program, for the LC.

National Association of Evangelicals (NAE)
701 G Street SW
Washington, DC 20024
http://nae.net

J. Elwin Wright of the New England Fellowship, along with 146 other evangelicals, met in St. Louis, Missouri, in April 1942 to establish the National Association of Evangelicals in order to bring unity to the various evangelical groups in the United States. These individuals did not wish to associate with the newly formed Federal (later National) Council of Churches, nor with Carl McIntire's dissident group, the American Council of Christian Churches. Seventy-nine denominations currently have memberships in the NAE. The NAE adheres to the basic tenets of conservative Christianity, including the belief that the Bible is the authoritative, infallible word of God. The organization's Office for Government Affairs interacts with all three branches of the federal government. The NAE takes conservative positions on various issues, advocating, for instance, a traditional definition of marriage against attempts to institute same-sex marriage.

National Coalition for the Protection of
Children and Families (NCPCF)
800 Compton Road, Suite 9224
Cincinnati, OH 45231
(513) 521–6227; (513) 521–6337 (fax)
http://www.nationalcoalition.org

Founded in 1983 and originally called the National Coalition against Pornography (N-CAP), the NCPCF assists communities to establish local coalitions to deal with the perceived problems of pornography, considering it a public health and safety issue. The Coalition asserts that research demonstrates that pornography promotes sexual violence and the degradation and abuse of children and adults. The organization encourages enforcement of laws against pornography and obscenity, while claiming that it does not support censorship. The Coalition's Legal and Public Policy Program assists those who wish to regulate sexually oriented businesses by drafting legislation, filing amicus curiae briefs, and contacting public officials.

National Legal Foundation (NLF)
P.O. Box 64427
Virginia Beach, VA 23467–4427
(757) 463–6133; (757) 463–6055
http://www.nlf.net

Founded in 1985, the National Legal Foundation involves itself in various court cases to defend the rights of Christian organizations and individuals. The NLF strives to inform people about what the organization considers dangers to religious liberty, in order to prepare people to become involved in the defense of Christians' rights. The organization considers the American Civil Liberties Union to be a major opponent in court cases. The NLF has become involved in cases dealing with the public display of the Ten Commandments, opposition to same-sex marriage, and use of public facilities by Christian groups. By responding to telephone calls and through *The Legal Alert,* its widely broadcast radio program, the NLF provides advice to churches on such topics as financial records, government employee reports, childcare facilities, and zoning questions.

National Right to Life Committee (NRLC)
512 Tenth Street NW
Washington, DC 20004
(202) 626–8800
http://www.nrlc.org

Established in 1973 as an independent lay organization by the Catholic Church in response to the U.S. Supreme Court decision legalizing abortion in *Roe v. Wade,* the NRLC attempts to limit the number of abortions performed in the United States. In addition to abortion, the organization lobbies against efforts to have euthanasia and assisted suicide legally permitted. The NRLC explicitly avoids taking official positions on such issues as contraception, sex education, or capital punishment. The NRLC's political action committee works for the election of political candidates that take an antiabortion position. The NRLC's federal and state legislative offices interact with elected representatives to pass legislation to limit abortions or to defeat legislation expanding abortion rights. The Committee acts as a clearinghouse for information for more than 3,000 chapters in all 50 states and for individual members.

Operation Save America (OSA)
P.O. Box 740066
Dallas, TX 75374
(972) 240–9370; (972) 240–9789
http://operationsaveamerica.org

Originally established in 1984 by Randall Terry as Project Life, and subsequently named Operation Rescue, Operation Save America focuses primarily on attempting to prevent abortions in the United States through demonstrations and through lobbying of public officials. Although Terry played a significant role in the early years, the organization is now severely critical of his behavior and tactics. Many in the organization objected to what was perceived as Terry's arbitrary decision making and self-promotion. In October 2003, OSA sponsored "ecclesiastical courts" in cities around the nation to protest six U.S. Supreme Court decisions, including the 1973 *Roe v. Wade* decision, and these ecclesiastical courts held the Supreme Court "in contempt of the Court of Almighty God." In many cities, demonstrators displayed six coffins to represent the six court decisions. The organization has also voiced its position on other issues, including the controversy over the removal of Terri Schiavo's feeding tube and over Roy Moore's refusal to remove a Ten Commandments monument from the rotunda of the Alabama state supreme court building. The organization maintains a nonviolent policy, backing the execution of Paul Hill, who was convicted of shooting and killing an abortion doctor and his bodyguard in Pensacola, Florida, in 1994.

Reasons to Believe (RTB)
P.O. Box 5978
Pasadena, CA 91117
(626) 335–1480
http://www.reasons.org

Hugh Ross, a former research fellow at the California Institute of Technology, established Reasons to Believe in 1986 as an organization dedicated to demonstrating that the Bible and the results of scientific research do not contradict each other. Although not adhering to a strict interpretation of the creation story in Genesis, as do other creationist organizations such as the Creation Research Society, RTB contends that the age of the Earth should be measured in billions of years, and they advocate an intelligent design theory of creation. The organization states that the Bible in its original writings is the error-free word of God, historically and scientifically as well as morally and spiritually. RTB staff members present lectures at various institutions, including schools, churches, and universities, and RTB produces books, audiotapes and videotapes, and DVDs on various topics related to science and religious belief. Although staff members do not lobby directly for the introduction of intelligent design approaches into public school systems, they provide materials to those supporting that position. The organization publishes a newsletter, *Connections,* containing reports of scientific research said to coincide with the organization's religious beliefs.

Religious Freedom Coalition (RFC)
P.O. Box 77511
Washington, DC 20013
(202) 543–0300
www.rfcnet.org

William Murray, son of atheist Madalyn Murray O'Hair, converted to Christianity in 1980 and later in the 1980s became director of Freedom's Friends, an organization ministering to people in Communist-governed nations. Murray established the Religious Freedom Coalition in 1996 to support the religious freedom of Christians in the United States and in other countries. Recently, the RFC has assisted Palestinian Christian families living in the Middle East. The Coalition asks supporters to send petitions to public officials regarding various issues of concern to the organization, such as limiting marriage to heterosexual couples, eliminating indecency in television advertisements, and supporting President George W. Bush's judicial nominations. Murray has supported legislation to remove federal regulations that prohibit clergy from supporting or opposing from the pulpit specific candidates for public office.

Traditional Values Coalition (TVC)
P.O. Box 940
Anaheim, CA 92815–0940
(714) 520–0300
http://www.traditionalvalues.org

Formed in 1982, the Traditional Values Coalition encourages Christians to become politically active to support Christian and profamily values. The TVC opposes gay rights legislation and supports right to life initiatives, such as the partial-birth abortion act approved by Congress in 2003. Louis Sheldon, the chair of the TVC, attended the ceremony at which President Bush signed the bill.

Vision America (VA)
P.O. Box 168
Houston, TX 77001
(866) 522–5582
http://www.visionamerica.org

Rick Scarborough established Vision America in 2002 in order to mobilize Christians to political participation. Holding that the major challenge to the United States today involves the preservation of moral values, the organization assists pastors in presenting this message from their pulpits. Vision America calls for changes in Internal Revenue Service regulations in order to allow pastors to speak out on political issues. VA opposes abortion, objects to any attempt by gay rights groups to establish same-sex civil unions or marriages, and calls for the enactment and enforcement of legislation restricting pornography.

WallBuilders
P.O. Box 397
Aledo, TX 76008–0397
(800) 873–2845
http://www.wallbuilders.com

WallBuilders states that it wishes to restore the moral and religious foundation upon which it claims the United States was founded. The organization gathers data to demonstrate the failure of public policies not based on fundamental Christian principles. WallBuilders has three major goals: to educate Americans about the godly foundation of the nation; to provide information to national, state, and local officials to help them develop biblically founded public policy; and to encourage Christians to become involved in civic affairs. Wall-

Builders' ProFamily Legislative Network gathers information about the legislative activities of states in such policy areas as marriage, abortion, education, gambling, and parental rights and responsibilities. The organization then makes this information available to legislators and activists in other states in order to further a profamily legislative agenda throughout the nation. The organization publishes the *WallBuilder Report,* a magazine that reports on family-related legislation and aspects of what it says is the nation's Christian heritage.

Groups Opposed to the Conservative Christian Movement

American Atheists (AA)
P.O. Box 5733
Parsippany, NJ 07054–6733
(908) 276–7300
www.atheists.org

Madalyn Murray O'Hair established American Atheists in 1963 to voice the interests of those who reject any belief in God. In 1995, O'Hair disappeared; ultimately, authorities charged a colleague with her murder. The organization has continued under the leadership of Ellen Johnson. AA has three main goals: to secure freedom from religion for those who have no religious beliefs; to work for the complete separation of church and state; and to defend the civil rights of atheists. The organization holds that religion is a private matter and should not be promoted by government. In March 2004, AA organized a demonstration at the U.S. Supreme Court building when the Court was hearing arguments in *Elk Grove Unified School District v. Newdow,* the court case in which the words *under God* in the Pledge of Allegiance were being challenged as a violation of the establishment clause of the First Amendment. AA claims that ever since those two words were added to the Pledge in 1954, atheists as well as members of religious minorities have been excluded from honest participation in patriotic ceremonies.

American Civil Liberties Union (ACLU)
125 Broad Street, Eighteenth Floor
New York, NY 10004
(212) 549–2585
http://www.aclu.org

Many conservative Christian groups consider the American Civil Liberties Union a major opponent on public policy issues. The ACLU supports a strict interpretation of the First Amendment's establishment clause, holding that it requires a rigid separation of church and state. The organization has challenged various public religious displays, including the exhibiting of the Ten Commandments. The ACLU opposes a constitutional amendment that would not allow same-sex couples to marry, arguing that such an amendment could deny government benefits to unmarried couples, whether gay or straight.

Americans United for Separation of Church and State
518 C Street NE
Washington, DC 20002
(202) 466–3234
http://www.au.org

Americans United for Separation of Church and State, by advocating the separation of religion from all aspects of public life, has become a major opponent of conservative Christian groups. The organization supports the removal of religious symbols from government buildings. Americans United has expressed concern about faith-based initiatives to provide public funds to religious institutions that offer social services, arguing that such organizations should not proselytize those seeking assistance and should follow hiring policies that are free of discrimination. The organization also has expressed support for maintaining the legal restriction that prohibits religious leaders from endorsing or opposing candidates in their churches. Americans United publishes *Church and State*, a monthly journal providing information about religious liberty issues and conservative Christian group activities.

Council for Secular Humanism (CSH)
P.O. Box 664
Amherst, NY 14226–0664
(716) 636–7571
www.secularhumanism.org

The Council for Secular Humanism challenges conservative Christian organizations, as well as all religious groups, advocating a life without religion. The very term *secular humanism* has become a battle cry for conservative Christians to represent their major foe in contemporary society. The CSH advocates strict separation of church and state, reproductive choice (including the right to abortion), and voluntary euthanasia. The organization publishes a magazine, *Free Inquiry*, containing articles on such topics as creationism, separation of church and state, and scientific advances; the *Secular Humanist Bulletin*, a newsletter reporting on the Council's activities; and *Family Matters*, a newsletter intended to attract families to the secular humanist movement.

End-of-Life Choices
P.O. Box 101810
Denver, CO 80250–1810
(800) 247–7421
http://www.endoflilfechoices.org

End-of-Life Choices works for a goal that is diametrically opposed to the beliefs of conservative Christian organizations. Originally established as The Hemlock Society, this organization lobbies for passage of state laws to allow for physician-assisted suicide for terminally ill individuals. The organization has defended the continuation of the Oregon Death with Dignity Act, originally passed in 1997. The organization, claiming a membership of 30,000 in 70 chapters throughout the nation, publishes a quarterly journal, *End-of-Life Choices*.

Freedom from Religion Foundation (FFRF)
P.O. Box 750
Madison, WI 53701
(608) 256–5800
http://www.ffrf.org

The Freedom from Religion Foundation supports the principle of separation of church and state and pursues educational activities relating to a nontheistic understanding of society. The organization describes its members as freethinkers, which include atheists, agnostics, and skeptics. The FFRF opposes prayer in the public schools; the use of public funds for religious purposes; government funding of sectarian institutions; and alleged attempts by conservative Christians to limit the rights of women, gays, and lesbians. The organization has engaged in various lawsuits, including those objecting to Bible instruction in public schools, faith-based funding, direct subsidies to parochial schools, and commencement prayers. The FFRF supports court decisions declaring unconstitutional the requirement that public school children recite the Pledge of Allegiance and requiring the removal of a Ten Commandments monument from the Alabama supreme court building. The Foundation distributes *Freethought Today*, a newspaper published ten times each year.

Human Rights Campaign (HRC)
1640 Rhode Island Avenue NW
Washington, DC 20036–3278
(202) 216–1572
http://www.hrc.org

Founded in 1980, the Human Rights Campaign claims to be the largest organization representing gays, lesbians, bisexuals, and the transgendered (GLBT). Its membership is estimated at more than 500,000. The HRC lobbies Congress, organizes grassroots political action, contributes to candidates who support equal rights for the GLBT, and conducts educational and communication campaigns. The organization's objective is to ensure that GLBT people are assured of equal rights and can enjoy safety at home and in public. The organization, which supports establishing the right of gays and lesbians to marry, is a major opponent of conservative Christian groups who wish to limit marriage to a union between a man and a woman. The HRC monitors national and state legislative activity relevant to its goals.

Interfaith Alliance (IA)
1331 H Street NW, Eleventh Floor
Washington, DC 20005
(202) 639–6370
http://www.interfaithalliance.org

The Interfaith Alliance describes itself as a nonpartisan, faith-based, grassroots organization committed to promoting a positive role for religious belief in the public realm. The organization encourages people to participate in the democratic process. The IA claims a membership of more than 150,000 people drawn from various religions, including Judaism, Christianity, Islam, Hinduism, and Buddhism. The organization contrasts its concerns, including religious liberty, civil rights, and environmentalism, to the claimed harmful agenda of the conservative Christian groups such as the Family Research Council and the Christian Coalition.

Lambda Legal
120 Wall Street, Suite 1500
New York, NY 10005–3904
(212) 809–8585
http://www.lambdalegal.org

As the push for gay rights has become more intense, organizations representing the interests of gays and lesbians have become a more significant opponent of conservative Christian groups. Lambda Legal works to achieve civil rights for lesbians, gay men, bisexuals, and people with HIV or AIDS. Attorneys associated with the organization work on cases dealing with discrimination in such areas as employment, housing, public accommodations, and the military. Lambda Legal opposes an amendment to the U.S. Constitution that would restrict marriage to heterosexual couples, arguing that such an amendment would limit the rights of gays and lesbians.

Log Cabin Republicans (LCR)
1607 17th Street NW
Washington, DC 20009
(202) 347–5306
http://www.logcabin.org

Log Cabin Republicans was established in the 1970s as an organization of gays and lesbians who support the basic platform of the Republican party. The LCR supports limited government, lower taxes, and a balanced budget. The organization calls for a more inclusive Republican party and opposes what it calls the bigotry of the party's right wing (including the conservative Christian movement), which the LCR claims is leading to a culture war. The organization blames the more conservative elements in the party for such proposals as the Defense of Marriage amendment to the U.S. Constitution, which would prohibit same-sex marriage. The LCR claims that gays and lesbians helped defeat Democratic candidate Al Gore in the 2000 presidential election by delivering more than 1 million votes for George W. Bush. However, they point out that Bush's support for conservative Christian groups by advocating the Defense of Marriage constitutional amendment may have made it difficult for the Log Cabin Republicans to muster electoral support for Bush in 2004. In March 2004, the group launched an advertising campaign criticizing the Bush administration for its efforts to ban same-sex marriage.

NARAL Pro-Choice America
1156 Fifteenth Street NW
Washington, DC 20005
(202) 973–3000
http://www.naral.org

A major foe of conservative Christian organizations, NARAL Pro-Choice America, formerly the National Abortion and Reproductive Rights Action League, campaigns to maintain the right of women to control their reproductive lives. Although the organization's main objective remains protecting the right to legal abortion, it has recently placed greater emphasis on providing access to effective contraception methods in order to reduce the need for the abortion option.

National Abortion Federation (NAF)
1755 Massachusetts Avenue NW, Suite 600
Washington, DC 20036
(202) 667–5881
http://www.prochoice.org

Established in 1977, the National Abortion Federation includes as members nonprofit and private clinics, women's health centers, Planned Parenthood offices, and private citizens. The Federation strives to keep abortion safe, accessible, and legal, goals that are antithetical to those of conservative Christian organizations. The organization offers assistance to abortion clinics, especially in providing security against potential violence. The NAF maintains a hotline that assists callers in dealing with the varying state restrictions on abortion.

National Council of Churches USA (NCC)
110 Maryland Avenue NE
Washington, DC 20002
(202) 544–2350
http://www.ncccusa.org

Founded in 1950 as the successor to the Federal Council of Churches, the National Council of Churches has been a focus for criticism by conservative denominations because of its emphasis on "social gospel" issues, including poverty, racism, protection of the environment, and promotion of relations with non-Christian religions. Members of the National Association of Evangelicals, as well as the more conservative American Council of Christian Churches, may not also hold membership in the NCC. The NCC is composed of thirty-six Protestant and Orthodox denominations. The organization holds an annual General Assembly, at which approximately 300 representatives from the member denominations meet to make organization policy.

National Organization for Women (NOW)
P.O. Box 1848
Merrifield, VA 22116–8048
(202) 628–8669
http://www.now.org

The National Organization for Women, an organization established in 1966 to work toward achieving equal legal, political, social, and economic rights for women, often advocates policies opposed to the agenda of conservative Christian groups. An organization of 500,00 contributing members, NOW supports the right of women to have the options of abortion and birth control and advocates rights for gays and lesbians. NOW strongly opposed the partial-birth abortion ban that President George W. Bush signed into law in 2003. The organization opposes other measures that conservative Christian groups support, such as fetal rights legislation, which NOW considers an indirect attack on abortion rights.

People for the American Way (PFAW)
2000 M Street, NW, Suite 400
Washington, DC 20036
(202) 467–4999
http://www.pfaw.org

In the 1980s, Norman Lear, with the assistance of political activists such as Barbara Jordan, established People for the American Way in direct response to the rise of conservative Christian organizations such as the Moral Majority, Focus on the Family, and the Family Research Council. PFAW has opposed attempts to censor public school textbooks, supported the teaching of evolution in public schools, opposed attempts to limit protection for gays and lesbians, and defended art exhibits against attacks from conservative groups. The organization works to mobilize supporters to oppose what are considered right-wing attempts to gain control of the judicial system by having conservative judges appointed.

Planned Parenthood Federation of America (PPFA)
434 West Thirty-Third Street
New York, NY 10001
(800) 829–7732
http://www.plannedparenthood.org

Conservative Christian organizations that focus primarily on an antiabortion agenda consider Planned Parenthood a major opponent. Planned Parenthood provides various health services for women, including cancer screening, HIV testing, and prenatal care. However, conservative Christians object to the organization's involvement in contraception and abortion. To counter what it calls antichoice fanatics, Planned Parenthood has begun the Responsible Choices Action Agenda to make available improved contraceptive methods and increase the availability of reproductive care for women.

Religious Coalition for Reproductive Choice (RCRC)
1025 Vermont Avenue NW, Suite 1130
Washington, DC 20005
(202) 628–7700
http://www.rcrc.org

Clergy and lay leaders from mainline religious groups founded the Religious Coalition for Reproductive Choice in 1973 as a means of defending the right to abortion. In addition to abortion services, the organization supports access to sex education, family planning and contraception, childcare, health care, and adoption services. The RCRC opposed conservative Christian support for, and the ultimate congressional passage of, the partial-birth abortion ban, which the organization claimed would deny women the ability to make medical decisions for themselves. Clergy for Choice, a subgroup of the RCRC, is an ecumenical group of clergy that supports reproductive choice.

Soulforce
P.O. Box 3195
Lynchburg, VA 24503–0195
(877) 705–6393
http://www.soulforce.org

Mel White established Soulforce as an interfaith organization dedicated to ending "spiritual violence" against gays and lesbians. The organization attributes such violence to both conservative and mainline denominations as well as to the Roman Catholic Church. In 1999, White and 200 followers met with Jerry Falwell and 200 fellow conservative Christians in Lynchburg, Virginia, and after the meeting, Falwell apologized for his previous antigay statements. The organization is dedicated to the principles of nonviolent resistance proposed by Mohandas Gandhi and Martin Luther King, Jr. In 2001,

Soulforce initiated a noncooperation campaign against Christian churches that their members had previously supported because the churches failed to recognize the legitimacy of gay rights.

Chronology

In this chronology, we focus primarily on the period after 1979. This was the year that Jerry Falwell, with the help of Paul Weyrich, Howard Phillips, and Edward McAteer, established the Moral Majority and thus initiated the contemporary conservative Christian movement that is the primary focus of this book. However, we have included some selected earlier events that contributed to conservative Christians' resolve to become more politically active.

1859   Charles Darwin publishes *Origin of Species,* in which he presents a theory of evolution based on the mechanism of natural selection and explains the origin of human beings through a random, exclusively physical process. Christians divide on this question, with some attempting to find compatibility between their faith and the new theory while others object strenuously to eliminating God from an account of human origins.

1886   Evangelist Dwight L. Moody establishes the Moody Bible Institute in Chicago to provide religious education that emphasizes more traditional Christian beliefs. The Institute serves as a model for many future Bible colleges that will teach the inerrancy of scripture.

1895   The Niagara Bible Conference declares the essential Christian beliefs that will thereafter guide fundamentalists. These beliefs include the inerrancy of the Bible, the deity and virgin birth of Jesus, the substitutionary atonement, the bodily resurrection of Jesus, and the second coming.

1910 The publication of twelve pamphlets titled *The Fundamentals: A Testimony to the Truth* begins; it continues until 1915. These pamphlets, written by noted conservative Christians, affirm the essential beliefs stated at the Niagara Bible Conference of 1895. The pamphlets also condemn the theory of evolution and criticize some other religious groups such as the Mormons and Jehovah's Witnesses.

1919 William Bell Riley, pastor of the First Baptist Church in Philadelphia, organizes a meeting to establish the World's Christian Fundamentals Association, which will lead the opposition to the teaching of evolution in the public schools.

1923 The Oklahoma state legislature approves the first law in the United States prohibiting the teaching of evolution.

1924 More than 1,200 Presbyterian church members sign the Auburn Affirmation, which rejects various fundamentalist beliefs, such as the inerrancy of the Bible, the virgin birth of Jesus, and the factual basis of miracles recorded in the Bible. The Affirmation represents the increasing split between more liberal and more conservative groups within mainline Christian churches.

1925 The Tennessee state legislature passes a law prohibiting the teaching of evolution in the state's public schools. John T. Scopes, a teacher in Dayton, violates the law and is placed on trial. The American Civil Liberties Union hires noted attorney Clarence Darrow to defend Scopes, and the World's Christian Fundamentals Association urges three-time presidential candidate William Jennings Bryan to work for the prosecution. Although Scopes is convicted, national publicity embarrasses more conservative forces and the World's Christian Fundamentals Association soon recedes into obscurity.

1926 The unfavorable publicity from the Scopes trial notwithstanding, the Mississippi state legislature approves a law prohibiting the teaching of evolution.

1928 Arkansas, by popular referendum, outlaws the teaching of evolution.

1933 American educator John Dewey and more than thirty other humanists sign The Humanist Manifesto, signaling to fundamentalists that secular humanism represents a belief opposed to Christianity.

1941 Presbyterian minister Carl McIntire establishes the conservative American Council of Christian Churches in response to the founding of the Federal (subsequently National)

Council of Churches, a more liberal coalition of mainline churches.

1942 The National Association of Evangelicals is established as an alternative to the fundamentalist American Council of Christian Churches and to the Federal Council of Churches.

1954 President Dwight Eisenhower signs legislation adding the words *under God* to the Pledge of Allegiance.

1956 Largely in response to the perceived Communist threat, the phrase *In God We Trust,* which was placed on American currency the previous year, becomes the national motto.

1960 Evangelist Pat Robertson establishes the Christian Broadcasting Network, which will become a major voice for conservative Christians.

Presidential hopeful John Fitzgerald Kennedy, a Roman Catholic, speaks before the Greater Houston Ministerial Association, assuring the members that his religious affiliation will not govern his decisions as president: "I believe in an America where the separation of church and state is absolute—where no Catholic prelate would tell the President (should he be Catholic) how to act, and no Protestant minister would tell his parishioners for whom to vote."

1962 The U.S. Supreme Court, in *Engel v. Vitale,* declares unconstitutional a New York state policy that public school students recite a nondenominational prayer written by the New York State Board of Regents. The general public as well as religious leaders strongly object to the ruling.

1963 In *Abington School District v. Schempp,* the U.S. Supreme Court again rules on religious ceremonies in the public schools, this time invalidating state policies in Pennsylvania and Maryland that require a Bible reading at the beginning of each school day. The Court declares that the Bible reading violates the First Amendment directive that government neither aid nor oppose religion, but maintain strict neutrality.

1971 In *Lemon v. Kurtzman* (403 U.S. 602, 91 S.Ct. 2105, 29 L.Ed.2d 745), the U.S. Supreme Court attempts to establish criteria to determine whether a statute violates the establishment clause of the First Amendment. To comply with this clause, a law must have a secular legislative purpose, and its primary effect must neither advance nor inhibit religion.

1973 The U.S. Supreme Court, in *Roe v. Wade,* declares unconstitutional laws limiting abortion in the first three months of pregnancy. Opposition to abortion, which prior to the *Roe* decision was limited largely to Roman Catholics, now begins to include a broad group of conservative Christians.

1976   In the presidential election, many conservative Christians support Jimmy Carter, a Southern Baptist. However, as president, Carter later disappoints many of those conservative Christians who supported him during the election.

1978   Jerome Kurtz, Internal Revenue Service commissioner under President Jimmy Carter, declares that the IRS will eliminate tax exemptions for private schools, including schools associated with churches, that apparently were established to avoid mandatory public school desegregation. Many conservative Christians consider the decision an attack upon religion.

1979   In response to the perceived lack of moral standards in government, as well as the perceived decline in moral standards in society as witnessed by the legalization of abortion, the prohibition of prayer in the public schools, and the spread of pornography, Paul Weyrich, Richard Viguerie, Howard Phillips, and Edward A. McAteer, along with Jerry Falwell, create Moral Majority, Inc. They hope to activate conservative Christians and bring into office public officials who are sympathetic with the organization's socially conservative agenda.

1980   Presidential candidate Ronald Reagan attends the National Affairs Briefing in Dallas, a gathering organized by conservative Christian leader Edward McAteer and the Religious Roundtable.

The Moral Majority claims to have registered 4 million new voters for the fall elections. Because the registration drive was conducted in church settings, the organization leadership assumes some credit for the election of Ronald Reagan to the presidency.

1981   Concerned about Sandra Day O'Connor's position on the abortion question, Jerry Falwell urges Christians to oppose her confirmation by the U.S. Senate to the Supreme Court. The Senate ultimately approves President Reagan's nomination of O'Connor.

1982   Delivering on a promise to conservative Christian organizations, President Ronald Reagan supports the passage of a constitutional amendment to allow prayer in the public schools.

1984   Randall Terry begins his career as a leader of the antiabortion movement. Accompanied by his wife, Cindy, Terry attempts to persuade women entering the Southern Tier Women's Services clinic in Binghamton, New York, not to undergo an abortion.

On March 20, after two weeks of debate, the U.S. Senate votes on President Reagan's proposed school prayer amendment. Although a majority of fifty-six senators support the amendment, it fails to receive the needed two-thirds majority in order to send it to the states for ratification. Senator Jesse Helms, a major supporter of the amendment, promises to continue the struggle to pass the measure.

Congress passes the Equal Access Act, a measure that guarantees access of religious organizations to public school facilities for voluntary religious events.

1985　In *Wallace v. Jaffree* (472 U.S. 38, 105 S.Ct. 2479, 86 L.Ed.2d 29), the U.S. Supreme Court invalidates an Alabama law that provides for allowing a moment of silence for schoolchildren for meditation or voluntary prayer. The Court declares that the law violates the establishment clause of the First Amendment.

1986　Jerry Falwell renames the Moral Majority, calling it the Liberty Federation, hoping to increase the appeal of the organization to a broader membership.

In *Smith v. Board of School Commissioners,* more than 600 conservative Christians file a suit in state court against Alabama state and local education officials, claiming that the Mobile public schools promote the religion of secular humanism. Phyllis Schlafly of the Eagle Forum supports the plaintiffs, arguing that if Christianity and Judaism cannot be taught in the public schools, secular humanism also may not be taught.

1987　In *Edwards v. Aguillard,* the U.S. Supreme Court invalidates a Louisiana law that provides for equal treatment of evolution and "creation science" in the public schools.

On March 4, in *Smith v. Board of School Commissioners,* U.S. District Court Judge W. Brevard Hand, in an interesting interpretation of the doctrine of separation of church and state, bans thirty-one public school textbooks in Alabama, agreeing with the plaintiffs that the books teach secular humanism, which, they claim, is a religion. Conservative Christians applaud the decision, but the Eleventh U.S. Circuit Court of Appeals soon reverses Hand's decision.

1988　*700 Club* host Pat Robertson decides to seek the Republican presidential nomination. Having an effective grassroots organization in Iowa, he does well in that state's caucus. However, Robertson is unable to attract conservative Christian voters in subsequent primaries and caucuses, and he later leaves the race.

Randall Terry, leader of Operation Rescue, conducts extensive antiabortion demonstrations in Atlanta, Georgia, site of the Democratic National Convention, during the summer. Terry uses such tactics as having his followers fail to carry identification, refuse to give their names when arrested, and attempt to crawl past police barricades. The summer-long demonstrations represent the organization's high point in the antiabortion protest movement.

1989   Jerry Falwell disbands the Moral Majority (Liberty Federation) after experiencing serious financial shortfalls. Some attribute the demise of the organization to its failure to establish an effective structure at the grass roots. With the demise of the Moral Majority, Pat Robertson uses his leftover campaign organization and mailing list to establish a new organization, the Christian Coalition, out of the ashes of his failed campaign for the Republican presidential nomination. Ralph Reed becomes the new organization's executive director.

1990   The Christian Coalition campaigns for Jesse Helms, who is running for reelection as senator from North Carolina. The Coalition takes some of the credit when Helms wins the election.

In *Board of Education of Westside Community School District v. Mergens,* the U.S. Supreme Court rules in favor of the Equal Access Act, which grants access to public school facilities to religious groups on the same basis as secular groups.

In *Oregon v. Smith* (494 U.S. 872), the U.S. Supreme Court declares that government must show a "reasonable interest" rather than a more stringent "compelling interest" in limiting free exercise of religion.

1991   When President George H. W. Bush nominates conservative Clarence Thomas to the U.S. Supreme Court, the Christian Coalition and other conservative Christian organizations lobby for Senate ratification of the nomination. Although Thomas's nomination becomes controversial when sexual harassment charges are brought against him, the Senate finally approves his nomination.

The U.S. Supreme Court rules in *Lee v. Weisman* that the public school system of the city of Providence, Rhode Island, has violated the religion clauses of the First Amendment by inviting members of the clergy to give invocations and benedictions at middle school and high school graduations. Conservative Christian groups object to the ruling.

1993 The Christian Coalition opens an office in Washington, D.C., in order more effectively to lobby Congress on the organization's political agenda.

Congress passes the Religious Freedom Restoration Act, and President Bill Clinton signs the bill into law. The legislation restores the compelling interest standard for determining the legitimacy of government involvement in limiting the free exercise of religion, a more restrictive criterion than the reasonable interest standard.

1994 Abortion rights groups successfully lobby Congress to pass the Freedom of Access to Clinic Entrances (FACE) Act, which prohibits demonstrators from blocking abortion clinic entrances.

Both the prochoice and antiabortion movements are shocked when Paul Hill, an anti-abortion activist, shoots and kills physician John Bayard Britton and his escort, James Barrett, outside a Pensacola, Florida, abortion clinic. Although more mainline prolife activists condemn Hill's violent actions, others express ambivalence, and more extreme members of the movement condone the killings.

With campaign assistance from conservative Christian groups, the Republicans succeed in regaining control of both houses of Congress for the first time in more than 40 years.

1996 At the urging of conservative Christian groups, Congress passes the Defense of Marriage Act, which President Bill Clinton signs into law. The measure defines marriage as a union between a man and a woman and authorizes states to refuse to recognize same-sex marriages performed in other states and to deny benefits to same-sex partners. Thirty-eight states ultimately pass similar measures.

Congress passes a welfare reform bill that contains a provision establishing charitable choice, which will allow faith-based organizations greater access to federal funding in order to provide social services such as drug rehabilitation and job training. The legislation, which Senator John Ashcroft (R-MO) strongly backs, does not require the faith-based organizations to adhere to strict separation of religious content from the social programs or to comply with equal treatment requirements.

In July, the Zionist Organization of America recognizes Pat Robertson for his strong support for the state of Israel.

1997   Ralph Reed leaves the Christian Coalition to establish Century Strategies, a political consulting firm. Randy Tate, who served as a member of the U.S. House of Representatives from 1995 to 1997, becomes the leader of the Coalition.

In *City of Boerne v. Flores* (117 S.Ct. 2157, 138 L.Ed.2d 624), the U.S. Supreme Court declares the Religious Freedom Restoration Act unconstitutional, arguing that Congress has violated the principle of separation of powers within the national government as well as between the national and state governments.

Following President Clinton's impeachment, Randy Tate of the Christian Coalition calls for Clinton's resignation despite attitude surveys indicating that the president continues to have significant public support.

1999   With polls continuing to show strong support for President Clinton, Pat Robertson advises Republicans to end the campaign to remove the president from office.

The Internal Revenue Service charges the Christian Coalition with inappropriate political activity and threatens to withdraw the organization's tax exempt status. The organization divides into two separate parts: the Christian Coalition of America, an educational organization, and the Christian Coalition International, a political action committee that will be more directly involved in politics.

Texas governor George W. Bush signs the Texas Religious Freedom Restoration Act, which requires the state government to demonstrate a compelling interest before it can legitimately restrict the free exercise of religion.

In response to the Fifth U.S. Circuit Court of Appeals decision prohibiting organized prayer prior to Santa Fe, Texas, high school football games, the U.S. House of Representatives passes a resolution calling for the Supreme Court to overrule the appeals court decision.

In the resolution of a lawsuit initiated in 1996 by the Federal Election Commission, the Christian Coalition loses its tax exempt status. However, a federal district judge dismisses many of the charges brought against the Christian Coalition.

The Kansas state board of education decides to make optional the teaching of evolution in the state's public schools.

The board also deletes the evolution topic from state assessment tests.

The Kentucky Education Department decides to substitute the phrase *change over time* for the word *evolution* in curriculum guidelines.

2000   The Christian Coalition reports having distributed 70 million voter guides during the year's election campaign. Jerry Falwell and Pat Robertson reportedly join forces to invest more than $18 million in mobilizing 35 million voters in support of George W. Bush.

The Governor Howard Dean of Vermont signs the first state law recognizing civil unions between same-sex couples.

The Family Research Council engages in a campaign to persuade state legislatures to allow the Ten Commandments to be posted in public schools.

During the presidential campaign, George W. Bush pledges that, if elected, he will bring about changes to allow religious organizations access to federal funds for social welfare activities. This is called the faith-based initiative. Many religious groups applaud the plan, but other, more conservative Christian leaders express concerns about possible government controls over religious organizations.

In assisting George W. Bush in the South Carolina primary, Pat Robertson of the Christian Coalition records a telephone message attacking Bush's major opponent, Senator John McCain, for being allied with anti-Christians.

Jerry Falwell announces a plan to register 10 million new voters for the November general election. He hopes to enlist the assistance of local pastors in the effort.

On June 19, the U.S. Supreme Court delivers a decision in *Santa Fe Independent School District v. Doe,* striking down the practice of having an officially sanctioned prayer prior to the start of football games. Following the decision, various conservative Christian individuals and groups announce their opposition to the decision. Presidential candidate George W. Bush announces his disapproval of the decision. Protests are scheduled for the first football game of the fall, but due to lack of organization, they fail to meet expectations.

The Sixth U.S. Circuit Court of Appeals invalidates the Ohio state motto, "With God, all things are possible," as a violation of the Second Amendment's establishment clause.

2001   In August, President George W. Bush announces his policy decision regarding the funding of stem cell research. Respecting the views of conservative Christians who believe that life begins at conception and that, therefore, the killing of a human embryo in order to obtain stem cells is immoral, the president agrees to allow the use of federal funds in research conducted only on already existing stem cell lines.

2002   The Ninth Circuit Court of Appeals, in a case brought by Michael Newdow on behalf of his 9-year-old daughter, rules that the saying of the Pledge of Allegiance in public schools is a violation of the establishment clause of the First Amendment because of the phrase *under God*. Conservative Christian individuals and groups add their voices to the general outcry against the decision. Members of Congress quickly schedule events at which the Pledge will be said.

    The U.S. Supreme Court, in *Zelman v. Simmons-Harris,* rules on a voucher program in the Cleveland, Ohio, city school district that distributes tuition aid to parents of students according to financial need. The Court rules that the program does not violate the establishment clause of the First Amendment even though both religious as well as nonreligious schools may participate. In the five-to-four majority opinion, Chief Justice William H. Rehnquist states that the voucher program is completely neutral with regard to religion and offers a choice of options, both public and private, to "a wide spectrum of individuals."

2003   In *Scheidler v. National Organization for Women,* the U.S. Supreme Court invalidates judgments against antiabortion protesters under the federal Racketeer Influenced and Corrupt Organizations Act (RICO) and other laws to regulate extortion by organized crime. The Alliance Defense Fund provides legal support for the antiabortion protesters.

    General William G. Boykin, deputy undersecretary of defense for intelligence, comes under attack when it is reported that he made statements at religious meetings about Islam and about the U.S. war on terror. Many believe that such comments harm U.S. foreign policy because they run counter to official policy stating that the United States is not at war with Islam. Conservative Christian groups come to Boykin's defense, arguing that the general has the right to practice freedom of speech.

In February, the U.S. Supreme Court refuses to hear an appeal from Indiana abortion clinics challenging an Indiana law placing restrictions on the ability of women to get an abortion. The law, passed eight years before, requires that women wait eighteen hours after first seeking an abortion, undergo face-to-face counseling about the risks of abortion, and be offered pictures of how the fetus might appear in the womb.

In May, Eric Rudolph is captured in Murphy, North Carolina. Rudolph is accused of a bombing at Centennial Olympic Park during the 1996 Summer Olympics as well as two bombings at abortion clinics, at one of which an off-duty policy officer was killed.

In June, New Hampshire clergy and parishioners of the Episcopalian Church USA elect V. Gene Robinson, an openly gay priest, as the state's new bishop. In August, a general convention of ECUSA bishops confirms Robinson's election. Conservative Episcopalians meet in Dallas, Texas, in October as the American Anglican Council, a conservative faction within the Episcopal Church, to discuss options for those who oppose the selection of Robinson. In November, at a ceremony held in Durham, New Hampshire, Robinson is consecrated as a bishop.

Terri Schiavo, a woman who has been in a vegetative state for years, receives the attention of several conservative Christian groups, including the Florida-based Center for Reclaiming America, when Schiavo's husband receives the support of a Florida state judge to remove his wife's feeding tube. The Florida legislature passes, and Governor Jeb Bush signs, legislation to force Schiavo's husband to replace the feeding tube. Conservative Christian groups view this incident as an example of the need to protect the right to life against proponents of abortion and euthanasia.

Americans United for Separation of Church and State, along with other civil liberties groups, challenge the placement of a 5,000-pound Ten Commandments monument in the Alabama Supreme Court building by the court's chief justice, Roy Moore. In August, a federal judge rules that Moore must remove the monument from public display. After he refuses, the Alabama Court of the Judiciary removes Moore from office in November. Many conservative Christian groups support Moore's cause, arguing that the American judicial system is ultimately based on the Ten Commandments.

The U.S. Supreme Court, in *Lawrence v. Texas,* strikes down a Texas antisodomy law in a six-to-three decision, thus legalizing homosexual relations throughout the United States. Justice Antonin Scalia writes a heated dissent, expressing the views of conservative Christians who believe that homosexuality is contrary to the moral foundation of the nation. Conservative Christians perceive that the consequences of the decision may be extensive, and they begin planning strategies to oppose further claims of homosexual rights such as the right to same-sex marriage.

A July Pew Research Center poll asks respondents about President Bush's public statements about his religious beliefs. Sixty-two percent of those interviewed say that Bush mentions his religious faith the right amount, another 11 percent want him to mention religion more often, and only 14 percent say he uses religious language too often.

In July, Pat Robertson responds to the *Lawrence v. Texas* decision by asking his television audience to pray for the retirement of three liberal Supreme Court justices.

In September, Paul Hill, convicted of killing a physician and his escort outside a Pensacola, Florida, abortion clinic, is executed. Hill continues until the end to say that he has obeyed a higher law by committing the murders.

In November, the Massachusetts Supreme Judicial Court, in a four-to-three decision (*Goodridge v. Department of Public Health*), declares that the state's ban on gay marriage violates the Massachusetts state constitution. The court grants the state legislature 180 days to enforce the decision. Conservative Christian groups uniformly condemn the decision and begin calling for a "Defense of Marriage" amendment to the Massachusetts state constitution. These groups also join with conservative politicians to initiate an amendment to the national constitution.

Roman Catholic bishops, in a November meeting in Washington, D.C., declare their opposition to same-sex marriage.

The Alliance for Marriage drafts a constitutional amendment that Representative Marilyn Musgrave (R-CO) and Senator Wayne Allard (R-CO) introduce into Congress. The proposed amendment would define marriage as a union between a man and a woman and thus would prohibit same-sex marriage.

President Bush signs a proclamation designating October 12 the start of Marriage Protection Week. Conservative Christians use the occasion to advocate the restriction of marriage to a union between one man and one woman.

In November, President George W. Bush signs the partial-birth abortion bill during a ceremony at which leaders of conservative Christian organizations, including Louis Sheldon of the Traditional Values Coalition, are prominently represented. The Center for Reproductive Rights, the American Civil Liberties Union, and Planned Parenthood of America immediately file objections to the new abortion legislation in federal courts around the country, which block enforcement of the new law, in part because it contains no health exception.

On November 12, Roman Catholic bishops, in a semiannual meeting, approve the document *Between Man and Woman: Questions and Answers about Marriage and Same-Sex Unions,* in which the bishops oppose a redefinition of marriage that would provide benefits to "those who cannot rightfully enter into marriage."

In December, two scientific advisory panels recommend to the Food and Drug Administration that an emergency contraceptive, the so-called morning after pill, or "Plan B," be sold over the counter without a doctor's prescription. However, the Food and Drug Administration delays approval, and some claim that antiabortion groups are responsible.

In December, the Sixth U.S. Circuit Court of Appeals, in a two-to-one decision, rules that an Ohio law passed in 2000 that bans a late-term abortion procedure does not violate the Constitution.

2004   President George W. Bush, in his State of the Union address, expresses his conditional support for a constitutional amendment limiting the definition of marriage to the union of a man and a woman. Conservative Christian groups continue to urge the president to give his explicit support to such an amendment.

In January, at a Woodbridge, Virginia, conference sponsored by the conservative American Anglican Council, 3,000 Episcopalians opposed to the elevation of gay priest V. Gene

Robinson to the position of bishop of New Hampshire discuss a possible separation from the ECUSA. A new organization is planned, tentatively called the Network of Anglican Communion Dioceses and Parishes.

In February, representatives of conservative groups, including Randy Thomasson, president of the Campaign for California Families, quickly criticize the new president of the Pasadena, California, Rose Parade for selecting "Celebrate Family" as the theme for next year's New Year's Day parade. The critics are concerned that gay organizations may attempt to enter floats in the parade.

In February, two U.S. senators, in response to the Alabama Ten Commandments controversy, introduce a measure that would prohibit federal courts from disallowing state court decisions favoring an acknowledgment of God. Conservative Christian groups favor the legislation.

On February 1, conservative Christians become increasingly upset with what they consider obscenity in the mass media when Janet Jackson, performing during the Super Bowl halftime show, has her right breast exposed before a vast television audience. Conservative Christian groups call for greater controls over the broadcast media, including increased punishment for violating decency rules.

On February 4, the Massachusetts Supreme Judicial Court responds to a request issued by the state senate to rule on whether legislation limiting same-sex couples to civil unions and not marriage will satisfy the state constitution. The court rules that anything short of marriage would violate the state constitution. This ruling increases calls for the state legislature to begin the process of amending the state constitution to define marriage as a union between a man and a woman.

On February 4, despite objections from Democrats, the U.S. House of Representatives votes to extend a policy that allows religious groups to limit employment opportunities to those who are members of the faith when hiring for community assistance programs funded by federal grants. The Bush administration threatens to veto the Community Service Block Grant Act if Congress removes the hiring autonomy of religious organizations from the Act.

On February 12, which gay activists declare National Freedom to Marry Day, Gavin Newsom, mayor of San Francisco, authorizes the issuing of marriage licenses and the performance of gay marriages by city officials. Conservative Christian groups, including the Campaign for California Families and the Alliance Defense Fund, begin immediate appeals to the California courts to halt the gay marriages.

On February 24, President George W. Bush, at the urging of conservative Christian leaders, announces his support for a "defense of marriage" constitutional amendment and calls on Congress to begin the process of amending the U.S. Constitution.

After failing to reach agreement on a state constitutional amendment in February, the Massachusetts legislature in March finally approves an amendment that would define marriage as the union of a man and a woman, but which would allow for same-sex civil unions to protect various rights of homosexuals.

On February 25, the U.S. Supreme Court, in *Locke v. Davey,* rules in a seven-to-two decision that when Washington denied a publicly funded scholarship to a college student enrolled in a program to prepare him for the ministry, the state did not violate the free exercise clause of the First Amendment. Those conservative Christians supporting the student's cause noted that the provision within the Washington constitution stating, "No public money or property shall be appropriated for or applied to any religious worship, exercise or instruction, or the support of any religious establishment" is similar to provisions in several state constitutions that discriminate against religious groups.

On March 7, V. Gene Robinson officially becomes the bishop of New Hampshire, the first openly gay priest to hold such a high office within the Episcopal Church.

On March 11, the California Supreme Court issues a stay to prevent San Francisco from issuing any additional marriage licenses to same-sex couples. Since February 12, more than 3,600 same-sex marriages have been performed in San Francisco.

In March, prosecutors in Salt Lake City, Utah, charge a woman with murder for refusing to undergo a caesarian section, which causes one of the twins she is carrying to die. The National Organization for Women, Planned Parenthood, and the American Civil Liberties Union object to the prosecutors' decision to bring charges, claiming that the action is another example of attempting to grant rights to the fetus and that it thus represents an attack on abortion rights.

On March 19, the House of Bishops of the Episcopal Church USA begins a six-day retreat in Navasota, Texas, in an attempt to arrive at a compromise in the controversy over the ordination of V. Gene Robinson, an openly gay priest, as bishop of New Hampshire. Robinson attends the retreat as a newly consecrated bishop. The bishops develop a plan to allow visiting bishops to serve conservative parishes with the approval of the resident bishop, but the conservative Anglican Council calls the plan inadequate. The bishops attending the retreat issue a statement repudiating the actions of five retired conservative bishops who participated in confirmations of new members without the approval of the bishop of the diocese.

On March 24, the U.S. Supreme Court hears arguments in the Pledge of Allegiance case in which the Ninth Circuit Court of Appeals previously ruled that the words *under God* in the Pledge are a violation of the establishment clause of the First Amendment. Michael Newdow, who brought the case before the courts on behalf of his daughter, argues the case before the Supreme Court. Supporters and opponents of the Pledge both lead demonstrations outside the Supreme Court building. Patrick Mahoney, director of the Christian Defense Coalition, leads supporters in prayer.

The American Civil Liberties Union files a lawsuit in the Multnomah County, Oregon, circuit court, challenging the decision of the Oregon Office of Vital Statistics not to recognize gay marriages performed in Multnomah County. Supporters as well as opponents of gay marriage consolidate their suits in the ACLU action, believing that it most directly confronts the issues and will more quickly be heard by the state Supreme Court.

On March 25, Congress approves a measure making it a separate crime to injure or kill a fetus during the commission of a federal crime. The bill defines the status of the fetus, beginning at conception, as a potential victim of violent crime. Abortion rights advocates consider this legislation to be another step taken by antiabortion forces toward banning abortion.

On March 27, a group of moderate and liberal Episcopalians from eleven conservative dioceses end a three-day meeting in Atlanta, calling for toleration of differing viewpoints on the ordination of a gay bishop in order to preserve church unity.

On March 29, federal judges in San Francisco, New York, and Lincoln, Nebraska, consider cases brought by the National Abortion Federation and Planned Parenthood to stop enforcement of the national Partial-Birth Abortion Act. A controversy arising from the cases involves the request from the U.S. Justice Department that abortion records be provided by hospitals as evidence in the government's argument. Federal judges in New York and Michigan rule that hospitals must comply, but two others in Chicago and San Francisco deny the request.

On March 29, the Massachusetts legislature gives final approval to a proposed state constitutional amendment that would prohibit same-sex marriages but sanction same-sex civil unions. Governor Mitt Romney states that he will ask the Massachusetts Supreme Judicial Court to delay implementing its ruling allowing same-sex marriages beginning May 17.

In May, Colorado Springs, Colorado, Roman Catholic Bishop Michael Sheridan states that voting for a politician who opposes church doctrine on such issues as abortion and same-sex marriage is a mortal sin.

On May 6, President Bush participates in a National Day of Prayer ceremony that is telecast nationally on Christian cable and satellite television networks. Barry W. Lynn, executive director of Americans United for Separation of Church and State, label the event as essentially political, commenting that the president is consolidating support among evangelical Christians for the November election.

In June, after several Roman Catholic bishops disagree over whether Democratic presidential candidate John Kerry, who is a Catholic and supports abortion rights, should receive Communion, Cardinal Joseph Ratzinger of the Vatican inform visiting U.S. bishops that they should exercise caution about denying Communion to Catholic politicians who support policies contrary to church doctrine.

In July, Richard Land, president of the Southern Baptist Convention's Ethics and Religious Liberty Commission, terms inappropriate a request from President Bush's reelection campaign organization to use church membership directories for campaign purposes, such as scheduling voter-registration drives at local churches. Barry Lynn, executive director of Americans United for Separation of Church and State, calls the effort an attempt to "abuse churches for partisan political ends."

After debate on a proposed Defense of Marriage constitutional amendment, the U.S. Senate on July 14, by a vote of 50 to 48, with 60 votes necessary, fails to permit further consideration of the amendment. Despite the failure, many politicians believe that the issue will influence the outcome of the November election. Meanwhile, Republicans in the House of Representatives are advancing legislation that would prohibit the federal courts from ordering states to recognize same-sex marriages performed in other states.

Glossary

born again   A Christian who claims to have had a personal reconciliation with God through Jesus is said to have been born again. As Jesus told Nicodemus (John 3:7), "Do not marvel that I said to you, 'You must be born again.'" Although Christians of various denominations may make the claim of being born again, conservative Christians perhaps are more likely to have this experience, especially those with a Pentecostal background.

charitable choice   In welfare reform legislation passed in 1996, faith-based organizations engaged in offering social services such as drug rehabilitation and assistance to the needy were granted greater opportunities to compete for federal grant funds. When George W. Bush campaigned for the presidency in 2000, he pledged to increase further the opportunities of faith-based groups to receive federal support. Critics express concern about the blurring of the line between church and state, and although many representatives of religious groups strongly support charitable choice, some conservative Christians express the fear that the federal government will acquire greater control over religious institutions.

Christian Reconstructionism   Based in part on Jesus's commission to his disciples in Matthew 28:19–20 ("Go therefore and make disciples of all nations, baptizing them in the name of the Father, and of the Son, and of the Holy Spirit, and teaching them to obey everything that I have commanded you."), this movement emphasizes the view that Christians can restructure society according to biblical principles. Rousas John Rushdoony, founder of the Chalcedon Foundation, an organization that claims to offer biblical solutions to the problems faced by the contemporary world, was a major proponent of reforming society according to biblical law. Those advocating Christian reconstructionism tend to be critical of premillennial believers, who expect progressively worsening conditions prior to the return of Christ and therefore tend to be politically passive, waiting for Christ's return.

Christian Zionism This is the belief of certain conservative Christians that Israel is still God's chosen nation. These Christians support Israel's claim to Jerusalem as that nation's capital and encourage the United States to back Israel in its conflicts with the Palestinians and with Arab nations. Conservative Christians believe that in the end times events depicted in Revelation, the nation of Israel will play a crucial role.

compassionate conservatism Attributed to conservative thinkers such as Marvin Olasky, this perspective supports social welfare policies that allow for ministering to the spiritual as well as physical needs of citizens. George W. Bush emphasized compassionate conservatism during his 2000 presidential campaign, advocating federal government funding for faith-based organizations that provide assistance to the poor.

creationism (creation science) Many of those who challenge the Darwinian theory of evolution advocate some form of creationism as an alternative explanation of the origin of the world and human beings. Some creationists hold to a literal interpretation of the six days of creation as described in Genesis, but others, although agreeing that God had a direct hand in creation, contend that the process took place over a much longer period of time. Advocates of creation science argue that creationism should be presented in the public schools along with evolution as an alternative scientific theory.

deism Having its origins in the eighteenth-century Enlightenment, deism is the belief that nature provides evidence to the rational mind for the existence of God. Deists hold that after creating the universe, God withdrew from the world, does not exercise control over natural events, and has given no supernatural revelation to human beings. Several prominent Americans in the late eighteenth century were associated with deism, including Thomas Paine, Benjamin Franklin, Thomas Jefferson, John Adams, and Ethan Allen. Although aspects of deism spread to the general population, the doctrine itself failed to achieve widespread acceptance.

dominion (kingdom) theology Those conservative Christians who are politically involved tend to appeal to dominion theology, the belief that the Bible calls for them to introduce Christian values to the nation's economic, political, and educational institutions. Advocates of Christian reconstructionism support this theological viewpoint.

establishment clause This clause in the First Amendment to the U.S. Constitution states that "Congress shall make no law respecting the establishment of religion." This clause has been used by those wishing to keep religious observance out of public life to support a strict separation of church and state. Conservative Christians tend to reject the idea of a strict separation, arguing that the same Congress that proposed the First Amendment also called on President George Washington to proclaim national days of prayer, thus indicating that the establishment clause does not mandate a strict separation of church and state.

euthanasia   Also referred to as mercy killing, euthanasia involves ending a person's life in order to avoid suffering in the face of imminent natural death. Believing that life is a sacred gift from God, conservative Christians object strongly to euthanasia in all its forms. Passive euthanasia, which involves disconnecting life support equipment or ending medical treatment necessary to continue life, introduces a more complicated circumstance. When, in 2003, the husband of Terri Schiavo, who had been in a vegetative state for thirteen years, obtained a court order to have his wife's feeding tube removed, several conservative Christian groups strongly objected. The Florida legislature passed, and Governor Jeb Bush signed, a bill ordering the reinsertion of the feeding tube.

evangelical   Originating in the Greek word meaning "good news," this term is used to designate those Christians who place great importance on a personal relationship with Jesus that they achieve through a born-again experience, acknowledge biblical authority to guide their faith and lives, and accept the commission to share their faith with others.

faith-based initiative   This term is used to refer to proposals to allow the participation of faith-based organizations in providing federally funded social services. In January 2001, President George W. Bush announced the creation of the White House Office of Faith-Based and Community Initiatives as well as Centers for Faith-Based and Community Initiatives in five cabinet agencies. The faith-based initiative, like charitable choice, has raised concerns about the possible mingling of secular government and religious activities.

faith movement   Identified with such evangelists as Oral Roberts, Kenneth Copeland, John Hagee, Benny Hinn, and Frederick Price, the faith movement involves the proclamation of a "health and wealth" gospel and a doctrine of salvation and prosperity. Although Jim Bakker proclaimed such a doctrine during his PTL Club days, since then he has rejected the expectation of prosperity in return for faith as a dangerous focus on the material at the expense of the spiritual. Spokespersons for the faith movement find support for their position in the Bible, such as the Old Testament references to covenants between God and the Israelites in which the people were promised prosperity in return for obedience. Followers of the faith movement are admonished to "plant a seed" (contribute money) in order to receive wealth.

free exercise clause   The free exercise clause of the First Amendment to the U.S. Constitution states that "Congress shall pass no law . . . prohibiting the free exercise [of religion]." Both conservative Christians as well as their critics emphasize the importance of religious freedom. However, conservative Christians argue that the First Amendment protects freedom *of* religion, not freedom *from* religion. This view allows for greater religious involvement in the public realm than opponents of the conservative Christian movement are willing to accept.

fundamentalism   Although the terms *fundamentalist, evangelical,* and *conservative Christian* have been used as synonyms, *fundamentalism* more narrowly refers to acceptance of the essential tenets of Christianity, including biblical inerrancy, the deity and virgin birth of Jesus, the substitutionary atonement, the bodily resurrection of Jesus, and the second coming of Christ either before or after the thousand-year reign of Christians here on earth.

Great Awakening   There have been in American history three extensive religious revivals call Great Awakenings. The first began in the 1730s with the highly effective preaching of Jonathan Edwards in New England and subsequently spread throughout the colonies. This Great Awakening is credited with increased opposition to the Anglican church and its associated royal officials, a democratic spirit in religion, and the first significant movement against slavery. The second and third Great Awakenings occurred in the early nineteenth century and in the 1880s, respectively. In the 1990s, some scholars suggested that there were signs that a fourth great spiritual revival was about to begin.

higher criticism   Scholars who engage in higher criticism examine the Bible in its historical and cultural context, attempting to determine authorship and probable dates for texts. Higher critics ask such questions as whether Moses wrote the first five books of the Bible, and even whether there was someone named Moses. They also search for similarities between beliefs and traditions recorded in the Bible and those recorded in texts from other cultures. Conservative Christians have tended to reject higher criticism, arguing that the enterprise undermines the authority of the scriptures.

inerrancy   This is the belief that the Bible is free of error, at least in the original texts, which admittedly are no longer available. Therefore, the claim to inerrancy amounts to holding that the translations available today, although not error-free, provide sufficiently accurate renditions to maintain the authority of the scriptures. Some argue that the Bible must be considered inerrant in order for it to have authority in the faith and life of contemporary Christians.

intelligent design   Intelligent design is the belief that scientific theories of physical phenomena cannot provide a complete explanation for the universe's origins and that scientists can discover within the physical universe signs of an intelligent creator. Organizations such as Reasons to Believe provide what is considered evidence in specific scientific research for the intervention of a transcendent force in the creation of the universe. Some conservative Christians argue that the intelligent design perspective is truly scientific and therefore should be included in the public school curriculum.

***Lemon* test**   In *Lemon v. Kurtzman* (1971), the U.S. Supreme Court established a three-part test to determine the constitutionality of policies challenged as violations of the establishment clause. First, the policy must have a "secular purpose." Second, it must not have the primary result of "inhibiting or advancing religion." Finally, the policy must "avoid excessive government entanglement with religion." During the 1970s and 1980s, constitutional scholars frequently criticized the Court for applying the test inconsistently. Later, although not abandoning the *Lemon* test, the Court appeared to use greater flexibility in its application.

millennialism   The millennium is a thousand-year reign of God's kingdom on Earth that is prophesied in the biblical book of Revelation. Christians disagree about the timing of the millennium, whether it will occur before Jesus' second coming (people who believe this are termed *premillennialists*) or after Jesus' second coming (people who believe this scenario are called *postmillennialists*). Although not considered essential to Christian belief, this disagreement has had political consequences, with postmillennialists calling for greater political involvement associated with instituting God's law here on Earth.

partial-birth abortion   This abortion procedure was outlawed by the Partial-Birth Abortion Ban Act of 2003. The procedure involves the physician partially delivering the fetus and then puncturing its skull. Supporters of abortion rights argue that *partial-birth abortion* is not a medical term but was coined by abortion opponents as a pejorative way to refer to a sometimes necessary procedure. However, supporters of the ban contend that the procedure is never medically necessary.

Pentecostalism   This Christian perspective emphasizes believers' possession of the gifts of the spirit, including speaking in tongues, prophesying, and healing. Conservative Christian denominations disagree over the significance of such phenomena subsequent to the first generation after Jesus. The Assemblies of God is the largest Pentecostal denomination in the United States.

Plan B   This emergency contraceptive (levonorgestrel) can be taken within 72 hours after unprotected sex in order to prevent pregnancy. Advocates of reproductive choice have supported implementation of a policy to allow Plan B to be dispensed without a prescription. However, abortion opponents have resisted such a move, even though the use of the medication could reduce the number of abortions performed.

RU-486   Also called the abortion pill, RU-486, or mifepristone, is a steroid hormone similar to the natural hormone progesterone, which is necessary for establishing and maintaining pregnancy. The medication induces abortion during the first 9 weeks of pregnancy by affecting the woman's progesterone level. Conservative Christian groups have been strongly opposed to the use of RU-486 because they hold that life begins at conception and that the medication ends the pregnancy. Opponents often argue that RU-486 represents a danger to women's health.

postmillennialism   This belief holds that the world will experience a thousand-year reign characterized by obedience to God's law as expressed in the Bible, which will bring peace and prosperity, and that Jesus' second coming will occur following this period. Advocates of the social gospel and reform efforts in the late nineteenth century held this view, as do contemporary reconstructionists.

premillennialism   This is the belief that increasing sinfulness, disorder, and warfare will occur before Jesus comes again to establish his thousand-year reign on Earth. Although postmillennialism expresses a more optimistic view of future world events and the role of Christians in social and political affairs, premillennialism evokes a more pessimistic assessment of the future and the ability of human beings to create a better world without God's direct intervention in human events.

progressive Christianity   This belief, expressed by Christian theologians in the late nineteenth and early twentieth centuries, held that the world was progressing physically and spiritually according to God's plan. Conservative Christians, especially those of a premillennialist bent, doubted the optimism expressed in the progressive perspective. Contemporary reconstructionists and their emphasis on a postmillennial eschatology have inherited the optimistic worldview of the progressives, but with greater emphasis on remaking the world according to biblical law.

pro-life movement   Originating with the formation in 1972 of the National Right to Life Committee by the National Conference of Catholic Bishops, today the prolife movement includes both Catholics as well as Protestants and others opposed to laws and court rulings allowing abortion. The ultimate objective of the movement is to overturn the 1973 Supreme Court ruling in *Roe v. Wade* legalizing abortion during the first two trimesters of pregnancy. Various organizations within the movement use differing strategies, including lobbying the national Congress and state legislatures, bringing lawsuits before state and federal courts, and protesting at abortion clinics.

rapture   This aspect of premillennialism holds that before the time of great suffering prior to Christ's return, the righteous will be removed from the world. After this removal, called the rapture, a seven-year period of tribulation will occur. Those critical of premillennialism argue that belief in the rapture leads to political quiescence, because Christians assume that they will not experience the tribulation and they therefore fail to contribute actively to establishing a truly Christian society based on biblical principles.

Sabbatarianism   This is a belief, especially strong among evangelical Christians, that the Sabbath should be properly observed. Sabbatarianism became a part of the religious reform movement in the early nineteenth century. In the twentieth century, calls for the observance of Sunday as a day of rest and worship resulted in passage of state and local legislation, known as blue laws, that banned certain business activities and sporting events on that day. Such laws have largely been repealed.

secular humanism   This belief system teaches that the application of human intelligence, reason, and science offers a sufficient understanding of the world and that technology can provide solutions to human problems without a belief in God. Conservative Christians argue that the secular humanist creed has caused many of the social disorders today, and the term *secular humanism* is often used to represent the enemy of Christianity in the contemporary world. In opposition to the religious perspective adhered to by conservative Christians, the Council for Secular Humanism offers a secular perspective on various subjects, including morality, justice, and education.

social gospel   This movement developed among progressive Protestants in the late nineteenth century. Adherents of the social gospel argued that the gospel called for Christians to focus on the social and structural sources of evil, such as industrialization and urbanization, as well as individual human causes. Conservative Christians criticized this movement, holding that the social gospel ignored the primary cause of human suffering, which was the fallen nature of human beings.

solemnization   This means to dignify or formally observe an occasion. Those supporting the introduction of prayer at official public school events, such as graduation ceremonies, have advocated solemnization as a way of creating a more dignified atmosphere for the gatherings. In their desired scenario, students would vote to determine whether to have a speaker to solemnize the occasion, and if they chose to do so, they would select a fellow student to perform this duty. The U.S. Supreme Court has not been receptive to the notion of solemnization, especially if prayer is involved.

substitutionary atonement   This term refers to Christ's taking the place of human beings in paying the price for sin by suffering and dying on the cross. Substitutionary atonement is one of the fundamental beliefs of traditional Christianity.

Annotated Bibliography

Ackerman, David M., ed. 2001. *Prayer and Religion in the Public Schools.* New York: Novinka.

Ackerman presents information on various U.S. Supreme Court decisions regarding prayer and other religious observances in the public schools. The author distinguishes which activities are legally permissible and which are legally prohibited, and he identifies those issues that remain unresolved.

Alley, Robert S. 1996. *Without a Prayer: Religious Expression in Public Schools.* Amherst, NY: Prometheus.

The author presents several case studies of violations of the First Amendment prohibition of government establishment of religion through the official sanctioning of prayer. Alley focuses on the personal lives of those objecting to school prayer.

Baird-Windle, Patricia, and Eleanor J. Bader. 2001. *Targets of Hatred: Anti-Abortion Terrorism.* New York: Palgrave.

The authors, strong supporters of abortion rights, provide detailed case studies of antiabortion protests from 1966 to 1998. They provide information about the increasingly militant nature of antiabortion protests, especially in the 1990s.

Barton, David. 2002. *America: To Pray? Or Not to Pray?,* 5th ed. Aledo, TX: Wall-Builders.

Barton claims that, beginning with the U.S. Supreme Court decision in *Engel v. Vitale* declaring officially sanctioned prayer in the public schools unconstitutional, the United States has experienced a steady decline in moral values and an increase in objectionable behavior, such as premarital sex, rapes, and murders.

Black, Amy E., Douglas L. Koopman, and David K. Ryden. 2004. *Of Little Faith: The Politics of George W. Bush's Faith-Based Initiatives.* Washington, DC: Georgetown University Press.

Basing their findings on interviews with those in Washington, D.C., who have been active in the policy proposal to provide religious organizations with federal assistance to offer social services, the authors investigate the reasons why President Bush's proposal experienced significant resistance.

Blaker, Kimberly, ed. 2003. *The Fundamentals of Extremism: The Christian Right in America.* New Boston, MI: New Boston.

This group of eight articles presents a highly critical evaluation of the conservative Christian movement, portraying it as a threat to American society and politics.

Borst, William A. 1998. *Liberalism: Fatal Consequences.* Lafayette, LA: Huntington House.

Borst treats liberalism as the enemy in the so-called culture wars. The author portrays liberalism as the principal cause of moral decline in the United States and details what he considers its various evil consequences.

Boston, Robert. 1996. *Most Dangerous Man in America? Pat Robertson and the Rise of the Christian Coalition.* Amherst, NY: Prometheus.

Boston, who is associated with Americans United for Separation of Church and State, presents a highly critical look at the Christian Coalition, focusing on violations of campaign finance legislation, questionable business practices, and radical statements made by Pat Robertson. The author examines the Christian Coalition's impact on the 1994 election outcome.

_____. 2000. *Close Encounters with the Religious Right: Journeys into the Twilight Zone of Religion and Politics.* Amherst, NY: Prometheus.

Boston focuses on various conservative Christian organizations and individuals that take an active part in the political process. The subjects of investigation include D. James Kennedy, James Dobson, Jerry Falwell, the Christian Coalition, the Rutherford Institute, and the Family Research Council.

———. 2003. *Why the Religious Right Is Wrong about Separation of Church and State.* Amherst, NY: Prometheus.

Boston supports a strict understanding of the establishment clause and the free exercise clause of the First Amendment, arguing against the claim that the original intent of the amendment was to prohibit the establishment of a particular national church. The author discusses the historical tensions regarding separation of church and state and the current debates over the issue.

Brown, Ruth Murray. 2002. *For a Christian America: A History of the Religious Right.* Amherst, NY: Prometheus.

Brown relies primarily on 100 in-depth interviews with conservative Christians to track the development of the Christian right from its origins in the 1970s to the new century. The author focuses on conservative Christian opposition to the proposed Equal Rights Amendment.

Bull, Chris, and John Gallagher. 2001. *Perfect Enemies: The Religious Right, the Gay Movement, and the Politics of the 1990s,* updated ed. Lanham, MD: Rowman and Littlefield.

The authors claim that political activity in the 1990s involving social issues tended to be defined by the contest between conservative Christian groups and the gay rights movement. Bull and Gallagher examine the legal maneuvering of the Christian Coalition to defeat measures to provide rights to gays in various states and claim that the antigay activities of conservative Christian groups are responsible for much of their prominence in American politics.

Carroll, Vincent, and David Shiflett. 2001. *Christianity on Trial: Arguments against Anti-Religious Bigotry.* San Francisco: Encounter.

The authors examine the various charges made against Christianity, such as Christians' involvement in racism, genocide, and plundering the environment. They argue that such claims are unfounded, claiming instead that the Christian tradition introduced morality into the political realm.

Carter, Stephen L. 2001. *God's Name in Vain: The Wrongs and Rights of Religion in Politics.* New York: Basic.

In his discussion of the relationship between religion and politics, Carter sees both an enrichment for the larger social and political world and a spur to positive social change, but also a potential danger for those Christians who engage in the political process, and who may find their religiosity compromised. Nonetheless, Carter believes that Christians have much at stake and therefore rightly participate in politics.

Crawford, Sue E., and Laura R. Olson, eds. 2001. *Christian Clergy in American Politics.* Baltimore, MD: Johns Hopkins University Press.

The authors of these essays use the results of personal interviews and statistical data to examine the political preferences of clergy in mainline and evangelical Protestant, Catholic, and Mennonite communities. The essays focus on the roles of varied religious leaders, including whites, African-Americans, and women, in the local, national, and international political realms.

Cromartie, Michael. 2003. *A Public Faith: Evangelicals and Civic Engagement.* Lanham, MD: Rowman and Littlefield.

The contributors to this volume investigate the beliefs, values, and public involvement and influence of conservative Protestants in many areas, including bioethics, homosexuality, abortion, same-sex marriage, public school policy, race relations, welfare reform, and international human rights.

Deckman, Melissa M. 2004. *School Board Battles: The Christian Right in Local Politics.* Washington, DC: Georgetown University Press.

Deckman investigates the influence of the conservative Christian movement on the politics of local school boards. Basing her investigation on a national survey, the author focuses on the motivation of conservative Christian school board candidates, their rate of electoral success, and, when elected, their level of influence on school boards.

DelFattore, Joan. 2004. *The Fourth R: Conflicts over Religion in America's Public Schools.* New Haven, CT: Yale University Press.

DelFattore recounts the disputes over prayer in the public schools from the early nineteenth century to the present. The author focuses on the conflict in the courts, Congress, and among various advocacy groups. An appendix identifies various contemporary groups concerned with the issue of prayer in the public schools. DelFattore interprets the issue as a struggle between majority rule and individual rights.

Diamond, Sara. 1998. *Not by Politics Alone: The Enduring Influence of the Christian Right.* New York: Guilford.

Diamond investigates the cultural origins of the conservative Christian movement and focuses on the ability of leaders to keep the movement cohesive during times of apparent political defeat. The author identifies the close relationship between Christian groups and the Republican party as a key to the movement's longevity.

Dionne, E. J. Jr., and Ming Hsu Chen, eds. 2001. *Sacred Places, Civic Purposes: Should Government Help Faith-Based Charity?* Washington, DC: Brookings Institution.

The various contributions to this volume investigate the possible roles of faith-based organizations in such policy areas as preventing teen pregnancy, fighting crime and substance abuse, aiding community development, improving education, and providing childcare. A concluding section evaluates the possible ways in which government can support faith-based organizations in performing social services.

Djupe, Paul A., and Christopher P. Gilbert. 2003. *The Prophetic Pulpit: Clergy, Churches, and Communities in American Politics.* Lanham, MD: Rowman and Littlefield.

This volume presents detailed survey results, based on a sample of 2,400 Episcopal and Evangelical Lutheran Church in America clergy, that identify the opinions of mainline Protestant clergy and the types of political activity in which they take part. The authors identify the various factors, including personal beliefs, perceptions of congregational needs, and denominational influences, that affect the level of clergy's political activity.

Djupe, Paul A., and Laura R. Olson, eds. 2003. *Encyclopedia of American Religion and Politics.* New York: Facts on File.

This work contains 600 entries on such topics as religious leaders and denominations, political activists, major historical events, court cases, elections, and significant issues such as prayer in the public schools.

Durham, James R. 1995. *Secular Darkness: Religious Right Involvement in Texas Education, 1963–1989.* New York: Peter Lang.

Durham recounts the effort of conservative Christians in Texas to influence the nature of public education in the state. The author argues that although conservative Christian groups failed to gain control of the educational structure, they had a significant effect on programs and on those involved in education policymaking in Texas.

Formicola, Jo Renee, Mary C. Segers, and Paul Weber. 2003. *Faith-Based Initiatives and the Bush Administration: The Good, the Bad, and the Ugly.* Lanham, MD: Rowman and Littlefield.

The authors explore the social and political backgrounds to President George W. Bush's establishment of the Office of Faith-Based Initiatives. They examine the political influences on the legislative process surrounding the policy proposals to provide religious organizations with federal funding so that they might offer social welfare benefits more effectively.

Fowler, Robert Booth, Allen D. Hertzke, and Laura R. Olson. 1999. *Religion and Politics in America: Faith, Culture, and Strategic Choices.* Boulder, CO: Westview.

The authors describe the relationship between religion and politics in contemporary American society as well as in the history of the nation. The book focuses on the motivations for political activism and participatory strategies pursued by religious actors who engage in such areas as voting, interest groups, and government.

Gamble, Richard M. 2003. *The War for Righteousness: Progressive Christianity, the Great War, and the Rise of the Messianic Nation.* Wilmington, DE: Intercollegiate Studies Institute.

Gamble recounts the development of the social gospel ministry, focusing on the efforts of clergy to promote an activist Christianity engaged with the world. The author associates advocates of the social gospel with an evangelical fervor for the spread of democracy and the redemption of the world through U.S. participation in World War I.

George, Robert P. 2002. *Clash of Orthodoxies: Law, Religion and Morality in Crisis.* Wilmington, DE: Intercollegiate Studies Institute.

George challenges what he considers the liberal claim to represent the only source of rational interaction in the public realm. The author argues that a Judeo-Christian perspective offers a rationally superior approach to such issues as abortion, homosexuality, same-sex marriage, and civil rights and civil liberties. George argues against the position that the state should remain neutral on such questions as the nature of marriage.

Gilbert, Christopher P., Paul A. Djupe, David A. Peterson, and Timothy R. Johnson, eds. 1999. *Religious Institutions and Minor Parties in the United States.* Westport, CT: Greenwood.

This volume investigates the effects of churches on the success of third parties and independent candidates in U.S. elections. The authors conclude that religious institutions have tended to support the two major parties at the expense of minor parties and independent candidates.

Gold, Philip. 2004. *Take Back the Right: How the Neo-Cons and the Religious Right Have Hijacked the Conservative Movement.* New York: Carroll and Graf.

Gold, who was active in conservative politics for more than thirty years, discusses his decision to separate from the conservative movement. The author criticizes cultural conservatism and the conservative Christian movement for alienating the Republican party from what he considers its true origins and objectives.

Green, John C., James L. Guth, Corwin E. Smith, and Lyman A. Kellstedt. 1996. *Religion and the Culture Wars: Dispatches from the Front.* Lanham, MD: Rowman and Littlefield.

In the seventeen articles included in the volume, the authors investigate various aspects of the political activity of conservative Christian groups. The topics covered include the participation of conservative Christians in congressional campaigns from 1978 to 1988, religious voting blocs in the 1992 election, the influences on the political mobilization of conservative Christians, and the relationship between religious belief and foreign policy attitudes.

Green, John C., Clyde Wilcox, and Mark J. Rozell, eds. 2003. *The Christian Right in American Politics: Marching to the Millennium.* Washington, DC: Georgetown University Press.

The authors of this collection of essays concentrate on the political activities of conservative Christian groups at the state level. The articles concentrate on those states, including South Carolina, Virginia, Texas, Florida, Iowa, and Kansas, in which such groups were especially active from 1980 to 2000. Therefore, the study is not necessarily representative of conservative Christian political strength nationwide.

Hanegraaff, Hank. 2003. *Fatal Flaws: What Evolutionists Don't Want You to Know.* New York: W. Publishing Group.

This brief book summarizes Hank Hanegraaff's arguments against the theory of evolution. The author contends that Darwinism contains numerous factual and logical errors and has fatal consequences for human beings. Hanegraaff attributes various harmful trends to Darwin's theory of evolution, including skepticism about the Bible and increases in divorce, adultery, drug abuse, and abortion.

Hart, Darryl G. 2003. *That Old-Time Religion in Modern America: Evangelical Protestantism in the Twentieth Century.* Chicago: Ivan R. Dree.

Hart describes the separation and alienation of evangelical Christians from the mainline Protestant denominations during the twentieth century, from the fundamentalist controversy over evolution in the 1920s to the movement's marginalization in the 1930s, and on to the rise of the religious right in the 1970s and 1980s.

———. 2004. *Deconstructing Evangelicalism: Conservative Protestantism in the Age of Billy Graham.* Grand Rapids, MI: Baker.

Hart recounts the formation of the evangelical movement after World War II. The author finds fault with the use pollsters have given the term *evangelical,* making the category vague and inclusive of many varied religious groups. Hart recommends abandoning the term as a method of identifying Christians.

Haught, James A. 1994. *Holy Hatred: Religious Conflicts of the '90s.* Amherst, NY: Prometheus.

Rather than seeing religion generally as a positive force, Haught, a journalist, posits a universal tendency for religious movements to become involved in serious conflict with political opponents. Among the discussed subjects is the murder of an abortion clinic doctor in Florida and the Branch Davidian tragedy in Waco, Texas. The author is concerned about the perceived increase in fundamentalist Christian influence in U.S. politics and advises the reader to avoid involvement with intense religion.

Heclo, Hugh, and Wilfred M. McClay, eds. 2003. *Religion Returns to the Public Square: Faith and Policy in America.* Baltimore, MD: Johns Hopkins University Press.

The essays in this volume explore the historical and social roots and the current status of the relationship between religion and American politics. The essays treat such subjects as religion's role in democratic politics, welfare reform and Catholic Charities U.S.A., charitable choice, public education, and American foreign policy.

Hoge, Dean R., Benton Johnson, and Donald A. Luidens. 1995. *Vanishing Boundaries: The Religion of Mainline Protestant Baby Boomers.* Louisville, KY: Westminster/John Knox.

Employing the results of interviews with some 500 Presbyterian respondents, the authors focus on the causes for the decline in membership among mainline Protestant churches since the 1960s. Among the factors contributing to the decline of mainline churches, the authors identify changes in American culture and the openness of the churches to changing with the contemporary culture.

Hunter, Cornelius G. 2002. *Darwin's God: Evolution and the Problem of Evil.* Grand Rapids, MI: Brazos.

The issue of evolution versus creationism, or "intelligent design," if not a major concern in national politics, has become significant for several state and local governments. Hunter, by arguing that Charles Darwin as well as contemporary supporters of evolution theory make religious assumptions in their work, contributes to the cause of conservative Christians who wish to introduce alternatives to the teaching of evolution in the public schools.

———. 2003. *Darwin's Proof: The Triumph of Religion over Science.* Grand Rapids, MI: Brazos.

In a sequel to *Darwin's God,* Hunter investigates further the religious presuppositions underlying Darwin's theory of evolution, adding further arguments helpful to those conservative Christians who wish to challenge the teaching of the theory of evolution in the public schools. The author provides various arguments that challenge the validity of the evolution theory.

Jelen, Ted G. 1991. *The Political Mobilization of Religious Beliefs.* Westport, CT: Greenwood.

Jelen investigates what motivates certain people with strong religious beliefs to become involved in conservative politics and deals with the possible consequences of such involvement to the democratic process. Employing data from members and clergy of fifteen churches in the Midwest, Jelen notes that disagreements among fundamentalists, evangelicals, charismatics, and Pentecostals tend to prevent the formation of more effective political coalitions.

———. 2000. *To Serve God and Mammon: Church-State Relations in the United States.* Boulder, CO: Westview.

Jelen investigates the supposed friction between the First Amendment establishment and free exercise clauses. The author discusses the history of church-state relations, the activities of interest groups concerned with the issue, and the shift in focus of the church-state debate from the establishment clause to religious free exercise issues.

Jelen, Ted G. ed. 1995. *Perspectives on the Politics of Abortion.* Westport, CT: Greenwood.

These essays, originally presented at a 1993 conference at Illinois Benedictine College, deal with various aspects of the politics of abortion, including abortion as an example of self-defense, the political involvement of the Catholic church, and the impact of the issue on partisan politics. The authors tend to recommend compromise between the two major sides of the abortion controversy.

Johnson, Curtis D. 1994. *Redeeming America: Evangelicals and the Road to Civil War.* Chicago: Ivan R. Dee.

Johnson presents the history of evangelical Christians before the Civil War, focusing on such issues as the treatment of Native American tribes, the observance of Sunday as a day of rest, and slavery. The early involvement of evangelicals in politics provides interesting parallels to the more recent political involvement of religious groups.

Jurinski, James John. 1998. *Religion in the Schools: A Reference Handbook.* Santa Barbara, CA: ABC-CLIO.

In this reference work, Jurinski offers an introductory chapter that provides a summary of the major areas of conflict regarding religion in public education, including school prayer, access for religious groups to the public schools, religion in public school curricula, and public support for church-affiliated schools. Subsequent chapters present a chronology of events, biographical sketches of individuals involved in the issue of religion and schools, and relevant documents, including Supreme Court decisions.

Kennedy, D. James, and Jerry Newcombe. 2003. *What If America Were a Christian Nation Again?* Nashville, TN: Thomas Nelson.

Kennedy and Newcombe present a common theme among conservative Christians regarding the Christian foundation of the United States. They observe that the nation is involved in a cultural war, and they claim that so-called progressive individuals and organizations misuse statements of the founders to misrepresent the founders' actual intentions. The authors note that although the founders wished to achieve freedom of religion, many today want to establish freedom from religion. They also distinguish between liberty, the goal of the founders, and licentiousness, the objective that they assert motivates many in contemporary society.

Kintz, Linda, and Julia Lesage, eds. 1998. *Media, Culture, and the Religious Right.* Minneapolis: University of Minnesota Press.

Attempting to explain the increasing influence of conservative Christian organizations in the United States, the authors of these essays focus on the use of the mass media, including television, radio, and videos, to communicate in a highly effective way the conservative Christian message.

Kohut, Andrew, John C. Green, Scott Keeter, and Robert C. Toth. 2000. *The Diminishing Divide: Religion's Changing Role in American Politics.* Washington, DC: Brookings Institution.

The authors employ survey data from the Pew Research Center and the National Election Studies to explore the interaction between religion, political attitudes, and political behavior in the United States. They conclude that the trend since the 1960s toward secularization presents a major challenge to religious groups.

Ladd, Everett Carll, and Karlyn H. Bowman. 1997. *Public Opinion about Abortion: Twenty-Five Years after Roe v. Wade.* Washington, DC: American Enterprise Institute.

The authors provide findings from public opinion surveys regarding the issue of abortion. They assert that although Americans clearly do not want to ban abortion, the circumstances vary under which they find the procedure acceptable.

Lader, Lawrence. 1995. *A Private Matter: RU–486 and the Abortion Crisis.* Amherst, NY: Prometheus.

Lader covers the history of abortion policy in the United States, the political battles over legalized abortion (including attacks on abortion clinics), and attempts to introduce RU–486, the "abortion pill," into the United States and the resulting opposition from various sources, including conservative Christian groups.

Limbaugh, David. 2003. *Persecution: How Liberals Are Waging War against Christians.* Washington, DC: Regnery.

In an attempt to encourage Christian activism, Limbaugh focuses on what he considers the agenda of anti-Christian forces to remove God from the public schools. Describing the influence of Christianity on colonial culture and education, Limbaugh argues that education today fails to meet the intentions of the founders. The author describes attempts to prohibit display of religious symbols in schools and to keep any account of Christianity from textbooks.

Livingstone, David N., Darryl G. Hart, and Mark A. Noll, eds. 1999. *Evangelicals and Science in Historical Perspective.* New York: Oxford University Press.

These essays deal with various aspects of the interaction between scientific advancement and evangelicalism. The book provides the background to such contemporary conflicts as that between the teaching of evolution and the counterclaims of so-called creation science.

Manatt, Richard P. 1995. *When Right Is Wrong: Fundamentalists and the Public Schools.* Lancaster, PA: Technomic.

Manatt recounts what he considers attempts by Christian fundamentalists to conduct a culture war against the nation's schools, especially educational reforms such as outcome-based education.

Mapp, Alf J. 2003. *Faiths of Our Fathers: What America's Founders Really Believed.* Lanham, MD: Rowman and Littlefield.

Mapp details the religious beliefs of prominent Americans at the time of the constitutional founding, demonstrating that these individuals varied considerably in their beliefs. Among the individuals treated are Thomas Jefferson, Benjamin Franklin, George Washington, James Madison, Patrick Henry, Charles Carroll, and Haym Salomon.

Martin, William. 1997. *With God on Our Side: The Rise of the Religious Right in America.* New York: Broadway.

Martin examines the involvement of religious organizations in American politics from the civil rights movement to the ascendancy of the Christian Coalition. Based on interviews with those active in the conservative Christian movement, the author discusses the religious right's influence in such policy areas as race relations, abortion, public school curricula, and family issues.

McConkey, Dale, and Peter Augustine Lawler, eds. 2003. *Faith, Morality, and Civil Society.* Lanham, MD: Lexington.

The contributors, who are from various religious and moral traditions, discuss the possible influences that religious faith and morality can have on society. The authors suggest that religion can make positive contributions to educational, economic, and political institutions.

Meier, Marianne M. 2002. *Understanding the School Prayer Issue and the Related Character Education and Charter School Movements.* Pittsburgh, PA: Dorrance.

Meier, a United Methodist minister, discusses the contemporary debate over separation of church and state in the context of the historical relationship between education and religion. The author discusses key court decisions as well as the attempts of Christian groups, including establishment of the charter school movement, to provide a religious educational environment for children.

Morken, Hubert, and Jo Renee Formicola. 1999. *The Politics of School Choice.* Lanham, MD: Rowman and Littlefield.

The authors examine the school choice movement, in which conservative Christians play a key role. The movement employs a wide variety of tactics, including lobbying for desired legislation; taking their cause to the courts; and appealing for local community support in order to achieve the establishment of tax credits, public vouchers, and charter schools.

Morone, James A. 2003. *Hellfire Nation: The Politics of Sin in American History.* New Haven, CT: Yale University Press.

Morone investigates the history of the influence of religion on American politics. The author describes the differential effects of religion on the politically more conservative as well as more liberal Christians. One group preached against moral decline and for individual responsibility, and the other, supporters of the social gospel, advocated government intervention to reform society.

Noll, Mark A. 2002. *America's God: From Jonathan Edwards to Abraham Lincoln.* New York: Oxford University Press.

Recounting the development of religious thought in the United States from the colonial era to the Civil War, Noll emphasizes the influence of republicanism on religious leaders. The author claims that deep religious beliefs in the North and the South set the stage for a conflict in which both sides claimed biblical support.

Oldfield, Duane Murray. 1996. *The Right and the Righteous: The Christian Right Confronts the Republican Party.* Lanham, MD: Rowman and Littlefield.

Oldfield examines the influence of conservative Christian groups on the Republican party at the national, state, and local levels. The author focuses on the difficulty faced by the party and the conservative Christian leadership in attempting to maintain the core membership while also attracting a broader coalition.

Pegram, Thomas R. 1998. *Battling Demon Rum: The Struggle for a Dry America, 1800–1933.* Chicago: Ivan R. Dee.

Pegram recounts the religious, moral, and political campaign for temperance in the United States from the early years of the nation through the repeal of Prohibition. The author details the ability of a Christian movement to achieve victory when policy preferences are strong, but also the limitations of attempting to enforce morals through political action.

Provenzo, Eugene F., Jr. 1990. *Religious Fundamentalism and American Education: The Battle for the Public Schools.* Albany: State University of New York Press.

Provenzo investigates the competition between conservative Christian groups and others regarding such public education issues as creationism versus evolution, textbook content and selection, the role of the family in education, school prayer, and state regulation of private Christian schools.

Reichley, A. James. 2002. *Faith in Politics.* Washington, DC: Brookings Institution.

Reichley presents an analysis of the major religious traditions in the United States, offering an account of the history of the varied interactions between religion and politics. The author concludes with a discussion of the role of organized religion and religious belief in the operation of American democracy.

Reiter, Jerry. 2000. *Live from the Gates of Hell: An Insider's Look at the Anti-Abortion Underground.* Amherst, NY: Prometheus.

Reiter, a former conservative Christian activist, recounts his experience with the antiabortion underground, including meetings with members of the Ku Klux Klan, Operation Rescue, and militias, all of whom justify extreme action to prevent abortions. The antiabortion cause has attracted many to political activism, but here Reiter is dealing primarily with the radical fringes of the movement.

Richardson, Stephen. 1998. *The Eagle's Claw: The Church and the IRS.* Lafayette, LA: Huntington House.

Richardson, a certified public accountant, has represented Christian organizations for several years before the U.S. Internal Revenue Service. In this book, he offers advice to religious organizations to deal effectively with IRS disputes. The author argues that many IRS challenges to churches are illegitimate and are intended to limit church activity.

Risen, James, and Judy L. Thomas. 1998. *Wrath of Angels: The American Abortion War.* New York: Basic.

The authors, who are news reporters, provide a detailed account of the rise of the militant antiabortion movement, describing the religious backgrounds of movement leaders. Risen and Thomas explore the divisions within the antiabortion movement and the shift toward more violent tactics.

Rozell, Mark J., and Clyde Wilcox, eds. 1997. *God at the Grass Roots, 1996: The Christian Right in American Elections.* Lanham, MD: Rowman and Littlefield.

This collection of essays analyzes the influence of conservative Christian organizations on the 1996 national, state, and local elections. The authors identify trends that developed since the 1994 elections in which the Republican party gained majorities in both the U.S. House and Senate.

Ruse, Michael. 2001. *Can a Darwinian Be a Christian? The Relationship between Science and Religion.* New York: Cambridge University Press.

Ruse, a professor of philosophy at Florida State University, asks whether an adherent of Darwin's theory of natural selection can simultaneously subscribe to the basic claims of Christianity. The author examines both Darwinism and Christianity as well as the ideas of other noted representatives of science and religion. In attempting to bridge the gap between the theory of evolution and religious belief, Ruse argues that it is not impossible for a Darwinian to adhere to Christian belief, and also that a Christian believer can accept evolution and Darwinian natural selection.

Schultz, Jeffrey D., John G. West, and Iain Maclean. 1998. *Encyclopedia of Religion in American Politics.* Phoenix, AZ: Oryx.

The entries in this volume treat various political issues of importance to religious groups, including abortion, sex education, prayer in the public schools, and religious freedom.

Segers, Mary, and Ted G. Jelen. 1998. *Wall of Separation? Debating the Public Role of Religion.* Lanham, MD: Rowman and Littlefield.

Segers and Jelen debate the influence of religious institutions on the character of political discussion in the United States, the development of public policy, and the democratic process generally. They examine constitutional issues regarding the involvement of religion in developing a public morality and citizenship in a pluralistic society.

Smith, Christian. 1998. *American Evangelicalism: Embattled and Thriving.* Chicago: University of Chicago Press.

Employing a national telephone survey in addition to personal interviews with evangelicals and other Protestants, Smith investigates the ways in which evangelicals attempt to affect the secular society in which they find themselves. Smith discovers a strong ability of evangelicals to interact effectively with a pluralistic society, and he attributes this ability to such factors as strong commitment to beliefs, group involvement, and effective recruitment and retention of members.

———. 2000. *Christian America? What Evangelicals Really Want.* Berkeley: University of California Press.

Smith's analysis is based on data collected from interviews with 130 churchgoing Protestants in six locations around the United States. The author deals with such topics as the goals of evangelicals as they perceive them, the possibility that evangelicals will come to dominate the Republican party, and evangelicals' thoughts about prayer and the teaching of creationism in the public schools.

Smith, Christian, ed. 1996. *Disruptive Religion: The Force of Faith in Social Movement Activism.* New York: Routledge.

The articles in this collection present comparative analyses of social and political movements, such as Operation Rescue in the United States and Solidarity in Poland, that have been largely defined and energized by religious faith.

————. 2003. *The Secular Revolution: Power, Interests, and Conflict in the Secularization of American Public Life.* Berkeley: University of California Press.

Contributors to this volume reexamine the causes of secularization of American public life from 1870 to 1930, arguing that the decline of religious authority can be associated not primarily with the phenomenon of modernization, but rather with various secular groups, including scientists, academics, and literary figures who competed with religious institutions to gain prominence and cultural authority.

Solinger, Rickie, ed. 1998. *Abortion Wars: A Half Century of Struggle, 1950–2000.* Berkeley: University of California Press.

This series of eighteen articles treats various aspects of the controversy over abortion policy in the United States. Taking a sympathetic position regarding abortion and reproductive rights, the authors discuss such topics as the militant antiabortion demonstrations of Operation Rescue, prochoice activism, and the electoral politics of abortion.

Solomon, Lewis D. 2003. *In God We Trust? Faith-Based Organization and the Quest to Solve America's Social Ills.* Lanham, MD: Lexington.

Solomon discusses the proposal for funding private, faith-based organizations to deal with social problems, considering the various practical and legal objections. The author concludes that faith-based organizations can play an important part not only in delivering needed social services, but in reforming the American "underclass."

Sprigg, Peter, and Timothy Dailey, eds. 2004. *Getting It Straight: What the Research Shows about Homosexuality.* Washington, DC: Family Research Council.

This volume was prepared because of the Family Research Council's concern for what the organization considers the affirmation and subsidization of homosexual relationship and for the prospect of same-sex civil unions and marriage. The selections deal with various issues regarding homosexuality, including research on the causes of homosexuality, the number of homosexuals in the population, the health risks of homosexuality, and homosexuals as parents.

Sproul, R. C., and Abdul Saleeb. 2003. *The Dark Side of Islam.* Wheaton, IL: Crossway.

Based on radio broadcast interviews, Sproul and Saleeb discuss the doctrinal differences between Christianity and Islam on such topics as the Trinity, sin, salvation, and the deity of Christ. They defend the Christian position. The last chapter discusses the asserted roots of terrorism in the Qur'an and in the Muslim cultural tradition.

Strehle, Stephen. 2000. *The Separation of Church and State: Has America Lost Its Moral Compass?* Lafayette, LA: Huntington House.

Arguing that human beings cannot live independently from God, Strehle disputes the idea that religion can be separated from politics. The author discusses the Christian roots of various concepts associated with democracy, such as inalienable rights and egalitarianism.

Thibodaux, David. 1994. *Beyond Political Correctness: Are There Limits to Lunacy?* Lafayette, LA: Vital Issues.

Thibodaux claims that, due to an emphasis on political correctness, education in the United States has become indoctrination. He argues that the political correctness movement has targeted valued ingredients of the American culture, including the Judeo-Christian tradition and the traditional family.

Vinz, Warren Lang. 1997. *Pulpit Politics: Faces of American Protestant Nationalism in the Twentieth Century.* Albany: State University of New York Press.

Vinz examines the American experience with nationalism from 1900 to the time of Vietnam, and he discusses the role that Protestant clergy, from fundamentalist to liberal, played in introducing a messianic component. Vinz notes that Protestant clergy did not provide a consistent message regarding the identity and objectives of the American people.

Wald, Kenneth. 2003. *Religion and Politics in the United States,* 4th ed. New York: Rowman and Littlefield.

Wald investigates the wide influence of religious belief on U.S. government and political decision making and discusses the rise of the conservative Christian political movement as well as the political activity of other religious traditions.

Wallis, Jim. 1995. *The Soul of Politics: Beyond "Religious Right" and "Secular Left."* New York: Harvest.

Finding fault with the basic emphases of both the religious right and secular interests, with the seculars overemphasizing structural problems while ignoring individual responsibility and the right focusing on individual virtue while minimizing the importance of structural evils, Wallis calls for these groups to overcome their opposition and complement each other in such areas as assisting the poor.

Walsh, Andrew, ed. 2001. *Can Charitable Choice Work? Covering Religion's Impact on Urban Affairs and Social Services.* Hartford, CT: Leonard E. Greenberg Center for the Study of Religion in Public Life.

The eight articles in this volume deal with the past performance and future prospects of charitable choice, which involves religious organizations receiving public support to play a role in offering social welfare programs.

Waters, Brent, and Ronald Cole-Turner, eds. 2003. *God and the Embryo: Religious Voices on Stem Cells and Cloning.* Washington, DC: Georgetown University Press.

The issue of cloning has become a significant public policy issue on which various denominations have taken a stand. The contributors to this volume provide a wide variety of views, from Roman Catholic to liberal Protestant, evangelical, and Jewish. The editors include official statements from religious organizations, including the Roman Catholic church, the Southern Baptist Convention, the United Church of Christ, and the Presbyterian Church (USA).

Watson, Justin. 1999. *The Christian Coalition: Dreams of Restoration, Demands for Recognition.* New York: St. Martin's.

Watson begins this book with a brief history of evangelicalism in the United States, recounting nineteenth-century social activism, increasing conservatism in the early twentieth century, and the return to activism beginning in the 1970s. In presenting the development of the Christian Coalition, Watson notes a tension between the goal of reestablishment of a nation under God and a conceptualization of the movement as striving for fair treatment in a society dominated by liberal values.

West, John G., Jr. 1996. *Politics of Revelation and Reason: Religion and Civic Life in the New Nation.* Lawrence: University Press of Kansas.

Given the increasing activism of conservative Christians, West examines the proposed solution of the constitutional framers regarding the place of religion in American politics, which involved a balance between the realms of reason and revelation. The author traces the political activity of reform-minded evangelicals from 1800 to 1835, including opposition to dueling and Sunday mail delivery. West concludes that the moral consensus, which is based on an accommodation of reason and revelation, has eroded in recent decades.

Wilcox, Clyde. 1996. *Onward Christian Soldiers? The Religious Right in American Politics.* Boulder, CO: Westview.

Wilcox identifies those conservative Christians who have organized politically, presents a history of their political involvement, and indicates what might be their future activity in politics. Wilcox discusses what may be the appropriate role of religious groups in American politics.

Wilcox, Clyde, and Ted G. Jelen. 1995. *Public Attitudes toward Church and State.* Armonk, NY: M. E. Sharp.

Employing the results of a national survey, Wilcox and Jelen investigate attitudes regarding the establishment and free exercise clauses of the First Amendment. The authors focus on the role that public opinion ultimately plays in policymaking in this area.

Wilson, Ken M. 2001. *The Moral Mandate to Vote: God's Priorities in Government.* Lafayette, LA: Huntington House.

Wilson argues that Christians have a moral obligation to vote and to cast their votes to achieve a higher moral purpose. Concentrating on the abortion issue, the author believes that Christians should exercise their right to vote to elect officials who will oppose abortion and protect the handicapped and the elderly.

Wuthnow, Robert, ed. 1998. *Encyclopedia of Politics and Religion.* Washington, DC: Congressional Quarterly.

This collection of more than 240 articles covers the subject of religion and politics from a cross-cultural and cross-national perspective. Topics covered include individuals, institutions, cults, and issues such as the relationship between church and state.

Zacharias, Ravi K. 2002. *Jesus among Other Gods: The Absolute Claims of the Christian Message.* Nashville, TN: W. Publishing Group.

Consistent with conservative Christian tendency following the September 11, 2001, terrorist attacks, Zacharias compares Christianity to Hinduism, Buddhism, and Islam, arguing that the claims of Christianity are unique. The author also argues against atheism. In his discussion of Islam, Zacharias focuses on grammatical and other difficulties in the Qur'an.

———. 2002. *Light in the Shadow of Jihad: The Struggle for Truth.* Sisters, OR: Multnomah.

This brief book represents the type of arguments that conservative Christians made following the September 11, 2001, terrorist attacks, comparing and contrasting Christianity with Islam. Zacharias notes that terrorists have misused the idea of jihad for their own purposes.

Index

About the Authors

Glenn H. Utter, Ph.D., is professor and chair of the political science department at Lamar University, Beaumont, Texas, specializing in American politics and political thought. His published works include *The Religious Right* (second edition, 2001), *Campaign and Election Reform* (1997), *Encyclopedia of Gun Control and Gun Rights* (2000), *Religion and Politics* (2002), and *American Political Scientists: A Dictionary* (second edition, 2002), as well as several articles for political science journals.

James L. True, Ph.D., holds the Brooks Chair of Government and Public Service and is associate professor of political science at Lamar University, Beaumont, Texas. He retired from the United States Air Force with the rank of colonel after serving positions in air operations, financial management, and professional military education. True has published several articles for political science and public policy journals.